The Complete Guide to
SUCCESSFUL
GARDENING

Published 1978 by Sampson Low
Berkshire House, Queen Street, Maidenhead, Berkshire, SL6 1NF
Designed and produced for Sampson Low by Intercontinental Book Productions

 Copyright © 1978 Intercontinental Book Productions
and Floraprint Limited, Nottingham

SBN 562 00114 X

Printed in Italy

Acknowledgements

This book has been compiled from the following ten titles which were originally published in 1977: *Gardening for Beginners* by Violet Stevenson; *Feeding, Pruning and Pest Control* by Brian Walkden; *Garden Flowers* by F. A. Boddy; *Balcony, Patio and Window Box Gardening* by Leslie Johns; *Fruit Growing* by Roy Genders; *Vegetable Growing* by Keith Mossman; *Herb Growing* by Violet Stevenson; *Indoor Gardening* by Leslie Johns; *Greenhouse Gardening* by Lovell Benjamin; *100 Gardening Questions and Answers* by Ronald Menage.

The photographs in this book were supplied by Floraprint Limited (copyright I.G.A.), Leslie Johns & Associates, Harry Smith, Syndication International, DP Press Limited, Suttons Seeds, John Topham, J. E. Downward, Bernard Alfieri, Kenneth Scowen, Marshall Cavendish, W. Schacht, Unwin's, Brighton Borough Council, Humex, Halls Homes and Gardens, Harry Hebditch, Baco Leisure Products, N.H.P.A., Spectrum Colour Library, Elizabeth Whiting, A–Z Collection, Picturepoint, Kim Sayer. Cover photographs were supplied by Floraprint (copyright I.G.A.).

The Complete Guide to
SUCCESSFUL GARDENING

Sampson
Low

CONTENTS

Gardening for beginners 6

1 Why garden?   8
2 Planning a large garden   11
3 Adapting average-sized gardens   15
4 Creating tiny backyard gardens   24
5 Fixtures and fittings   30
6 Tools   34
7 Creating the background   36
8 Trees and shrubs   40
9 Coping with pests   50

Feeding, pruning and pest control 52

1 Basic techniques   54
3 Feeding plants   56
3 Compost   62
4 Watering   68
5 Pruning   72
6 Weeds and weed control   77
7 Controlling pests and diseases   83

Garden flowers 84

1 Floral display   86
2 Making and preparing beds and borders   88
3 Raising your own plants   90
4 Purchasing plants   94
5 Planting   95
6 After-care   96
7 Sowing hardy annuals in situ   98
8 Window boxes, plant containers and hanging baskets   100
9 Selecting plants   101
10 Plant associations   140

Balcony, patio and window box gardening 144

1 The pros and cons of container gardening   146
2 Containers   160
3 Techniques   170
4 Plants   173
5 Roof gardens   192

Fruit growing 196

1 Planning the fruit garden   198
2 Apples   202
3 Pears   210
4 Plums and gages   215
5 Damsons and bullaces   220
6 Cherries   221
7 Apricots, peaches and nectarines   224
8 Grapes   227
9 Figs   232
10 Raspberries   234
11 Blackberries   237
12 Loganberries   240
13 Gooseberries   241
14 Blackcurrants and redcurrants   245
15 Strawberries   248
16 Blueberries and cranberries   252
17 Rhubarb   253
18 Pests and diseases   255

Vegetable growing 258

1 Soils and digging 260
2 Planning your own vegetable plot 262
3 Sowing and planting 264
4 Caring for growing crops 266
5 Watering and mulching 268
6 Harvesting and storage 269
7 Pests and diseases 270
8 The vegetable garden month by month 272
9 Cabbage family (brassicas) 276
10 Peas and beans 282
11 Permanent crops 287
12 Salad crops 289
13 Root crops 296
14 Miscellaneous crops 305

Herb growing 312

1 What is a herb? 314
2 Herb gardens 322
3 Colour in the herb garden 330
4 Herbs from seed 340
5 Herbs in limited spaces 348
6 Herbs in winter 353
7 Cosmetic and potpourri herbs 356
8 Drying herbs 362
9 Wild herbs 365
10 Uses of herbs 366

Indoor gardening 374

1 Indoor plants 376
2 Environment 402
3 Decorative uses 410
4 Treatment 418
5 Propagation 428
6 Pests and diseases 432

Greenhouse gardening 434

1 Why grow plants under glass? 436
2 Types of greenhouse 437
3 Choosing a greenhouse 441
4 Installing a greenhouse 442
5 Running a greenhouse 444
6 Fitments and equipment 449
7 Greenhouse culture 454
8 Growing plants under glass 458
9 Garden frames and cloches 480
10 Common pests and diseases 485

Gardening questions and answers 488
Index 508

Gardening for beginners

1 Why garden?

The present surging interest in gardening probably originated in the economic pressures of the recent recession – an interest which can reap profits to the order of at least one thousand per cent on a small outlay – the cost of a packet of seed. Such a return on outlay must be virtually unique. Furthermore, there can be few people who do not realise that cheap, home-grown food tastes infinitely better than its shop-bought equivalent. But what many people may not appreciate is that growing things is both easy and, done sensibly, relaxing.

As a whole generation of new gardeners has emerged within the last few years, there must be many who find themselves turning for the first time in their lives to tasks which, were it not for the necessity of doing them, would seem to be mere chores. But in gardening, the interest of developing a barren or overgrown piece of land into a colourful and flourishing garden cannot help but eradicate any initial reluctance to get

started – and once you have started, you will undoubtedly want to keep going.

In the garden, you are your own master – but nonetheless, you are a pupil, too, and you never cease to learn. You will ask questions: why do it that way? what is the best way of doing this? what can I do about that? And you will learn the answers to many of these questions through experience. You will not necessarily accept what you are told, but will make up your own mind. Sometimes you'll be right, sometimes wrong, but either way you will learn.

One of the most important lessons to learn is that a great deal of gardening lore is nonsense – nonsense that can frequently involve unnecessary time and labour, and maybe expense too. Before long, you will find the easy or the quick way, and though your flowers may not always be up to flower-show standards or your vegetables

There is no better place for children to play than in the safety and convenience of their own garden.

8

The not-so-young can enjoy the gentle exercise afforded by gardening and at the same time economise by growing their own vegetables.

top-grade, you should find that your more realistic approach (in terms of time, effort and money) can still produce a very satisfactory result.

People have surely never been as busy as they are today. There is always so much to do. The working week and the commuting to and from work take up so much time and energy that alternative activities should, whenever possible, act as a restorative. Many types of sport, educational interests, books, music, social activities, trips, home improvements – all these things make one wish for a longer day and greater reserves of energy. Gardening may seem, especially to those who have seen neighbours giving up an inordinate amount of their spare time to the cultivation of their gardens, a further drain on what little spare time they have. But it need not be. A little know-how, practice and determination can make a plot of ground productive with very little labour –

A patio can become an extension of the home. Here, people gather and rest while meals are served in a relaxed outdoor setting. A barbecue is an easy and delightful way to make the most of a patio.

and labour of a type so much in contrast with one's normal work that it is both pleasurable and relaxing. Before long, it will dawn on the new gardeners *why* their friends and neighbours spend so much time in their gardens: they enjoy it!

Advance planning

We only enjoy what we do well, and as a newcomer to gardening you would be wise to consider the future before beginning to plan your plot. Make up your mind what you want from your garden. Do you want it to be economically profitable, producing food crops to stretch the family budget? Do you want a pleasure garden with flowers and shrubs to delight the senses? Do you want a children's play area, an extra 'room' for outdoor living, an exercise yard for the dog, a place to practise a golf swing, or a showplace? The probability is that it will be none of these things, but rather a compromise, with a little space set aside for the children, an area for fruit and vegetables and a place in which to lie in the sun or enjoy a barbecue.

But our dreams must be limited by reality. The space available may be small or steeply sloping. Pressures of work may not allow the time needed to convert the area to some special purpose. Money may be short, or the land may be waterlogged and need draining. So aspirations must be tempered by practicalities; yet equally, a little sensible planning can facilitate the task ahead. It is often possible to do two things at once, to take advantage of one activity to lay the basis for another.

Perhaps you may decide to have an ornamental pool in the garden, stocked with water lilies and colourful fish. But because the children are young you may feel that the water could be a dangerous temptation. In that case, dig the pool and prepare for it in every way, but fill it with sand instead of water. When the children are older take out the sand and pour in the water. Or again, perhaps the idea of a pool appeals to you. If the notion of a rock gar-

A patio should link the house and garden.

den is also attractive, then use the soil excavated for the pool to help build up the raised area for the rock. Do you want a paved area, a terrace or patio, to link house and garden? Then use as a foundation for the paving slabs the builders' rubble and waste that you picked up while clearing the site and the stones you threw aside as you dug the vegetable plot.

Try always to think ahead. A large area of grass is always a perfect foil for garden plants and it makes a splendid playground for the children, but can you afford the time to mow it perhaps twice a week? And if you have built sharply angled flower beds into the grass, can you manoeuvre the mower around them without wasting time and temper? Are you sure you would rather have a hedge than a labour-saving fence or wall? Must you grow tall, floppy plants that require staking and tying in? Why fly in the face of nature and try to grow rhododendrons on a soil which is so rich in lime that they cannot possibly live more than a few weeks?

Gardening should be fun, and it can be if you know a little about it and can find the quick and easy way, the profitable way, to carry out the necessary work. The following pages are an attempt to help you find the short-cuts to managing your own garden, whatever its size and type.

10

2 Planning a large garden

The larger the garden the more vital the planning, for not only does the greater area demand a larger number of plants, but there is more opportunity to go wrong. Today a large garden can be defined as one more than about 200 sq m (2000 sq ft) in area, and one of this size will accommodate almost any normal feature that can be desired – lawns, a pool, a rock garden, woodland or shrubbery, flower beds, fruit and vegetable plot, play area, patio and

A flower border of annuals such as marigolds, petunias and salvia brightens a garden all summer long.

perhaps even a small greenhouse. It can involve a considerable amount of work and in certain circumstances could justify the employment of a part-time gardener. It would certainly require one or two power tools such as a mower, cultivator, hedge cutter and chain-saw.

But given careful planning and a few power tools it should be possible for one person to handle an area of this size, to keep it attractive and productive on a very few hours a week. The first thing, as already indicated, is to decide exactly what is

A garden area can be broken up into separate sections so there is always curiosity about what lies just around the corner.

wanted from the garden and then ask if this can be achieved with the time and labour available. Gradually a compromise will be reached and the following advice may be helpful in deciding what can and what cannot be done.

In the first place, if you have a large plot do not attempt to make a park out of it. Understand that gorgeous flower beds and rolling lawns cannot be made ·or maintained on a few hours' work a week. Try to make the areas nearest the house as neat

and pleasant as possible and keep other parts relatively simple and undemanding so that they take up little time. Bear in mind always that the parts of the garden that are nearest to the house are, in effect, an additional room to the house and they must be kept as tidy and as pleasant as any of the rooms indoors. Keep this part of the garden simple, peaceful and not too strident with flowers. Green lawns with neat edges are the main requisite. If you wish to have flowers, keep them in relatively small beds that can be easily reached so that planting and weeding are a simple matter. Or grow your flowers in containers on the patio, for this way they are easy to keep looking their best and are simple to replace. If you wish to grow a specimen tree or two on the lawn, make sure that the branches do not hang so low that the mower cannot conveniently travel beneath them. Make sure also that the grass at the foot of the tree can be cut without trouble. Remember that this tree will receive star treatment, so make it a worthy one. Grow a tree of size and dignity, not a flowering cherry or a laburnum but an evergreen that will look dominant in any season.

Although the garden near the house should be kept neat and simple, the remainder of the plot can be as varied and as complex as you like. No garden other than the smallest should ever reveal all its secrets at a glance. There should always be hidden corners, little surprises tucked away to be stumbled upon accidentally, unsuspected features as evidence of the gardener's taste and talent. Some gardens can be almost a series of rooms, each in some way specialised: perhaps dominated by a pool or a rock garden, or by a particular plant, say roses in one and delphiniums in another. This way you gain the greatest impact and arouse immediate interest.

Also, this way you can justify a small area of the garden being neglected and full of weeds. In fact, a good gardener with plenty of space available will do well always to leave some portion to grow local weeds,

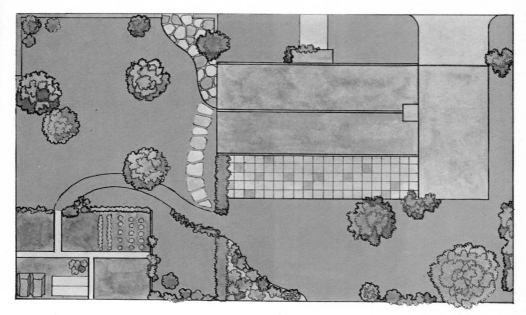

Where space permits, a large patio is always better than a small one as it gives extra freedom of movement and greater possibilities for plant decoration.

for these are very often the host plants and the food of butterflies and moths, the nesting places of birds and the haven of insects. An over-gardened plot, always neat, clean, tidy and almost polished, will not give opportunity for the birth and nurture of some of the butterflies that are as bright and as pretty as any of the flowers that grow in their regimented and disciplined rows.

But it is also possible to compromise. Too much space given to lawns, for example, will demand too much time spent on mowing, but groomed lawns near the house can lead on to longer grass mown just two or three times a year. Through this grass can curve paths or rides that need the passage of the mower only once or twice to cut the entire width. Grasses left to flower can have an interesting elegance and beauty that is all too seldom seen. Above them can grow trees and shrubs which will require the minimum of attention at any time of the year.

It is always wise to make a 'service area'

in a large garden – a place where the tools can be kept, where supplies of peat, lime and insecticides can be stored, where the compost heap can be built and the occasional bonfire made. Choose this area with great care, making sure that it is concealed from the pleasure parts of the garden and also that it is conveniently accessible. There is much to be said for creating this area more or less in the centre of the garden rather than at one end or the other, for this will save much time and energy in travelling to and fro with the mower or to fetch a trowel or sprayer. Allow plenty of room and if possible pave those parts which will be most frequently used, to save churning up mud in bad weather.

Plants for large gardens

Trees and shrubs are the best friends of the gardener with a large area to look after, for after their first few formative years they require little or no attention. Remember, though, that when they are originally planted they are small, yet they will grow large, perhaps very large, in the course of time. It is possible to create a more

13

Welsh poppies (*Meconopsis cambrica*) grow best where summers are moist and cool. They provide ground cover and colour.

immediate effect by close planting, but this will mean that after a few years either some of the trees or shrubs will have to be removed or they will grow into each other and become misshapen. Most nursery catalogues give the mature height and span of trees and shrubs and it is wise to take note of these facts when planting.

Close planting can also reduce weeding, but it is better and easier in the long run to smother weeds by ground-cover plants rather than by making use of trees and shrubs. Ground-cover plants are those that creep or sprawl on the surface of the soil, growing thickly enough to inhibit the growth of weeds. Ivy makes a good ground cover and it is quick-growing yet easily controlled. Heathers make good ground covers and there are even some low-growing or prostrate conifers which look attractive, being evergreen, require no attention, yet smother the soil so effectively that weeds cannot manage to grow.

3 Adapting average-sized gardens

The average-sized garden is less than 200 sq m (2000 sq ft) in area and is probably either suburban or a part of a group or estate of houses, all more or less similar in size and design. There is still sufficient space for several different features such as a lawn, play area and the like, but these may sometimes have to be scaled down in size and there is only limited opportunity to create the series of 'rooms' and multiple features possible with the larger garden.

A compact garden like this necessitates a real discipline in planning, for to attempt to pack too much into the little space available will result only in a confused, untidy, irresolute plot without theme or purpose. Try instead to decide what is to be the one dominant feature and give this prominence, keeping the minor factors well to the background.

Choose carefully which trees and shrubs you will grow in this smaller garden, for

A lavish use of paving enables one to walk to any corner of the garden without having to tread on damp grass. Stark paving slabs can be offset by bordering plants and labour-saving shrubs. A medium-sized garden lends itself well to the use of paving and to other decorative touches such as miniature pools and bird baths.

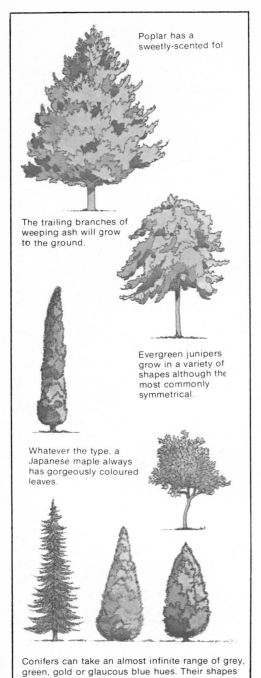

Poplar has a sweetly-scented fol

The trailing branches of weeping ash will grow to the ground.

Evergreen junipers grow in a variety of shapes although the most commonly symmetrical.

Whatever the type. a Japanese maple always has gorgeously coloured leaves.

Conifers can take an almost infinite range of grey, green, gold or glaucous blue hues. Their shapes are equally diverse in variety.

over-ambition here could mean that in a few years the area is overcrowded, dark and difficult to move through. In catalogues or at garden centres look for tall and slim ('fastigiate') trees shaped like a Lombardy poplar. Keep in mind that the only part of the garden where there will always be space to spare is upwards into the sky.

Planning the area nearest the house

Once again, the area nearest to the house is the most important and should be kept simple, for easy and quick maintenance, and restful rather than jazzy in appearance. In the average, fairly small garden this area may well take up the greater part of the available space, so it should be both attractive in appearance and as useful as another room to the house. A paved area next to the house is almost essential here, although if space is very limited this need be no more than a pathway. It is important, however, to be able to walk around the house or from house to garden with clean shoes in any kind of weather.

If you are having a terrace or patio this must certainly be paved, and there should be a slight slope (1 in 40 is sufficient) away from the house to avoid any damage from heavy rain. This area can be given greater importance by covering or partially covering it with a pergola or some similar structure, possibly roofed over to provide shelter, or possibly more open with climbing plants such as roses or wisteria to soften and decorate the pillars. If this pergola, or arbour structure, is covered with plants and the side of the house also has climbers on it, there may be no necessity for further plantings in or on the terrace, which can be given up entirely to non-gardening activities.

But certainly the terrace or patio needs some plant material growing in or on it, to soften what might otherwise be a somewhat bare and arid area of paving. If trailers, creepers and climbers are not on the wall or decorating struts and props of the pergola, some plants should be grown elsewhere.

Coloured paving loses its stridency when brilliant flowers grow nearby. Pelargoniums, for this reason, are splendid patio plants. They are always full of colour and they are able to withstand full sun and occasional dryness at the roots.

The floor area would need to be considerable to allow for the establishment of one or two beds to grow brilliant annuals, so on the whole it would be best to leave the floor space free for chairs, tables and other impedimenta of outdoor living. Grow a few plants, probably decorative annuals, in tubs or other containers, to stand on the terrace. They can be moved about according to season or function.

To emphasise that the terrace is really another outdoor room to the house, it is helpful to construct around it a wall, linking it to the house and separating it from the garden. This wall should be mainly symbolic – certainly not high or impenetrable, anything from 30 cm (1 ft) or so high, depending on proportions – and opening on to the lawn and possibly at the sides around the house. On this low wall

can be grown further plants, either in box-like containers or possibly even on the wall itself. A number of plants like aubrièta will grow quite happily in chinks in the wall, and provision can be made for them during the building of the wall.

Planning the main garden area

Away from the house the area outside the terrace is best taken up by lawn, as this gives a feeling of space. Once again it is important to divide the lawn from the terrace by some means, such as a low wall or possibly some contained plants. But at the same time it is helpful to prepare an adequate and formal opening from the terrace to the lawn, perhaps in the semblance of a gateway or, if levels permit, a step or two. This gives the impression that the garden proper has been reached, passing from the house to the halfway point of the terrace and then out into the open space of the garden itself.

This lawn area is important, and, even if

17

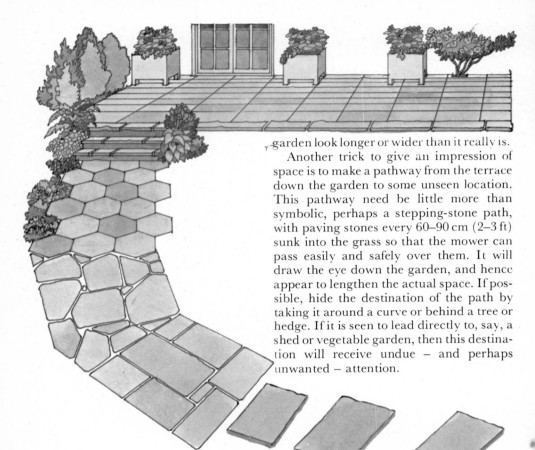

garden look longer or wider than it really is.

Another trick to give an impression of space is to make a pathway from the terrace down the garden to some unseen location. This pathway need be little more than symbolic, perhaps a stepping-stone path, with paving stones every 60–90 cm (2–3 ft) sunk into the grass so that the mower can pass easily and safely over them. It will draw the eye down the garden, and hence appear to lengthen the actual space. If possible, hide the destination of the path by taking it around a curve or behind a tree or hedge. If it is seen to lead directly to, say, a shed or vegetable garden, then this destination will receive undue – and perhaps unwanted – attention.

space is limited, as much as possible should be given to it, for this open area will create the strongest impression of the size of the garden. So keep beds, borders and individual plantings at the edges to allow clear and uncluttered space. If you wish to bring colour to what might otherwise be an all-green background, keep flower beds either in the background or filled only with low-growing plants so that the eye can travel over them to the further distance. White, yellow and orange are advancing colours which appear to make the bed or border come nearer, and dark colours such as blue, purple and even dark red are recessive, giving the impression that the bed is farther away than it really is. You can take advantage of little tricks like these to make a

However, paths in a moderately small garden can be unsatisfactory features, for they can assume greater importance than they should have in the design of the plot. To be effective a path must have a good surface, and a good surface is necessarily more or less permanent. A permanent path of concrete can sometimes look like a motorway, quite alien in the garden. Paving stones of various kinds are to be preferred if they are laid well. If necessary, these can always be lifted and replaced elsewhere, while the site they occupied can be dug and seeded for lawn or planted up otherwise. It is true that a properly laid path will enable you to walk from place to place in the garden with dry and clean feet in any weather; even more important, a good path will greatly ease the task of pushing a heavy barrow about. But paths too often have a tendency to become permanent divisions or barriers in a garden, and where space is comparatively limited, the apparent size of the garden should not be further sub-divided.

A grass path is usually quite effective for the greater part of the year under most conditions. But in some cases it is not very practical – for example, if elderly and possibly infirm people wish to stroll in the garden. Here a firm non-slip surface is essential, one which is dry and steady to the feet. Another possibility is that the children wish to have a place to ride their tricycles, which is likely to cut up the grass and in wet weather, bog the tricycles down as well.

Looking ahead

By all means always bear in mind the functions of the various parts of the garden and the people who use it, but also look ahead to a certain extent. The children will not always be small, so do not make the facilities you provide for them too permanent. Consider, too, your own position. While young you may have plenty of energy and a reasonable amount of time free for gardening. But heavier work loads and greater responsibility may reduce the amount of time you can give the garden, and muscles will not always retain the power and elasticity of youth. So, when planning your garden, bear in mind possible limitations that may occur in the future.

To some extent all gardening is a process of thinking for the future, because unless some dreadful error is made each gardening act is a means to an end. Each time you dig a bed you make it a little easier to dig next time. But there are more positive, creative and permanent means of thinking of tomorrow. For example, extend your paved area near the house or by the 'service area', for this will decrease the amount of mowing or planting necessary and at the same time simplify and ease your movements. Consider the building of one or two raised beds, so that in later years you can

A paved path gives way to paving stones in the lawn and leads toward a conveniently raised bed of flowers that are neatly paved around and securely walled.

still indulge your pleasure in gardening but at waist height to save the strain of bending. Grow more plants in containers: doing this gives you much greater control than you have over plants growing in the open garden. Install an irrigation system or provide the facilities for one, so that watering can be carried out in any part of the garden without having to waste time and energy carrying heavy buckets or cans of water. Install one or two electricity points at strategic places so that you can use cheap, efficient, silent and easy-starting electric power tools to trim your hedges or mow your lawns.

The installation of labour-saving facilities like these may be expensive and may involve some upheaval. Beds must have trenches dug through them, for example, when special insulated power lines are laid. But comfort yourself with the knowledge that you will be making life easier and more pleasant for yourself in later years, and that you are appreciably increasing the capital value of your property.

Convenience and aesthetic appeal

Try to gain as many comforts and conveniences as you can without at the same time increasing the complications. Why, for example, make and maintain a path to the front door from the street if you must also have a driveway for the car from the street to the garage? Why not make the latter serve both purposes? And why plant fruit trees down the garden if you have to buy climbers to disguise the hideously blank walls of the garage? Instead, train espalier trees on the garage walls where they will conceal and disguise the surface, save space, and gain from the release of the warmth absorbed by the walls.

Plants, being a part of nature, generally blend pleasantly with their surroundings. It is important, therefore, to ensure that building work achieves the same result. For example, use the same materials in making your drive, your patio or your garage as were used in the building of your house, or at least use a material which is compatible. If you

Patio containers have every virtue; hygiene, good drainage, size and a clean, clear-cut appearance.

have to employ alien materials for reasons of economy, then hide the worst elements of the conflict by a lavish planting of creepers and climbers, making sure at the same time that you do not over-dress a wall and so use up space that should be open to the passage of people or vehicles.

Although the house and its garden should look right aesthetically, it is equally important that they should fit into their neighbourhood and surroundings. The use of brick where everything is of stone is unsympathetic. The installation of modern plastic ranch-style fencing where hedges are the rule is again an unhappy lack of understanding. It is quite possible to indulge one's creative spirit and express one's personality in the making of a garden without at the same time violating the principles of unity and design that prevail in the neighbourhood as a whole.

Privacy in the garden

As suggested earlier, the less open and public parts of the garden belong very much to the gardener and his family. They should be treated as another room to the house and as such afforded all the cosiness and privacy that are needed. It is pleasant to be able to rest or fall asleep in the garden, or to have family meals on the terrace, without the knowledge that you will be watched by curious eyes.

Happily a dense screen is not necessary to provide privacy in a garden. The lacy branches of a silver birch, through which the sun can sparkle, will screen a garden quite satisfactorily from neighbours. A wall or fence need not be tall, for it can be topped with a lattice-work fence of timber or plastic slats, through which a Russian vine can twine itself, its creamy foam of flowers cascading downwards. Too heavy a screen will darken a small garden and will make it oppressive.

Providing shade

Many people are content to lie in the heat of the sun for hours, which will mean that our

The Russian vine, or mile-a-minute plant, is a rampant climber bearing a froth of creamy flowers.

plantings must be made with the sun's journey through the skies in mind. But there are also those who, by reason of preference or possibly for health reasons, pre-

21

The shade from small trees can be used to give a flower border a welcome respite from the hot sun.

fer to rest in the shade. It is therefore wise, if not essential, to carry out any significant planting of trees or shrubs with the orientation of the sun in mind. Work out the eventual spread and height of the tree and then gauge the movement of its shadow across the garden. It is possible to make use of this shadow to cool the patio at the hottest part of the day or to shade one of the rooms from the low and penetrating beams of the setting sun. But if you miscalculate it is also possible to keep a room in deep shade all day or leave the terrace always hot and arid.

Never plant any tree so near to the house that it will significantly darken any room for long. Falling leaves from trees too near a house can block drain pipes. The roots of some trees can break walls and crack foundations. Roots can also enter and choke underground drains. If the local soil is heavy clay, roots will sometimes extract moisture from the soil until it cracks, moves and affects the stability of house or garden walls. It is pleasant to plant a small and immature tree where it can be seen and enjoyed from the windows of a house, but too many of these trees will grow too large, block out any other view and make a room so dark that you will have to prune the tree in order to let in light. The character and beauty of the tree will be spoiled and eventually the only thing left to do will be to have the tree out completely, always a considerable and unpleasant task.

Wind protection

Sunshine and light are not the only elements which we sometimes enjoy and from which, at other times, we seek protection. On occasion it is very pleasant to enjoy a light breeze on a hot sunny day, but there are other days when the wind, cold or hot, can cause both irritation and damage. In most areas there is a prevailing wind, most frequently coming from one section of the compass. This being so, it is often possible to build a windbreak for protection from this prevailing wind. Like the sun screen, it need not be heavy, for a light screening is most effective in softening or breaking the power of a wind so that it filters through instead of rushing over a barrier.

But when constructing a windbreak make quite sure that you are not creating a wind tunnel which increases the force of the wind into your own garden or that of a neighbour. Even as light a screen as wire netting can effectively break the force of wind without channelling it into narrower and more violent pathways. Some screening of this kind is most helpful to those parts of the garden which are normally occupied by the very young or the elderly, as it provides them with the warmth and comfort that they need when they are outdoors.

The brilliant bed of begonias is easily tended from the stepping-stone path and is also protected from strong winds by a contrasting evergreen hedge.

4 Creating tiny backyard gardens

If your garden consists of a tiny backyard, with no more than about 25 sq m (270 sq ft) in which to create your elysium and raise garden produce, you will need to be the most creative and imaginative gardener of all. The limitations are so severe that success will depend primarily upon your flair for design. As a general rule you will not be able to grow the same plants as are suited to larger locations, either for lack of space or lack of light. Almost certainly, the situation will be urban, with tall buildings blocking most direct light. Here, being entirely visible from the house, the garden area will be more genuinely an 'extra room' than in any other case.

Lawns, flower beds and shrubberies, tall, stately trees – these are out of the question.

Always brilliant, mixed pansies (right) provide the concentrated mass of colour that is essential in a large container. Soil should never be allowed to show.

Even in the smallest of spaces (left), everything from a full-sized garden can be included if grown in containers. Container plants are compact, easily cared for and can be moved according to season and the dictates of convenience.

Instead, everything must be miniaturised, each item selected with the greatest of care for its ability to grow under the poorest light conditions and to give of its decorative best where space restrictions are inevitable. In such circumstances, there can be no room for a sprawling plant, a tiny overflow of fallen leaves, a leaning branch or a drooping bough. Nor will there be anywhere to conceal such mundane but necessary items as dustbins, oil tanks, compost bins and so on.

Unquestionably, the floor of the garden will have to be paved (see pages 37–9). There will be no room for grass, nor would it grow well under such conditions. There could be a tiny bed or border containing a flowering plant or a shrub which will tolerate poor light conditions, and perhaps a climber or two growing up the wall towards the source of light. There could be a miniature pool, perhaps with its own little fountain. And there could be a number of plants in containers of various kinds. It may be possible in certain circumstances to remove these from time to time from the poor light of the garden to the brighter light of the roof

or a balcony. This will give them the opportunity to make good, healthy growth to sustain themselves during the periods when they enhance the true garden below.

Soil, light and artificial stratagems

Another drawback will probably be that the soil of town gardens or backyards is usually poor, undernourished, thin, sour and contaminated by years of deposits from the polluted air of the city. It would be wise to dig out 50 cm (18 in) or so of the top soil wherever plantings are to be made and replace it with fresh soil, either a stabilised soil mixture bought by the sack or a natural soil made up of leafmould, loam, peat and sand. It will not be advisable, nor will it be helpful, to make this soil mixture too rich – the light available will not normally be able to balance the stimulus at the roots, and plants will find it difficult to grow as they would do under more normal circumstances. Watering will have to be almost completely artificial.

Despite the difficulties and drawbacks in this type of gardening, the problems to be faced should, in fact, serve to stimulate the

keen gardener. Obviously, everything possible should be done to overcome them. For example, walls can be painted white or a pale colour to trap and reflect as much light as possible. A powerful but – for its gardening value – comparatively inexpensive artificial lighting system could be installed. Ample benefit will result from switching on only one or two floodlights or fluorescent tubes for the darkest parts of the day; it is not necessary to extend the hours of natural daylight.

The soil in which the few plants grow can be improved, and plants selected so that they decorate the space available without stealing too much space or light from other floral residents. You could even take advantage of the sheer artifice of your activities and paint murals on the walls, make a small dark moss-and-fern-encrusted grotto, or install a miniature pool, lit from beneath, which will glow gently in a spot not often in sunlight.

Coping with what a spacious garden can usually conceal – dustbins, a compost bin, a place for gardening tools – is not such a problem in a small garden as it may appear, for the entire area is almost certain to be paved, and much of it can be built up with raised beds and spaces for wall plants. If you can make what looks like a bench covered in against one wall, part can hold the necessary spade and rake, and other parts can conceal the compost and the rubbish – even the oil storage tank for the central heating if necessary. If an ivy or a Virginia creeper is grown around the portions of the structure that do not have to be opened, the deception will be complete.

Advantages of a small, enclosed garden

Apart from temperature there will be little difference between the seasons. Because space is so limited, you could possibly allow yourself the luxury of changing the contents of the various pots, tubs, troughs and boxes more frequently than you might otherwise. A single box of early-season primulas bought from a street market or a garden centre can bring spring to the area when it is still winter-enshrouded. Instead of growing evergreens, concentrate on evergolds or everwhites or greys – those plants that will reveal their strong and healthy foliage at all times of the year in glowing colour rather than a drab green.

One particular benefit of the small town garden is that it is unlikely to suffer from strong winds. So climbers, for example, need only minimal support, easily provided by wires attached to the walls. Taller trees, especially if young, will need no staking. The soil will not dry out as quickly as it would with a similar space on a roof, for example, and hence watering will be less important and need not be so thorough. The somewhat damp atmosphere will tend to encourage mosses and ferns – which is just what you want, for they will be natural to the surroundings. Plants of this kind will grow in comparatively shallow containers because of their root structure, and again this is an advantage because little watering will be required.

Frosts are unlikely to be a problem, owing to the proximity of warm, inhabited buildings, so the range of containers nor-

The patio (left) should be a transition zone from the house to the garden. It is a place where both plants and living space can be happily combined.

A good rich soil in a town garden (right) will support a surprising array of flowers such as marigolds, petunias and geraniums. Here, a constant succession of brilliantly coloured flowers can be raised.

27

mally used for outdoor conditions can be extended. Glazed pots and tubs will bring an extra splash of colour to brighten up the paving on which they stand, and white paint can be used to lighten pot stands or supports. Do not attempt elaborate architectural effects with your containers, however. Keep the area homely and unpretentious.

The front of this town house is richly and ingenuously decorated with simple, cottage-type flowers.

Tidiness

Under all conditions the tiny city garden must be kept meticulously clean and well groomed. Every trace of debris must be removed as soon as possible or the overall effect will tend to be slovenly and unkempt. To make the task easier, avoid using deciduous trees or shrubs, for they serve to emphasise winter gloom when their leaves fall, and the leaves themselves create untidiness. (In any case, in such a small area there would only be room for one or two plants of this type.)

Paving

The basic paving which is usually found to form the floor of a garden of this type is nondescript, dark in colour and utilitarian rather than attractive. There are times when it might prove possible to move some of this paving – when electricity cables are installed, for example – and this could provide the opportunity to create a more exciting floor. Paving slabs when removed can be used to create raised beds or other features. With only slight reorganisation it may be possible to re-pave a corner using glazed and patterned tiles, or some other more interesting and more attractive means of adding to the overall brightness of the scene. If you consider this to be carrying things a bit too far and making something resembling a bathroom in the garden, there is no reason why a dozen different textures cannot be imported. Paving slabs are available in many different shapes, colours and textures. It is possible to pour concrete into the space available and brush the surface to create an attractive aggregate finish. Cobbles can be laid, pebbles inserted into concrete, and bricks laid in many patterns. Any changes in the overall paving pattern will combine to add interest to the general effect of a garden of this nature. Whatever the type of paving, however, it should be laid so that there is a very slight slope to a drainage channel in one corner. Once established, it is important to keep it clean.

A large area of paving (above) is stark and harsh unless softened and made interesting by some plants. But where a paved area is comparatively small (below) keep it clear and uncluttered.

29

5 Fixtures and fittings

Plants are not the only materials used to fill and furnish a garden: paths, terracing, sheds, compost bins, fences or walls – all these are practical aids to the creation and maintenance of the plot. It is possible to manage without any of these aids and frequently new garden-owners find they have to, either because there is insufficient time to organise their purchase and installation, or because after acquiring the house and moving into it there is too little money available.

Basic improvements

It is possible at first to do without paths and paved areas, but bear in mind the fact that the hardest of all gardening work is making a start. A laden wheelbarrow or truck travels much more easily on a path than on grass or muddy soil and saves the soil from being churned up further. It may seem a simple matter merely to measure out the path or the paving and then order paving slabs, bricks, gravel or bituminous surfacing material. But it is not quite so easy as that, for the path or area to be paved must first be dug and possibly levelled. It must have a base or foundation installed and it must then be prepared to accept the type of final surfacing decided upon. This can involve ordering such materials as gravel, sand, cement and possibly timber. If foundation materials such as broken bricks, large stones, pieces of concrete and the like are not to be found in sufficient quantity on the site, a load may have to be delivered by a local builder. It may be necessary to install a drainage system in the garden, which means buying agricultural drainpipes and installing them in channels of rough stone.

These basic improvements should be

All permanent garden fixtures in the garden should be installed with care so that they will give no trouble during their lifetime and will make life easy for the gardener. Fences need to be made of weather-treated wood. Paths, patios and terraces must be evenly laid so that weeds and grass do not take root in the cracks. Walls must be solid, built to drain well and sited away from young trees whose roots might grow into them. A three-stage compost bin is best for providing a continuous source of compost.

carried out before any major planting scheme has been started. Otherwise you may find yourself destroying work already done in order to install drainage or a path. The physical details of laying paving, building walls and so on are discussed in chapter 7.

Work centres

It is of the greatest assistance to have a work centre (or at least a power point) in a new garden. The basis of this area should be a shed or other covered place where materials (tools, peat, lime, sand, insecticides and so on) can receive protection from the weather. Drainage from the roof of this shed can flow into a rain barrel to provide a water supply. A compost bin or heap can be built nearby, and all vegetable rubbish can be placed there to turn into useful and rich garden soil.

It is not necessary to have electricity and water laid on to this centre, but it is always helpful. If you hope to install it one day, then the earlier the better as once again it can involve digging up a part of the garden. Electricity running through the garden must be buried and protected in special metallic fittings to avoid injury in the event, for example, of a spade being driven through the soil on to the wire. Always obtain professional advice about this.

Garden sheds are inexpensive, usually made from timber and, if correctly installed and treated with moderate care, they should last many years. The shed must be erected on solid and level foundations, preferably of concrete or paving slabs. Choose a site which is level and equally accessible from all parts of the garden. If it has only one door, face this in the direction from which the shed will be most frequently

The working sections of the garden (a) should be grouped in a corner so that everything is immediately to hand.

To receive the best light, a greenhouse (b) should be sited in a north-south direction.

Soil, sand and peat are best kept in convenient storage bins (c).

A compost bin divided into three sections (d) provides a constant supply of well-rotted humus.

approached, otherwise you may find that each time you go to the shed for a tool or appliance you have to walk right round it.

The way in which you lay out your garden shed will depend on several factors, such as its size, the number of appliances it will have to house, the number of windows, the type of flooring and other similar factors. Heavy machines such as mowers and cultivators will have to stand on the floor, of course, and if there are several it may well be worthwhile to move them about until you discover how they can be fitted together to occupy the least floor space. But remember also to make sure that the tool or implement you use most often will be most nearly to hand and that you do not have to go to the trouble of wheeling one machine out

of the shed to enable you to get to another.

Hand tools such as spades, forks and rakes can be hung on a wall. Try to keep them neat and tidy and always in the same place, for this way you will know at a glance where a tool will be or which tool is missing if one has been left in the garden at the end of the day. Beside the hand tools keep a scraper of some sort with which to remove any mud adhering to them and an oily rag with which to give the tools a final wipe over. The latter will serve both as a cleaner and rust preventer.

Erect shelving to hold the cans, bottles or packets of weedkillers, insecticides, fungicides and other preparations that are helpful in the garden. Avoid confusion by grouping them according to category, all

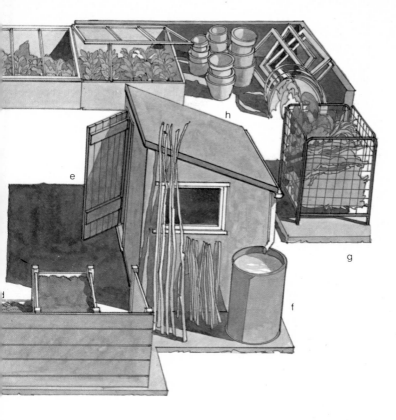

A garden shed (e) for storing tools, fertilisers and weedkillers is a key part of any work area.

Sheds and greenhouses, when adapted, are natural traps for collecting rainwater (f).

A small storage bin (g) is essential for keeping unwanted garden rubbish that cannot be used in the compost heap.

The area around frames (h) should be arranged to provide storage space for empty plant pots and extra frame covers as well as having an area for standing young plants.

the herbicides in one place, the insecticides in another, and so on. If a packet bursts or if a label is lost always throw the contents away, to avoid the danger of using the wrong substance on some occasion and causing damage. Always bear in mind that all insecticides are necessarily poisons. Keep them in the least accessible place and certainly where they cannot be reached by children. Never place any material, solid, powder or liquid, in a container which is not actually made for that material. In other words, if you have a little insecticide left over from a mixing, either use it up or throw it away; never pour it into, say, an empty lemonade bottle. Examine your garden chemicals every month or so to make sure that no packets are broken and leaking

their contents. Garden sheds can become very hot in summer and very cold in winter, and sometimes damp, which can cause bottles to crack and cans to rust.

Outside the shed it is possible to have two or three bins such as those used for storing small quantities of coal. These are readily available, inexpensive and very useful for storing supplies of peat, sand, sifted soil, leafmould or similar materials. Beside them can be the compost heap. This can either be free-standing or contained in purpose-made wire mesh or plastic frames or contained by home-made timber, brick or plastic walls. Home-made compost can be a vital source of good humus for the garden and it would be unwise not to establish your own supply.

6 Tools

A stainless steel spade slips easily through heavy soil.

An efficient digging fork must have strong, flat tines.

A garden line is an invaluable aid for laying out straight rows and beds.

On heavy soil, a draw hoe must be used for most jobs.

The Dutch hoe is more useful where the soil is light.

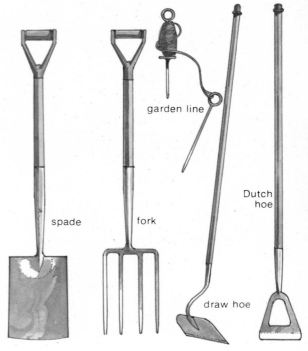

spade   fork   garden line   Dutch hoe   draw hoe

Essential tools

The basic tools needed in order to garden efficiently will depend on the individual and the type of garden he intends to create. They will almost certainly include a spade and a fork, a rake, a trowel, a hoe, a line and a watering can. The list of tools needed for a particular garden can be extended from here.

Stainless steel hand tools are best because they do not rust and hence tend to pick up less mud on their smooth surfaces. They should be selected with some care according to the size and physique of the gardener, much as one would choose a set of golf clubs or a sporting gun. Tools that are comfortable and convenient, that are not too heavy and fit the hand easily are a tremendous assistance in some of the heavier garden tasks. Never choose a large spade, to take one example, in the belief that by moving a large quantity of soil at one time the task will be completed more rapidly. It will usually be found that a smaller spade or the removal of smaller lumps of soil will enable you to work more quickly and with less expenditure of energy.

Powered tools

Don't be in too much of a hurry to seek the assistance of a powered machine for your gardening. Many cooks have found that it is easier and quicker to use a fork than to get out, assemble, use and finally dismantle and clean a mixer or blender. Similarly, by the time a machine has been removed from the shed, filled with petrol and oil as necessary, started, wheeled to the site and then set to work, many a task could have been completed using a spade or a fork alone.

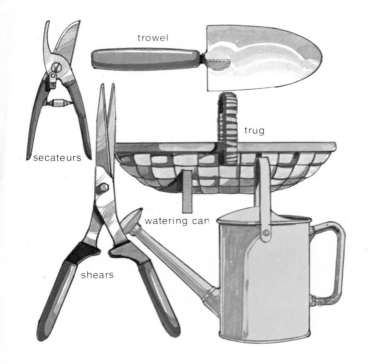

trowel

trug

secateurs

watering can

shears

Keep secateur blades
sharp to avoid damage
when pruning plants.
Wipe and oil the blades of
shears each time after
using them.

A trowel is an essential
tool for transplanting
young plants and setting
out bulbs.

A garden trug is useful
when weeding or
gathering vegetables,
flowers and fruit.

A hand-held watering can
is convenient for spot
watering.

A powered mower is probably the most useful machine for the garden so long as the lawn is more than about 10 sq m (100 sq ft) in area. The size of the mower can be increased according to the size of the lawn and generally speaking a small lawn is probably more easily maintained with an electric-powered machine than one driven by an internal combustion engine. Electric mowers are almost foolproof, light in weight and nearly silent, as well as being less expensive in the first place and less liable to deterioration. So long as the modest techniques of handling a vacuum cleaner indoors have been mastered, handling the electric cable of an electric mower on the lawn will present no problems, except that where considerable areas are involved the sheer weight of the cable can render it somewhat impractical.

A powered cultivator is only justified in a garden where there is a comparatively large area (again, say 10 sq m or 100 sq ft) which will require frequent cultivation, such as an intensively gardened vegetable plot. If the machine is required only for occasional but intensive use, as for example when a new lawn is being made and the whole area requires thorough digging more than once, then it will be found cheaper and considerably more convenient to hire a machine for a day or two and use it for all the cultivating tasks in the garden at one time.

More likely to be of use are powered hedge trimmers and possibly powered chain saws, both of which can be obtained in different sizes according to the tasks to be carried out. There are models powered by electricity and some trimmers are also available with a built-in battery.

7 Creating the background

Establishing a lawn

Nothing makes a better background for your plants than a green lawn, and the sowing of grass seed or the laying of turf is often one of the first activities of the new gardener. Because the grass may be there for many years it is worth making sure that it is as perfect a lawn as is reasonable.

Dig the area thoroughly, removing all weeds and stones and levelling it roughly. After a few days another crop of weeds will be seen and these can be removed when the area is dug once again, this time breaking up the soil more finely and checking the levels. Finally rake over the surface several times, breaking down the soil even more finely and making quite sure that there are no hills or valleys. With this last raking it is helpful to rake in one bucket of peat per square metre (per square yard).

If you are sowing seed, make sure that the soil surface is just moist on a warm, still, spring day. Sow the seed evenly on the surface, 50 g per sq m (1½ oz per sq yd). The best way to do this is to sow one half of the quantity up and down the chosen area and then the other half across it. Rake the seed in very gently and sprinkle over it just the finest layer of a peat and soil mixture. Most seed is pre-treated with a chemical that will make it unpalatable to birds. But the fine soil alone is attractive to them for taking dust baths, so if you have the patience, wind black cotton over the area on little pegs in the soil.

The grass seed will begin to germinate in a few days or a few weeks depending on the weather. With it are almost certain to be some more weeds and these should be carefully pulled out by hand. Each day the grass will grow thicker but there should be no attempt to mow it until the spears are at least 5 cm (2 in) tall. Make sure your mower has sharp blades and that these are set high for the first two or three cuts. Only after the young grass has been growing for at least six months will it be absolutely safe to use chemical weedkillers on the lawn.

If you prefer to turf the area, a process which will give quicker results but will cost appreciably more, the soil preparation is exactly the same as for seed sowing. The turfs will probably be delivered in rolls about 1 m (3 ft) long and 30 cm (12 in) wide. Lay them as soon as you can, depending on the weather, so that the joins come alternately, like bricks. Keep each turf close to its neighbour and make sure that one is not thicker or thinner than another. If this *is* the case, make the necessary adjustment with the soil. When the whole area has been finished, sprinkle a little fine soil and peat

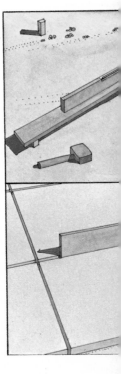

Well-laid paving should never need attention again. Make sure that the ground is level (1) then put down an even bed of gravel and sand (2). Carefully place the concrete slabs in place (3) with even spaces (4) left around each. Brush cement into the cracks (5) and water (6) so it sets in place and fills all the spaces where weeds might otherwise sprout.

mixture over it and give a gentle watering if necessary. Make sure for the next few weeks that the turf is not allowed to dry out or the roots will be killed and patching will be necessary.

Plan your lawn area with a view to the mowing you will later have to do. Keep the site simple and uncluttered so that the mower can go over it freely and easily without having to stop to negotiate a tree or a bed. Make angles wide or better still substitute gentle curves.

Where paving joins the lawn make sure that the levels are compatible so that the mower blades do not become damaged. If this is not possible, allow a space between lawn and paving.

Lawn-mowing

The time and labour involved in mowing a lawn would be considerably reduced if it were unnecessary to dispose of the grass cuttings in some convenient place. But this task can be eased by using several large plastic or hessian sheets placed at strategic points on the grass. If each is used as a dumping ground on passing, they can quite easily be dragged to the main deposit when the mowing has been completed. Grass mowings can be used as a mulch in the vegetable garden, around the roses and at the base of trees and shrubs where there is space. Spread it quite thickly, to a depth of 5 cm (2 in) or so over the ground. It will help to keep down weeds and conserve moisture in the soil, and in time it will rot down and improve the soil structure.

Laying paving

All paving should be laid on a foundation both for the sake of stability and for drainage purposes. This foundation should ide-

ally consist of some 10 cm (4 in) of well consolidated rubble topped by 5 cm (2 in) or so of gravel or sand. Paving slabs can be laid directly on this but it is generally more satisfactory to lay the slabs on a concrete foundation.

When marking out the area to be paved, remember that a very slight fall in one direction or another should be allowed for, so that rain water can drain quickly and easily from the surface. It is essential that levels should be accurately worked out and the only way to do this is to drive pegs into the ground, their tops being levelled by means of a plank and a spirit level. If this is done carefully and all the work is carried out according to these pegs, much subsequent work will be saved.

Precast paving slabs come in several shapes and sizes, and it is well to work out in which pattern they are to be laid before placing your order so that you can order exactly the right quantity. Handle the slabs with care for they can be surprisingly brittle if dropped. They are also exceedingly heavy, so do not try to save time and trouble by using slabs which are too large: 60 cm (2 ft) or so square is quite large

For an informal country garden effect, crazy paving is ideal. Always make sure that the surface is even and that the stones are firmly bedded in concrete.

enough, but they can be rectangular, hexagonal or round. A mixture of sizes produces the most appealing result.

If the paving is laid in concrete no weeds can grow through the cracks, but otherwise it is almost certain that weeds of one type or another will grow between the slabs, either up through the soil far below or from seeds caught in the shallow cracks between the stones. One way to avoid this without actually laying in concrete is to fill the spaces between the slabs with a sand and cement mix, applied dry. If it is mixed with water it is certain to stain or otherwise disfigure the slabs on each side, but if brushed into the cracks while still dry this will be avoided. After the dry mix has been carefully brushed into the cracks, water the area gently with a watering can with a fine rose. The moisture will be sufficient to make the cement mix harden in a day or two.

This stone wall blends well with the shrubs growing above it and is attractively stepped to suit the sloping contours of the land as well as enhancing the appearance of the landscape.

Wall construction

As with paving, the most important element in the construction of other architectural or structural features, such as walls or pergolas, is the base or foundation. If the wall does not stand on a solid foundation it will be apt to crack, to lean or to fall, and equally if the pergola posts are not firmly anchored in suitable holes so that they are meticulously vertical, the whole pergola will look unsightly and be exceedingly difficult to erect.

Walls can be of several types, whether they be retaining or free-standing. A retaining wall is one which is built into the soil, as for example when a garden is on a slope and is terraced to give level areas next to

each other. If a retaining wall is to retain or hold back a bank of soil it must obviously be solid and secure; the foundation should therefore be of up to 10 cm (4 in) of concrete laid on a base of well consolidated ballast. A retaining wall should also be built with a slight *batter*, or receding slope, towards the bank or soil, which is to say that it should lean slightly into the bank, for added strength. During periods of heavy rain some of the moisture in the bank behind the wall will force its way outwards through the wall, and it is a good idea to make provision for this happening by allowing a few 'weep' holes in the wall while it is being constructed.

Materials from which a wall can be constructed are brick, stone and reconstituted stone.

A retaining wall is particularly suited to the growing of certain plants on its surface, and indeed so suited is it to this purpose that wild plants or weeds will find their way into the wall naturally after a time. It is possible to squeeze the roots of little plants such as sedums and sempervivums into cracks in the wall, but more satisfactory results can be obtained by inserting the plants as the wall is being built.

A free-standing wall has space on each side. This makes it easier to build, but also creates new difficulties. Again, a sound foundation is essential and the same materials for its construction can be used. However, whereas a retaining wall is supported to some extent by the soil, a free-standing wall has no such strengthening background. Where it is of a considerable height or length it will be necessary to insert at regular intervals a pier or buttress to give added solidity. A free-standing wall also requires a protective capping to keep water and frost from entering the interior of the wall and breaking it down.

It is best to make the foundation of a wall wider than the wall itself, so that weeds cannot grow through the soil immediately next to the wall – where they are difficult to remove.

39

8 Trees and shrubs

Apart from the more or less permanent, or architectural parts of the garden, there are the plants, the real purpose or meaning of the garden as such. These vary widely, from trees and shrubs, some of which once planted will outlive the gardener, to the bright and brilliant little annual flowers which will bloom fleetingly. It is true that all of these can be raised from seed, even the largest tree. But it is likely to be so difficult and to take so long that normally specimens already between two and ten years old are bought from a nursery or a garden centre and planted in the garden.

The basic difference between a tree and a shrub is that the former grows on a single stem or trunk and the latter sometimes (though not always) rises from the soil with several main stems. Both can be evergreen or deciduous: evergreen kinds retain their leaves in winter, shedding them gradually all the year round; deciduous kinds shed theirs more dramatically, in autumn.

So a tree is worth planting well to give it the start in life it deserves.

When buying a tree you must first decide on the type and variety of tree and its site. Should it be an apple or a pear? A conifer?

Garden centres (above right), with their comprehensive selections of plants and equipment, are invaluable to beginner gardeners. They offer an inspiring array of flowering plants and trees that are ready to set out (below).

A blossoming cherry? A variegated-leaved maple? What should be its ultimate height? Width? Where will it cast its shade? Will it block window light? Will its roots penetrate drains or wreck the foundations of walls?

Most of·these questions will depend on the gardener's desires, the garden space available, and possibly, his economic position in his decision whether or not to grow fruit. Ultimate heights and widths are frequently given in nursery catalogues and both are important, for a tree that is delightful in its young and immature state can prove a nightmare of obstruction when it begins to reach maturity.

Catalogues The gardener can choose his trees and shrubs from a catalogue issued by a specialist nurseryman. The catalogue entry, possibly illustrated, will probably give all the information necessary: the name, family, type, size and whether the tree likes an acid or alkaline soil, or a mild and sheltered position. Unless the gardener has seen this particular plant growing, it may be difficult for him to picture exactly what it will look like growing on his own land. The nurseryman will always be able to advise him, and tell him whether the plant is suited to his soil and his conditions. Having placed his order, the gardener will be told when it will be ready for collection or delivery. This will generally be during winter, the dormant season when the leaves have fallen from deciduous trees and shrubs and when all plants of this nature are comparatively inactive. The plants will be dug from the soil where they have been growing in the nursery, packed with soil around their roots, protected, staked and wrapped for a journey by road or rail.

Garden centres For the new gardener or the gardener who demands immediate results or year-round working, garden centres are a real help, for here every type of gardening material may be seen, examined and bought, from abutilon to zinnia seeds and including many plants from annuals through to roses, trees and shrubs. It is

41

possible to see many of them actually in full leaf and flower, always a help to a new gardener. Plants can be bought in this state, taken home and planted without disturbing the root ball. Quite literally, it is possible to make an instant garden, a whole plot planted and growing in a single afternoon. Naturally prices of plants are somewhat higher because of the extra attention they have been given.

It takes only a visit to a botanical garden or a park to indicate that the choice of plants that can be grown in a garden is extremely wide. Most of us like trees and shrubs but do not know the names of those we see frequently, to say nothing of those that we admire in a park. We may have a better knowledge of some flowers, but others, though attractive to us, are unfamiliar, and we may assume that those plants which we seldom see must be exotic or difficult to grow under normal circumstances. Similarly, we may fear that some plants we admire may grow too large for our gardens or demand a more equable climate than we can provide.

But all of this is merely a matter of finding out and checking, and normally nursery catalogues plus a visit to a good garden centre will provide the answer to almost every question.

Planting trees and shrubs

Having chosen your plants with due care, it is only sensible to be just as thorough when it comes to planting them. Trees and shrubs are a major investment and it really does pay to give them a good start – then they will last in good health and fine appearance from some ten to twenty years to several hundred, and they will grow from only a metre – a very few feet – or so in height to about 20 m (60 ft) for garden varieties and more for those trees grown commercially or in parks and arboreta.

A tree on which one lavishes something like two hours' work can last a lifetime, which indicates the real value it can give. If it is planted with moderate care it may

require no further attention for the remainder of its life. It will seek its own water and its own food, will grow to ten times or more its original height, will provide shade in the garden and in some cases will provide more fruit than can reasonably be consumed by the average family.

How far apart you plant your trees will be decided by the number of trees you can fit into a site unless you are prepared to remove some of them when they begin to brush against each other. A very general rule about planting intervals says that one should add together the mature widths of two adjoining trees and divide by two. An example might be an autumn blooming cherry, *Prunus subhirtella autumnalis*, which can grow to a mature height of some 7 m (23 ft) with a spread of 5 m (16 ft). Planted next to a hornbeam, *Carpinus betulus fastigiata*, with a mature height of about 10 m (33 ft) and spread of 6 m (20 ft), then the distance apart should be 5 m + 6 m divided by 2, or 5.5 m (about 18 ft).

No tree should be planted too close to a house, a major wall or drain pipes. In times

Japanese maples, such as this *Acer japonicum* 'Vitifolium' (above), give us some of our brightest and most beautiful autumn colours. A hedge of mixed shrubs and small trees (left) is attractive where there is a suitable space in a garden.

of drought tree roots seek out moisture and some can penetrate drains and break them up. But the most frequent cause of damage is where the soil is heavy and made up mainly of clay, for here tree roots will absorb all existing moisture, causing the soil to dry out, to crack and to subside, thus causing cracks in walls and broken foundations. Poplar and ash are the most liable to cause this kind of damage.

Having chosen the site, dig the planting hole a little deeper and slightly greater in circumference than is needed and, if the weather is dry, fill it with water. While this is soaking into the surrounding soil, examine your tree and trim away any broken or damaged twigs and any broken

43

roots. Stand the tree in the hole to make sure that the roots can be accommodated comfortably and that the old soil mark on the trunk will come at soil level. Place the stake in the planting hole to make sure that it will not damage the roots and then drive it in securely, making sure that it is absolutely vertical.

Now begin the actual planting. Into the bottom of the planting hole sift some well rotted farmyard manure or homemade compost and on top of this a little soil, then place the roots in position and cover them

When a variegated maple sends out a branch which has plain leaves, cut it back to the main stem to keep the tree from going green.

gradually with soil, shaking the tree occasionally to make sure that no air pockets are formed. Tread down the soil at intervals. When the soil has reached the top of the hole tread it down again. If the weather is dry leave a slight dish around the trunk so that rain water can be caught and absorbed, and if it is wet bank up the soil slightly in a little mound to shed excess water. In either case a final mulch with peat will be helpful. Only after the tree has been planted and is in its permanent position should it be attached to the stake, preferably using a standard plastic tie. If string, rope or wire is used, make sure that the stem of the tree is protected so that it does not cut into the bark.

The method of planting a shrub is exactly the same except that a stake is not always necessary for a subject which is comparatively low and spreading. But both trees and shrubs should have close attention for the first few weeks, being sprayed daily in hot weather, perhaps even shaded and protected from strong winds. After the first few months, which are critical, the tree will begin to look after itself but it will make little or no growth in the first couple of years while it puts down strong roots.

To space out two trees correctly, add the mature width of both trees and divide the total in half. This will ensure that each tree has enough room to grow without touching the other.

Heeling-in a tree gives the roots short-term protection from drying winds or surface frosts until permanent planting is done.

45

Some popular trees and shrubs

The following is a brief list of trees and shrubs suitable for a small garden. Though suitable for a large garden also, no really large trees are included. Nor does the list mention roses, the most popular shrub of all. They can be in flower for about seven months of the year, they are tolerant of most soils and of weather, their blooms are of many colours and are frequently scented.

Moreover, roses can be grown as bushes, as standards, as climbers, as ramblers and as ground covers. However, although some of the old-fashioned or shrub roses produce wonderful scented blooms, many varieties only flower once a year. They are not continuous-flowering as are modern varieties. Also, many shrub roses take up more room than can be spared, and on the whole they do not respond well to pruning.

Name		Evergreen	Season	Mature height and spread (metres)
Acer palmatum Japanese maple			Spring, autumn	2–6; 3–4
Amelanchier canadensis			Spring, autumn	3–4; 2–3
Arbutus unedo strawberry tree		√	October-November	5–6; 2–3
Aucuba japonica Japanese laurel		√	All year	2–3; 2–3

Name		Evergreen	Season	Mature height and spread (metres)
Berberis several varieties		some	Spring, autumn	1–2; 1–3
Betula birch, several varieties			All year	3–6; 4–5
Buddleia butterfly bush, several varieties		some	July, August	2–3; 2–3
Buxus box, clipped to size		√	All year	1–6; 1–3
Camellia japonica		√	Spring	1–3; ½–2
Chaenomeles flowering quince several varieties			Spring	1–3; 1–3

Name		Evergreen	Season	Mature height and spread (metres)
Fatsia japonica false castor oil plant		√	All year	1–3; 1–3
Hydrangea		√	Summer	1–2; 1–2
Laburnum several varieties			Spring	3–5; 3–4
Laurus nobilis sweet bay		√	All year	1–3; ½–1
Ligustrum privet, several varieties		some	All year	1–3; 1–4
Malus flowering crab, several varieties			Spring, autumn	3–5; 1–3

Name		Evergreen	Season	Mature height and spread (metres)
Philadelphus mock orange, several varieties			Summer	2–4; 1–3
Prunus plum, cherry, almond, etc., many varieties		some	Spring	1–7; 1–5
Pyracantha firethorn, several varieties		√	Spring, autumn	2–4; 2–4
Ribes flowering currant, several varieties		some	Spring	3–4; 3–4
Syringa lilac, several varieties			Spring	1–5; 1–4
Viburnum guelder rose, several varieties		some	Summer, winter	1–5; 2–4

49

9 Coping with pests

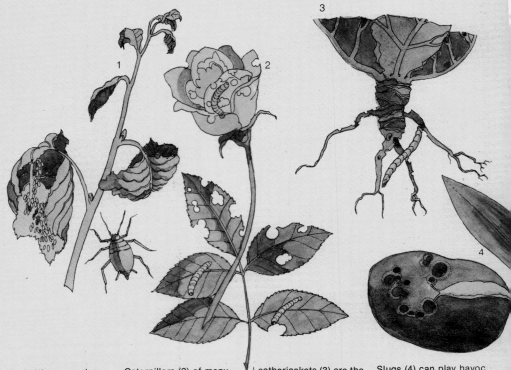

Aphids (1) can produce millions of offspring in a matter of a few days.

Caterpillars (2) of many pests do untold damage to leaves and buds.

Leatherjackets (3) are the grubs of the cranefly or daddy-long-legs.

Slugs (4) can play havoc with lettuce and leaves of other tender foliage.

Just as a healthy person can quickly and easily shake off many of the infections that may attack him, so a healthy plant will frequently withstand the onslaughts of disease or insects. Your aim should be to grow all your plants so well that they remain strong and healthy for the whole of their useful lives. Unlike humans, however, any plant that is sickly and likely to infect others should be cured or ruthlessly thrown away.

Owners of relatively small town gardens have fewer problems in the field of plant sickness than those who garden in the country. In the first place there is less chance of infection if plants in a locality are comparatively few in number, as they are in towns. Secondly, most plants in town gardens are surrounded by an atmosphere that is to some extent disease-preventive. All city air contains and carries a proportion of factory smoke and vehicle fumes. These are largely composed of sulphur, a product used for the treatment of several plant diseases, notably mildews, fungi, blights and similar infections. Furthermore, if a garden is fairly small you can pay closer attention to individual plants than when you have large areas under your control. You can spot, identify and take action against any disease or pest attack as soon as it starts instead of overlooking the trouble until it has reached dangerous proportions and has affected many plants in one area.

There exist proprietary cures and pre-

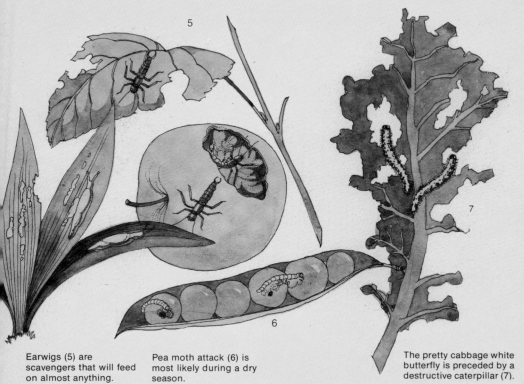

Earwigs (5) are scavengers that will feed on almost anything.

Pea moth attack (6) is most likely during a dry season.

The pretty cabbage white butterfly is preceded by a destructive caterpillar (7).

ventives for all plant illnesses – or almost all, for some diseases are so troublesome or so easily spread that it is better to destroy the affected plant than to try and cure it.

All reputable manufacturers subject their products to long-range tests to ensure that they are as safe for the specified purpose as they can be made. They look for a product that is safe to handle when mixing or preparing, one that can safely be applied, one that will carry out its specific task without harming plants or beneficial insects, and one that breaks down quickly into harmless compounds without leaving dangerous residues on plants, in the soil or in the bodies of insects it may have killed.

Apart from the ill effects which arise from human error in growing plants, such as failing to water a thirsty plant or wounding a tree trunk by the careless use of a mower, nearly all plant troubles can be put down to pests or diseases. Most diseases are some form of fungus, mildew or virus.

This being so, you have only to kill or prevent insects and either prevent or cure fungus diseases to keep your garden plants in good health. Pests are usually biters, suckers or borers and if we apply a poison to the plant it is likely that these pests will be killed. Most fungus trouble can be prevented, and on the basis that prevention is better than cure we can apply fungicides to those of our plants which are susceptible to this type of attack.

Feeding, pruning and pest control

1 Basic techniques

For every gardener, there are certain techniques which can be said to lay the foundations of a beautiful, healthy and successful garden – the techniques which, being unglamorous in themselves, are rarely the subject of a special book: feeding plants, using compost, watering, pruning and keeping gardens free of weeds, pests and diseases. Yet these are the very areas in which many gardeners feel their knowledge could be improved. Among the questions often raised are:

why should it be necessary to feed plants?

what is the difference between the various types of compost?

how much should plants be watered?

how do I know where, when and how much to prune plants, and why does it have to be done?

how can I keep my garden weed-free without hours of back-breaking labour?

how do I recognise what pest or disease is destroying my plants, and what can I do about it?

The general principles for successful gar-

Compost is invaluable; site the compost heap in the vegetable plot.

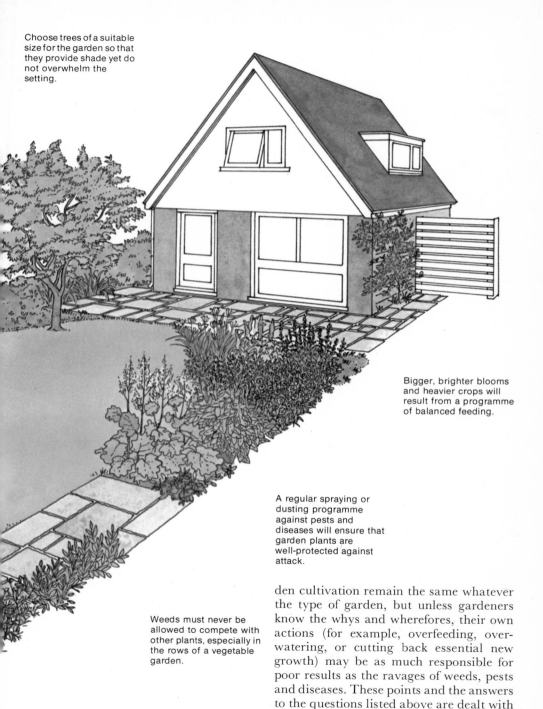

Choose trees of a suitable size for the garden so that they provide shade yet do not overwhelm the setting.

Bigger, brighter blooms and heavier crops will result from a programme of balanced feeding.

A regular spraying or dusting programme against pests and diseases will ensure that garden plants are well-protected against attack.

Weeds must never be allowed to compete with other plants, especially in the rows of a vegetable garden.

den cultivation remain the same whatever the type of garden, but unless gardeners know the whys and wherefores, their own actions (for example, overfeeding, overwatering, or cutting back essential new growth) may be as much responsible for poor results as the ravages of weeds, pests and diseases. These points and the answers to the questions listed above are dealt with here in detail chapter by chapter.

2 Feeding plants

Successful plant growth depends on good feeding. Soils differ widely in their content of foods or chemicals which are beneficial to plants but there must be adequate organic matter (humus) in the form of the compost to keep the soil in good condition. In addition, sufficient artificial or chemical feeds will be needed to maintain a balanced growth.

Even in an uncultivated garden, soil is manured or provided with organic matter by the action of worms, which bring decomposed leaves into the subsoil. There is also a natural process of decay or rotting down within the surface vegetation. However, where the soil is required for intensive cultivation, it is necessary to apply plant foods in a more concentrated form and more frequently, since plants quickly use up the food which is in the soil.

Most soils contain reserves of essential chemicals which slowly become available to plants by the action of soil organisms and weathering. It is still necessary, however, to add to these chemicals. In many cases, more of one chemical than another must be added in order to provide the plants with a good 'diet', to encourage sturdy, healthy growth, high crop yields and beautiful floral displays.

Frequent plant feeding is required for most garden plants so that they receive chemicals that can be used straight away by their root systems or which will be available in suitable forms, after some basic changes, in as short a time as possible.

Plant foods

There are certain foods which are essential to good plant growth. Top of the list are four chemicals – nitrogen, potassium, phosphorus and calcium. There are also some which are known as trace elements. These include magnesium, sulphur, iron, manganese, zinc, copper, boron and molybdenum. The first four foods, the chemicals, are the ones which gardeners need to supply to the soil, as many of the trace elements are probably already there in adequate amounts and are, in any case, only required in quite small amounts in comparison with the essential ones.

All the prime foods must be applied as a *balanced* feed to plants. Too much of one or too little of another will cause poor growth. By feeding back into the soil the correct proportions of plant foods the balance is restored. The results can be quite amazing.

Nowadays, it is possible to check the soil quite easily to find out what foods are lacking and how much of one particular food is required to bring the soil back into a bal-

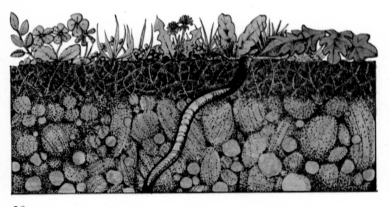

Even uncultivated gardens are enriched by the natural processes of fertilisation. Earthworms work decayed plant matter into the subsoil, providing new organic material. Their tunnelling also aerates the soil.

Pink-flowered hydrangeas are an indication of an alkaline soil, while blue-flowered hydrangeas indicate an acid soil.

which are relatively acid. Cabbages and Brussels sprouts, on the other hand, will grow successfully only in soils which are neutral or slightly alkaline.

Fortunately, there is a very simple way in which the acidity of soils is classified. This is by a scale that measures the soil's pH value. A reading of pH 7·0 indicates that the soil is neutral – neither acid nor alkaline. A reading above this figure indicates that the soil is alkaline, while below 7·0 the soil is acid.

The best values for most garden plants lie between pH 6·5 and 7·0. To make the soil more alkaline, lime must be added; to make it more acid, sulphate of ammonia is applied. An example of the effect of an acid or alkaline soil is demonstrated in the case of coloured hydrangeas. If blue flowers are produced all the time, this is an indication that the soil is acid. If, on the other hand, the flowers are pink, this is a sure sign that the soil is alkaline.

anced state. This is done with a soil-testing kit, which costs only a few pounds and is a very good investment – especially when planting a new garden.

The test outfit provides a colour code reference for small soil samples, which are treated with special chemicals in tiny test tubes. After shaking up the contents of each tube, the mix is allowed to settle and then a colour comparison is made against a special chart.

The deficiency (if any) can immediately be read off, while a check-off column at the side of the chart tells how much of a particular fertilizer is required to bring the soil back to its correct balance. These tests are only relevant for vital plant foods.

Acid and alkaline soils

When tackling the problem of plant foods it is also important to know whether the soil is acid, neutral or alkaline. This condition will have an influence on the fertility of the soil and on what types of plant can be cultivated.

Plants such as the heathers and rhododendrons will grow well only in soils

The degree of acidity or alkalinity of soils can be determined with a soil-test kit. A pinch of soil is mixed with the test chemicals and the resulting colour matched against a standard chart. Each colour indicates the degree to which a soil is acid or alkaline.

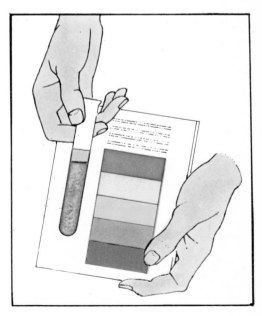

Let us now take a closer look at the individual plant foods which can be used to good effect in the garden. The nitrogenous feeds are very quick-acting. In other words, the effect on growth can be appreciated soon after application. The rate of growth increases, leaves take on a dark green colour and become large and luscious (fleshy). By comparison, lack of sufficient nitrogen results in small stunted plants and poorsized foliage, which may also take on a pale bluish colour.

Nitrogen promotes the rate at which plants grow. Leaves will become fleshier too.

Potash encourages better ripening and adds colour to fruits and flowers.

Phosphorous is a plant food that produces a vigorous root formation, especially with root crops.

Phosphorus is needed to promote good root development, without which the plants cannot obtain enough good food from the soil. It is a very important substance for root vegetables too. The phosphorous content in the soil is vital for seedlings to form a vigorous root system – thus building up an excellent plant for planting out later on in permanent quarters. Phosphorus is also essential for the satisfactory ripening of fruits, as is potash – an even more important plant food in this respect.

Potash adds colour to fruits, flowers and certain vegetables. It also encourages better ripening and enhances the quality of food crops in terms of flavour and properties. This is especially the case with apples, pears, potatoes and carrots. Plants deficient in potash become poor bearers and yield smaller crops. Leaf margins – especially those of fruit trees – can become scorched where potash is lacking.

The other top-priority food for plants is calcium, which already exists in many soils in adequate quantities. Calcium helps to stimulate essential bacterial action in the soil, which makes other foods readily available to the plants. It also helps to improve the physical condition of soils, corrects acidity and provides a good 'grounding', as it were, for other plant foods.

Feeds can be purchased individually or they can be bought in pre-mixed bags.

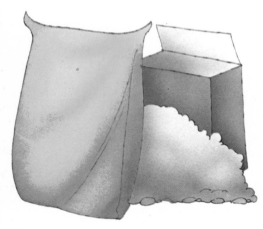

Fertiliser should be scattered along rows and should be raked in well.

Applying foods

Plant foods can be applied to the soil as individual types, or as balanced or specially blended mixtures which contain all the essentials, such as nitrogen, phosphorus and potash. Some mixtures also contain several important trace elements. Nitrogen is available as a plant food in the form of such fertilisers as sulphate of ammonia, nitrate of soda and nitro-chalk. Phosphorus can be obtained as superphosphate of lime, as basic slag and as bonemeal, which should be of the sterilised kind. Potash is supplied in the form of sulphate of potash. This is the best form of potash for the gardener to use as it is also relatively quick-acting.

Here is a check-list of some of the most popular plant foods available together with the details of their composition, the way in which they are used and their application rates. These are all 'dry' feeds which are applied as fine granules or powder and should be either well watered or carefully worked into the soil with a fork or rake, depending on whether they are applied as initial soil preparations or as feed to plants which are already growing.

Popular plant foods

Type	Use
Basic slag	This is a rather slow-acting fertiliser which supplies plants with phosphates and lime.
Bonemeal	Provides phosphates and is slow-acting. Use like basic slag in the winter and autumn. For safety it is important that only sterilised bonemeal is used as this eliminates the possibility of anthrax disease.
Lime	The quickest-acting form is hydrated lime. Chalk (calcium carbonate) is slower acting but is good for light soils because it holds moisture. Gypsum (calcium sulphate) is excellent for the improvement of the soil, especially the heavy clay types, as it helps to break them down.
Nitrate of soda	This is a highly nitrogenous fertiliser which is quick-acting. It can be used very successfully during the main summer growing period and is ideal for the leafy plants such as lettuce and cabbages. Care must be taken when using it as it has a caustic effect (burns) on foliage – especially tender young plants.
Nitro-chalk	Another quick-acting fertiliser which supplies nitrogen and lime. Nitro-chalk is ideal for acid or lime-free soils. Best used in early summer.
Sulphate of ammonia	Similar in use to nitrate of soda. This plant food is for boosting green growth. It is not so caustic as nitrate of soda and is best applied in spring or early summer. Must not be mixed with lime as a chemical reaction will occur. Can be mixed safely, however, with sulphate of potash and superphosphate of lime.
Sulphate of potash	It is an ideal fertiliser which supplies potash to plants. It acts quite rapidly and is non-caustic. Can be used at any time of the growing season.
Super-phosphate of lime	For the supply of phosphates to plants in the quickest form, this is the fertiliser to use. Will not affect the acidity of the soil and is best used in the spring or early months. Use carefully as it is inclined to scorch foliage.

mposition	Application rates
good sample is over 80 r cent soluble, a poor e less than 40 per cent.	It is best applied in the autumn and winter at rates of 110 g–220 g per sq m (4–8 oz per sq yd).
5 per cent nitrogen, –25 per cent osphoric acid.	Use at rates of 110 g per sq m (4 oz per sq yd) or 84–110 g (3–4 oz) in a bushel of potting soil (box with internal dimensions of 10 × 10 × 22 in).
	Use at rates up to 0·5 kg per sq m (1 lb per sq yd). Use at rates up to 1 kg per sq m (2 lb per sq yd). For the latter purpose, a dressing of 220 g (8 oz) is required.
per cent nitrogen.	The rate of application is 14–30 g per sq m (½–1 oz per sq yd). It can also be diluted in water and applied as a liquid feed. For this purpose it is used at the rate of 7–14 g per 4 litres (¼–½ oz per gall) of water.
per cent nitrogen, 48 r cent carbonate of ne.	Rate of application is 28 g per sq m (1 oz per sq yd).
per cent nitrogen.	Applied at the rate of 14–28 g per sq m (½–1 oz per sq yd).
B per cent potash.	Applied at the rate of 14–28 g per sq m (½–1 oz per sq yd).
B per cent phosphoric cid.	Rate of application is 28–84 g per sq m (1–3 oz per sq yd).

3 Compost

In gardening terms, there are two types of compost. The first is the special soil mixture which is made up for the cultivation of a wide range of plants. Then there is the compost we are concerned with here – the finished product, as it were, which results when waste vegetation is collected and allowed to rot. Both kinds are invaluable for soil and crop improvement.

Quite often compost is referred to as humus material. It is, without any doubt, a most important product and is essential if good results are to be expected from your garden, no matter what you are growing. It is something which is easy to provide because most of the ingredients for making

A garden can virtually feed itself. All the essential materials for making good compost can be obtained from the plants raised there. Trimmings from the vegetable plot can be used for compost as can leftover kitchen scraps.

compost are harvested from the garden itself.

Any soft material can be used to form compost. This includes hedge trimmings, grass cuttings, trimmings from the vegetable garden, autumn leaves and many waste scraps from the kitchen – for example, tea leaves, peelings, etc. When the waste material is decomposed efficiently it becomes a dark brown, fairly friable mass.

Of course, if it is not made correctly compost can become a rather nasty evil-smelling pile of slimy material which is pretty useless. In these days of natural manure shortages it is vital that as much compost as possible be made for the garden. Here is how to go about preparing your own.

Making compost

The amount of compost you will be able to make depends on the quantities of basic material you can obtain from your garden. It is surprising how many grass mowings can be collected over the cutting season.

Bracken, seaweed, leaves, dead flower heads and other trimmings can all go into the compost heap. Such plant material is a rich source of chemical nutrients.

62

This material can form quite a large part of a compost-making scheme. If you have a busy vegetable plot there will be lots of 'bits and pieces' you can gather here such as leaf trimmings from cabbages, lettuces and Brussels sprouts, and the tops of various root crops such as carrots, turnips and beetroot.

Then there are the bean and pea growths (haulms, as they are technically called) that can be added to the compost when the crop has been gathered. When you tidy up the garden, cutting off the dead flower heads, for instance, you can add the refuse material to your compost. In the autumn, there is usually a great clearing up effort made when the dead top-growth of plants, especially in the herbaceous borders is removed. All this can be used to make compost.

Many annual weeds can also be incorporated, but *never* incorporate the perennial ones, which could take root again. Try to

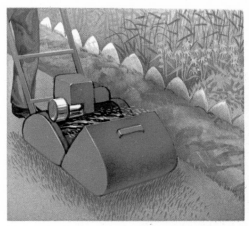
It is amazing how much rich compost material can be obtained from the clippings gathered in a mower's collecting box.

place weeds in the compost before they have made their seeds otherwise you will be sowing more weeds in the compost, and once such compost has been dug in a large proportion of the weed seeds it contains will grow again.

It is possible that you may be able to obtain other materials for your compost-making. Some bracken and seaweeds are useful but are best used in a moist condition as they will not rot down easily if too dry. Small amounts of straw can be included too. This should be wet or watered before it is incorporated.

There are a few items which should not be used in making compost. These include tough stumps or roots, and bits of plastic. Very hard prunings or trimmings from hedges are not suitable either as they do not decompose well.

Material for compost-making should be placed in a compost area or heap in order to rot down. The success of a compost pile depends to a great extent on the way in which the heap is made and contained. The use of special compost bins or containers is thoroughly recommended. These not only hold your compost heap neatly – this is very important in smaller gardens – they also encourage more efficient decomposition.

The autumn fall of dead leaves can also be used in the compost heap. Hedge clippings, but not the woody twigs, are another valuable source of compost matter.

63

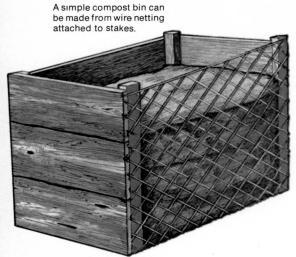

A simple compost bin can be made from wire netting attached to stakes.

Compost containers The material in a compost heap is broken down by bacteria and many other organisms that will only work well if there is adequate air, moisture, nitrogen, non-acid conditions and plenty of warmth. The modern compost bin is specially designed to promote the best conditions for the activity of bacteria. Holes in the sides of the container ensure adequate air penetration.

Of course, you can always make your own container. This will be particularly practical and money-saving if you are fortunate enough to obtain large quantities of waste material for your compost-making. The simplest container consists of wire or plastic mesh netting supported at four corners by strong posts driven into the ground. The smallest practical and efficient size is a little over 1 m × 1 m (3 ft × 3 ft). Usually a heap which is some 2 m (7 ft) in length and

A compost heap should have a base made of coarse matter that permits proper drainage.

The first layer of material about 23 cm (9 in) deep is then laid in the bin.

The next layer is made up of manure or a rich fertiliser that serves to activate the decaying process.

The 'sandwich' effect is achieved by adding additional layers of plant matter and activator.

about the same in depth is the best size.

Avoid placing your compost heap in a low-lying damp location. Good drainage is important. Avoid deep shade or a place where there is no free movement of air, for here stagnant conditions may prevail. On the other hand, a place directly in the sun will cause the material to dry up too quickly and poor rotting will result.

Building the heap No matter what type of container is used, always start the heap with the coarsest or roughest materials so that they form a natural drainage system for the rest. This material will rot eventually but initially will do its work well. After this your heap is built up 'sandwich fashion' – that is to say, a layer of waste material followed by an application of a special compost accelerator and so on.

The accelerator is a special preparation which encourages a more rapid decomposition of the waste and ensures a better and

sweet-smelling end product. The depth of each layer should be about 20 cm (9 in).

Place the material lightly on the heap – ideally, scatter it over the surface with a fork. Also, try to balance the material so that the weight distribution is fairly even. This will prevent heavier areas from settling down more than lightly loaded ones. Also decomposition will be encouraged if a balanced heap is made up.

The other big advantage with the use of special accelerators is that there is no need to turn the compost heap to ensure even and thorough decomposition.

Natural forms of accelerator include fresh manure – chicken, horse or farmyard

Quicker decomposition in the heap is obtained by scattering an accelerator in with the plant material.

The ingredients of a compost heap must not be allowed to dry out. Water the heap when it becomes necessary

manure. This can be applied on each 20 cm (9 in) layer of material. Such a heap will need turning to ensure thorough rotting down. This can be done after some six to eight weeks. Throw the material to one side, making sure that the outer sections are placed towards the middle of the new heap to rot down better. Keep the heap tidy and compact by retaining it in a wire enclosure – the original one can be used.

You can make up your own compost accelerator by applying 14 g per sq m (½ oz per sq yd) of sulphate of ammonia to the surface, then covering it over with about 4 cm (1½ in) of soil. This should be done after each 20 cm- (9 in)-deep layer of material has been laid down on the heap.

Rotting down will be much quicker in the warmer summer and early autumn months than in winter and early spring. A heap

started in early spring will be ready to use some time in the summer. With a good accelerator, many heaps of soft material will be well rotted after seven weeks. A heap started in summer should be ready in the late autumn. For spring use, a winter heap can be made up.

Keep an eye on the layers as they are built up. If they look rather dry, give them a light watering, using a rose on the spout.

If the weather is exceptionally wet it is a

This specially designed container has removable sides.

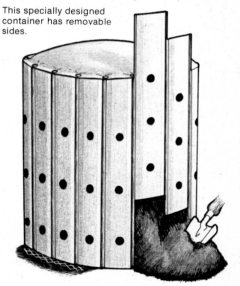

Both light and heavy soils will benefit by digging in compost. This helps to retain moisture and aerates the soil.

heap has rotted down well the bin can be removed and a new heap started.

The benefits of compost

Prepared compost will do many things for your garden. In the first place it is a soil conditioner. Light soils tend to dry out quickly, especially in the summer. If plenty of compost is dug in when the ground is being prepared in the winter or spring, and at any time when beds are being made ready for sowing or planting, the compost will act like a sponge and retain valuable moisture for the plants' roots.

Heavy clay soils are those which have their soil particles packed tightly together. If compost is worked in frequently it will help to space out these particles and make the soil easier to work or cultivate. It takes a little time for an improvement to be noticed but it is well worth doing.

Roots Compost also encourages the formation of vigorous roots, which in turn produce a healthy plant, one which is capable of taking in more food and water. Lining the bottom of planting holes or drills with compost is an excellent way to ensure a good start for plants. The larger holes for trees and shrubs can be treated the same.

good plan to provide a temporary 'roof' over a heap in the form of a sheet of plastic or sheet of corrugated iron to keep off excess water. Some commercial bins or containers have a sort of top or roof. Some also have removable sides so that the progress of the heap can be judged and also so that the contents can be easily removed. When one

Rotted compost matter should be incorporated into the bottom of the trenches made while preparing a planting site. It provides a source of nutrients for the plants.

Compost is ideal as a mulch or dressing along plant rows. It keeps the base of plants and their roots moist.

Quick-growing crops such as lettuce depend on a high moisture content in the soil. The inclusion of compost in the bed preparations for these crops will promote rapid growth, which in turn will result in crisp leaves.

Top dressing Compost is ideal as a mulch or top-dressing around plants or along plant rows. Applied to a depth of about 5 cm (2 in), the covering will reduce water loss from the surface of the soil and also suppress a lot of tiny weed seedlings. For many vegetable crops, mulching with well-rotted compost is an excellent idea. Crops which benefit especially from this system are peas and beans.

Root crops, such as carrots, benefit from a generous layer of compost in their drills at seed-sowing time. The compost retains soil moisture and encourages the formation of first-class tender roots.

Lawns Composted vegetable waste can be used for the preparation of lawn sites if the ground is enriched with the material by forking it in as the soil is cultivated. In light, sandy types of soil, this preparation is vital if the grass roots are to grow strongly and are not to suffer from very bad dehydration during hot weather.

Under glass Where plants are grown under glass – in greenhouses, frames and cloches – enriching of the soil beds is important as they tend to dry out more quickly under glass owing to the persistent high temperatures. For pots or other containers which are used for tomato and cucumber cultivation, the compost can be mixed with soil at the rate of one part compost to three parts soil. This, and some basic fertilisers, will produce an excellent growing medium with which to fill the containers.

When preparing soil borders or beds, outdoors or under glass, the same proportion can be used. Wherever the soil is light and tends to dry out badly the compost ingredient can be increased by one part.

This also applies to the use of window boxes and larger containers or tubs for flower displays. The one-to-three mix has proved successful for a wide range of plants when used with fertilisers. (These will be discussed in chapter 4.)

Compost is also useful as a top-dressing for lawns, where it is applied in the autumn or spring. The material is scattered as evenly as possible over the surface of the grass at the rate of a small- to medium-sized barrow load to every 3–4 sq m (3–4 sq yd). Afterwards, the compost is carefully worked or 'rubbed' into the surface with to-and-fro motions using the back of a rake or a stiff brush. A large proportion of the compost will be incorporated in this way and the remainder will gradually be washed in by the rain.

The lawn will benefit from a dressing of compost worked into its surface, especially in sandy soils that tend to dry out rapidly and that tend to be relatively poor in nutrients.

4 Watering

One of the most important gardening operations is watering. A plant must have a regular intake of water in order to grow well. In the case of fruit-bearing crops water is essential in order to swell the fruits.

Watering is vital where plants are being grown under glass and where they cannot benefit from natural rainfall. Plants grown in containers under glass dry out surprisingly rapidly, especially in high temperatures. Without the correct amount of water all plants will suffer, since the nourishment which the plants are obtaining from the soil is in solution.

The art of watering Watering is something of an art, because too little will hinder good growth whereas too much can cause the soil to become water-logged so that the plants' roots do not grow well. Too much water in the ground also cools the temperature and chills the soil, making for very poor plant progress.

If there is any 'golden rule' it is that the gardener should water little and often: the aim should be to keep the soil just nicely moist at all times. Remember that fruit-bearing plants such as tomatoes, cucumbers and melons need increasing amounts of water as their fruits swell.

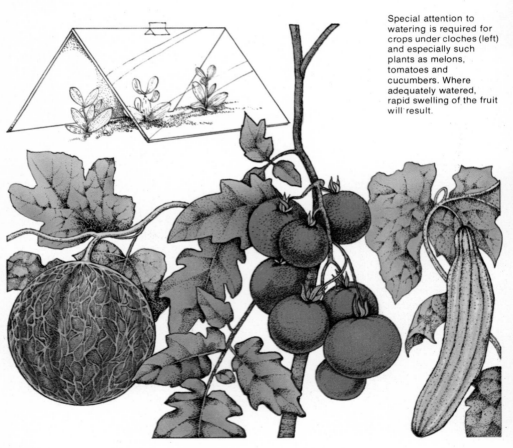

Special attention to watering is required for crops under cloches (left) and especially such plants as melons, tomatoes and cucumbers. Where adequately watered, rapid swelling of the fruit will result.

In the greenhouse, a good test for watering requirements is to pick up a pot and give it a tap. If there is a ringing note the pot needs watering. A dull ring, on the other hand, means that the soil is wet enough. This system applies only to the old (clay) type of pot. Unfortunately plastic ones provide no such practical clues.

However, a well-watered pot always feels heavier than a dry one, so this could be a fair means of gauging the condition of plants in plastic pots. It is now possible to purchase a special moisture indicator from your local garden shop or garden centre. The probe of this device is pushed into the soil in the pot, and straight away a light indicates whether conditions are wet, moist or dry. The device works from tiny batteries which will last many months. This is a very handy gadget, especially for house plants, which need constant checking for their watering requirements.

In the home, the dry atmosphere of a

A moisture indicator (**below**) will reveal the moisture level of the soil at a glance.

In the warmth of the home, stand pot plants (above) on top of a water-soaked gravel bed in order to give them more moisture.

heated room quickly dries out the soil in plant containers. One method of overcoming this is to place plant containers in shallow dishes filled with small pebbles or gravel. Run in some water so that the level is just below the stones. If the pot is care-

69

fully placed on the stones its base will not rest in the water causing the soil to become waterlogged. However, the air around the container will be kept cool and moist and will provide a better growing atmosphere for the plant.

Methods of applying water

The two most common methods of watering are by hose and by watering-can. For indoor use a smaller-capacity can is much easier to handle. With the hosepipe it is a good idea to have an attachment on the end which will provide a spray or a jet that can be easily controlled, either by a trigger or by turning the head of the attachment one way or the other.

With special connectors, a permanent hose system can be laid out for watering large gardens. Watering points can be attached so that all parts of the garden are watered at once.

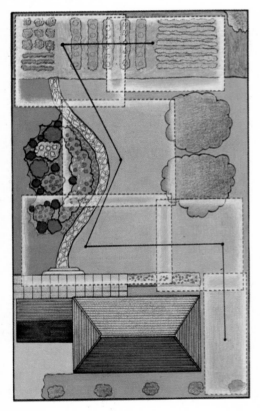

To conserve soil moisture, black polythene sheeting can be used as a mulch. Slits are cut out for the plants.

Sprinklers For watering large areas, such as a lawn or vegetable garden, sprinklers should be considered. These range from the very simple stick-in-the-ground designs with a central hole through which the water is emitted in a spray pattern, to the more sophisticated adjustable sprinklers which move their spraying bar from side to side and whose direction is controlled by a switch system. The latter can be 'dialled' or set to water certain patterns. Their greatest advantage is that application can be controlled with accuracy.

Hosepipes are very versatile and can be hooked up with connectors, some of which provide T-junctions. Quite a complex layout can be quickly set up to reach various watering points in the garden. There, a tap can be attached so that only short lengths of hose are required to water any part of the garden.

Watering requirements can be reduced if the soil around plants is mulched. Rotted manure or waste vegetation from the compost heap can be used for mulching, applying it over beds or around plants to a depth of at least 5 cm (2 in). This prevents a lot of water evaporation from the surface of the soil. Black polythene sheeting can also be used for the same purpose. Turning a little soil over the edges as the sheets are laid down will hold them in place.

Watering under glass In the greenhouse, under cloches and in frames, automatic watering devices can play a useful role, especially at holiday times. A simple system is one known as capillary matting. Capillary mats are capable of absorbing and retaining a considerable amount of water. If laid on the benching or staging with pot plants standing on top, each plant will be able to draw up its own water requirement.

The mat is kept supplied with water via a tank fitted with a simple float device. This piece of equipment is attached to the water trough, into which one end of the mat is placed. The mat absorbs water from the trough. To be completely automatic, the water tank can be attached to the main water supply. The floating ball valve in the tank will always keep it topped up with water.

For another simple system, a perforated hose or small-bore hose is used, fitted with an adjustable nozzle that can be regulated to provide a drip of water to plants in pots or in soil borders. This device can also be connected to a water-supply tank.

In a frame or under a cloche a trickle irrigation line with adjustable nozzles can be laid out and connected to a hosepipe. The tap can be turned to slightly open to maintain a trickle of water to the system. Shading glass, whether in a greenhouse, frame or cloche, will reduce the amount of evaporation from the soil.

Watering times

Water should not be applied during the heat of the day. It is far better to water in the evenings or early in the morning before the sun is high. Make sure, too, that the outdoor soil is *thoroughly* watered. It may look wet and dark, but it may well be quite dry below the surface if you scratch down a bit.

Newly-bedded plants should be well watered, especially larger plants such as trees and shrubs. A good idea is to pre-soak the planting hole a few hours before placing the tree or shrub in position. As light soils tend to dry out more rapidly than others, they in particular *must* receive plenty of water.

In the open garden it is possible to apply a liquid feed at the same time as watering. This is accomplished by using a simple diluter which is attached to the end of the hosepipe. The concentrated feed is put into the diluter and as the main flow of water passes through the hose the correctly diluted liquid is emitted from the end in the form of a fan-like spray.

Capillary matting and a self-regulating water-supply device will provide an automatic watering system which is ideal for the greenhouse

5 *Pruning*

Why do we need to prune? Basically, there are three very good reasons. The first is to produce the best possible fruits or flowers. The second is to maintain a tree or bush in good shape, and the third is to keep the plant as healthy as possible by removing dead or diseased growth.

There are, of course, several other advantages with pruning. It will keep a tree or shrub within predetermined bounds and will also maintain the attractive shapes which are so essential for fruit trees grown as cordons or fans.

The simplest forms of pruning are carried out purely to keep a tree or shrub in good shape. However, when fruit trees are pruned it is essential that certain rules be followed as each type has its own special requirements. If these are not followed closely a loss of fruit may result, simply because the branches which would have borne that fruit have been cut off.

Pruning is used to train such trees as this cordon apple. Unwanted shoots are pruned back to maintain the desired shape.

Raspberry canes which have fruited (dark outlines) should be cut right back to soil level. In general, cut canes back after harvesting except for everbearers that fruit in summer, autumn and again the next spring. Only cut these after the second crop has been harvested.

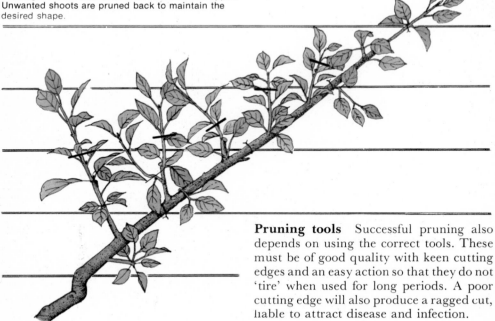

Pruning tools Successful pruning also depends on using the correct tools. These must be of good quality with keen cutting edges and an easy action so that they do not 'tire' when used for long periods. A poor cutting edge will also produce a ragged cut, liable to attract disease and infection.

There are two types of pruning shears. One has a so-called 'anvil cut'. Here the pruner has a sharp upper blade which comes down on to a bottom flat-edged blade. Pruners of this kind that have a slight sliding action are particularly good as they produce a natural, knife-like cut. The other type of pruner cuts with a scissors action. The two blades cross over each other as the cut is made. Both upper and lower blades have sharp cutting edges.

For tough wood, lopping pruners should be used.

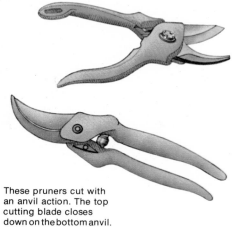

These pruners cut with an anvil action. The top cutting blade closes down on the bottom anvil.

There may come a time in a tree's or shrub's life when some large, tough branches must be removed. This is frequently necessary in neglected gardens. For this type of pruning special cutters, or 'loppers', will have to be used. These have short thick handles and very strong blades. Some have a special action which gives the user extra cutting power.

For taller trees and shrubs it is a good plan to have a special set of long-reach pruners. These have long tubular or flat metal shafts extending their handle, with a rugged cutting blade at the top. The blade is connected to a handle in the base of the shaft by a cable or rod. Some of the more sophisticated designs have extendable handles and can reach up high into a tree.

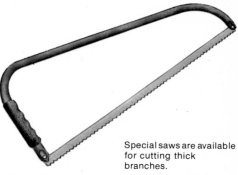

Special saws are available for cutting thick branches.

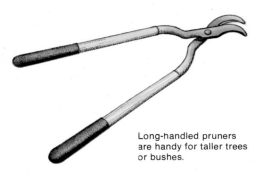

Long-handled pruners are handy for taller trees or bushes.

For the removal of very large limbs or branches a saw will be required. The best ones have specially-shaped handles – many of them of tubular construction with a bow shape for easy handling.

Successful pruning depends on an appreciation of what a good pruning cut is and the ability to identify various types of buds, especially on fruit trees and bushes.

Pruning cuts   These must always be made close to a selected bud with the slope or angle of the cut pointing away from it. The cut should never be made so that it slopes into the bud as this can cause moisture to lodge there and rot to set in.

Buds   The difference between a fruit bud and a growth bud must also be recognised. The former is quite plump whereas the latter tends to be thinner and often lies a lot closer to the stem it grows on. The fruit bud is responsible for producing the blossom which in turn becomes the fruit. The growth bud, on the other hand, makes new shoots or growths and thus extends the size of the tree or bush.

Other pruning terms   Leaders and laterals are two terms with which you should familiarise yourself before pruning. A leader, as its name implies, is a leading shoot or branch of a tree or bush. A lateral

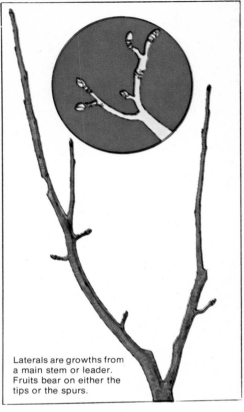

Laterals are growths from a main stem or leader. Fruits bear on either the tips or the spurs.

Bud identification: Plump buds (left) are the fruit buds. Thinner, pointed ones (right) are growth buds. The latter often lie closer to the stem.

is the growth or shoot which forms from the side of a main branch.

There are also the terms spur and tip. Some varieties of plant bear their fruits on short shoots or growths called spurs. Quite often, these spurs appear in clusters of more than one. Two well-known kinds of apple are spur-bearers: these are James Grieve and that delicious apple Cox's Orange Pippin.

Although some plants bear their fruit on spurs, there are many which have their fruits at the tips of shoots that have been made the previous summer. These are the tip-bearing plants. The apple, Worcester Pearmain, is a good example of this type of tree.

Ornamental trees and shrubs sometimes raise doubts but are dealt with separately.

Shrubs

Usually, shrubs need little pruning, except to maintain their pleasing shape or to remove dead or diseased wood. Where a neglected garden has been taken over it may well be necessary to cut back shrubs quite ruthlessly if a lot of weak, straggly growth has been produced. The centres of the shrubs will most likely be very over-crowded and some drastic thinning in the area will have to be carried out. Crossing and badly-placed branches will need to be removed.

It is useful to know that some shrubs produce their flowers on new growths and others on the previous year's wood. In the case of the former, spring treatment is best, cutting all the previous year's growth back to three buds from the base.

For the latter type of shrub, pruning is carried out only after flowering. Seek out the branches which have just borne their flowers and cut back to about three buds from the base. There are some shrubs such as clematis which need 'sorting out' as far as their rather complex growth is concerned. This plant can get out of hand over the years unless the growths are cut back. For the large-flowered hybrids February treatment is required, and for those var-

Floribunda roses (above) and climbing roses (below left) are both pruned in the spring.

ieties which flower twice in a season, cut back lightly after the first bloom of flowers has finished.

Another rambling type of shrub is the wisteria. In July, cut back side growths to six leaves, and in winter shorten them again, to two buds.

Roses

New roses Plants which require no attention after planting are ramblers, climbers and the species types. Old roses should also be left alone for the first year.

For others, such as the hybrid teas and the perpetuals, pruning should be quite drastic. Cut the stems right down to 10 cm (4 in) from ground level.

Treat floribundas a little more gently by cutting down to about 15 cm (6 in). Prune the polyanthus types back in the spring, cutting them to about a third of their original length.

Established roses Shorten the young shoots of hybrid teas to four buds. Medium-vigour shoots should be cut back to two buds. Do the work in March–April, the latter month being better in cold areas.

With floribundas study the different types of growth on each plant, distinguishing between strong-, medium- and weak-vigour growths. For strong growths, cut back to about six buds; for medium growths cut to four buds, and for the weaker ones prune to one or two buds. The latter treatment should encourage the production of sturdier shoots later in the year. Prune in March and April.

Prune polyanthus roses in March. Cut out all weak or thin shoots. Then cut back all other stems to about half their length.

Climber roses must have all their old or diseased growths cut out in March. Then cut the young branches back by approximately two-thirds their length. Prune the climbing 'sports', as they are called, in March–April, cutting strong shoots back by a quarter, medium growths by a half, and weak ones by at least two-thirds in order to encourage the production of much stronger growths.

Prune shrub roses from October to March. Thin out badly-placed growth and dead or diseased shoots at this time too.

Trees

Tree roses usually require very little pruning. For the most part pruning can be confined to the removal of dead or diseased branches and of any growths that are so badly placed that they spoil the shape or appearance of the tree. An open centre to a tree – especially the round-headed types – should be the aim. For this reason some thinning out of the central branches may be required from time to time.

Deciduous trees (those which lose their foliage in the winter) should be pruned after their leaves have fallen. Evergreens (those which do not lose their leaves) should be pruned, if necessary, in April.

Climbing roses (above) should have old and diseased wood cut out and thin wood removed. Make all cuts back to a good bud. Remove any old flower stems.

Cutting lines show how to prune an established hybrid tea rose (left). The extent of cutting depends on the vigour of each shoot. Remove dead and diseased wood.

76

6 Weeds and weed control

It is a great pity that weeds grow just as well as other plants in the garden. In fact, many weeds grow a lot *better*, and thrive in even the poorest growing conditions. Because weeds grow so prolifically, careful organisation is needed so that they can be controlled with the minimum of effort and time.

Unless weeds are promptly dealt with, they will quickly seed themselves, thus adding to the misery of keeping them out of the garden. Weeds are generally vigorous

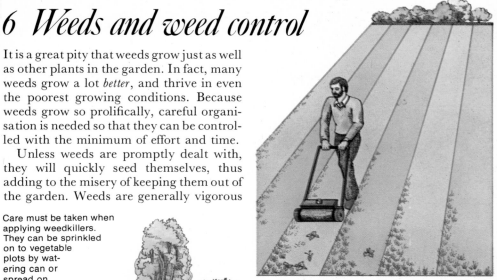

Care must be taken when applying weedkillers. They can be sprinkled on to vegetable plots by watering can or spread on lawns by special spreaders.

plants and will quickly smother crops if allowed to grow. Of course, they vie with other plants for food and moisture, often to the detriment of these plants, and ruin the garden's general appearance.

Weedkillers

Fortunately, there exists a wide range of chemicals which, if used sensibly, will greatly reduce the effort required in the battle against weeds.

A number of sensible and important precautions must be taken when using weedkillers. Keep them well away from children and animals. Always follow the instructions to the letter and always wash out containers thoroughly after use. Never use the same watering-can for ordinary watering as well as weedkillers. An *old* can, and one marked as such, should be kept especially for this purpose.

Specially-designed applicators for weedkillers can be purchased. These take the form of a large container with a long neck at the bottom of which is a special perforated bar which allows a very fine application of weedkiller to fall on to the weed area. This type of applicator is very useful as the bar end can be kept very close to the ground, where it cuts down the danger of wind drift.

For large lawn areas, there is another type of applicator, in which a diluted weedkiller mixture is allowed to fall on to a roller, which in turn spreads the preparation evenly on to the grass and weeds.

Lawn weeds

Chickweed This annual weed reproduces by seed. It has tiny heart-shaped leaves under 3 cm (1 in) in length. Use mecoprop or, for a recently-made lawn, a weedkiller specifically recommended for new lawns.

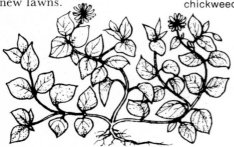

chickweed

Cinquefoil This is a perennial – in other words, a plant which continues to live for many years and which, in many cases, flowers time after time. Cinquefoil has a five-leaf pattern of a serrated form. Flowers are yellow with tiny reddish stamens. Cinquefoil seeds itself. Several applications of mecoprop should keep it in check.

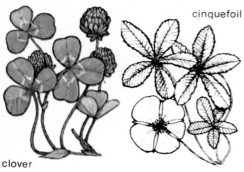

cinquefoil

clover

Clover Many lawns look lovely and green from a distance even in drought – but a closer inspection often reveals the fact that most of the growth is clover. This plant is a perennial with a three-leaf pattern formation (occasionally four-leaved). Clover has creeping stems and so spreads very rapidly. It has white ball-like flowers and also seeds itself. Use mecoprop to control clover, and feed the lawn with sulphate of ammonia in the spring.

Creeping buttercup A perennial which, as its name implies, spreads quite rapidly by its creeping stems. It also seeds itself. It has triangular, serrated leaves and bright yellow flowers. Treat it by watering on a 2,4–D mixture.

creeping buttercup

Field woodrush A perennial found most commonly on lawns which have been made on light soils, especially acid ones. It creeps along, roots rapidly and also seeds itself. Poorly-fed grass suffers from this weed. Its leaves are very thin and pointed and its head brown. Mecoprop will control this plant but several applications will be needed.

field woodrush

Meadowgrass A tough type of annual grass with broad leaves and green heads. Meadowgrass spreads all too easily by its seeds. The only way to control it is to dig out bad patches and use new, good-quality grass seed. The spread of its seeds can be limited by using the collecting box on your mower.

Dandelion   This perennial has serrated leaves and bright yellow flower heads. The plant reproduces itself freely by seeds. Even if a new plant is cut down, its fleshy tap root will soon produce a new growth. Repeated application of mecoprop or 2,4–D should be effective in keeping down dandelions.

dandelion

meadowgrass

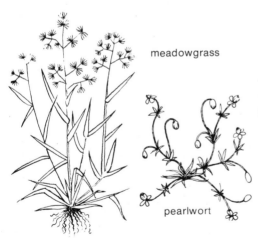

pearlwort

Pearlwort   This perennial is a very common invader of lawns. It seeds a great deal, has very thin narrow leaves on spreading stems and tiny yellow flower heads. Use mecoprop to control it.

Ribwort   This perennial is to be found in many lawns which have been uncared for. It has tapering leaves and rather insignificant brownish heads. Ribwort seeds itself. Control it by using mecoprop or 2,4–D.

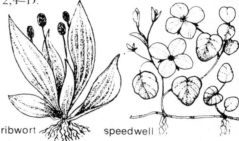

ribwort   speedwell

Speedwell   This is a perennial weed often found in lawns. It has pretty, tiny blue flowers and small, heart-shaped foliage. It takes root along its long stems and is generally quite fine in growth. Apply ioxynil or mecoprop weedkillers – preferably in the spring.

Trefoil   An annual weed, which seeds itself, trefoil indicates that the soil lacks an adequate nitrogen content. The answer is to apply sulphate of ammonia in the spring at rates which must not exceed 14 g per sq m (½ oz per sq yd). Regular applications of mecoprop until the weed has gone are also recommended.

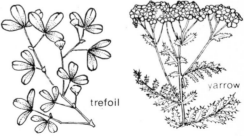

yarrow

trefoil

Yarrow   Another perennial, this plant has ferny-type leaves and tall heads of tiny white flowers. Several applications of mecoprop will control it. Sulphate of ammonia feedings will also help reduce infestations of this weed.

Flower and vegetable plot weeds

While you have been keeping an eye on your lawn weeds, other weeds have probably been settling in elsewhere in the garden. Let us take a look at the more common types which you may discover in your flower and vegetable plots.

Bindweed A really nasty weed which can really take over a garden, bindweed climbs to fantastic lengths and smothers plants with its heart-shaped leaves. It can be recognised by its trumpet-shaped white flowers. Bindweed is a perennial that comes up early each year. It is easily spread by its fast-rooting underground stems. Concentrate the weedkiller application around groups of plants. Spot treatment, on the other hand, is a somewhat tedious but very effective method of attack. To spot-treat, take a paintbrush and dab concentrated weedkiller on to it. Use 2,4–D for this.

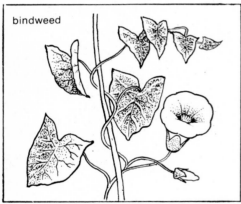

bindweed

Couch grass This is another nasty perennial weed which is difficult to deal with if it is allowed to get out of control. Like ground elder, it makes life very difficult for a gardener, especially if he is taking over a new or neglected garden. It has broad, pointed leaves and green heads. Use dalapon to control it. Couch grass also has masses of creeping stems which can easily be rooted out. Deep digging and then forking out and burning of roots is another method of dealing with this weed.

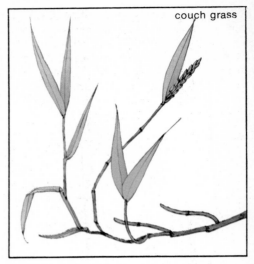

couch grass

Dock The broad-leaved dock, which is a perennial, has long spikes of brown heads. It seeds only too easily. If the long tap root is cut off but left in the ground, this too will take root and continue the infestation. Take your time and patiently spot-treat the weed. This means taking a paintbrush and dabbing concentrated weedkiller on to it. For large infestations, however, the best method is to apply a watering or spray of dichlobenil. Spot treatment should be done with 2,4–D.

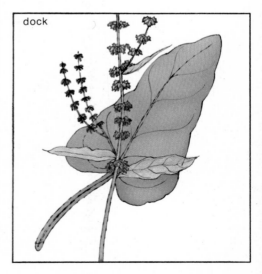

dock

Ground elder This is a difficult one to control as it spreads rapidly by means of its readily rooting stems. It is a perennial plant, has oval, pointed leaves and flat heads of yellow flowers. It can be controlled by 2,4–D and 2,4,5–T mixes of weedkiller. It is necessary to make several attacks on this weed for control to be successful.

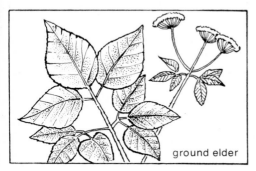

ground elder

Groundsel An annual weed which spreads by its seeds, groundsel has serrated foliage and bunches of yellow flower heads. It can be dealt with by applications of propachlor or dichlobenil.

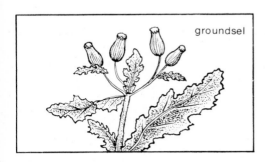

groundsel

Horsetail Another quite nasty perennial weed with fir-tree-like growths that start off as closed spikes of brownish shoots, horsetail spreads quickly by its root system. Repeated applications with dichlobenil will check it, although it is a very difficult weed to deal with and unfortunately there is no foolproof answer.

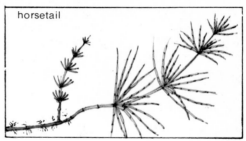

horsetail

Nettle This plant is a real nuisance. Not only is it a perennial which seeds easily, but it has stinging oval leaves. Several applications of 2,4–D or 2,4,5–T are effective control measures. A spring application is always a good idea.

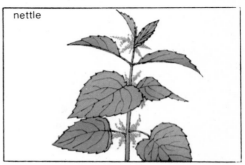

nettle

Oxalis A perennial which soon spreads by means of the tiny bulbs at its base, oxalis also seeds a lot. It has clover-like leaves and tiny pinkish flowers. Unfortunately there is no chemical available to control it. Forking up and burning the weed as soon as it is found is the best method of keeping its spread in check.

oxalis

Petty spurge A very common weed, petty spurge is an annual with pale-yellowish oval foliage on spreading branches or stems. Regular hoeing will cut it right down, although this work must be kept up throughout the season so that all tiny seedlings are killed as well.

petty spurge

Plantain A perennial plant with broad leaves and spikes of brown heads, plantain seeds easily. It is controlled by mecoprop or by using 2,4–D.

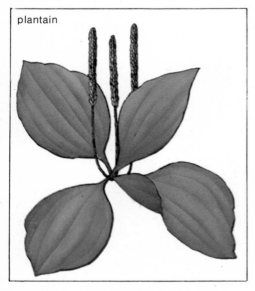

plantain

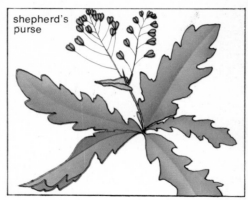

shepherd's purse

Shepherd's purse This plant is an annual with deep-toothed leaves and tall greenish heads. It seeds all too easily. Apply successive treatments of propachlor or dichlobenil to control it.

thistle

Thistle There are two types of thistle – the sow thistle, which is an annual, and the creeping thistle, which is a perennial. The creeping thistle seeds and also spreads by its vigorous roots. Both the sow and the creeping thistle have long serrated leaves, the sow thistle having yellow flowers while the creeping type has reddish flower heads. In both cases use dichlobenil to control it.

7 Controlling pests and diseases

One of the 'wars' all gardeners have to wage from time to time is against the pests and diseases which can attack your plants.

There are several pests and diseases which can be termed 'common' to the garden. That is to say, they are most likely to be present in your garden at some time or another, and it is as well to be able to identify them early so that the best methods of control can be put into practice. Most pests and diseases you are likely to come across will be found in this book under the crops they may attack.

Spraying There is a lot to be said for taking precautionary measures in good time – even before an attack has begun. A regular spraying programme can prevent

A powerful mist or spray is needed for trees so that a good penetration is assured.

A hand sprayer is useful when spraying smaller plants such as rose bushes.

troubles. With some types of preparation that are assimilated by plants early spraying can fortify the plants and make them reasonably resistant to attacks.

Successful control of pests and diseases also depends on spraying or dusting when conditions are favourable. Choose a windless day so that the material being applied is not blown all over the place. Care must be taken to reduce the drift of spray or dust to a minimum to prevent contamination of food crops (and your neighbours' gardens).

Garden flowers

1 Floral display

For many home gardeners the highest achievement is a garden full of flowers – a riot of floral colour from spring to early autumn, to which herbaceous borders, rockeries, trees, and shrubs contribute. Annuals and other plants, assisted by spring bulbs, raised and planted out twice a year in beds and borders, will produce the most colourful displays. There is, however, a vast difference between a tasteful picture

A riotous mixture of colourful summer-blooming flowers is here dazzlingly combined with flowering rock plants.

and the mere jumble of vivid floral colour that random planting will produce.

Enthusiasm for shapes, colours and scents is not enough in itself. The importance of plant form, and of the form, colour and texture of foliage should not be overlooked. These aspects can help to modulate the sheer brilliance of the blooms, and make possible tasteful arrays in which the different types of flower will complement

Far Left: A more modest mixture of flowering plants can be equally pleasing if planned with care.

A cheerful bed of attractively arranged spring flowers heralds warm days ahead.

Bedding plants graded in size and in contrasting colours relieve an otherwise austere design.

each other rather than set up in competition.

This can only be achieved by choosing good, healthy plants, creating for them the right setting in beds and borders which harmonise with the rest of the garden, and caring for them properly.

It is hoped that this book will help all gardeners to practise this popular form of gardening with understanding and inspiration. Better, more subtle effects can result from the same amount of effort and outlay (sometimes even less), yet will provide infinitely greater satisfaction. Working in this way, and knowing exactly what effects can be achieved, the gardener will be rewarded in ample measure by the results which ensue.

2 Making and preparing beds and borders

Sensible beds and borders in proportion to the surrounds and other features of the garden are the first essential. A few large beds are better than numerous small ones. They allow a greater range of plants to be grown without producing either a very flat or a top heavy picture and usually a much better effect is obtained, often with fewer plants. After-care is generally easier, too.

Avoid making beds of intricate shapes

like those shown here. They add to the difficulties of preparing, planting, edging round, and mowing between, and produce no better effect than beds of simple outline.

Also, avoid narrow ribbon borders of 60 cm (24 in) wide or less skirting a path or lawn or in front of the house. However planted, they will only emphasise straight lines; if a few plants make poor growth, the borders will look as if they are full of gaps, and they will also tend to dry out very quickly in times of drought.

When one display is over the old plants should be removed as quickly as possible and the beds dug over one spit deep. Well-rotted farmyard or mushroom-bed manure or compost can be incorporated at the same time, in the autumn for heavy and medium soils, in the spring for light, open soils.

Before raking down to produce a fine, level surface for planting, the soil must be made firm by treading. Use your heels rather than the balls of your feet for the greatest, most even pressure.

Beds and borders should be finished slightly higher than the surrounding ground but should never be mounded up. The finished level after treading and raking should be concave, sloping down gradually to just below the level of the turf or path. It should never be left like a plateau with steeply sloping sides, otherwise the soil round the edges may erode and the outer plants will suffer accordingly.

Intricate shaped beds make for hard labour and do not necessarily add to a garden's beauty. Simple designs are usually best.

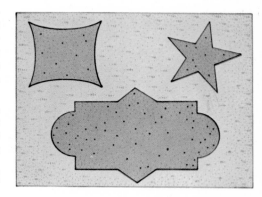

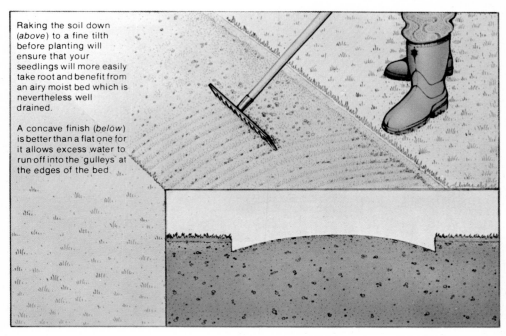

Raking the soil down (*above*) to a fine tilth before planting will ensure that your seedlings will more easily take root and benefit from an airy moist bed which is nevertheless well drained.

A concave finish (*below*) is better than a flat one for it allows excess water to run off into the gulleys at the edges of the bed.

3 Raising your own plants

A small greenhouse is valuable but not vital.

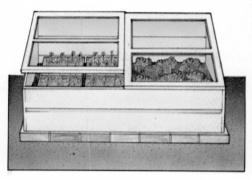

A cold frame is needed to harden off the plants.

Glass on flat or edge-side-up bricks makes a useful temporary frame.

Cuttings can be rooted and seedlings can be raised on a window sill.

Anyone can raise at least some of the plants they require and thereby save some expense and often disappointment, of purchased plants.

With the aid of a small greenhouse, even an unheated one, or a lean-to conservatory attached to the house, one can raise a wide selection of plants, provided these temporary occupants are not deprived of light by the other, more permanent plants.

A cold frame is essential for hardening off

plants. Even a knock-up frame constructed of boards nailed together or loose bricks with a polythene-covered light can be invaluable. Frames should be placed in a sunny position.

Cuttings of bedding geraniums, fuchsias, and other plants can be rooted in a small propagating case and grown on a window-sill. Marigolds, asters, alyssum and other plants which do not need to be sown until March can be raised in boxes. Turn them round each day to achieve balanced growth, eventually transferring them to the cold frame to harden off.

Suitable pans, pots and boxes will be required to accommodate plants, and compost in which to grow them. John Innes seed and potting composts can be bought ready mixed or you can use a soilless compost, i.e. peat with nutrients added.

Put roughage from the compost over the bottom of each receptacle to assist drainage, and fill to the rim with compost.

Press down lightly with the fingertips and level off.

Lightly firm to just below the rim with a levelling board or an empty pot.

Stand receptacles in water before sowing and allow to drain off. Sift a little fine compost over the surface if fine seeds are being sown. Scatter seeds very thinly over the surface. Large pelleted seeds may be spaced out separately.

Sift sufficient fine soil over the seeds to just cover them, and lightly press down. Leave very fine seeds uncovered. Cover with glass or polythene, and shade until seeds germinate.

Seedlings must be given plenty of light as soon as they germinate.

Prick out about 6 cm (2½ in) each way in other boxes as soon as large enough to handle. Lightly firm each seedling with forefinger and dibber.

Handle by the seed leaves, never the stem, which is easily damaged.

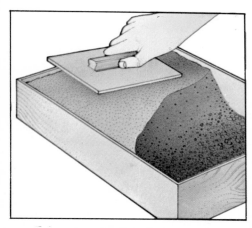

Left: First layer the bottom of the seed box with coarse material from the compost heap, then fill it to the brim with compost. Tamp down and smooth off.

Below left: Sow the seeds thinly in rows over the fine surface of the compost. Space pelleted seeds further apart. Cover both with a fine layer of soil.

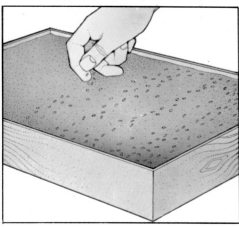

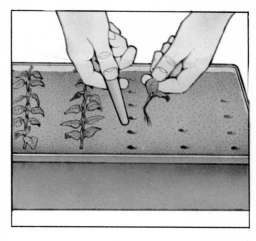

Above: To prick out seedlings successfully, pick them up carefully by the leaves to avoid damaging the delicate stems, insert the roots gently into holes prepared at regular intervals and press them gently in with the fingertips.

Above: Trim off the bottom leaves of the cutting and cut to a suitable length immediately below a node.

Above: Dahlia cuttings are best taken with the heel of the old stem.

Below: Insert the cuttings a reasonable distance apart in pots of peat and sand compost.

Below: When the cuttings have rooted, pot them individually into separate pots.

Lightly tap box to level the surface. Water in and keep as close to the light as possible. Take cuttings of such plants as fuchsias, zonal and ivy-leaved pelargoniums, *Iresine* and *Helichrysum rupestre* from plants in the beds at the end of August. Use a compost of 2 parts peat and 1 part sharp sand, and root under a propagating case in a greenhouse or on a shady windowsill. The pelargoniums do not need a propagating case and should be given very little water until rooted. Give the young plants full light and the minimum of heat during the winter. Pot off separately into small pots after the turn of the year using John Innes potting or a suitable soil-less compost. Pinch if necessary to obtain bushy plants and harden off by transferring to a cold frame in spring.

To obtain dahlia cuttings, cover old tubers with peat or soil, water and give heat to start them into growth in spring. Take the cuttings with a heel of the old stem and root in a shaded propagating case.

Wallflower (*Cheiranthus*) and *Myosotis* seed can be sown outside in shallow drills, about 25 cm (10 in) apart, in a prepared seed-bed in late May and June. Pansies, double daisies, aubrieta and Brompton stocks are best sown in boxes at about the same time and germinated in a cold frame. Polyanthus, primroses and *Primula denticulata* should be sown in April and also need a cold frame for germination, pricking off into boxes and hardening off as for summer bedding plants.

As soon as they are large enough, plant out the young plants for the summer 25–30 cm (10–12 in) apart, in rows about 30 cm (12 in) apart on any spare piece of ground or corner where they will get full sun. Polyanthus and primulas, however, should be planted in a more shaded position. Water in well and keep free from weeds. Daisies, pansies and aubrieta may be spaced out and grown on in deep boxes if spare ground is not available.

Later, lift them out carefully and plant in the beds and borders in the autumn when the summer bedding plants have finished flowering.

Polyanthus, primroses and *Primula*

Sow spring bedding plants in shallow drills in the open.

denticulata may be grown on from year to year. When they have finished flowering, lift carefully with a fork, remove all old flowering stems and gently pull them apart into single crowns, each with some root attached. Plant out as many of the best crowns as required on a shady piece of ground for the summer, and make sure they do not lack water.

After flowering, propagate polyanthus and primroses by dividing the roots.

4 Purchasing plants

Choose your plants for bedding out with care. Choose healthy, robust plants which grow together thickly. Avoid spindly plants (left) selecting instead well-grown plants (right).

It is not usually safe to plant out summer bedding plants before the third week in May, later in cold districts. Plants are often on sale at garden centres and shops long before this – do not be tempted to buy even if your beds are ready to receive them.

Plants kept in boxes until sold are often weak and spindly by the time they are really ready to be planted out. It is then difficult to separate them without serious damage to the roots. Neither they nor pot-bound plants make rapid root growth when planted out and so suffer more from the move, especially if the weather is hot and

dry. Spindly plants also tend to flop about and may not regain their natural bushy habit; likewise plants already well in flower, except, perhaps, *Alyssum, Tagetes* and French marigolds, which habitually start to flower when quite small. If it is possible to remove some of the flowers without spoiling the plants, this will be helpful.

In the autumn choose dwarf, bushy, sturdy plants, of wallflowers especially rather than large, lush ones which take longer to recover from the move and may not come through the winter so well.

5 Planting

The outer row excepted, slightly irregular staggered spacing is better than precise planting on the square system in straight rows or concentric circles. It is easier and quicker, and bare soil is not so obvious if the plants, for some reason or other, do not make their full growth.

Distances apart should be about 20–25 cm (8–10 in) each way for the dwarf edging plants; 30–35 cm (12–14 in) for salvias, petunias, intermediate antirrhinums, wallflowers and others of medium stature; 40–45 cm (16–18 in) for African marigolds, bedding geraniums, penstemons, annual rudbeckias and the ·taller zinnias; and 60 cm (24 in) or more for bedding dahlias. Tulips and narcissus bulbs which are to grow up through wallflowers, etc., need be no closer than 35 cm (14 in) each way.

If the ground is dry, water thoroughly some hours before planting. Plant at the correct depth, being careful not to plant too shallow. Firm well by hand and/or the handle of the trowel, and level out the soil between plants as you go.

Water in thoroughly, preferably individually, using an extension spout to the watering-can or an improvised lance to the hosepipe, to avoid treading on the beds. Water again as necessary until the plants are established. If the whole of the bed is watered, as the surface starts to dry, stir lightly to halt evaporation.

Above: Irregularly staggered spacing of the plants gives better coverage of the beds and promotes a fuller effect.

Below: An extension to the spout of the watering-can saves treading on the beds.

6 After-care

Careful hoeing on a dry day between the plants until they close up will keep down seedling weeds. When the plants meet they should effectively stifle most weeds; any weeds which do survive should be pulled out by hand.

Specimen or accent plants such as standard fuchsias and geraniums may need supporting, as inconspicuously as possible, with single stakes and ties, especially if the situation is exposed.

The ground-covering plants seldom need any support, but if for some reason they start to flop about and become untidy they are best held up by inserting a few bushy

Hoe on a sunny day to keep down weeds.

Support specimen plants with single stakes.

twigs which do not protrude above the plants.

Where practical, dead flowers or flowering heads are best removed as soon as they fade, for tidiness' sake and to prevent seeding and encourage continued flowering. This is very important in the case of antirrhinums, pansies, scarlet salvias, stocks and dahlias, where seed heads are conspicuous and soon affect flowering. It is not practical or necessary with *Alyssum, Lobelia, Impatiens,* begonias and others with numerous small flowers. Marigolds, petunias and verbenas usually continue to flower without any such aid, while asters and nemesias

tend to expend themselves in one long flush of bloom.

Spring bedding plants do not warrant this attention, as theirs is a comparatively short display with no follow on. It pays, however, to snap off the flowers of tulips just below the head either before or when they are lifted from the beds, so that the

Remove dead flowers for continuous blooming.

formation of seed pods does not hinder the building up of the bulbs for another year.

Insect pests are not usually much trouble. Greenfly is an occasional problem and is best controlled by spraying with a systemic insecticide. Sometimes the greenhouse whitefly is brought out on geraniums and fuchsias and continues to breed in a hot, dry summer. Malathion gives a better control than a systemic insecticide. Some plants are damaged by these substances, so read the directions carefully. Earwigs can be troublesome, especially on dahlias. Spraying against the other pests may help to keep them at bay, or they can be trapped in pots with a little dry moss laid inside among the plants. Inspect daily, destroying any catches.

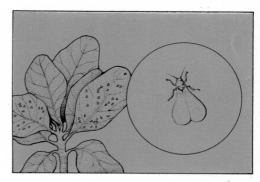

White fly

Antirrhinum rust

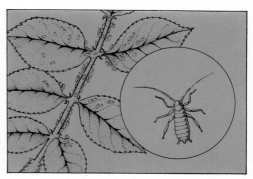

Aphis

Diseases are not much of a problem and one does not generally have to take any active steps to keep them in check. However, in southern areas of Britain, the brown fruiting bodies of antirrhinum rust on stems and leaves can be very crippling. This can be countered by planting modern rust-resistant varieties such as those in the Regal and Monarch strains. Wilt of China asters can mean the complete loss of plants. The stem blackens and shrivels just above ground level or a little higher, and the whole plant wilts and dies. Where it tends to be prevalent, it can also be countered by growing only resistant strains and varieties.

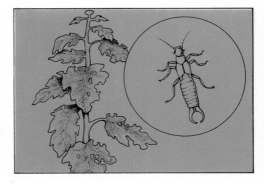

Earwig

7 Sowing hardy annuals in situ

If you do not wish to raise or purchase plants to bed out in the usual way, you can still have a lasting display of summer flowers by sowing seeds of hardy annuals where they are to flower. However, this means foregoing an April and May show of spring-flowering plants and bulbs. Dig the ground in the usual way, firm and rake down to a fine tilth, and then mark out irregularly shaped patches to a preconceived plan, with the tallest kinds in the centre – or at the back if the bed or border has one face only.

If necessary, thoroughly water the soil some hours before to ensure it is moist for sowing. Sow the seeds thinly from the end of March to early May. Either broadcast the seeds carefully over the surface and very lightly rake in; or sow in very shallow drills (little more than depressions in the soil) 25–40 cm (10–16 in) apart, according to the dimensions of each kind, carefully covering

To identify the flowers in the stylised border, see the diagram on the right and the key below: 1. *Clarkia* 'Salmon Queen' 2. *Linum grandiflorum* 3. *Phacelia campanularia* 4. *Chrysanthemum* tricolour 5. *Gypsophilia elegans* 'Pink' 6. *Godetia* (mixed) 7. Cornflower 'Blue Diadem' 8. Candytuft (mixed) 9. *Calendula* 'Orange Cockade' 10. *Nemophila insignis* 11. *Nigella* 'Miss Jekyll' 12. *Layia elegans* 13. *Eschscholzia* 'Ballerina' 14. Shirley poppy 15. *Chrysanthemum* 'Golden Gem'

each drill with fine soil when complete. Germination is often better by this latter method if a dry spell follows.

Weed seedlings usually germinate before the plants; remove them carefully by hand when quite small. Thin the plants in two stages – the first, when about 2–3 cm (¾–1¼ in) high, to half the final spacing, according to each kind's ultimate size. At the second and final thinning some

unwanted plants can, if necessary, be carefully lifted and used to fill any large gaps.

After-care consists of little more than hand weeding until the plants can take care of themselves, and supporting with bushy twigs if necessary. Sometimes these twigs can be confined to the perimeter of a group of plants merely to prevent them flopping over their neighbours. With some deadheading will help to prolong the display.

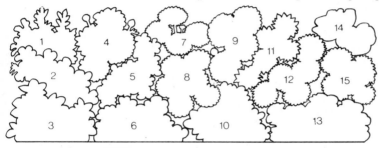

8 Window boxes, plant containers and hanging baskets

Even if you have only a backyard, or not even that, you can still enjoy the floral beauty of bedding plants by growing them in a variety of containers. If you have a garden, you may also like to decorate the house with window boxes and hanging baskets and have a few containers of plants on the terrace or patio.

cissi and the various tulips can be grown along with the usual bedding plants such as wallflowers, forget-me-nots and polyanthus. Crocus, miniature daffodils, blue squills, dwarf iris and a host of other miniature bulbous subjects are very useful for window boxes. Aubrieta and *Arabis* are especially useful for draping over the sides.

Above: A summer window box will brighten the barest window and is ideal for city flat dwellers.

Many of the summer bedding plants lend themselves to this form of culture. Bedding geraniums, fuchsias, begonias, *Impatiens*, heliotrope, marigolds, salvias and petunias are especially favoured. Dahlias, antirrhinums, nemesias, pansies and some of the hardy annuals are less suitable. Ivy-leaved pelargoniums, trailing lobelia and *Mesembryanthemum criniflorum* and others of a low spreading nature are invaluable for draping the sides of the containers. Climbing plants of annual duration can be successfully grown in containers for clambering up supports on the house walls. Many permanent plants can be grown in large containers, on their own or associated with bedding plants.

In the spring hyacinths, daffodils, nar-

Top: Brick pillars make attractive stands for plants.

Above: Group spring bulbs in containers.

100

9 Selecting plants

Summer bedding plants from cuttings

Note Throughout the following pages botanical names are shown in italics. In some cases, for simplicity, only popular names are given.

As most of the half-hardy plants propagated annually by vegetative means require a start in a greenhouse, less emphasis will be placed on plants grown from cuttings than on those plants readily raised from seed. Some in limited number can be raised on windowsills and in lean-to conservatories (see page 90) including the popular zonal pelargonium or bedding geranium and its forms, grown mainly for their coloured foliage.

In most cases cuttings have to be rooted in late summer and over-wintered under glass. A few quick-growing subjects such as *Iresine* can be can be left until spring. Bedding dahlias can be raised as previously described but they are now very easily raised from seeds annually.

The hardy blue fescue grass (*Festuca glauca*) makes an excellent edging and foil for geraniums and other brightly-coloured flowers. Stock plants can be lifted in autumn, divided and, for convenience's

Festuca glauca

(*Pelargonium zonale*)

sake, wintered in a cold frame. Other accent foliage plants such as *Abutilon striatum* 'Thompsonii', with golden variegated leaves, and the silver-leaved *Helichrysum rupestre* and *H. microphyllum* are easily raised from late summer cuttings and none are more simple to root or quicker to develop than *Iresine lindenii*, with deep crimson foliage, and *I. herbstii* 'Aureo Reticulata', whose leaves are green splashed with gold with reddish veins.

101

Pelargonium, ivy-leaved

plants in the beds or as specimens in large tubs. Varieties with a natural pendant habit are most g·aceful when trained as pyramids or standards.

Ordinary bushy plants of many of the indoor varieties of fuchsia are splendid for window boxes and containers, for which purpose it is best to raise them annually from late summer cuttings. Compact growing, free flowering varieties should be chosen. The single-flowered are often more adaptable than the large doubles. Many other plants which can spend summer in the beds can be grown by those with greenhouses and some means of providing heat

The ivy-leaved pelargoniums are good value for those with the means for propagation and overwintering. In beds they can be well spaced out as their trailing growths will cover quite a large area. This makes them excellent for hanging baskets and for draping over window boxes and other containers.

Those with a greenhouse can train up their own standard geraniums, fuchsias, *Helichrysum rupestre* and *Lantana*. This may take a couple of years, but by lifting before frost damages them, potting up and wintering in a cool greenhouse, and cutting back and shaping just prior to growth starting in the spring, they will last for several years.

Fuchsias in window box

Pelargonium crispum 'Variegatum', with small silvery, lemon-scented leaves, can be easily trained into close pyramidal form. Many fuchsias also make ideal pyramids, in which form they can be used as accent

when necessary. For the majority of home gardeners, however, plants which can easily and cheaply be raised from seed will be more practical and economical, and these are covered much more fully in the following pages.

Summer bedding plants from seed

Throughout the succeeding pages the following abbreviations are used: H.A., hardy annuals; H.H.A., half-hardy annuals; H.B., hardy biennials; H.P., hardy perennials; H.H.P., half-hardy perennials. An asterisk denotes hardy annuals which can also be sown where they are to flower.

Ageratum. H.H.A. 12–25 cm (5–10 in). First-class edging plant. Fluffy flowers mainly in shades of powder-blue, some with mauve cast. Also white variety. Sow February/March in heat.
Alyssum maritimum. Sweet alyssum. H.A. 8–12 cm (3–5 in). The white varieties are the most popular but there are also lilac, purple and rose-pink forms. Sow in March and April.
Amaranthus. H.H.A. 60–90 cm (24–36 in). Varieties such as 'Molten Fire' and 'Illumination' make spectacular accent foliage plants. Sow in February/March in heat.
Anchusa capensis. H.A.* 20–25 cm (8–10 in). Dwarf and compact. The variety 'Blue Bird' is an intense shade of true blue. Good for window boxes. Sow in March.

Amaranthus 'Molten Fire'

Alyssum maritimum

Anchusa capensis 'Blue Bird'

Antirrhinum. Snapdragon. H.P. The old and still popular intermediate kinds ranging in height from 30 cm (12 in) to 45 cm (18 in) have been joined by such modern strains as the rust-resistant Monarch and Regal series. Entirely new types include the Coronette hybrids, with the first central spike surrounded by a cluster of laterals, the hyacinth-flowered, with pyramidal spikes, and varieties with open, penstemon-like flowers lacking the usual pouch.

The new Pixies, with open flowers on plants a mere 25 cm (10 in) high, are an attractive addition to the very dwarf Nanum Compaction and Carpet types.

Antirrhinum 'Floral Carpet'

Taller varieties around 60–75 cm (24–30 in) in height include the original penstemon-flowered 'Bright Butterflies' and 'Madame Butterfly' (a variation with double, azalea-like flowers), base-branching varieties and others going up to 90 cm (36 in) in height.

Sow in January and February in heat.

Antirrhinum 'Madame Butterfly'

Antirrhinum, penstemon-flowered

104

Aster. H.H.A. Bedding or China aster belonging to the genus *Callistephus* and not to *Aster* proper which includes the popular Michaelmas daisies. There is a wide range of types and heights, including disease-resistant strains. All make an excellent display in beds from midsummer onwards.

The flowers of the taller strains, 45–75 cm (18–30 in) high, vary in form from the neat rounded blooms of the Ball or Bouquet strains to the large shaggy flowers of the old Ostrich Plumes. Most, especially the single-flowered varieties, make excellent long-lasting cut flowers.

Aster 'Powderpuffs' (Bouquet type)

The dwarf asters are ideal for formal beds. Modern strains such as Milady have large double flowers on bushy plants no more than 30 cm (12 in) high and as much across. Pinocchio is even more dwarf and has neat little flowers. Then there are the somewhat taller, pompon-flowered Lilliputs, the semi-double Pepite strain and others.

All the foregoing are available in well-varied mixtures, some of them in separate colour varieties. Sow in March and early April.

Aster, dwarf bedding type

105

Begonia semperflorens.
Fibrous-rooted begonia.
H.H.P. 15–25 cm (6–10 in).
Many modern strains and
cultivars are now available,
either in mixture or individual varieties in colours
from white through shades of
pink to deep scarlet, some
with deep purple/maroon
foliage. Continuous-
flowering but not always
successful in colder districts.
Sun or partial shade. Sow
December/January
in heat.

Begonia, intermediate bedding. 20–30 cm (8–12 in).
Hybrids such as the Danica
series, which make rather
larger plants than *B.
semperflorens*, have a good
range of colours, some with
shiny bronze foliage.

Begonia, intermediate bedding

Begonia semperflorens

Strains of tuberous begonias
and others, ideal for hanging
baskets and window boxes,
can now be raised from seed
to flower the same season.
They require sowing in
December/January, so a
heated greenhouse is really a
necessity.

Cineraria maritima

Coleus

Coleus. Flame nettle.
30–40 cm (12–16 in). Dwarf
strains of these greenhouse
foliage plants are now available from seed and used to
supplement flowers in summer beds of more favoured
districts. Sow in heat in
February.

Cleome spinosa

Convolvulus 'Tricolour'

Cleome spinosa. Spider flower.
H.H.A. 90–100 cm
(36–40 in). Unusual flowering plants for the centres of
large beds, for use as accent
plants or for large
containers. They flower
throughout the summer.
Purple, rose and white forms.
Sow February/March in
heat.

Cineraria maritima. H.H.P.
15–30 cm (6–12 in). Not to
be confused with the popular
greenhouse annuals. Several
different varieties, all with
elegant silver foliage, which
are very useful for accent
plants and for toning down
bright floral colours. Sow in
February in heat.

Convolvulus. H.A. 20–30 cm
(8–12 in). Forms of C. minor
are non-climbing plants
allied to the bellbine.
Trumpet-shaped flowers in a
mixture of colours. Deep
blue variety with white
throat also available. Good
for tubs and window boxes.
Sow in February in heat.

Dahlia. H.H.P. 30 cm (12 in) plus. Bedding dahlias of various heights with flowers of most of the popular types, i.e. single, double, cactus, collarette, pompone, etc., can now be so easily raised from seeds annually that it is not worth while storing the tubers and raising plants from cuttings each season. Sow in February in heat.

Dianthus. Pink. 15–30 cm (6–12 in). Modern bedding strains derived from perennial species are grown as H.H.A., flower early and freely and produce brilliant displays in mixture or as separate varieties. Sow February/March and grow cool.

Echium. H.A.* Bugloss. 30 cm (12 in). Open flowers on bushy plants in a mixture of soft tones of pink, blue, lilac, purple and white. Blue available as a separate variety. Sow in March and in April.

Dahlia, Coltness hybrids

Dahlia, Unwin's hybrids

Dianthus sinensis 'Magic Charms'

108

Gazania splendens 'Grandiflora'

Echium, dwarf hybrids

Euphorbia marginata. Snow-on-the-mountain. H.A.* 60 cm (24 in). Soft green leaves variegated with silver. Inconspicuous flowers surrounded by white bracts. Good accent plant. Sow in March.

Gazania. H.H.P. 24–30 cm (10–12 in) South African daisies in brilliant mixtures of yellow, orange, pink, red and bronze shades, many attractively zoned. They revel in full sun. Good for window boxes and tubs. Sow in February in heat.

Euphorbia marginata

109

Geranium 'Sprinter'

impatiens, mixed

Geranium. Zonal pelargonium. H.H.P. 45 cm (18 in). Now possible to raise these popular bedding plants from seed. New dwarf early-flowering varieties such as 'Chérie', 'Sprinter' and 'Ringo' are now taking the place of the original varieties and are very free-flowering. Sow in heat January/February.

Heliotrope. Cherry pie. H.H.P. 40–45 cm (16–18 in). Lavender to deep purple flowers, some varieties with purplish foliage. Highly valued for its sweet scent. Good for window boxes and containers. Sow in February in heat.

Impatiens. Busy lizzie. H.H.P. 10–25 cm (4–10 in). Dwarf, spreading and continuous-flowering. Does well in shade. Suitable for window boxes and containers. Sold as mixtures or separate varieties in white, orange, salmon, pink, rose and scarlet, some with striped flowers, some with bronze foliage. Sow in early March in heat.

Heliotrope 'Marine'

Lobelia 'Kaiser Wilhelm'

Lobelia. H.H.P. 10–15 cm (4–6 in). Along with sweet alyssum the most popular edging subject, especially the deep blue, Cambridge blue and blue/white eye varieties. Also available in white, red with white eye and a mixture of colours. The trailing forms are invaluable for draping hanging baskets, window boxes and other containers. Sow January/February in heat. Do not cover the seed when sowing and prick out in groups of 2–4 rather than individual seedlings.

Mesembryanthemum criniflorum. Livingstone daisy. H.H.A. 8–15 cm (3–6 in). Sprawling plants of a succulent nature specially suitable to a hot dry position, thus ideal for trailing over the edges of window boxes and containers in full sun. The type is rose pink but modern mixed strains include other brilliant colours. Sow February/March in heat.

Mesembryanthemum criniflorum

Lobelia 'Sapphire'

Marigold. H.H.A. The African or American marigolds have arisen from *Tagetes erecta* and are available in heights of 20–90 cm (8–36 in). Those of medium height are probably the most valuable for the home garden. All have large almost globular heads of flower varying from pale primrose through lemon and gold to deep orange.

The French marigolds are forms of *Tagetes patula* and are smaller in all their parts than the Africans. Heights vary from the 15 cm (6 in) dwarfs suitable for edging to those around 35 cm (14 in). Mahogany-red, in whole or in part, is the latest addition to the colour range and the flowers may be fully double, single or have a distinct central crest.

A new race of hybrids between the Africans and the French has been introduced recently. In habit and type of flower these hybrids more closely approach the French but the flowers are larger and the plants grow to 25–35 cm (10–14 in) high.

All these marigolds are quick to develop. To avoid them becoming tall and drawn before planting out they should not be sown earlier than late March or early April.

Marigold, African, 'Gold Coins'

Marigold, French, 'Naughty Marietta'

Matricaria. Feverfew. H.P. 20–25 cm (8–10 cm). Modern dwarf kinds may have ball-shaped flowers, or the boss of disc florets may be surrounded by a single row of flat florets. Very adaptable, they flower over a long period. Sow in March.

Nasturtium. H.A.*
20–30 cm (8–12 in). Non-climbing forms now available in a variety of bright colours. Good for poor dry soil and for hanging baskets and window boxes. Sow in March in small pots, one seed per pot.

112

Nemesia. H.H.A. 20–30 cm (8–12 in). Most popular as a mixture but can be had in separate colours of yellow, orange, scarlet, pink and blue, also bicolours. Early and profuse of flower. Sow in March

Pansy and viola. H.P. 15–20 cm (6–8 in). Available in mixture or in separate colours. Violas generally have smaller flowers in a more limited colour range but stand heat and drought better. Sow from January to March.

Nemesia hybrids

Pansy, mixed giants

Nicotiana. Flowering tobacco. H.H.A. 25–90 cm. (10–36 in). Available in different heights with white or crimson flowers, also strains including pastel shades and an attractive lime green variety. Sow in February in heat.

Nicotiana affinis hybrids

113

Penstemon hybrids

Petunia Multiflora 'Pale Face'

Penstemon. Beard tongue. H.P. 45–75 cm (18–30 in). Sold as a mixture in mainly pink, red and purplish shades, some with white or striped throats. Long season of flowering and good for cutting. Sow January/February in heat.

Petunia. Multiflora type. H.H.A. 25–30 cm (10–12 in). These have smaller flowers and are rather more profuse of bloom than the Grandifloras on page 115. Also they are rather less susceptible to bad weather so more reliable for bedding purposes. Good weather-resistant strains have been developed. Wide range of brilliant colours, including striped and chequered varieties. Sow January to March in heat.

Petunia Multiflora 'Starfire'

114

Petunia Grandiflora

Petunia Multiflora Double

Petunia. Grandiflora type. H.H.A.
25–35 cm (10–14 in). These have larger
flowers than the Multifloras, some with
waved petals, and are available as
individual varieties in a range of brilliant
colours – self, chequered or bicolour.
They are better for window-box and tub
culture than for planting in the beds, but
weather-resistant strains are being
developed. Sow January to March in heat.
Petunia. Double-flowered type. H.H.A.
30–35 cm (12–14 in). Both the Multifloras
and Grandifloras have double-flowered
strains with large, ruffled flowers up to
10 cm (4 in) across in a wide range of self-
and bicolors. Some strains are sweetly
scented. Generally used for pot culture but
also suitable for window boxes and tubs in
the more favoured districts, if not for
display in the beds. Sow from January to
March in heat.
Phlox drummondii. H.H.A. 15–30 cm
(6–12 in). Both tall and dwarf strains are
available as individual varieties or
mixtures in a wide range of colours
including blue and violet. The dwarf
strains are good for window boxes. Sow
February/March in heat.

Phlox drummondii, Beauty strain

115

Ricinus zanzibarensis

Portulaca. Sun plant. H.H.A. 15 cm (6 in). Dwarf and spreading with fleshy leaves. Likes a hot, dry, sunny position so is very suitable for filling in on the rockery and for tubs and window boxes. Generally sold as a mixture of brilliant shades of rose, orange, scarlet, crimson, rosy purple, yellow and white, many with double flowers. Sow February/March in heat.

Ricinus. Castor-oil plant. H.H.A. Will reach 130 cm (52 in) or more when planted out. A splendid accent plant with large shiny leaves but suitable only for limited use in large beds or as a tall architectural plant in a tub. *R. gibsonii* has deep bronze leaves and stems while *R. zanzibarensis* has green leaves with prominent mid-ribs. Sow singly in small pots January/February in heat.

Rudbeckia. Cone flower. H.H.A. 40–90 cm (16–36 in). Dwarf forms, such as the Rustic Dwarfs with large flowers in rich yellow, bronze and mahogany, and 'Marmalade' (golden-yellow with black central cone), make the best bedding plants. The Gloriosa Daisy type are taller with larger flowers. All are excellent for cut flowers. Sow in February and grow cool.

Rudbeckia, annual form

Salpiglossis. H.H.A.
45–70 cm (18–28 in).
Delightful mixture of
colours, many flowers veined
and chequered with different
shades. Must have plenty of
sun, therefore suitable only
for more favoured areas. Sow
January-March in heat.
Stock. H.H.A. 25–60 cm
(10–24 in). Ten-week and
other summer-flowering
stocks vary mainly in height,
season of flower and size of
spike. With some strains it is
possible to obtain a higher
percentage of doubles by
discarding either the weaker
or the dark green seedlings.
Sow February-March.
Salvia splendens. H.H.A.
15–30 cm (6–12 in). Several
different scarlet varieties
varying only in height, time
of commencing to flower or
foliage. Purple, rose and
pink forms also available.
Sow January-March in heat.
Tagetes signata 'Pumila'
H.H.A. 15–20 cm (6–8 in).
Differs from French
marigolds in its finer foliage
and its very small flowers in
shades of lemon, yellow,
orange or red. A useful
edging plant. Sow in March.

Salvia splendens

Salpiglossis

Tagetes signata 'Pumila'

117

Verbena hybrida 'Nana Compacta'

Ursinia. H.H.A. 15–20 cm (6–8 in). *U. anethoides* is a South African daisy with orange flowers and reddish central zone. Other hybrid strains in lemon to orange tones. Requires a sunny position. Sow February/March in heat.

Venidium. Monarch of the Veldt. H.H.A. 60–90 cm (24–36 in). *V. fastuosum* is a South African daisy with orange flowers with black centres. Hybrid strains have white, cream, lemon and orange shades. Pleasing woolly foliage. Sow February/March in heat.

Verbena. Vervain H.H.A. 15–30 cm (6–12 in). Available in mixtures or separate colours including violet-blue; some have conspicuous white eyes. Useful for window boxes and tubs. Sow January/March in heat.

Venidium fastuosum

Zinnia. H.H.A. Zinnias do best in warm, sunny summers. Weather- and disease-resistant strains are now being developed. The tallest varieties are suitable for large beds and cut flowers. They may have flat or quilled florets. The dwarfer kinds range from the Lilliputs, 30 cm (12 in), with ball-shaped flowers, the Persian Carpet type, 30 cm (12 in), with small double and semi-double flowers, many of them bicoloured, the compact Buttons strain 25–30 cm (10–12 in), the newer Peter Pan hybrids with large flowers on 25–30 cm (10–12 in) high plants down to the Thumbelina varieties with small double and semi-double flowers on 15 cm (6 in) plants. Some are available in separate colour varieties. Sow in March in heat.

Zinnia 'Lilliput'

Calliopsis

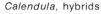

Calendula, hybrids

Hardy annuals for growing in situ

Amaranthus caudatus. Love-lies-bleeding. 60 cm (24 in). Long red drooping racemes of flower like lambs'-tails. A form with greenish-white flowers also available. Best on a soil that is not too rich. Thin to not less than 35 cm (14 in) for the best effect.
Calendula. Pot marigold. 30–60 cm (12–24 in). An old favourite now available with double, quilled centre and incurved flowers in lemon, yellow and orange selfs and mixtures of cream, apricot, flame and bicolors. Remove dead heads regularly for long flowering. Thin to 25–50 cm (10–20 in) apart.
Amàranthus caudatus

Candytuft. 25–35 cm (10–14 in). One of the most popular hardy annuals, quick to come into flower. Thrives in most soils and will succeed in sun or partial shade. Available in mixture or separate colours of white, red, pink, rose, lilac and crimson-purple. Sweetly scented. Thin to 25–30 cm (10–12 in).

Chrysanthemum. 15–75 cm (6–30 in). Several different annual chrysanthemums have excellent garden strains. There are the dwarf spreading *C. multicaule* with yellow flowers, *C. carinatum* (tricolour) varieties with zoned flowers in bright colours, the garden versions of the corn marigold, *C. segetum* and the double-flowered *C. coronarium* in yellow and primrose. All have finely cut elegant foliage and are useful for cutting. Thin to a distance slightly less than their height.

Candytuft 'Mercury' ('Giant Tetra')

Chrysanthemum carinatum
(Tricolour)

Calliopsis. Annual coreopsis. 25–50 cm (10–20 in). The taller varieties have mainly golden-yellow and orange-yellow flowers, some with a maroon zone. The dwarf forms also include dark red shades, some with a gold border. Thin dwarf forms to 25 cm (10 in), taller varieties to 35–45 cm (14–18 in).

121

Cornflower. 30–90 cm (12–28 in). The dwarf – 30–40 cm (12–16 in) high – varieties are the most suitable, although the really tall ones can be used in a wide border and their flowers are very useful for cutting. Both can be had in mixture or in separate colours including white, shades of red, pink and rose, and true cornflower blue. Thin the dwarfs to 25–30 cm (10–12 in), the taller kinds to 40–50 cm (16–20 in), at which height they should support each other.

Clarkia elegans. 50–60 cm (20–24 in). Long, slender stems of double flowers on bushy plants which usually need a little support. Long season of bloom. Can be had in mixture or in distinct varieties with white, pink, rose, salmon, orange-scarlet, scarlet and purple flowers. Do not thin too closely: at 35–45 cm (14–18 in) apart, the plants should support each other without detriment to the display.

Cornflower (*Centaurea cyanus*)

Clarkia elegans

Dimorphotheca aurantiaca hybrids

Cynoglossum amabile 'Firmament

Eschscholzia californica hybrids

Cynoglossum. Hound's tongue. 45–55 cm (18–22 in). Small true turquoise-blue flowers are freely produced, also a white form. Flowers throughout the summer and is not averse to partial shade. Thin to about 30 cm (12 in) apart.

Dimorphotheca. Star of the Veldt. 25–35 cm (10–14 in). Large daisy-like flowers in yellow, orange, salmon-orange shades and white. Comes into flower quickly and continues throughout the summer if dead blooms are removed. Thin to about 25 cm (10 in) apart.

Eschscholzia. Californian poppy. 15–30 cm (6–12 in). Free-flowering plants with finely cut foliage and single, semi-double or double flowers in a brilliant range of colours. Likes plenty of sun and is not particular as to soil. Thin to about 20 cm (8 in) apart.

123

Godetia. 20–60 cm (8–24 in). Long-flowering colourful annuals with single, semi-double or double flowers, many with frilled petals, in colours from white through pink and red shades to crimson plus lavender-blue, some composed of more than one colour. Some are available as separate varieties. Thin the dwarfer kinds to about 20 cm (8 in), the taller ones to 30–45 cm (12–18 in) apart.

Helianthus annuus. Sunflower. The common annual sunflower growing to a height of 2 m (6 ft) or more is obviously much too tall for the average annual border. There are now dwarf forms no more than 60 cm (24 in) high, some with single, and some with double flowers. They are good plant-makers, so thin them to about the same distance as their height.

Helianthus annuus 'Yellow Pygmy'

Gypsophila elegans. 45 cm (18 in). Graceful sprays of small white or pink flowers which are also useful for mixing with larger flowers in floral arrangements. Thin to about 35 cm (14 in) apart.

Lavatera. Mallow. 75–90 cm (30–36 in). Suitable for large borders. Needs little or no support. Large rose, pink or white trumpet-shaped flowers. Good plant-makers, they should be thinned to stand not less than 60 cm (24 in) apart.

Gypsophila elegans alba

Leptosiphon. Stardust.
10–15 cm (4–6 in). Finely cut foliage and masses of tiny star-like flowers in various shades. Very dwarf and ideal for the front of the border or for temporarily filling bare spots on a rockery. Thin to 15 cm (6 in) apart.
Larkspur. Annual delphinium. 75–120 cm (30–48 in). Invaluable for the character of its long spikes of white, pink, salmon, rose, scarlet, lilac and blue flowers. A dwarfer form has recently been introduced. Available as mixtures or separate colours. They can be thinned to distances much less than their height.

Larkspur, Giant Imperial mixed

Lavatera trimestris, mixed

Leptosiphon hybridus, mixed

Lupinus, Hartwegii strain

Linum. Flax. 30–40 cm (12–16 in). *L. grandi-florum* in crimson-scarlet or white with crimson centre is an excellent hardy annual. The slightly taller common blue flax is also well worth growing. Thin to 25–30 cm (10–12 in) apart.

Lupinus. 40–90 cm (16–36 in). The annual lupins can be had as a colourful mixture of tall kinds or as the dwarf Pixie strain and, like the perennial kinds, they are very showy border plants. Thin to 30–40 cm (12–16 in) apart.

Lonas inodora. 30–35 cm (12–14 in). A South African daisy with small, tightly packed heads of yellow flowers on branching stems with finely cut foliage. A useful secondary plant when grown as an H.H.A. and also good for drying for winter decorations. Thin to 30 cm (12 in) apart.

Linaria. Toadflax. 20–30 cm (8–12 in). Spikes of small snapdragon-like flowers in mixtures of pink to red, purple and yellow shades, including bicolours. Suitable for the front of the border and for cutting. Thin to 20 cm (8 in) apart.

Linaria 'Fairy Bouquet'

126

Nemophila insignis

Nemophila insignis. Baby Blue Eyes. 15 cm (6 in). Sweet little plant for the front of the border. Sky-blue flowers with white centres. Likes a hot, dry situation. Thin to 15–20 cm (6–8 in) apart.

Nigella. Love-in-a-mist. 40–45 cm (16–18 in). Cornflower-like flowers within a ring of fine leaves followed by attractive inflated seed pods, but better succession of blooms if these are removed. Blue and rose-pink varieties, also mixture of these colours with lavender, mauve and purple. Good for cutting. Thin to 35–40 cm (14–16 in) apart.

Mignonette (*Reseda odorata*). 30 cm (12 in). An old favourite valued more for its sweet fragrance than the form or colour of its spikes of reddish or yellowish flowers. Germinates best when the soil has been well firmed before sowing. Attracts bees. Thin to 25–30 cm (10–12 in) apart.

Nigella damascena 'Miss Jekyll'

Mignonette

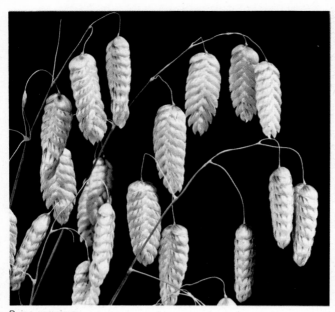

Ornamental grasses. Groups of annual grasses with ornamental flowering plumes can add to the distinction of the annual border and provide valuable material for drying for winter decorations. They may be used in mixture, or preferably, in distinct kinds. One of the most popular is the quaking grass, *Briza maxima*, with nodding spikelets. The cloud grass, *Agrostis nebulosa*, has broad feathery panicles, the hare's-tail grass, *Lagurus ovatus*, oval white downy plumes and the squirrel-tail grass, *Hordeum jubatum*, 5 cm- (2 in-) long silky tassels with even longer barley-like awns.

Briza maxima
Hordeum jubatum

Poppy. 45–90 cm (18–36 in).
The Shirley poppies with
single, semi-double or fully
double flowers, the
carnation-flowered and the
peony-flowered are all first-
class, fairly tall, long-
flowering annuals available
in mixtures of bright warm
colours. Thin to a little less
than their height apart.

Poppy, Shirley mixed

Sweet william 'Indian Carpet'

Phacelia campanularia

Phacelia campanularia. 22 cm (9 in). Dwarf
plant for the front of the rockery with true
gentian-blue bell-shaped flowers beloved of
bees. Thin to about 20 cm (8 in) apart.
Sweet william. 15 cm (6 in). Very dwarf
forms of the popular early summer-
flowering sweet william flower very quickly
when grown as hardy annuals. Sold as a
mixture in shades of pink and red with
white. Thin to 15 cm (6 in).

129

Viscaria, mixed

Sweet sultan. 45–60 cm
(18–24 in). Long-stemmed,
sweetly-scented fringed
blooms in a mixture of many
colours. Good for cutting.
Thin to a little less than their
height.

Sweet scabious. 40–90 cm
(16–36 in). Generally sold as
a mixture of many colours
from white to deep maroon.
Thin to a little less than their
height.

Viscaria. 20–40 cm (8–16 in).
Single flax-like flowers in
blue, pink, red and white in
mixtures or separate colours.
Thin to a little less than their
height.

Virginian stock. 22 cm
(9 in). Useful little plant for
the front of the border or the
rockery. Small flowers in
mixture of many colours.
Thin slightly.

Sweet sultan

Morning glory (*Ipomaea*)

Annual climbing plants

Annual climbers are particularly useful for tub culture on patios to grow up wires or other supports on walls or fences.

Canary creeper (*Tropaeolum canariense*)

Canary creeper. H.A. Fringed canary-yellow flowers all summer. Grows in sun or shade and is also useful for draping window boxes and tubs in addition to covering fences or walls. Sow in situ in April or early May or, if more convenient, in small pots for planting out later. Sow one or two seeds in each pot and later thin to one plant.

Morning glory. H.H.A. A lovely climber for a sunny position, especially the variety 'Heavenly Blue'. White, scarlet and blue-striped white varieties also obtainable. The flowers last for a morning only, hence the name, but are produced in succession for many weeks. Soak seed in water for 24 hours before sowing in small pots in heat in March as for Canary creeper.

131

Nasturtium. H.A. The climbing forms have single or semi-double spurred flowers in a variety of colours. They are less rampant and more floriferous in dry rather poor soils. They do well as hanging plants in window boxes and containers. Sow in situ in April or early May or if more convenient in small pots as for canary creeper and plant out later.

Nasturtium (*Tropaeolum majus*), Gleam hybrids

Sweet pea. *Lathyrus odoratus.* H.A. Very popular with numerous varieties and colours. Usually grown primarily for cut flowers but also make splendid plants for summer covering of walls and fences growing in the open ground or in tubs. Flowers must be cut off as they fade to maintain a succession of blooms. Soak seeds in water for two days before sowing in small pots from January to March in heat, or in September and October and winter in a cold frame.

Sweet pea, mixed

132

Spring bedding plants from seed

Bellis perennis 'Monstrosa' white

Aubrieta. H.P. 10 cm (4 in). This popular rockery plant makes an excellent subject for the spring beds with its low cushions of mauve, purple, pink or carmine flowers, most colours available separately. Sow as advised on page 11 or lift after flowering, divide and plant out for the summer.
Bellis perennis. Double-flowered daisies. H.P. 10–15 cm (4–6 in). The Monstrosa type has flowers up to 2·5 cm (1 in) across. The Pomponettes are dwarfer and have smaller pompon-like flowers with quilled florets. Pink, rose-red and white flowers in mixture or separately. Ideal for edging or under dwarf tulips.
Cheiranthus allionii. Siberian wallflower. H.P. 30–40 cm (12–16 in). Slightly later flowering than the ordinary wallflower, extending its season into June. The type has rich orange flowers and there are golden and apricot versions.

Aubrieta, mixed

Myosotis. Forget-me-not. H.B. 15–40 cm (6–16 in). The only true blue spring bedding plant. Pink and white varieties are available but these do not have the same appeal. The taller varieties vary in the depth of tone of their flowers. The dwarf forms, including a good rose-coloured variety, make very compact plants ideal for edging or for small beds.

Pansy. Heart's-ease. H.P. 15–20 cm (6–8 in). Numerous strains and varieties are available as mixtures or separately in white, yellow, orange, apricot, rose, red, rich wine, blue, violet-blue and purple. Some are completely self-coloured, others have the typical dark purple

Pansy, winter-flowering type
Pansy, 'Clear Crystals' type

Myosotis, dwarf type

or purplish-black blotch in the centre. Winter and spring strains are used for spring bedding and are seldom without a few flowers during any mild spell in winter, coming into full flower in April and May.

Polyanthus. H.P. 20–30 cm (8–12 in). Most popular as a brilliant mixture in white, yellow, pink to rose, red to crimson and blue, many with yellow eyes. Some colours are available separately, of which blue is very valuable. Beware of the very large-flowered strains grown for pot work; they are generally less profuse of bloom and do not always stand cold weather well.

134

Polyanthus, mixed

Primrose. H.P. 15 cm (6 in).
Differs from the polyanthus
in that the flowers are
produced singly instead of in
heads. Generally a little earlier to flower. Now available
in much the same range of
colour. Choose only the fully
hardy strains for bedding.

Primrose, modern strain

Primula denticulata. Drumstick primula. H.P. 30–40 cm (12–16 in). Not used for spring bedding as much as it might be. Can be raised and treated in the same way as polyanthus. The type has medium mauve flowers, but there are much deeper-coloured versions, also pink, red and white forms, the latter the tallest of all. Narcissi and the earliest flowering tulips are its best companions. Not really suitable for container cultivation.

Wallflower (*Cheiranthus cheiri*). H.P. 20–45 cm (8–18 in). Spring bedding is incomplete without the seductive scent of wallflowers. The standard kinds are available in white, primrose, yellow, orange, pink, scarlet, ruby, blood-red and purple shades. 'Eastern Queen' is of a shade in which apricot predominates and there are other pastel shades usually incorporated in mixtures. The dwarf or Tom Thumb forms have many uses and often stand the winter better than the taller kinds in exposed places, although their range of colours is not quite so extensive. They are better than the taller kinds for container cultivation.

Primula denticulata

Wallflowers, mixed

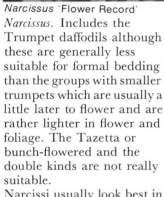

Narcissus 'Flower Record'

Spring bedding bulbs

Hyacinths. Probably best planted on their own in beds as they do not mix too readily with the usual spring bedding subjects. Ideal for colourful effects in window boxes and other receptacles. Choose bedding-type bulbs, i.e. those of second size, which are cheaper and produce rather smaller and more graceful flowering spikes.

Narcissus 'Sempre Avanti'

Hyacinths, mixed

Narcissus. Includes the Trumpet daffodils although these are generally less suitable for formal bedding than the groups with smaller trumpets which are usually a little later to flower and are rather lighter in flower and foliage. The Tazetta or bunch-flowered and the double kinds are not really suitable.

Narcissi usually look best in a natural setting – in grass, or on a rockery, for example. They can, however, be used in the beds with early-flowering subjects such as *Primula denticulata* and prim-roses as groundwork. They are always acceptable for bringing an early breath of spring to window boxes and other receptacles.

The bedding season begins with the large brilliant blooms of forms of *Tulipa fosteriana* and the early single tulips which can be used either on their own or grown with primroses or *Primula denticulata*. For the latter the taller varieties of the early singles, such as 'General de Wet', 'Dr Plesman' and 'Prince of Austria' should be chosen, all of which are sweetly scented.

Early single tulip 'Pink Beauty'

Early double tulips

The Triumph tulips flower second and being of medium height are fine for growing with polyanthus. The early double tulips flower about the same time. Being quite dwarf they are best used over a low groundwork of pansies, double daisies or dwarf forget-me-nots.

138

Lily-flowered tulips

Darwin tulip 'Queen of Bartigon'

The glorious Darwin and Cottage tulips and the elegant lily-flowered varieties are the right companions for wallflowers, *Cheiranthus allionii* and the taller forget-me-nots. The majestic Darwin hybrids and the late double or peony-flowered group are very striking but only suitable for beds large enough to take their height and 'weight'.

Those with a flair for the unusual can try the parrot and fringed tulips with waved and crested petals, the Rembrandts which are flamed and feathered in different colours and the Viridiflora tulips which are blazed and feathered with green.

10 Plant associations

It is not difficult to put seasonal bedding plants together to form a colourful display. However, much of the satisfaction of this form of gardening lies in creating harmonious combinations of form and colour, with the plants enhancing each other's beauty.

Summer bedding plants can be divided into:

(a) main groundwork, e.g. geraniums, petunias, antirrhinums, salvias;

(b) secondary groundwork, i.e. plants of open, slender growth with small leaves and flowers to percolate through the main groundwork, such as nemesias, *Anchusa capensis*, *Echium* and, among hardy annuals which can be treated as general bedding plants, *Viscaria*, *Linum*, *Lonas*, *Cynoglossum* and others;

(c) dwarf edging plants such as *Lobelia*, *Ageratum* and *Alyssum* (these can also be used for the main groundwork in very small beds);

(d) accent plants spaced at widish intervals to give height and character proportionate to the area, e.g. standard geraniums, fuchsias, etc., pyramidal fuchsias, *Pelargonium crispum* etc. and foliage plants of various habits such as *Ricinus*, *Cineraria maritima*, *Amaranthus*, etc. In spring bedding bulbs, especially tulips, take the place of these accent plants.

Bedding plants can be associated with the permanent occupants of the garden if beds and borders cannot be set aside for special bedding schemes. Although this style of planting is less formal, the harmonising of plant forms and colours is equally important.

Left: the *Yucca* is the character plant of this display. Salvias, *Alyssum*, *Lobelia*, begonias and other permanent and seasonal plants are tastefully planted in association with both the spiky leaves and the plumes of creamy-white flowers of the *Yucca*.

When individual beds and borders are devoted to seasonal bedding, the happy associations created in them should also blend in with other features in the garden. Although personal taste will naturally enter into colour blending, there are certain basic principles to follow. The colour extremes are the soft tones of blue, mauve and pink and the harder tones of white, orange, deep yellow, crimson and scarlet. A soft tone can be used to relieve the intensity of a hard one, e.g. pale pink with crimson or blue with deep yellow. Dark purples also require some relief. Magenta tones are difficult to associate with other colours.

Foliage is particularly useful as a foil for floral colour. Grey and silver especially will effectively break up and tone down bright and the less sociable colours. Golden and variegated foliage must be used with care: too much can produce effects which are either harsh or spotty. That of a deep crimson or purple tone has many uses but must not be overdone otherwise the picture will become sombre. The surrounds of adjacent permanent plants may decide whether a quiet harmonious combination or something rather more vivid is required. A dull situation will almost certainly call for a bright combination of colours.

Above: A bright association of scarlet salvias interplanted with *Coleus* 'Golden Ball', with the variegated *Abutilon savitzii* as an accent plant. The whole is surrounded by an edging of white *Alyssum*.
Left: A low and more subtle blend of the soft colours of pink fibrous-rooted begonias with white and violet *Alyssum* and dot plants of the silver-foliaged *Cineraria maritima*.

141

Although the range of subjects is much more limited spring bedding offers great scope for colour planning. It is difficult to avoid a two- or three-tier effect in the beds but this seldom becomes boring. The blue of forget-me-nots (*Myosotis*) is invaluable either as a main groundwork or in combination with any tone of wallflower. Use wallflowers on their own either in a single colour or in two harmonising tones mixed together. Fully mixed strains are seldom as pleasing as individual colours or planned combinations – either of wallflowers on their own or overplanted with tulips.

Polyanthus and primroses must be kept on their own, with tulips of suitable type as their sole companions – for they flower somewhat earlier than wallflowers, *Myosotis*, *Bellis* and pansies. The last two subjects, together with the dwarf compact forms of *Myosotis*, make ideal edgings for wallflower combinations, providing blue, purple and white tones to offset the more dominant yellow and red shades of wallflowers. Alternatively, both *Bellis* and pansies make good groundwork for the shorter-stemmed tulips in the smaller beds. The *Fosteriana* hybrids and the early single

Left:
'Royal Blue' forget-me-nots filtering through the wallflowers make a suitable 'base coat' for the deep maroon of 'Giant' and the creamy-yellow of 'Niphetos' Darwin tulips.
Below:
The brilliance of Darwin tulip 'Charles Needham' is softened by the pastel chamois-rose of wallflower 'Eastern Queen' and the forget-me-nots.

tulips are the best companions for primroses and for *Primula denticulata*; the Triumph tulips blend well with polyanthus; the Darwin, Cottage, lily-flowered and other tall, late-blooming tulips are best for wallflower associations, and the dwarfer varieties of these together with the early double tulips look attractive over a ground-coat of pansies, *Bellis* or dwarf *Myosotis*. Purple and mauve tulips are particularly effective over yellow, prim-rose or white wallflowers. Separate var-ieties or a mixture of two to harmonise with

the groundwork are always more pleasing than full mixtures.

The more thought devoted to the initial planning of flower beds and borders, the more satisfying will be the finished result: a mere conglomeration of different plant col-ours and shapes can rarely be as pleasing in a garden as the beautiful, well-balanced picture that will emerge when the relation-ships of one plant to another have been thought out with care and sensitivity. Very little extra effort is needed – and the results will be infinitely more rewarding.

Above:
A delicate combination of tulips 'Smiling Queen' and 'Northern Queen', with pink and white daisies inter-planted with *Myosotis* 'Dwarf Royal Blue'.
Right:
Pomponette daisies with *Myosotis* 'Dwarf Royal Blue' make a charming picture in a small bed or used to furnish a corner.

143

Balcony, patio and window box gardening

Diversity makes this patio a place of interest at all seasons, yet there is space left which is open and which is uncluttered.

Some people whose gardening activities are restricted to filling a few pots on a balcony, a few tubs on a patio or a roof, or to tending a window box might feel that they are under-privileged gardeners, deprived of their right to get their fingers into the real soil, to get mud on their boots and thorns in their fingers. But they would be very wrong.

This type of gardening could with advantage be called container gardening, for it must be carried out almost entirely in containers rather than in mother earth. Container gardening is probably the easiest, most rewarding, most exciting and most foolproof type of gardening there can be, for the gardener is in complete control over everything except the weather, and even this he can command to a certain extent.

The gardener can choose his own containers, their size, shape, colour, material. He can decide where they are to be placed, in this corner or that, at this height or that.

He can decide what kind of soil he will put in them, sandy or peaty, acid or alkaline, heavy or light. He can decide which plants he wishes to grow and even though his residence may be in a belt of the most uncompromising lime, he can grow in his containers fine plants of rhododendrons, azaleas and ericas. He can change his display at will, moving his containers from place to place or emptying them according to season and replacing their contents with fresher, more colourful plants. If frosts come he can even bring a container into the home for a night or two or place it where it will otherwise receive some shelter. He can plant spring-flowering bulbs in his containers at the end of the summer and overplant these with ericas, happy in the knowledge that he will have a certain amount of winter colour and all the promise of a glorious spring, yet during the colder and darker months he need never step out on to his balcony, say, to tend his plants, for they will look after themselves.

What limitations, then, face the container gardener? What problems will he find? In the first place it will be apparent that he is limited by size. Almost any plant,

Pelargoniums can be maintained in vivid, colourful bloom for most of the year.

Contrast of colour and shape on this balcony ensures a peaceful beauty with minimum attention.

147

even trees of considerable size, can be grown in a container so long as it is large enough. But one cannot grow a tree in a window box, nor on most balconies, unless it be either one that can be kept under strict control – such as a clipped bay tree – or perhaps one of the dwarfed bonsai trees. The gardener is also limited by weight, for a container filled with moist soil can be heavy indeed, certainly too heavy to move about with ease, and sometimes too heavy structurally. There is, then, a tendency for gardeners to choose fairly small containers made from some lightweight material (rather than stone, concrete or other durable but heavy material), for the sake of convenience.

The fact that the containers used are mainly on the small side presents another problem, for small containers dry out very quickly and in warm or dry weather can require watering twice a day. This can be an awkward chore and a considerable tie, for it may mean that one is unable to go away for a weekend, for example, without making arrangements for the plants to be watered or without installing some automatic watering device.

But these are comparatively minor problems when one considers that no heavy digging, no constant weeding, no regular mowing of the lawn, no hedge trimming, and no carting away of piles of garden refuse are involved.

Although the three types of gardening mentioned here have been grouped together under the title of container gardening, certain minor differences exist, owing mainly to physical conditions. The balcony is larger than a window box but probably smaller than the patio. So let us have a brief look at each of these locations.

Balcony gardens

With a balcony one must make up one's mind right at the beginning whether the

The use of masses of vivid colour in containers is well suited to hot, sunny climates.

garden is to be for the benefit of the residents or for the pleasure of passers-by. Are the plants to be enjoyed from indoors or are they to be placed on the exterior of the building so that they are hardly seen from indoors? A balcony is almost always bounded by a wall or a balustrade of some kind. Plants in their pots can be placed against this so as to leave as much room as possible, or they can be hung or otherwise fastened to the outside of the wall or railing. If both locations are used – growing plants *on* the balcony for the benefit of those indoors and at the same time *outside* the balustrade for the benefit of strangers – there will be problems of handling, reaching and stretching. There will also be problems of watering and the danger of debris falling into premises below or on to the street, something which must always be avoided.

On the whole it is probably better to create the balcony garden so that it can be seen at its best by the residents of the apartment. By using raised boxes, hanging baskets and the like there will be every opportunity of adding to the decoration of the building and the district at the same time.

There are several little problems which will face the new balcony gardener. For example, until one has experienced living

A variety of containers: *from left*, an evocative urn; a classic trough; a coopered half-barrel; a simple, shallow saucer; and a terracotta jar with planting holes.

high above street level it is impossible to imagine how much more wind there is, not only in quantity and strength, but – more important – in unpredictability. One never knows from which direction it will arrive, regardless of prevailing winds. So it is vital to take this wind into account. In certain positions a hanging basket may swing so violently in the wind as to be a positive danger, yet moved further back or against a wall it may do no more than rock gently in the breeze. Dry soil or peat may be blown away and a jet of water from a hose can easily find its way into a neighbour's windows. Plants usually have to be well staked or otherwise supported. Better still they should be comparatively dwarf so they will not snap off or rock in their pots.

Another problem that can face the balcony gardener concerns the sun. Some balconies can be in full sun for almost the entire day, others can be so affected by shade that certain plants just cannot be grown successfully. There is nothing that can be done about this other than adapting one's style of gardening to the existing conditions.

There is also the question of weight. A box of pansies bought from a street market may weigh only a kilo or so, but once they have been removed and planted in several pots or troughs of soil the total weight will have increased considerably, and when freshly watered they will be even heavier. Although this extra weight will not affect the structural safety of your balcony, you

Wooden window boxes are long-lasting, and a metal tray underneath will catch excess water.

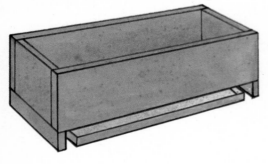

A built-in tray prevents having problems with drips when hanging baskets are being watered.

may find that if you have to move pots or tubs they may be heavier than you can conveniently manage; and if they are to be lifted above floor level and fixed in position, you may find that soil and plants have to be removed first.

Debris can be a nuisance on a balcony. Dust and soil crumbs, fallen leaves, dead flowers, a broken pot, seed packets and labels – all these can be a nuisance, disfiguring an otherwise pleasant scene if they are allowed to blow about in the wind. For this reason it is always wise and helpful to maintain a covered trash-can into which rubbish can be placed at the first opportunity so that the place is kept clean and tidy and so there is no likelihood of annoying neighbours.

Plants growing on a balcony should normally be in containers with drainage holes in them, although if they can be protected from rain this is not essential. Drainage holes will allow water to trickle through and on to the floor. However, this water can stain some surfaces, and it may linger in puddles and become a nuisance. Again, the copious watering needed at some times of the year means that fertilisers are constantly leached from the soil and require

150

replacing. For all these reasons it is helpful to stand pots on the balcony inside a saucer or some other container or to fit drip trays underneath them to catch and contain any excess water. This can then be returned to the plant soil at the next watering and will help to reduce the fertiliser bill.

Window boxes

Window boxes offer rather less opportunity for gardening than the space of a balcony. They also offer additional problems, the greatest and most important of which concerns the actual box or container and the way in which it is fixed in position. There can be no half measures with window boxes; they must be sound and undamaged, they must be securely held in their positions and they must have means for the collection of excess water or for its safe removal. This water must not be allowed to drip down into the street because of the damage or danger it might cause.

There are restrictive clauses in the leases of some city buildings prohibiting window boxes and it is worth checking this out before installing any. Insurance policies should also be examined, for if you are not covered for any possible damage or injury you could be open to heavy costs. It is therefore only prudent to make sure that if you do install window boxes they should both fit the windows for which they are intended and they should be securely fixed in place so that they cannot possibly fall.

It is this necessity for careful fixing that has led to the use of timber almost exclusively for the construction of window boxes, for this is a material which is easy to cut to size and easy to fix to walls or windowsills. The timber should be sound and not less than 25–30mm (1in) thick and it should be well preserved with several coats of paint. The window box should be not less than 15cm (6in) deep and wide, preferably more. If possible it should be fixed in position slightly above the actual sill so that a removable drip pan can be placed underneath it to catch any excess water. This should be of metal, and, once again, it should be either fixed in position or so secure that no wind or casual knock can send it

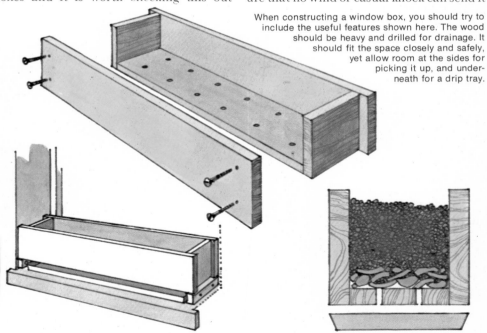

When constructing a window box, you should try to include the useful features shown here. The wood should be heavy and drilled for drainage. It should fit the space closely and safely, yet allow room at the sides for picking it up, and underneath for a drip tray.

falling to the street below; yet it should be easily removed and replaced from inside the room, rather than accessible only by means of a ladder in the front of the building.

A filled window box can be very heavy, so it is essential to fix it in position empty, and then fill it. It should have drainage holes in the base and there should be a drainage layer on the floor at least 2–3cm (1in) deep, with the soil above this. The soil mixture should be rich and well drained, yet with sufficient peat to hold moisture well. Too much peat or a soilless compost will almost certainly mean moisture loss by wind erosion.

Do not attempt to sow seeds in a window box, for uneven temperatures and the almost inevitable occasional dryness will inhibit their germination. Grow your plants indoors and then plant them out or buy ready-grown plants. Make sure that they are always at their best, for a shabby window box with half-dead plants is an eyesore. Any plant past its best should be removed and replaced.

Above: Window boxes need not be empty in winter. Evergreens such as ivies, aucuba, skimmia and heathers can be underplanted with dwarf spring-flowering bulbs like crocuses, daffodils and tulips. *Below:* Zinnias, calendulas, mesembryanthemums and pelargoniums will flourish in a window box in hot sun if watered regularly.

Above: Where shade is a problem for part of the day, pansies can be persuaded to flower, as can begonias and calceolarias.

Keep window boxes going in winter as well as in summer. Use evergreens such as skimmia, winter-flowering heathers, aucuba, ivy and similar plants, possibly underplanted with spring-flowering bulbs which can come up through the foliage to bring early flowers. Choose dwarf varieties of daffodils and tulips, for tall-stemmed kinds will almost certainly snap in the wind.

In summer the plants you grow will depend largely on whether the site is mainly in the sun or the shade. In the first condition use calendulas, zinnias, mesembryanthemums and the always useful pelargoniums. If shade is a problem, try pansies, begonias and even calceolarias.

Patios

A patio is less likely to present shade problems, unless it conforms to the narrow definition of this site as a courtyard completely surrounded by buildings. The name has come to mean what is almost an outdoor room attached to the house, frequently linking the house and the garden,

153

lying as it does between the two. It has also come to mean the backyard of a town house, an area too small to be labelled a garden and probably paved overall, with perhaps a few gaps in which plants are grown. But having considerably more space than is available either on a balcony or in a window box, shaded parts of the patio can be used for shade plants and the sunnier portion filled with sun-loving plants. It is also possible to use light-coloured paints to cover some or all of the walls, which will considerably increase the intensity of the available light.

Patio gardening gives the best of all worlds, for it makes it possible to plant some material directly in the soil, yet it also encourages the use of containers. The containers can be large and weighty. There is no need to worry about drips of excess water from any containers. Some plantings can be on a semi-permanent basis, while others can be as temporary as desired.

Unless one inherits a patio which has been used with intelligence and thoroughness, it is probable that the soil on the site will be cold, thin, sour and unproductive, so it will be well worth digging out the top layer where you intend to plant and replacing it with some fresh and healthy loam. It is easy enough to replace the soil in containers of growing plants, except where the containers are built-in or permanent structures, which might be more difficult.

Only in the most fortunate of conditions can a patio be made to look like a garden or even made into a green and pleasant retreat from the world. As a general rule one cannot escape from a certain formality, from straight lines, from flat paving, from a built-in and slightly claustrophobic atmosphere. Yet on these bases it is perfectly possible to build an outdoor room of charm and beauty, to disguise the straight lines, conceal the flatness, and soften the surrounding walls with green growth.

It may be that the patio has to hold such unsightly objects as an oil tank or a dust bin. It will probably have a pile of soil and perhaps some sand or a bale or two of peat, perhaps some tools and a roll of hose pipe. The thing to do is to build the patio in such a manner that these necessities can be concealed yet readily available for use at any time. This is not a difficult thing to do so long as it is done at the beginning and the work is carried out with the overall appear-

Before': It would seem impossible to transform this small, enclosed, obstructed place into a spacious and elegant garden.

154

'After': Tank and dustbin are hidden; the wall is lightened and heightened; and paving, plants and containers have been selected with care.

ance in mind. A light screen can cover the oil tank, for example, with a rampant *Polygonum baldschuanicum* growing on and through it, the plant's exploring tendrils and foam of creamy flowers concealing the functional interior. Seats with removable lids can hold tools. A wall with a built-in flower strip along the top can have concealed in its belly a cavity which will hold a good sack of soil or peat. All this is a matter of good design and imagination, and where space is so limited it is essential that every square metre of it should be used both to give pleasure and to ease normal house- and garden-keeping. If the patio is made into an exquisite retreat from life at the expense of comfort in the home, or if it becomes unrealistic in its demands for constant clearing and cleaning, then it will be more of an irritation than a pleasure.

Planting in soil If the area has been paved overall and you want to make certain plantings direct into the soil, it will probably be possible without too much trouble to remove one or two paving slabs here and there. The soil beneath is certain to be poor and unproductive, so it should be removed to a depth of at least 15cm (6in) and more if this is not too difficult. In order to check that drainage will be sufficient or suitable, pour a bucket or two of water into the hole just excavated to make sure that it runs away satisfactorily. If the drainage is poor

155

and the water lies in the hole for more than a very few minutes, it will become necessary to dig out more soil and to break up the subsoil.

Fill the hole with fresh soil according to what you intend to plant. If you have in mind a small tree or a shrub, then fill the hole with a soil mixture which will provide nourishment to the plant over a long period. Place in the bottom of the hole a spadeful of well-rotted farmyard manure, if you can get it, and mix a few handfuls of peat with your loam or leafmould which you sift in around the roots of your tree. Firm the soil well around the roots and then cover the naked soil with pebbles or something similar to give the finishing touch of

A pavement planting such as this should be bursting with plants, packed tightly so no soil shows through. This means a rich, well fed soil, regular watering and constant dead-heading of the flowers.

smartness and to keep soil off the paving.

If you intend to grow something more brightly coloured and cheerful, such as a little rectangle of vivid annuals, then plant these in a soil and peat mixture, about half and half, which has been well enriched with a slow-acting fertiliser, perhaps bonemeal or one of the proprietary types available. Make sure that the little patch is watered regularly and that all dead flowers are removed as soon as they begin to look faded. This will ensure that the bed always looks neat and it will help the production of further blooms.

When winter comes the occupants of this summer bed will have to be removed and one is then left with a vacant space. It can be filled with some hardy material such as heathers or ivy, but one cannot continually be lifting and planting in this manner, so a possible answer to this winter problem is merely to replace the original paving. This need not be done with any great thoroughness for it will be a temporary measure, but it will help to disguise the vacant space until the spring comes around again.

Herb gardens It is possible on a patio to grow a few of the most useful herbs for the kitchen. Some can be grown in pots but, if there is space, most will do better in the soil. A tiny section can be marked out like a chess board and different herbs grown in each of the squares. In this way you can also help to provide the type of soil enjoyed by the different herbs, a deep rich loam for the apple mint, a well-drained sandy soil for a little sage bush and so on. Some of the herbs will quickly outgrow the small space allotted to them, so it will be as well to take cuttings constantly and bring them along to replace a plant which has grown too large for its square.

Raised beds Consider also making a herb garden on a raised bed at waist height. Raised beds are useful for several reasons and they can give vast pleasure because the plants grow almost at nose level so one can

A raised bed such as this allows fragrant, colourful flowers and plants to be enjoyed almost at nose level.

pinch and smell easily. Waist-high gardening is also ideal for those who through age, accident or illness cannot bend to do their gardening at ground level. At this height they can plant and weed from a chair or even from a wheelchair, or they can stand, using a cane, to pluck out an invasive weed. In some cases the incapacitated can even perch on the broad side of an elevated garden and carry out simple operations from that position.

This last suggestion presupposes not so much a raised container as one which is built into a raised portion of the patio – in effect where there are two walls with an interior trough, usually planted up with bright plants to make a colourful band along the top of the wall. The actual soil container is seldom more than about 30cm (1ft) deep and this rests on top of the otherwise solid or core-packed wall.

If a flower bed is to be raised to waist level then it must be quite secure and there must be no danger that the sides will crumble and give way. For this reason the building of raised beds can be a somewhat lengthy business. The easiest and one of the most foolproof methods is to use prefabricated paving stones, square or rectangular. Once the size of the bed has been decided, the ground should be excavated about 20–30cm (8–12in) deep to this size. The paving slabs should be stood on edge around the perimeter. Spend some time making sure that they fit well together and are at the same height and angle. Hardcore rammed around the bases of the slabs should hold them securely in position, but if there is any doubt they can be concreted in. The interior of the square should then have rubble, coarse ash, half bricks and any other filling and draining matter dumped in place until within 30cm (1ft) or so of the top of the paving slabs.

This space can then be filled with soil,

157

preferably after placing some sealing material on top of the rubble to prevent the soil from trickling down too far. Turf squares are excellent, as are peat bricks. The type of soil used will depend on what is to be grown.

A more attractive appearance will be given if the walls are made from natural or reconstituted stone, although this is a more lengthy process normally requiring a concrete foundation for the considerable weight of the stones.

A lower bed can be built on a patio making use of peat blocks. Naturally these do not have the strength or stability of stone, but once they are built and planted the roots of the plants will take hold and the bed will become stable. This type of bed has several advantages. It is sufficiently solid to be a permanent fixture and yet it is

A raised bed is easily made with regular paving slabs, which because they are strong and slim allow large areas of soil to be used. Natural stone walls are attractive but need a foundation and greater space.

sufficiently portable to be moved should this be necessary. It is also naturally acid, so the filling-in with an acid soil will allow the planting of acid-loving plants in what might otherwise be an area where azaleas or ericas cannot be grown. A slightly raised bed of this nature can be an excellent spot on the patio in which to plunge some of the house plants from the home during the summer months. They will benefit from this access to fresh air and sunlight and the patio will gain through a new exotic appearance.

Electricity on the patio Try always to bear in mind the fact that a patio is an extension of the house, an outdoor room meant to be lived in, to be used and occupied. If you remove your furniture rather than leave it on the patio at all times and in all seasons, then make it easy to get out so that you waste no time and do not find it too much of a chore. Eat out of doors whenever weather encourages this activity.

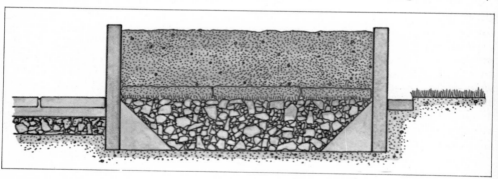

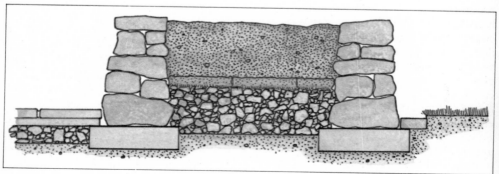

Peat bricks should be thoroughly soaked in water before being used to make a retaining wall. This makes them more stable and workable.

Install lighting, its type depending on the area available, but always bear in mind that glaring, overall flood-lighting will annoy or disconcert neighbours and will certainly not be attractive to anyone sitting out in it. It is far better to use just two or three smaller lighting units concealed among your plants, so that they are high-lighted. At the same time you have a useful but not obtrusive lighting of certain parts of the patio while other parts are kept dim and mysterious.

If you are going to install exterior light-ing on the patio make sure that your electri-cal wiring is both safe and unobtrusive. Engage the services of a competent electri-cian if you are not sure of what you are doing. You can either install a permanent system of electricity with one or two basic power points into which you can plug your electric lights as and when you wish to use them, or alternatively you can merely drape electric cable along the garden from the house for use on special occasions and remove it again at the earliest convenience.

A permanent system will probably leave the house and travel through the garden to the required spots in a specially armoured and insulated cable which is expensive but safe and long-lasting. If a spade should accidentally descend upon cable of this type it will do no damage. The points it is connected to would be of a special water- and weatherproof type, suitable under all conditions.

Electricity in the patio space can widen the uses to which you put this outdoor room. You can have a small pool with a few plants, a few fish and a little fountain of some sort that can drip, dribble or jet water in an attractive manner so that you get not only the shimmer and the twinkle but also the sound of the water – just another way of making the most of the patio space and its sophisticated equipment.

In fact, the possibilities open to exploita-tion by the possession of a patio are limited only by the amount of money and time available, and it has been known for a patio to be changed into a conservatory by the erection of a glass roof over the area, as the ultimate in garden luxury.

2 Containers

Materials

Above: Containers are available in a wide variety of shapes and a large choice of materials.

Under normal gardening conditions, when plants are grown in pots or containers of any kind, these look best if they have some affinity with the soil – that is, if they are of stone, clay, terracotta, even metal. But gardening on a balcony or in a window box is not normal gardening and this enormously widens the list of materials available for use as containers. On the ground-level patio, though, stone still looks best.

Stone Stone flower containers are often prohibitively priced. They must be made by hand and consequently they are seldom produced today. Old models come from antique shops with price tags suggesting that the stone used is precious rather than mundane. Fortunately the problem has been recognised and is being rectified by the use of reconstituted stone. Its main vir-

160

tue is that it can be moulded, which means that many copies of a single model can be made instead of just one. Inevitably this leads to a limited number of designs and the fact that one is likely to see one's own containers in a neighbour's garden, but this matters less today than it used to do. Designs are chosen which have a universal appeal and will suit most surroundings and conditions, and it is from these that the artificial stone duplicates are made. Sometimes they tend to be somewhat grainy, crumbly and soft at first, but normal weathering can be expected to harden and mature them so that they become safe under conditions of normal handling. Harder and tougher are those models which are cast in concrete rather than moulded in stone; when new, these seem to have a somewhat unsympathetic surface texture, yet this again weathers to become a great deal more appealing.

Above: Unusual containers always appeal, but they should be practical enough to hold sufficient soil.

Below: Terracotta is used for all these containers.

161

All stone containers by the nature of the material are bound to be somewhat large and heavy, an impressive addition to patio design. They need to be placed carefully and are often improved if stood on a plinth or formal base. Various plinths, bases and balustrades are also available in reconstituted stone, as indeed are a range of statuary and ornaments that do much to bring back into the garden or even the patio a grace of decoration that was for a time lost because of the expense.

Asbestos A material similar in some respects to stone but lighter in weight and thinner in section is asbestos sheeting, and this is used by one or two manufacturers to produce containers which are pleasant in shape, comparatively light in weight,

Left: Purpose-made half-sphere containers made from reconstituted stone are available at reasonable cost.
Below: Precast concrete and preformed asbestos will complement the brilliant flowers they contain.

neutral in colour and flexible in design. Being thinner this material is suitable for making smaller containers, and some of the most useful of these come in a series of long, narrow shapes eminently suited to use as window boxes. The range of sizes of these shapes means that you can choose one that will fit almost exactly into the window. The material is one that can easily be drilled to make fixing holes, although one should remember that the material is also some-what brittle and should be handled with a certain care. With care, however, it is quite possible to fix an asbestos window box quite securely into position so that it is safe and cannot fall into the street. If drainage holes are not provided (for many of these products can equally be used indoors and out) they can easily be drilled, and an asbestos window box made in this way will almost certainly require a drip tray under-neath it. This is best made from metal and ready-made trays are available at garden centres. There are plastic trays which are also suitable, but unless these can be firmly anchored they may prove too light-weight

Above: Containers on a balcony should always be heavy or well balanced enough to avoid being blown over.
Below: New shapes and materials are constantly being produced for the patio or terrace.

Above: Choose containers to fit the atmosphere of the site. *Below:* Always conceal the mouths of containers like this with masses of plant growth.

for a window and tend either to blow away or to rattle and become an irritation.

Timber   The most common material for a window box is timber. This is because a wooden box can be made exactly to measure and can be fixed in position with brackets or screws without trouble. If using timber, make sure that it is stout enough to last for more than one or two seasons. It should normally be at least 2–3 cm (1in) thick and of a dense timber such as oak, teak or elm, suitably matured so that it does not warp or crack. The exterior will probably be painted, but before this is done the entire surface should be coated inside and out with one of the copper naphthenate solutions, normally available as solutions in green, brown or natural. Do not use creosote, which is toxic to plants until it is old. If the box is painted, make sure that the paint has dried and all fumes have dissipated before doing any planting. The copper naphthenate solution will add years to the life of timber because it inhibits attack by all fungi and many insects.

Plastic and fibreglass Various types of plastic substances have been used for the production of containers, from the traditional flower pot to larger and more elaborate designs. Few of these plastic containers are suitable for window box use, mainly because of their lightness in weight and the fact that they are not easy to fix permanently and safely in position. A stronger material than most plastic is glass fibre, and apart from the fact that this again is dangerously light in weight, a fibreglass window box can generally be fixed securely in position. Fibreglass can be made in the widest possible range of shapes and designs, and finishes can also be controlled to some extent so that the completed con-

Above: This plastic container is in the style of a coopered timber tub but is longer lasting.
Below: A few potted plants and a climber or two will quickly furnish an otherwise stark patio.

Where a container is unlikely to be moved, it can be as large as you like and can hold anything up to a tree.

cause their weight renders them unsuitable.

In addition, on a charming and sophisticated town patio, plastic containers would seem to strike a wrong note unless the design is also sophisticated. But plastic on a balcony seems much more at home, probably because it is functionally correct in its lightness and its easily cleaned surfaces. The balcony is more an extension of the house than is the patio, for it is connected to the home, whereas the patio proper is a link with house and with garden.

On a balcony it is almost certain that a container of growing plants will have to be moved on occasion. This means that it must be as light in weight as possible. One should also remember, when buying, that all containers have to be first transported to the spot where they are to be filled. This again suggests that, to say the least, lightness will be a convenience.

Clean colours suit balcony use because they fit into any decorative scheme. Plastic surfaces can easily be kept clean, wiped down quickly with a damp cloth or sponge. Some plastic surfaces will accept the growth of algae, moulds and moss unless they are cleaned down regularly. This may not be of importance in a garden or even on occasion on some patios, but as a general rule a soiled container like this would not be acceptable on a balcony.

Because a balcony is normally smaller than a patio it cannot accommodate the cumbersome containers of large plants that might be appropriate for the patio. So to get the same effect of flower and plant colour on the balcony, one is forced to use a greater number of containers. There is nothing wrong with this so long as they are mainly massed together and not dotted about piecemeal. On a patio it is possible to cover an entire wall with a single plant growing either in the soil or in a large container. As far as the balcony is concerned neither the wall space nor the large container is available, thus for concentrated impact a large number of pots must be massed together, some raised or banked to be easily visible.

tainer can look like plastic, timber or, most successfully, like antique lead. Fibreglass is not as cheap as most plastic, but on the other hand it is virtually everlasting, whereas some of the less expensive plastics tend to degrade under the influence of sunlight and lose their colour and strength so that eventually they begin to split and must be replaced.

Choosing containers

Containers should be chosen carefully, partly for their suitability to the task and partly for aesthetic reasons. It has already been said that stone and other materials taken from the soil seem to have a certain feeling of rightness as patio plant containers. Equally, stone containers appear quite wrong on a balcony, as they do when fitted into a window space. This is simply be-

166

they might be in a whalehide pot or in soil.

The plastic sack is waterproof and the growing medium, normally a specially enriched peat mixture, is clean, sterile and balanced. All that is needed is the addition of water. Although these growing bags appear to be expensive and make the cost of the tomatoes or lettuces grown in them no cheaper than those in the shops, they are highly convenient and easy to use, and the actual growing medium can be used in the

Left and below: Why empty the growing medium out of the sack into a container if you can use the bag itself as the container? These growing bags are used mainly for the convenient culture of vegetables and salads.

Containers for growing crops

The plants grown on a balcony, in a window box or on a patio are nearly always purely decorative. The exception might be a few herbs grown on the patio. This is traditional, but there are a number of other, less traditional crops that can be grown in these locations. For example, there is no reason why the gardener should not grow, say, strawberries in his window box, lettuces on his balcony or tomatoes on his patio.

In comparatively recent years a new method of growing some of these crops has been developed, a method which for various reasons has proved so successful that it has been widely adopted by the commercial growing world, which we can accept as an indication of its viability. Basically, the idea is that instead of buying a special soil mixture and scooping this out of its sack into containers, the sack itself is used as the container. It is laid flat on the floor, and is slit open. Then the crop, such as tomato plants, for example, are placed in it just as

garden or to fill other pots once the crop has been harvested. (It is not advisable to use the bag for a second crop.)

It is a clean, easy and efficient way of growing and one eminently suited to use on the patio or the balcony. The sacks are not, perhaps, attractive in appearance, but they can be disguised or hidden and it is, after all, the crop that is most important.

Hanging baskets

Hanging baskets are a useful and charming addition to a balcony display and they can provide colour high on a wall, helping to make the most of the limited space available. They are unusual decorations which bring welcome splashes of colour where they are not normally expected.

The usual type of frame for a hanging basket is a half sphere of galvanised wire 30–45cm (12–18in) in diameter and provided with chains and a ring for hanging. There are also types, usually made from some plastic material, which involve fewer problems. In either case the bracket from which the basket is to be hung must be strong and firmly fixed to the wall, for the basket, when planted and watered, can be very heavy indeed. Although they should be placed high enough to be out of the way of people walking below, they should not be so high that they are difficult to water, for they dry out quickly and will require water both morning and evening on a dry and sunny day. Make sure that any drips that might fall cannot harm other plants that are growing below, and, if the baskets are in a position over a roadway, see that they do not drip on passers-by.

When you are using a wire frame basket it must have a lining to serve as a cup or container for the soil. Moss is the best material for this, but as this is not always available or easy to obtain, other materials will suffice. Thin turves of grass, laid so that the grass is on the inside and the soil on the outside, will be a useful substitute. Alternatively, coarse sacking will usually last for a season and, if it is coarse enough, will allow shoots of some plants to grow through it and so clothe the basket in growing green, for the purpose will be to have flowers and foliage everywhere.

Having lined the wire basket, fill the interior with a good, rich soil. Knock the plants from their pots and plant them in this compost, positioning them to trail prettily over the edges or even to grow downwards through the lining. Water the basket thoroughly and make sure that it is never allowed to dry out. You will find that on some days this will mean watering twice or even three times, so it may be worth your while to fix a hose on to a cane so that it can be lifted easily, to water from a window above or to have the hanging basket on a rope and pulley so that it can easily be lowered. In the last case it will sometimes be helpful to water the basket by immersion rather than by pouring water from above. Simply drop it into a bucket or basin and leave it there until uniformly moist, then allow to drain and restore it to its correct position.

Plastic hanging baskets will not normally allow plants to grow through the base, so it is more than ever necessary to have plants or trails hanging over the sides so as to conceal what might otherwise be a rather ugly naked material. On the other hand, plastic hanging baskets usually have a drip tray incorporated, which means that not only do you have fewer worries about water falling on other plants or on the heads of people, but a single watering will last longer, for the moisture that collects in this tray is more or less a reservoir for the main basket, the water being released slowly.

Useful plants for hanging baskets include several varieties of the ever-popular pelargonium, some of the smaller-leaved ivies, alyssum, lobelia, tropaeolums, selaginella and some of the begonias. Among the perennials choose from *Columnea banksii*, several of the more pendulous fuchsias, *Hoya bella*, the quick-growing plectranthus with its glossy leaves and some of the tradescantias and zebrinas.

Left: Line a hanging basket, then fill with a moisture-retentive soil. Allow some plants to trail.

Below: Fix hanging baskets securely and high enough to be out of the way of passers-by.

3 Techniques

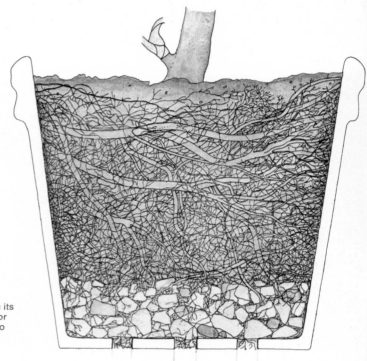

A plant's roots travel round in its container searching always for fresh moisture and fertiliser to keep it in good health.

With few exceptions, plants for patios, window boxes and balconies usually have to be grown in containers. A plant growing in a container can be killed in a day by neglect: it depends entirely on the gardener for its life because it cannot send its roots out in search of food and drink

Needless to say, the soil in which plants grow is important. But this is not enough, for plants, like humans, need food and moisture, light, air, warmth and a degree of shelter. And the roots have as much need of these benefits as do the branches, foliage and flowers.

Aeration

Plants in containers need more water than

plants in the ground, and this will affect the soil. Some of the soil is washed away, the fertiliser content is leached out, the surface may become panned down and brick-like, and the drainage holes may become clogged up.

Attention must be paid to the top and bottom of the soil. Scratch the soil surface lightly every now and again to open it up to the air. It also helps to mulch the soil surface once or twice a year with a rich leaf mould, well rotted farmyard manure, spent hops or even a handful or two of moist peat.

Drainage

The base of the soil cannot be reached, of course, but at the time of initial planting,

before the soil is poured in, be sure to include a layer of drainage material such as broken crocks, pebbles, or pea gravel. This will allow moisture to course through quickly and easily. A spongy material, such as coarse peat or well rotted farmyard manure, between the drainage layer and the soil will prevent over-quick drying out of the soil in larger containers.

Light and shade

It is not always easy to provide enough light when growing plants on an enclosed patio, on a shaded balcony, or in a window box on the north side of a building. Most plants will grow, but they cannot be expected to give their best. In some circumstances it may be possible to paint one of the walls in a light colour which will reflect more light. But the important thing is to choose plants which will grow happily and well under conditions of constant shade. It will also help where possible to give the container a

Above: Poor light can be considerably improved by painting nearby walls a light colour.
Below: If it is impossible to improve the light, grow only plants which tolerate shady conditions.

Roots can be kept at an even temperature by surrounding the plant pot with insulating material.

Pests and diseases

Container-grown plants are less open to trouble from pests and diseases than those grown in garden soil. We can quickly and easily clear our plants from any pest infestation with proprietary pesticides. Frequently, it is possible to pick off caterpillars from a plant, or to wash off greenfly or blackfly with soapy water.

Diseases can be brought by insect attack or can be the result of physiological disorder. They are less easy to cure than insect attack, but just as easy to prevent. Any plant susceptible to mildew or other fungal trouble should be sprayed before the disease is apparent, thus keeping it at bay.

Town sparrows can cause damage to town-grown plants, especially as they love to take dust baths in beds of fine soil sown with seeds. Large areas can have black cotton strung over them, just 5-10cm (2-4in) above the soil. Small plants can be protected with a temporary dome of wire netting, and the sparrows can be kept off some plants by spraying or dusting the plants with one of the modern deterrents, which will not harm the birds.

A wire netting dome can easily and quickly be slipped over a plant if it is being attacked by birds.

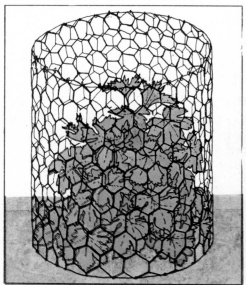

quarter turn once a week or so to ensure that light strikes all sides of the plant, so that it grows upright instead of leaning towards the light. It is sometimes possible to move plants around so that, by rotation, each plant will have a chance of receiving sunlight.

Temperature

Plants must be selected according to the climate and the situation or aspect in which they will be placed. Many plants like to have their head in the sun and their feet in the shade, and this should not be difficult to arrange. In hot sunshine, the heat from the container may be transferred to the soil and then to the roots. To keep the soil cool, small containers can be placed inside larger ones, with the space between filled with dry peat or some other insulating material. Larger containers will have to be protected from the sun by some kind of portable shelter such as a sun umbrella.

172

4 Plants

There are a lot of hybrid Japanese maples, many of them dwarf and suited to tub culture, and all particularly attractive because of the shape and colour of the rich foliage.

The right plant for the right container

Any plant which will grow in the soil will grow in a container. Surprisingly large trees and shrubs will grow in comparatively small containers, but not for long. It is wise to try to match the size of the plant with the size of the container. Bear in mind the fact that the roots of a plant are roughly the same size as that part of a plant which grows above ground. A tree's roots will extend more or less to the same area as that occupied by the branches. This means that in a tub or pot the roots must coil round and round, and this indeed they do until they just cannot grow any longer or find any more space open to them. They will then sometimes break the container but more often they will begin to die.

However, really large trees or shrubs do not look right except in a container so large that it is fitted for a park, stately home or town square rather than the confined patio. Because so large a container cannot be fitted into limited space, we might be tempted to employ a smaller but lightweight container and here we will again run into

173

Camellias require an acid soil if they are to flourish, which is easily provided in a tub.

trouble, for it will be found that the least puff of wind will overbalance the tree and send it over on its side. There is also the fact that a large or tall tree or shrub will probably require staking, and a stake in a container looks hideous and is exceedingly difficult to fix firmly into place.

Because any contained plant attracts more attention than a comparable plant growing in a bed or border in the garden, it should preferably be an evergreen. A winter skeleton in a tub is not an attractive object and to move it out of sight during the colder months should be unnecessary.

Choosing plants for window boxes, balconies and patios

It is impossible to list usefully the herbaceous plants that can be grown in containers on a balcony, in a window box or even on a patio, for there are so many and the choice must always be one of personal taste. It might help, however, to emphasise that, in all locations other than the garden proper,

tall and floppy plants cannot be considered because they will need staking, and a stake in a container is an abomination. Certain other tall plants may be strong enough to stand on their own in some situations but will look out of proportion when growing in a container.

Plants for the patio Some of the most useful plants for the patio are those which cover a considerable area yet leave the limited floor space almost entirely free – climbers. They take up little space yet give a vast return in providing leaves and sometimes flowers in abundance. This softens outlines, blurs sharp angles and helps to bring peace and quiet.

The most useful climbers are those which are both evergreen and self-clinging, but unfortunately there are only a few of these. Probably the best is the ivy, available in a wide range of varieties, colours and leaf sizes. The ivy will cling to a wall yet do little or no damage to it except after many years. It will make no demands in the way of special feeding or watering so long as it is growing in the soil and not in a pot. It can quite easily be trained to travel in any direction you choose and is quite simple to prune.

Among some of the other evergreen climbers there is *Eccremocarpus scaber*, with attractive fern-like foliage and, in the summer, orange-red tubular flowers, followed by unusual seed pods shaped like a small sack or bladder.

Berberidopsis corallina, the coral plant, has dark green, heart-shaped leaves, their undersides a glaucous blue-grey. It provides pendulous clusters of dark red flowers in summer.'

Still another good evergreen climber is the lobster claw plant, *Clianthus puniceus*. It gets its name from its bright red flowers, similar in shape, size and colour to a lobster's claws. It climbs easily and well.

Shrubs which are grown on the patio will have to be fairly small, whether they are grown in the soil or in a container. This is

The vivid scarlet berries of *Pyracantha coccinea* show at their best against a wall. Not strictly a climber because the plant needs support, the pyracantha responds well to training.

just as well for, if any shrub is to be grown in a space where its roots have little room to travel, it will tend to stay rather smaller than if given plenty of space. Yet although dwarfed to a certain extent by the environment, there is no reason why most suitable shrubs should not live and give every satisfaction for a number of years.

Once again evergreens are useful because they are decorative at all times of the year and one that has several uses is the sweet bay, *Laurus nobilis*, which can be pruned into shape so that it becomes living sculpture. It also provides the occasional leaf for the kitchen pot when needed. It will grow in sun or shade.

Another evergreen that will stand shaping is the small-leaved box, *Buxus sempervirens* and the rather more decorative *Buxus* 'Elegantissima' a silvery grey. These again will grow in sun or shade.

If there is space for two or more plants of aucuba, you can have small, tough, evergreen shrubs which will grow in sun or shade and in grossly polluted air, and at the same time will provide glossy green and gold leaves and shining red berries.

There are a considerable number of evergreen cotoneasters which will do well in soil or in containers on the patio, most of them bearing white flowers to be followed by scarlet berries, the flowers loved by bees and the berries by birds. Many of the cotoneasters are shrubs, some can be trees and there are others that can be either prostrate or will lean happily against a wall almost like a climber. They make excellent cover or concealing plants to hide a drain or an oil tank.

Similarly happy against a wall or as a prostrate ground-cover plant is the blue-flowered *Ceanothus thyrsiflorus repens*, sometimes a little tender where the winter is very cold and long and so should be given just a little shelter.

Two evergreen species of the normally deciduous euonymus, or the spindle, are *E. fortunei* and *E. japonica*, both with a number of varieties with differing leaf shape, size and colour. Both of these are tolerant of soil, sun or shade.

And finally in this brief list of evergreen

175

Top: The young foliage of *Pieris forrestii* is a vivid red, even outshining the little white flowers.
Above: Euonymus fortunei, the spindle, has several forms, green or variegated, prostrate or upright.

shrubs suitable for growing in the soil or in a container on the patio, consider the glorious pieris, hardy evergreens with the most dainty appearance. *Pieris forrestii* and *P. taiwanensis* are two species that come immediately to mind but there are several more and a number of useful varieties. Some of these produce pretty racemes of little white flowers like lily-of-the-valley and are noted also for their young springtime growth of vivid scarlet shoots. The pieris like a moist and peaty soil and a lightly shaded position.

Trees and shrubs

In the next few pages a number of trees and shrubs are briefly examined, most of them evergreen. It is suggested that, except under the most favourable circumstances, they are suitable only for growing on a patio. They are too large for all but the most magnificent balcony and of course unsuited to any window box. Plants suited to these sites will be discussed in detail later.

Useful because it flowers in winter, *Erica carnea* has many varieties with coloured flowers and foliage.

Some of the dwarf Japanese maples make first-class patio plants. Often gnarled and twisted they appear almost like bonsai and the vivid colours of their leaves attract immediate attention. They are deciduous. *Acer palmatum* 'Atropurpureum' is thickly covered with reddish purple foliage. Keep them out of strong sun.

A really tough evergreen that will grow in sun or shade, in winter or summer, in city or country, is *Aucuba japonica*, available in several forms, large and small, with white, yellow or red berries and yellow and green splashed foliage. You must have bushes of both sexes to get the berries.

If you have space and are prepared to go to a little trouble to find and select your plants, some of the Japanese varieties of evergreen azaleas can present you with rich and vivid flowers in late spring and early summer and plenty of foliage colour at other times of the year. Choose from a specialist catalogue or go to a nursery or garden centre to pick out your own. Give these plants a moist, peaty soil and a situation where they will not be baked by too

strong a sun or blown by too strong a wind.

Box will grow on a balcony as well as a patio, for it can be clipped and controlled so that it does not grow too large. It can be rather fun clipping formal shapes in box, and these plants grow easily. *Buxus* 'Elegantissima' has cream and grey foliage, *B. sempervirens*, the common box, is plain green. Both are evergreen.

Starry-white flowers are produced in May on plants of *Choisya ternata*, which will grow as tall as 2 metres (6½ft) in a favourable spot sheltered from the coldest winds.

There are a number of cotoneasters which grow well in containers and which give not only masses of little flowers in the spring but follow these with berries, usually scarlet. Bees love the blooms and birds the berries. Most cotoneasters are evergreen but they can be in the form of trees, shrubs or sprawling plants. Most can be trained to grow as you want them.

Most daphnes are evergreen and they are particularly useful because they are easy to grow and are small, neat and covered with

Fatsia japonica makes an excellent pot plant, producing large distinctive palmate leaves.

Ruta graveolens 'Jackman's Blue' is a variety with a low compact habit of growth and bright blue-grey foliage.

perfumed flowers. These appear mainly in spring but can bloom as early as January on a species such as *D. mezereum*, unfortunately deciduous.

Most ericas or heathers must have a lime-free soil in which to grow, but this is not so with *E. carnea*. Nevertheless, with container-grown plants, it is easy enough to tailor the soil to the plant, so ericas should be attended to very closely because so many of them will give excellent winter colour. Several varieties bear foliage which is as colourful as flowers. Choose them by examining growing plants rather than from a catalogue.

A splendid architectural plant for the patio is *Fatsia japonica*, bearing large, dramatic, glossy green palmate leaves. The flowers are insignificant and even the berries are subordinate to the foliage.

Culinary bay leaves are picked from plants of the sweet bay, *Laurus nobilis*, which is also decorative and useful. It is not a spectacular plant and is best grown clipped or pinched to familiar and formal shape. It will grow in sun or shade, and it is an evergreen.

A shrub that will withstand strong winds but is not happy under really cold and frosty conditions is the New Zealand daisy bush, *Olearia haastii*, a silver-leaved, round-growing bush which in early summer is covered with a mass of white daisies. The bush tends to grow large and sprawling if allowed, but a careful clipping over each spring will both help to keep the size under control and to encourage plenty of flowers.

Another shrub with a pearly-grey foliage is the culinary herb rue, *Ruta graveolens*. The variety 'Jackman's Blue' is probably the best for growing in a container on a patio. Keep the shrub trimmed back each spring and concentrate on getting good foliage by removing the yellow flowers, which begin to appear in the early summer, before they open.

Santolina is yet another silver, grey or almost white leaved bush that will benefit from being cut back in the early spring, almost to the previous year's growth. The best form is *Santolina chamaecyparissus* 'Nana', small, thick growing and producing masses of yellow flowers in midsummer. Remove these flowers as they pass their best and you will achieve a constant succession almost all summer through.

There are so many conifers suitable for patios that it is difficult to name them all. They have great architectural value with their formal shapes: they can be upright, conical or low and spreading; they can be green, glaucous blue, gold or silver. They are easy, tolerant plants to grow so long as they are not allowed to become dry at their roots. There are dwarf and slow-growing varieties of conifer that will live for many years in a large pot and will hardly seem to move yet will always give good value. A golden conifer in the wintertime can be just as bright as a tree of flowers.

Bonsai trees

Not suited to growing in a window box, but almost tailored to a life on balcony or patio are examples of the ancient Japanese art of bonsai, the art of dwarfing trees. Although bonsai trees are sometimes thought of as

The container is as important as the tree in creating a beautiful bonsai specimen, and the two should therefore be selected to harmonise with each other.

indoor subjects, they are just as much outdoor trees as their fully-grown brothers. They can be brought indoors for brief periods to be enjoyed in the comfort of the home but must be taken out again in a day or two, for the home is normally too hot and dry for them.

And even outdoors they must receive some protection against the elements. They must not, for example, be placed where the sun will be on them for more than a short period each day, for their root system is short and shallow. Even if the handful of soil around the roots is kept moist, this moisture cannot be taken up to the leafy extremities at the pace necessitated by the warmth of the sun. They must also be placed in a position where they do not stand in a strong wind. This can knock them over, break their sometimes frail leaves and once again lead to transpiration at a rate which cannot be compensated by the dwarf and delicate root system.

However, if you enjoy bonsai trees and wish to grow them on the patio or the balcony and can give them the necessary

elementary protection, the following notes may be of assistance.

There are four basic ways of starting a bonsai collection, and in order of descending expense these are as follows. At the top is the purchase of genuine, old, trained examples of bonsai already planted up in suitable containers. This can be a very expensive matter indeed and unless you have some basic experience of handling these miniatures it would seem to be unwise. But on the other hand the basic training work will have been completed and your tasks will simply be of maintenance. Any reputable dealer will guarantee your trees, give you advice and assistance, and some will take your tree annually for what could almost be called servicing.

Next in order comes the purchase of trees some five to ten years of age, with a certain minimum of training already given to them. They will have been dwarfed and root pruned several times and their basic

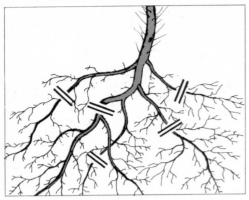

Above: Some of the heavy anchoring roots can be pruned away to save space in the bonsai container.

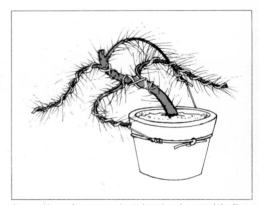

Above: With a careful eye to the final shape desired, cut away some of the excess stem growth.

Above: Use soft copper wire to bend and control the line of the branches, but never make this too tight.

shape will have been decided and will be apparent. These trees will be comparatively inexpensive, although the price will reflect the work that has been carried out on them. They will probably not be planted in a decorative container but will be growing in a flower pot and it will be up to the new owner to transplant them and to grow them on.

You can buy young trees through the post from specialist nurseries for suspiciously low prices, and by doing so you may waste your money. They are inexpensive because they have only recently germinated and they are weak, quite incapable of travelling and being brought up in a completely different atmosphere.

If you wish to start from the beginning it is much better to find and grow on your own trees. Any gardener will know that young oak trees, cotoneasters, ashes and one or two others are constantly appearing in flower beds as the result of bird, mouse or squirrel activity. If these are carefully dug up, potted, cared for and gradually trained they are far more likely to grow into something useful than trees bought from a nursery many miles away.

The best thing to do is to go to a specialist nursery, examine the examples of bonsai that they have for sale and choose your own. Look for healthy growth with no signs of disease, damage or insect attack. Make quite sure that you see and understand the purpose and the shape of the preliminary shaping and training that have been done. See that any cuts made were cleanly done without snags or shredding. Check that the soil in which the plant is growing is moist yet aerated and well drained, that no roots protrude above soil level and that the tree is held firm without any trace of rocking. If training wire is wound around branches see that it is fulfilling its purpose without cutting into the surface.

Buy your container at the same time, making quite sure to choose one that the young tree will be able to grow in for many years and that conforms to it in shape and size.

The training of the bonsai tree consists of a somewhat complex balance of maintaining good growth and pinching out growing tips, of bending and splinting to shape, of pruning roots to keep them small in bulk yet capable of feeding the plant with the necessary food and moisture. The details are too lengthy to explain here and, although the process could not be described as difficult, a certain talent and a certain sensitivity are necessary in order to obtain really good results.

Herbaceous plants

The world of herbaceous plants suitable for growing in containers on the patio, on the balcony and even in certain window boxes is a huge one and it is necessary to be selective. In the first place one must turn down any plants which will grow very tall or will fall and flop about unless they are disciplined and staked. Secondly, one does not wish to make use of plants with so brief a life that they constantly need replacing. This can be the case with a number of herbaceous favourites if they do not get enough moisture at their roots. In general it will be found that it is best to stick to just a few species. Too many plants of too many colours can tire the eye and give a restless, hot and over-busy appearance.

The following list comprises suggestions for plants which can be grown on the patio, on the balcony or, in many cases, in win-

An old bonsai specimen makes a good patio plant.

dow boxes. The average growing height is given for each and there are occasional comments and suggestions. It is impossible to cope here with every combination of conditions which might be met and for this reason it is probable that certain varieties or species will not be successful in certain places. Little will be lost. Experiment will be helpful because it will reveal sometimes surprising results. Where only the genus of a plant is given, this indicates that although some species or varieties will be suitable, others will not, and a choice must be made.

Ageratum

Names	Measurement	Comments
Achillea	25–40 cm (10–20 in)	Choose dwarf varieties of this perennial.
Aconitum monk's hood	25–50 cm (10–20 in)	
Ageratum	10–50 cm (4–20 in)	Half-hardy annual.
Ajuga bugle	12–36 cm (5–15 in)	Perennial. Makes a good ground cover and will clothe a large tub.
Alyssum maritimum	10–15 cm (4–6 in)	Hackneyed, perhaps, but easy and excellent for carpeting and for odd corners.
Amaranthus love-lies-bleeding	50–100 cm (20–40 in)	
Anemone japonica Japanese windflower	25–50 cm (10–20 in)	A pretty perennial.
Antirrhinum snapdragon	25–125 cm (10–50 in)	

Asperula

Begonia

182

Antirrhinum

Armeria

Names	Measurement	Comments
Arabis rock cress	5–15 cm (2–6 in)	A perennial which will more or less take over a tub or window box.
Armeria thrift	5–45 cm (2–18 in)	Perennial with flowers of long and lasting life.
Asperula woodruff	7–23 cm (3–9 in)	There are several varieties, all of them useful and decorative.
Aubrieta	5–10 cm (2–4 in)	
Begonia		The widest range of sizes, shapes and colours of any flower.
Bellis daisy	10–40 cm (4 – 15 in)	The common daisy, but with varieties which live long and provide constant decoration.
Campanula bellflower	25–150 cm (10–60 in)	A wide choice of varieties is available.
Centaurea cornflower	40–150 cm (15–60 in)	Several good, hardy, compact varieties.

Bellis

Campanula

183

Cheiranthus

Chrysanthemum

Names	Measurement	Comments
Cheiranthus wallflower	25–50 cm (10–20 in)	Dwarf and colourful.
Chrysanthemum	30–60 cm (12–24 in)	A wide choice of types and varieties, most long-lasting, is available.
Coreopsis	50–100 cm (20–40 in)	There are some excellent varieties among the American perennials.
Dianthus	15–50 cm (6–20 in)	Among these, there are many sweet-smelling pinks that will do well as long as they have good sun and a well-drained soil.
Dicentra bleeding heart	50–80 cm (20–30 in)	Best kept in a situation where this dainty plant will not be too buffeted by the wind.
Dictamnus burning bush	50–75 cm (20–30 in)	Often confused with kochia, for both are known as burning bush, but this perennial is always better than the annual.

Gaillardia

Iberis

Dianthus

Eschscholzia

Names	Measurement	Comments
Eschscholzia Californian poppy	30–60 cm (12–24 in)	Many good varieties.
Gaillardia	25–75 cm (10–30 in)	
Geum	25–50 cm (10–20 in)	Long-lasting flowers of red, orange or yellow.
Godetia	15–60 cm (6–25 in)	Bright single or double flowers.
Iberis candytuft	25–50 cm (10–20 in)	Several useful evergreen perennial varieties.
Impatiens busy lizzie	50–125 cm (20–50 in)	Popular as an indoor plant, this will do well in its many new varieties but must be grown as an annual outdoors.
Linaria toadflax	50–100 cm (20–40 in)	Many varieties available.
Lysimachia	3–6 cm (1–2 in)	Perennial trailer that can be somewhat invasive if grown in the soil but is safe confined to a pot.

Impatiens

Lysimachia

Pelargonium

Petunia

Names	Measurement	Comments
Lythrum loosestrife	50–100 cm (20–40 in)	Several good new varieties.
Matthiola stock	15–60 cm (6–24 in)	There are several types and many good varieties of stocks.
Nemesia	23–30 cm (9–12 in)	Many colourful hybrids.
Pelargonium geranium		Variable height according to how the plant is grown. This is perhaps the best-known and most used container plant in many parts of the world. It is also one of the best.
Petunia	23–60 cm (9–24 in)	Many types, many sizes, many colours, all of them good.
Phlox drummondii	15–40 cm (6–15 in)	The annual phlox provides a wide and useful range of plants for many locations.
Reseda mignonette	15–30 cm (6–12 in)	The sweetly perfumed mignonette is fine for window boxes and balcony pots.

Sedum

Sempervivum

Phlox drummondii

Saxifraga

Names	Measurement	Comments
Saxifraga saxifrage	15–30 cm (6–12 in)	There are many kinds and many colours.
Sedum stonecrop	5–20 cm (2–8 in)	Stonecrops of many kinds, shapes, textures and colours are natural inhabitants of troughs and tubs of many kinds. They are tolerant of neglect.
Sempervivum houseleek	10–30 cm (4–12 in)	Sometimes difficult to differentiate from the stonecrops.
Thymus thyme	5–10 cm (2–4 in)	There are a large number of thymes, mainly creeping or mat-forming, most in vivid colours and all easy to grow.
Verbena	25–40 cm (10–15 in)	Scented plants are always worth growing.
Viola	10–20 cm (4–8 in)	The violas do not always make a significant mass effect, but are worth growing for their individual impact.

Thymus

Viola

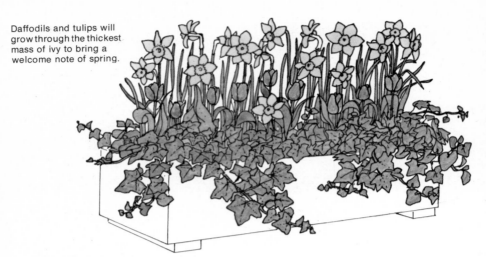

Daffodils and tulips will grow through the thickest mass of ivy to bring a welcome note of spring.

Plants for window boxes

Some of the preceding plants will grow well in a window box, but circumstances vary here and it is difficult to make recommendations without knowing details. Sun and shade, wind, size of box and depth of soil, all these and other matters affect what plants can most successfully be grown. There is also the personality and the courage of the owner to be taken into account, for some growers will attempt anything and will frequently succeed, whereas others will grow only the tried and tested plants and even then will fail. Window boxes are always tricky because their situation makes them liable to freak winds, which can either break and batter the plants or can sear them and burn them so that they either die or at the best fail to grow as they otherwise could.

In winter, window boxes can be planted with winter heathers, with the broad-leaved green of aucuba and skimmia, with ivy and similar plants. These will not give much colour other than a pleasant green and they will have to be washed or hosed down every so often to remove from the foliage the gritty dust that is almost certain to settle on them if they are being grown in a city. They will, nevertheless, be growing plants and they will be evidence that life still exists in a cold and bleak world.

Before installing your winter plants anticipate spring by underplanting with bulbs. Snowdrops, crocuses, daffodils and tulips, these and others will grow quite successfully in window boxes, and as they appear the drab winter occupants can be

Below: Petunias are excellent window-box flowers so long as they are carefully groomed and dead-headed.

removed or allowed to stay with the green leaves of the bulbs growing through them. But when choosing and planting your bulbs make sure you select only the dwarf kinds. Do not attempt to grow any daffodils or tulips with long stems in a window box, for they will almost inevitably snap in the strong winds.

As the bulbs die, so the fear of frost becomes less and when all danger of this has passed you can prepare for the real glory of summer. Trite and commonplace they may be, but the magnificent, easy and showy pelargoniums or pot geraniums take a lot of beating and will last the whole of the summer until the frosts come again. There is the widest possible choice of colour, shape and form, including some of the fancy-leaved types that look so well when seen at close range.

If the site is sunny and the soil can be watered frequently, you will find that calendulas, zinnias and even mesembryanthe-

Above: Clematis like their heads in sun and their feet in shade. One like this requires fresh soil each year.
Below: Pelargoniums will grow well almost anywhere.

mums will flourish. Petunias will grow lush and colourful if you feed and water them well. Lobelia, alyssum, verbena and the new strong, dwarf and rust-free varieties of antirrhinum will be in constant bloom.

Where the boxes are on the shady side of the house you will probably have more success with pansies, begonias and the fat, blowsy calceolarias, all of which will give you tremendous amounts of colour.

If you are both keen and ambitious as well as willing to take a chance against the elements, it is quite possible in many circumstances to grow one or two climbers to surround the window frame, particularly the quick-growing climbers and trailers of the tropaeolum family which gives us

Lobelia, pelargoniums, petunias, tagetes, alyssum, begonias and glecoma, all in a container of some kind, make a vivid and long-lasting display.

Canary creeper and the nasturtiums. Make sure that supports are available and that the tendrils are secured at all times, for it only wants a single long trail to break free and the whole plant will be in peril from the winds.

If you are not concerned about the view from the window or even the light which enters, it is perfectly possible to grow in the window box a series of climbers which will cover the entire space. A number of examples have been seen of French beans which have been grown mainly to conceal the view of the house next door, yet which have presented the growers with several meals of vegetables. In a case such as this, make sure that supports are firm, that the plants are secure in their growth and that you can get at them for attention and for picking without damage to the plants or danger to you.

Tomatoes in window boxes or small containers require watering two or three times a day in hot weather.

Food crops

It is perfectly possible to grow certain of the smaller food crops, mainly salads, in a window box. Lettuce, radishes, carrots are examples of this and certainly strawberries can be grown. If the appearance of the window box is of major concern, then these crops can be grown between flowering plants or, if there is space enough, they can be grown at the back (i.e., the window side) of the box. It is not suggested that any major contribution towards feeding the family can be made by this means, but it is always pleasant to have a freshly cut lettuce plant or crisp radishes straight from the soil.

The secret of all vegetable-growing is to hurry the plants along, grow them quickly, for they are then tender and succulent. To do this it is necessary to have a richer than ordinary soil and plenty of moisture, so incorporate plenty of humus-making material in your soil mixture and use frequent liquid feeds.

Little more can be grown on most balconies than one can raise in a window box, but a patio is a different matter and here, depending on size and inclination, it is possible to have one or two fruit trees, a miniature vegetable patch, a herb garden and other culinary crops.

191

5 Roof gardens

The main advantage of a roof garden over other forms of gardening above ground level is one of sheer space. On a roof the sky is literally the limit – at least in one dimension, and other boundaries depend on the size of the building. Yet all plants will have to be grown in some container, which means watering will be a constant exercise. Winds can be a problem on a roof, but shade will probably cause less trouble.

Preparation

Before beginning any roof garden it is vital that the actual roof surface be examined to

Rich soil and copious water will result in lush growth on the roof garden, and this in turn will help to keep the roots always cool and moist.

make quite sure that it cannot be damaged. The structure of the building should also be investigated, because if the garden is to be extensive in any way the extra weight which will be placed on the load-bearing sections may be very considerable. When it is wet, soil can be very heavy indeed. Where the roof is composed of some bituminous material, take care that all containers placed on it have rounded edges, rather than sharp for sharp edges can easily work into, cut and pierce sun-softened bitumin.

On some roofs it is possible to make beds around the circumference by containing soil with bricks, either of clay or of peat. Most roofs have a low retaining wall around them for safety reasons and soil can be placed against this wall and held in position by the bricks. Here it is especially necessary to make quite certain that the roof surface is sound and in particular that the junction of roof and wall is free from any cracks or faults. The roots of plants will easily find their way into any crevice or crack and quickly enlarge the opening until water can seep through and cause damage.

Beds of this type present the greatest opportunities for effective roof gardening. One advantage is that with complete beds, all plant roots will have a wider area in which to roam. Also, the soil will take longer to dry out, so watering will be less of a problem. And because it is possible to have a greater depth of soil, taller trees can

The larger the size of the bed on a roof garden, the greater the moisture reservoir there will be and the less watering that will be necessary.

be grown without the danger that they will be blown over. Aesthetically it is more satisfying to grow plants in a long and comparatively wide bed than in a series of small containers.

It is possible, too, to install special soils for special plants. Azaleas, which require an acid soil, grow well on rooftops, and so do various pinks and carnations which prefer a more alkaline mixture. It would be unwise to try to grow bog plants on a roof, but the location admirably suits the drier and sandier soils demanded by cacti and other succulents. Herbs for the kitchen can quite easily be grown, as well as an occasional lettuce, some radish and perhaps even some carrots. If there is space to spare, it is quite possible to grow pots of tomatoes, so long as you can find a place for them that is protected from strong winds.

Watering

The greatest problem on a roof garden, as with gardening on a balcony or in a window box, is watering. Whether plants are being grown in containers or in artificial beds, neither has any quantity or depth of soil, which means that evaporation in the sun and air is quick. Watering must be thorough and frequent, sometimes twice a day. Not all roof gardens have facilities for such frequent watering, but with a little ingenuity it is usually possible to rig up a hosepipe from some convenient spot on the floor below and lead this on to the roof. Take care when watering that gusts of wind do not send showers into open windows nearby or on to the streets below. Make sure also that all drainage pipes are kept free of fallen leaves or other debris that might block them and cause trouble.

Other roof-garden features

Every roof garden should provide space for leisure. Arrange plantings so that at the hottest part of the day the leisure area is in shade. A strategically placed tree or a vine-covered pergola, both perfectly possi-

Below: Cacti and other succulents grow well on a roof because there they get the hot sunshine they need.

194

ble on a large roof, can provide shade and add interest to the area.

Some roof gardens have space for a small greenhouse. These are especially useful for the raising of seedlings and for the restoration of ailing house plants. Failing a greenhouse, it is almost always possible to install a frame or even a cloche in which to bring on seedlings or protect tender plants.

If attention is paid to their watering, vegetables and herbs will grow well and quickly on a roof. When you are harvesting your crops, make sure all city dust and grime are washed away.

All gardening produces waste vegetable matter. This can be converted into soil or compost and stored in a roof garden. With the necessary care, rooftop gardening, like other kinds of gardening in containers, can offer new and rewarding possibilities.

Fruit growing

1 Planning the fruit garden

Fruit-growing is a satisfying occupation and by careful planning it is possible to enjoy home-grown fruit all the year round and have sufficient in the deep freezer for out-of-season use.

Both dessert and culinary apples should be grown for they are the most useful of all fruits. Where space is restricted those which are spur-bearing may be grown as dwarf pyramids or as cordons. Ten or twelve apple trees will provide fruit from August until March if it is stored carefully.

Pears are best grown as espaliers (horizontal-trained), on a sunny wall or along one side of a path, and in this way will take up little space. For late dessert, plant William's (America's Bartlett pear) and Conference; these two pears will pollinate each other and are delicious straight from the tree or marinated.

Of the stone fruits, peaches need the most sunshine to ripen the wood, without which they will not bear well. They may be grown against a sunny wall as fan-shaped trees or as bushes in the open where the climate is warm and dry. Duke of York, Hale's Early and Peregrine are reliable.

Damsons are grown on the side of the prevailing winds, for they are hardy. The best is Bradley's King. Plums and gages can both be grown either against a wall, as fan-shaped trees, or in the open, in the bush or standard form. Czar is the best early plum and Denniston's Superb the best gage, followed by Victoria and Jefferson. If standard trees are used, plant gooseberries

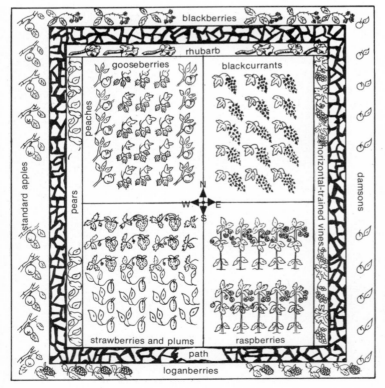

The plan makes the best use of a small area and takes into consideration the climatic aspects. For instance, on the sides where cold north-easterly winds are prevalent, blackberries are grown as a hedge and the hardy damsons planted as a windbreak. Horizontally trained vines and pears may be planted alongside a path to conserve space; and beneath, plums and peaches, gooseberries and strawberries are grown, for they flourish in semi-shade. Blackcurrants and raspberries are planted in full sunlight. Make the rows north to south so that all parts of the plants receive maximum sunlight.

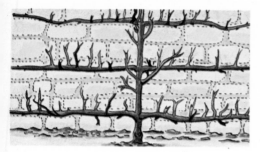
Espalier (horizontal-trained) tree on a warm wall.

beneath them, spacing them 90–120cm (3–4ft) apart in the bush form and 60cm (2ft) as cordons. For dessert, plant Whitesmith, Leveller and Gunner; for culinary use, Careless and Howard's Lancer. Gooseberries grow well in a cool climate; blackcurrants prefer warmth. They also require an open situation whilst gooseberries do well in semi-shade. For early fruit, plant 120cm (4ft) apart, Laxton's Giant and Wellington XXX, followed by Westwick Choice and Amos Black. Redcurrants require similar conditions to gooseberries and the best are Laxton's No. 1 (early) and Red Lake (mid-season) raised in the USA.

Plant strawberries in double rows between the bush fruits, spacing the plants and rows 30cm (12in) apart. The best early crops are Cambridge Premier and Royal Sovereign, which do not make too much leaf. For late summer, plant Montrose and Talisman.

The cane fruits crop later than the soft fruits, and the hardiest are blackberries, which may be used as a hedge, trained along wires, or alongside a path. They may be grown in semi-shade. Bedford Giant is the earliest, followed by Himalaya Giant and Oregon Thornless. All freeze well.

Loganberries are not so hardy. They do not like cold winds and the canes are more brittle. They also require full sun. Like raspberries, they fruit on the new season's canes; blackberries fruit on both the old and new wood, hence they bear more heavily. Plant loganberries and blackberries 240cm (8ft) apart, raspberries at 45cm

(18in). Glen Clova is the best early raspberry, followed by Malling Promise and Admiral. The autumn-fruiting varieties will prolong the season, and September and Zeva are both suitable for this purpose.

There should be a place for a vine, either against a trellis or trained along wires. Vines are able to withstand $-7°C$ ($20°F$) of frost, and varieties of the Chasselas type may be left outdoors until the first winter frosts. Outdoor grapes require a sunny position and they grow well in a greenhouse with a winter temperature of $6°C$ ($42°F$). Plant the following varieties in order to enjoy a long succession of fruit:

Apples (culinary)	Apples (dessert)	
Grenadier	Elton Beauty	Aug-Sept
Wealthy	James Grieve	Oct-Nov
Monarch	Golden Delicious	Nov-Dec
Wagener	Cox's Orange Pippin	Jan-Mar
Annie Elizabeth	Brownlee's Russet	Apr-May
Plums and gages	**Pears**	
Denniston's Superb	Clapp's Favourite	Aug-Sept
Victoria	William's (Bartlett)	Oct
Jefferson	Conference	Oct
Reine Claude de Bavay	Roosevelt	Dec
Cherries	**Gooseberries**	
Early Rivers	May Duke	May (late)
Merton Heart	Whitesmith	June
Amber Heart	Careless	July
Waterloo	Leveller	Aug (early)
Strawberries	**Currants**	
Cambridge Favourite	Laxton's Giant	June
Royal Sovereign	Wellington XXX	July
Montrose	Westwick Choice	Aug
Gento	Amos Black	Sept-Oct
Red Rich or		Oct-Dec
La Sans Rivale		
Raspberries	**Blackberries**	
Glen Clova	Bedford Giant	Early July
Malling Promise	Merton Thornless	Late July
Taylor	Himalaya Giant	Early Aug
Malling Admiral	Oregon Thornless	Late Aug
September	Lowberry	Sept
Peaches	**Apricots**	
Hale's Early	Alfred	Late July
Alexander	Early Moorpark	Early Aug
Peregrine	Hemskerk	Late Aug
Royal George	Moorpark	Early Sept

The tree fruits have been selected as suitable pollinators for each other – essential for heavy crops.

Types of fertiliser used in fruit cultivation.

Preparing the ground

Though each fruit requires somewhat different treatment as to soil and climate, the ground should be given a general preparation, so that if each fruit is planted at the right time, the minimum of attention will be needed to bring the soil into just the right condition for maximum crops.

Site and situation are important, for where frosts are troublesome, those fruits flowering early should be omitted unless their blossom is frost-tolerant. These apples are frost-resistant: Annie Elizabeth; Claygate Pearmain; Monarch; Edward VII; James Grieve; Pearl; Laxton's Superb; Howgate Wonder. (The best of all dessert apples, Cox's Orange, is highly susceptible to frost damage.) Some pears which are frost-resistant are Dr Jules Guyot; Catillac; Conference; Fertility. These plums bloom late or are frost-tolerant: Pond's Seedling; Belle de Louvain; Czar; Kirke's Blue; Severn Cross; Denniston's Superb.

The following blackcurrants are frost-resistant: Amos Black; Mendip Cross; Laxton's Giant. (Blackcurrants are more susceptible to frost damage than other soft fruits.) In strawberries, Cambridge Early Pine and Favourite are more frost-tolerant than most varieties. In raspberries, plant Malling Jewel instead of M. Promise where there are frosts, and Glen Clova if the garden is in a frost hollow. For reliable and heavy crops, select varieties to suit the district and the soil of your garden. Blackcurrants and blackberries require a heavy soil, containing potash. Plums and cherries do well in a limestone soil if given plenty of nitrogen; apples and pears do not, for they are often troubled by chlorosis (caused through iron starvation), in which the leaves turn yellow and the trees are stunted in growth.

Chalky soils are usually shallow soils and need liberal amounts of humus, such as material from the compost heap, composted straw or decayed manure. If the latter is in short supply it may be augmented by some peat or by 'green' manuring, in which rape seed is sown thickly over the surface in spring and the plants dug in when 7cm (3in) high.

Liming will not be necessary for chalk soils, but most town gardens should be

Below: raking in fertiliser. *Opposite:* essential tools.

When double digging soil is removed to a depth of at least 40cm (16in), or two spades' depth.

Manures and humus materials are shown here being incorporated into the trench.

given a liberal dressing before planting, to correct the acidity caused by deposits of soot and sulphur which may have fallen on to the soil over a long time. Give 0.5kg (1lb) of hydrated lime to every 6 sq m (6 sq yd).

Heavy clay soil may be broken up by treating it with caustic (unhydrated) lime obtained from a builder's merchant. If applied during the early winter just before digging the ground, the action of the lime as it dehydrates will also break up the clay particles of the soil. Then, in March, when frost has left the ground, dig in some peat or poplar bark fibre, old mushroom-bed compost, or decayed manure before any planting is done at the month end.

Soft fruits require plenty of moisture to make growth and for the fruit to swell, so it will be sweet and juicy. To supply the plants with humus, dig in whatever materials are available, such as clearings from ditches, straw composted with an activator, leaf mould and peat. Shoddy (wool and cotton waste), used hops (obtainable from breweries) and farmyard manure have the advantage over other forms of humus in

that they contain nitrogen, which is necessary for the plants to make plenty of new growth. Other forms of nitrogenous manure are bone meal, poultry manure and fish meal. Chopped seaweed is also valuable.

Working the soil

No amount of care in supplying the correct fertilisers will be of any value unless they are worked well into the soil. Clean ground is essential, for most fruits are permanent crops and it is difficult to clean the ground after planting without damaging the roots.

It is best to bring the ground into condition in autumn, whilst it is still dry and in a friable condition. Double digging or trenching is necessary, in order to work in the humus to a depth of at least two 'spits' or spades, about 40cm (16in).

As trenching is done, it is advisable to treat the ground for wireworms and millepedes, which feed upon the roots of raspberries and strawberries in particular. Everything must be done to ensure that the fruits are given the conditions necessary to crop well over a long period of time.

201

2 Apples

Apples are the most important of all fruit crops, for they have so many uses and can be stored or frozen to use all year. They are also the hardiest fruit, cropping well in cold climes where, apart from the gooseberry, little else would grow so well.

Apples may be grown as standards or as bushes, or in the cordon and dwarf pyramid form. Cordons and pyramids are suitable for the small garden. In recent years, British growers have followed the lead given by the Dwarf Fruit Trees Association of America, producing a ten-fold increase in density by using the new Malling rootstocks. On Malling IX, the trees will come quickly into heavy bearing. They bear fruit rather than make wood, which means growers should know how to prune them and provide the trees with a balanced diet. Bush trees on this rootstock may be planted 240–270cm (8–9ft) apart; pyramids 180–210cm (6–7ft); cordons 90–120cm (3–4ft). The most vigorous kinds, i.e. Bramley's Seedling and Newton Wonder, are unsuited to this rootstock. For these, Malling II Rootstock is suitable and after five to six years, the trees may be expected to yield up to 180kg (10 bushels or 400lb) of fruit compared with a maximum yield of 18kg (1 bushel) from all trees on Malling IX at whatever the age. Plant bush trees 3m (10ft) apart; standards 4.5m (15ft) apart.

Trees on the dwarfing rootstocks need careful staking, for they do not produce such large roots as on the more vigorous stocks. Stake the trees immediately they are planted, using strong wooden stakes driven well into the ground about 30cm (12in) from the roots and at a slight angle. Use one of the patented ties or strips of rubber 30cm (12in) long, cut from the inner tube of a tyre. The stake must not be in contact with the bark of the tree, or it may rub against it during windy weather.

Soil requirements

Apples require a balanced diet with plenty of humus in the soil to retain moisture – without which the fruits will not make any size and will lack juice. As apples require magnesium in the soil, lime is best given when the ground is prepared, as magnesium carbonate, about 525g per sq m (1lb per sq yd). Apples also require potash; for heavy soils give 33g per sq m (1oz per sq yd), doubling this amount where the soil is light and the potash easily washed away. The amount of nitrogenous manures will depend on variety. The most vigorous apples will need little, for they require no assistance in making new wood. But those of more compact habit need as much shoddy or farmyard manure as can be obtained, and cooking apples need more nitrogen than dessert kinds. Nitrogen will intensify the green colouring of the cooking apples, whilst potash will bring out the scarlet and crimson colourings of dessert apples. Where possible, use organic nitrogenous manures, which will supply the necessary humus.

To obtain heavy crops from limited space, plant cordons and train against wires. Spur-forming apples may be grown in this way.

Young trees will suffer a shortage of nitrogen if planted directly into grass. In its nitrogen requirements, grass will be in competition with the trees, so it is important when planting in grass first to make a circle of 60cm (2ft) diameter and to remove the turf from this area before preparing the soil. In areas of low rainfall, all apples will benefit from a thick mulch of garden compost or farmyard manure given in June to check moisture evaporation. Trees growing in dry districts will also require more nitrogen, and if after two years they have made less than 30cm (12in) of new growth, give each tree a 66g-per-sq-m (2oz-per-sq-yd) application of sulphate of ammonia early in spring when growth recommences.

Lack of potash may be shown by the leaves turning brown at the edges and becoming crinkled, whilst the fruit will be small. Potash will also release the phosphates in the soil, which are so important in building up the size of the fruit and stimulating root action. So in spring give each tree a 33g-per-sq-m (1oz-per-sq-yd) dressing of sulphate of potash. Magnesium deficiency, which causes the leaves to turn pale green, is corrected by spraying the foliage with magnesium sulphate (Epsom salts) at a strength of 25g to 1 litre (4oz to 1gal) of water. In difficult soils, these apples will do well: in limestone and chalk, Gascoyne's Scarlet, Barnack Beauty, Charles Ross, St Everard; in wet, badly drained soil, Lord Derby, Grenadier, Monarch, Laxton's Superb; in cold, heavy clay, Newton Wonder, Adam's Pearmain, Pott's Seedling, Wagener.

Pollination

This is important and it is little use planting several Cox's Orange, just because it is one's favourite apple, without a pollinator. It will set almost no fruit with its own pollen, but will set at least 15 per cent where one of these trees is grown nearby: James Grieve, Merton Worcester, Charles Ross, Discovery, Stirling Castle, Egremont Russet or Jonathan.

Bush apple trees usually bear heavily.

Triploids will not set their own pollen, nor will they pollinate others, so two pollinators should be grown with them to ensure heavy crops. Gravenstein, Blenheim Orange and Ribston Pippin are triploids. Plant with them Grenadier, a cooker, and either James Grieve or Lord Lambourne for dessert. These and most other apples are known as diploids. One of the best pollinators for all apples is Lane's Prince Albert, for it is in bloom longer than any, for at least 21 days. Others which are long in bloom and good pollinators are Rev. Wilks, Grenadier, James Grieve, Lord Derby and Annie Elizabeth. They will pollinate most other varieties.

Planting

Apples may be planted between November 1 and the end of March, but unless the soil is badly drained, the earlier the better

203

They will then be established before the hard frosts. The soil should be in a friable condition to allow for treading it around the roots when covered over.

Select a tree with a good head and a strong sturdy stem if planting a standard. But for cordons, bush and pyramid trees, plant maidens – i.e. one-year-old trees, which are readily established and may be trained and pruned to the requirements of the grower. They are also less expensive to buy than older trees. Cordons are usually planted in trenches, made perhaps on either side of a path; the rows should be 120cm (4ft) apart. The trees are tied in to strong wires held in place by strong stakes at intervals of 240–270cm (8–9ft).

After making the hole, which must be of ample size, plant by spreading out the roots. Shorten with the pruners any that are too long. This will encourage them to make more fibrous roots. Before replacing the soil, which should contain the necessary humus and plant food, sprinkle some peat over the roots; tread in the soil as it is replaced. Fix the stake in place, tie, and water in if the soil is dry. Before doing any training, select an efficient pair of pruners which feels comfortable in the hand; it will have to be in constant use.

Training and pruning

Training to the required shape will depend on the type of tree to be grown: standard, bush, dwarf pyramid or cordon.

For a **standard**, a 'feathered' tree should be obtained. This means the small 'feathers' or lateral shoots will have been removed by the nurserymen all the way along the stem. A full standard will have a 150–180cm (5–6ft) stem, a half standard a 90–120cm (3–4ft) stem. The formation of the head, which will be the same for **bush** trees, will be by one of two methods, the 'open centre' plan, or the 'delayed open centre'.

For the first plan, a bush tree should have a good 'leg' and, like standards, be allowed to grow unchecked the first year, at the end of summer 'heading' back the main shoot to 90cm (3ft) above soil level. This will persuade the tree to 'break' and form two or three shoots, which will form the head. Shoots appearing on the lower 45cm (18in) of stem with bushes should be removed. The following winter, the new shoots

Cordons may be used alongside a path where space is limited. Plant them 90cm (3ft) apart in the rows.

Dwarf pyramids give the heaviest crops in the quickest time and take up little room. Plant 120cm (4ft) apart.

Standards produce the heaviest crops over a long period but take several years before cropping heavily. Plant 360cm (12ft) apart.

Bush trees come somewhere between the pyramid and standard forms, have a long life and crop heavily. Plant 3m (10ft) apart.

204

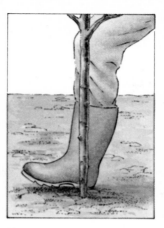

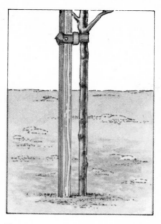

Spread the roots well out, removing any damaged roots before covering.

After covering with soil, tread firmly if the soil is friable, and water in if dry.

To make the tree secure, place a stake close to it and use a rubber tie.

should be cut back to half way, and the next year the newly formed extension shoots cut back half way, to about 22cm (9in) of their base. The head will now have formed.

The delayed open centre is made by removing only the top 15cm (6in) of the main stem. Then, along the entire length of the stem, buds will form from which new growth will begin and the tree will be built up. Remove any laterals where there is overcrowding, or if several close together are facing in the same direction.

The **dwarf pyramid** form will produce the heaviest crop in the shortest time. Unlike apples in the bush and standard form, there is no waiting several years. For the tree to make as much wood and as many fruit buds as quickly as possible, bud growth must be stimulated by making a nick in the bark just above each bud on the main stem. The shoots formed from the buds are pruned back to half the new season's growth each year to encourage the formation of fruiting buds. Throughout its early life, until well established, the central main shoot must be pruned back each year. This enables the tree to concentrate its energies on the formation of side shoots.

Cordons are single-stem trees, planted at an angle of 45° to restrict the flow of sap and prevent the trees from making too much growth. Maiden trees should be planted 90–120cm (3–4ft) apart, and tied in to wires stretched at intervals of 30cm (12in) above ground. Here, the main or extension shoot should never be pruned, only the laterals, which in August should be pinched back to 15cm (6in) of the main stem. This will ensure the formation of fruiting spurs as quickly as possible. When the main stem has reached 180–210cm (6–7ft), it should be cut back to persuade the tree to direct its energies to the side shoots. The removal of surplus fruiting spurs will maintain the quality of the fruit.

The trees should be allowed to grow away in their first year untouched, to form plenty of wood whilst making root growth. The next winter, pruning will begin.

There are three methods: the 'established spur' system, for the more restricted or artificially trained trees; the 'regulated' system, for trees of vigorous habit; and the 'renewal' system, for keeping the tree in continuous new growth.

In the established spur system, wood formed in summer is cut back to four buds. During the following summer, the two top buds will make new growth whilst the lower will develop into fruiting spurs. From the

205

Left: When renovating old fruit trees, use a tree saw to cut away dead wood. Remove entire branch so that the wound will callus over.

Right: To build up a healthy spur system, cut back wood formed in summer to three or four buds. The next year, the two uppermost buds will make new wood and the two lower buds fruiting spurs.

cut made above the top buds, two laterals will form which in turn should be cut back to two buds. Thus the balance is maintained whilst the tree channels its energies into making fruiting spurs. With trees over ten years old, some spur thinning is necessary to maintain the size of fruit.

The regulated system mostly applies to bush and standard trees. The idea is to keep the tree 'open' at the centre by removing crossing branchlets and all in-growing laterals. Commence by shortening the laterals to a third at the end of each summer. Then cut back the laterals as described for the spur system. The tip bearers (those which fruit at the ends of the laterals) are left unpruned until they have made excessive growth, when some wood must be removed.

The renewal system involves the replacement of old wood by new, thus maintaining the tree's vigour over many years. The side shoots are cut back to two buds from the base. These will produce two more shoots which will bear fruit. Afterwards, each is pruned back to two buds and the process continues indefinitely.

Old trees may be made more productive by removing all dead wood, using a tree saw. Where there is overcrowding at the centre, entirely remove any branches, to let in sunlight. Make the cut close to the bark so that it will heal (form a callus) quickly. To leave even a few centimetres of the branch will enable brown rot to take hold. Paint the wound with a fungicide or with white lead paint to guard against disease.

De-horning will also increase the yield of old trees. It is the top branches which are de-horned, cutting them back by a third of their length. Make a sloping cut so that moisture will drain away, and treat with a fungicide to heal the cut as described.

If you need to restrict a certain bud, make a notch in the bark just below it. To encourage a bud to 'break' into growth, make the notch above it.

Harvesting and storing

Knowing when to harvest calls for a degree of skill. Do not remove the fruit too soon: it will keep longer if you let it stay on the tree until it is fully mature.

An attic, shed or cupboard is suitable for storing fruit. It is important that it be cool but dry and frostproof. Place the fruit on a layer of straw making sure that they do not touch each other.

Varieties

Dessert

Acme The first apple to crop well on its own roots, it fruits freely from two years old. If gathered in November it keeps all winter, its yellow flesh possessing much of the Cox's flavour.

Cox's Orange Pippin This is the most popular apple ever introduced. It is a weak grower, susceptible to frosts, and crops well only where everything is in its favour. Yet the fruit has a more subtle blending of aromatic flavour and crispness than any apple, and is good for eating from November till March.

Egremont Russet An ideal variety for a small garden, it crops well and is of neat upright habit. It does well as a cordon and is at its best for eating in November, when its deep yellow flesh is crisp and juicy.

Golden Delicious It does well as a pyramid, and with its evenly shaped fruit and clear yellow skin, it is a favourite of the supermarkets. It is at its best for eating in December and January.

James Grieve One of the most reliable apples and a good pollinator. The green fruit streaked with red matures by mid-September.

Laxton's Superb A fine apple for Christmas eating, this is a tremendous cropper though for this reason tends to biennial bearing. The large handsome fruits have pure white flesh which is crisp and juicy.

Michaelmas Red Similar to its parent Worcester Pearmain, it matures three weeks later. But as it makes a small compact tree and is a spur bearer, it is more suitable for a small garden.

Left: In the regulated system of pruning (mostly for bush and standard trees) crossing branchlets and in-growing laterals are removed to keep the tree open at the centre. Shorten the laterals to a third at the end of summer, then cut back the laterals as for the spur system. Leave the tip bearers unpruned until they have made excessive growth, then remove some of the wood.

Above: In the renewal system of pruning, old wood is replaced by new to maintain vigour. Cut side shoots back to two buds from the base. These will produce two more shoots which will become fruit-bearing. Then prune each back to two buds, and so on.

Culinary

Annie Elizabeth A healthy tree of compact habit, it blooms late and is rarely troubled by frost. The large handsome fruits are popular on the show bench and cook well right through winter.

Bramley's Seedling It has the richest vitamin C content of all apples and is the best for cooking. It makes a large spreading tree, bears heavily, and its fruit will keep until April.

Left: One of the best dessert apples, Cox's Orange Pippin requires a warm garden, fertile soil and suitable pollinators.

Moss's Seedling Introduced in 1974, it was the first apple protected by Plant Breeders' Rights. Like an early Cox's Orange, ready in late September, it will bear heavily.

Mother This is an American apple which is for November use. Its crimson-yellow fruits with their aromatic pink flesh make for delicious eating.

Rival One of the best for use in November, when no apple is more juicy. It makes a spreading tree and needs ample space to develop.

Worcester Pearmain A tip bearer, it makes a vigorous tree as a bush or standard, its highly coloured fruits being crisp and juicy and ready in early September.

Crawley Beauty It makes a neat upright tree and blooms late. The handsome dark green fruit cooks well and, if allowed to hang until late November, it will keep until Easter.

Edward VII Flowering late, it misses the frosts and it makes a neat, upright tree which crops well. It will keep until May when the golden-skinned fruit is still crisp and juicy for dessert whilst being equally good for cooking.

Below: A well spaced and heavily laden branch, the result of good pruning and cultivation.

Right: Golden Delicious, one of the most reliable dessert apples, crops heavily in the cordon and pyramid forms.

Grenadier It makes a small, neat tree yet bears the largest of all apples, often as big as a dinner plate, which bake to perfection. But they must be used from the tree, when ready September – October.

Wagener This American apple, though 160 years old, is only now being widely planted in Britain. It makes a neat, upright tree and bears heavily, whilst it keeps until Easter.

Wealthy A fine American apple which crops well in Britain, the yellow skin being striped with scarlet. It makes excellent eating from the tree in November and it also cooks well.

3 Pears

Natives of the warm regions of the Mediterranean, pears require greater warmth than apples for the fruit to ripen correctly and so attain their full flavour and keeping qualities. Pears require the sunniest places in the fruit garden, where they may be grown as standards or bush trees and in the pyramid and cordon form, requiring similar culture to the apple in their pruning.

Pears are, however, at their best where grown as espaliers or in horizontal tiers, the arms being either fastened to a wall or to strong galvanised wires supported by posts at intervals of 240cm (8ft). Espaliers may be grown in the open, possibly alongside a path, or to divide one part of the fruit garden from another, but it is important that they have full sun.

Espalier trees

A maiden tree will form one pair of arms each year, which can be grown on to any length. Espaliers can also grow to any height and will often be seen covering the entire wall of an old house to a height of 9m (30 ft) or more. Long ladders must then be used for picking fruit and pruning at the top. In the garden, the topmost arms should be about 210–240cm (7–8ft) from soil level so that cultivation can be readily carried out.

After planting the maiden, make a nick in the bark above two buds, one on either side of the stem and pointing in opposite directions, to make them 'break'. These will form the first arms or tier. The leader shoot is allowed to grow away. Next season, in early spring, another two buds are selected on either side of the stem, and so on, selecting a pair of buds each year which are spaced about 40–45cm (16–18in) above each other.

At first, the new wood growing from the main stem will tend to grow upwards. It is advisable to fix canes to the wires, first at an angle of 45°, to which the shoots are fastened. The canes are gradually brought to the horizontal position, then fastened to the wires.

The first tier will grow to about 1m (3ft) on either side of the main stem in a year. The following year, early in August, to encourage the formation of fruiting spurs, which will bear fruit the next year, all shoots growing from the arms should be pinched back to 10–12cm (4–5in) of the main stems. The plant will then form fruiting buds instead of making excess wood. As the arms continue to grow, at the end of each summer, cut back the new season's wood to about half way, to a bud which will form the extension shoot to grow on next year. This may continue for several years, until the arms are about 180cm (6ft) in length, so that with espaliers it is desirable to plant them 3.5m (12ft) apart.

As pears bloom about two weeks before apples, many varieties should not be planted in frost-troubled gardens unless they are planted against a warm wall. There are, however, several which bloom late and in most years, will miss late frosts: they include Fertility, Dr Jules Guyot and Winter Nelis.

Pollination

Pollination is as important for pears as for apples. Though several will be in bloom at the same time, they are unable to fertilise each other. The fertile Conference is unable to pollinate Beurré d'Amanlis; neither will Seckle fertilise Louise Bonne. They need another pollinator such as Marguerite Marillat or Durondeau.

Certain pears are self-fertile, setting fruit with their own pollen, but they will set heavier crops with another in bloom at the same time. These pears bloom early and one or two should be planted together: Beurré Superfin, Conference, Durondeau, Louise Bonne, Marguerite Marillat. These

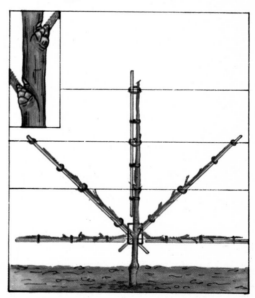

Opposite: Doyenne du Comice requires a warm garden and crops heavily when grown in espalier form against a wall.

Above: Buds on fan trees can be induced to develop or remain dormant by nicking either above or below them.

Gather pears dry before they're frosted.

Wrap in greaseproof paper, stand on end.

bloom in mid-season: Beurré Bedford, Glou Morceau, Merton Pride, Packham's Triumph, William's Bon Chrétien (Bartlett), Roosevelt. These bloom late: Doyenne du Comice, Dr Jules Guyot, Fertility, Gorham, Winter Nelis.

Early and mid-season varieties, and mid-season and late pears may be planted together, for their flowering times will overlap. Thus Conference and William's (Bartlett) will fertilise each other. The hardiest pears are Beurré Hardy, Jargonelle and Durondeau, which will crop quite well up to 300m (1000ft) above sea level. Conference, Dr Guyot and William's are almost as easy and are the four best pears for any garden.

Rootstocks

There are several rootstocks for pears which are grafted on to quince stock. Quince B is comparable to MII of apples, making large trees which crop heavily but take longer to come into bearing than the more dwarf stocks (such as Quince C, which is used for pyramids and cordons). Also, those pears which are slow to begin cropping, e.g. Comice and Beurré Hardy, should be worked on this stock. Quince A comes somewhere between these two stocks and is the rootstock mostly used.

Where a large standard tree is required, pears are worked on wild pear stock and this is also used for the weaker growers. It is the most vigorous rootstock.

Trees on quince stock must be planted with the graft at least 8cm (3in) above soil level so that scion rooting does not occur. Take out a large hole so that the roots can be spread out well, making it a depth such that the graft is comfortably above the soil after treading down. Sprinkle peat over the roots and mix in the nitrogenous humus before replacing the soil, treading it well down. Then stake the trees as for apples.

Pruning

As to their pruning, pears are divided into two sections: those of vigorous upright habit, and those of weaker, drooping habit. In the former group are Comice, Conference, Durondeau, Gorham, Marguerite Marillat and William's (Bartlett). In the latter group are Louise Bonne, Emile d'Heyst, Beurré d'Amanlis and Josephine de Malines. When pruning, the upright growers should be cut back to an outward-facing bud and the droopers to an upward bud. This will correct the 'drainpipe' habit of the second, weaker group and the 'umbrella' habit of those of the first group. Those of weeping habit are mostly tip bearers and light croppers and so require little pruning.

212

Each shoot or lateral will form both fruiting and wood (foliage) buds. The latter lie flat along the stem and are more pointed. Several years after planting, the spur bearers may need to have some of their spurs removed so as to maintain the size and quality of the fruit.

Harvesting and storing

Pears require more care in their harvesting than apples. They bruise easily and are harmed by frost, whilst they deteriorate quickly if over-ripe. They will be ready to gather if, when you take the fruit on the palm of the hand and lift it, it parts from the spur with its stem attached. Gather pears when dry and before they are frosted, between late July and the end of October. They require a temperature of $7°–10°C$ ($45°–50°F$) to store well and should be kept in a darkened room or a cupboard or drawer. Pears will sweat and quickly deteriorate in a too cold place. Carefully stored, some pears will keep until Easter.

Varieties

There are no pears grown especially for culinary use, though several – e.g. Jargonelle and Catillac – are better stewed. The latter will keep until Easter.

To ripen in late July and August

Clapp's Favourite An American pear of vigorous, upright habit. It bears heavily, and the pale yellow fruit, striped crimson, is ready late in August.

To ripen in early to mid-September

Dr Jules Guyot It blooms late and is a good pollinator. Its large fruits have a yellow skin dotted with black and should be eaten from the tree.

Gorham This American pear makes a neat upright tree and is resistant to scab. Similar to William's, it bottles equally well.

William's Bon Chrétien The Bartlett pear of America, this is possibly the best all-round pear ever raised. It makes a compact tree and crops heavily, the white flesh retaining its quality after bottling.

To ripen in October

Beurré Bedford It is self-fertile and makes a good pyramid, bearing heavy crops of golden fruits of good flavour.

Beurré Hardy It makes a strong upright tree, is hardy and is a reliable cropper. The rose-tinted flesh has a pleasant perfume.

Possibly the best all-round pear ever, William's Bon Chrétien makes a compact tree and crops heavily. The flesh retains its quality after bottling.

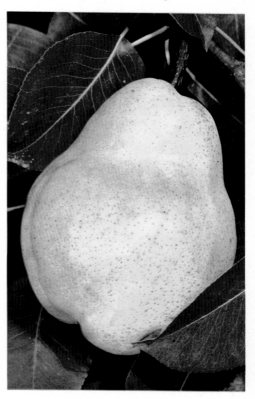

Bristol Cross Good in the pyramid form, it crops heavily. The large fruits are yellow covered with russet, and sweet and juicy.

To ripen in November

Conference It is hardy, is a valuable pollinator and none crops more reliably. The dark green fruits, heavily russeted, are of excellent flavour.

Doyenne du Comice This is the finest of all pears but is difficult away from its native France. It requires warmth and a long ripening season, when its melting cinnamon-flavoured fruit has no equal.

Durondeau It makes a compact tree and is hardy. If gathered in early October, the golden fruits will keep until late November.

Louise Bonne It needs warmth, when it will be a strong grower and regular cropper. The green fruits, flushed crimson, possess fine flavour.

To ripen in December/February

Glou Morceau A good pollinator for Comice. Under similar conditions it will bear good crops of juicy fruit, free from 'grit'.

Roosevelt An American variety, it is the largest of pears with a golden skin, flushed with pink. Of excellent flavour, it is at its best in December.

Winter Nelis It requires the same treatment as Glou Morceau and makes a small fruit, but is of outstanding flavour and has a delightful rose perfume. It keeps until February.

To ripen from February onwards

Catillac It is hardy, makes a large tree and bears heavily but is a triploid, so plant with it Beurré Hardy and Dr Guyot to fertilise it and each other. The large crimson-brown fruits are removed in late November and, if stored with care, will keep until Easter.

Conference, which ripens in November, crops reliably. A valuable pollinator, it is hardy and its fruits delicious.

4 Plums and gages

After apples, plums are the next most widely grown fruit, for they have both dessert and culinary uses. Plums do not keep for long but, by planting for succession, they may be enjoyed from late July until the end of October. Plums are the first fruits to bloom and in frost-troubled gardens only those which bloom late should be grown. Amongst those which bloom late are the following: Czar, Belle de Louvain, Marjorie's Seedling, Severn Cross and Late Transparent Gage.

The bush or standard tree suits the plum best and it will come quickly into bearing, whilst it does not require the same degree of pruning attention as either the apple or pear. The plum fruits mostly on the new wood and, apart from the removal of any dead wood, excessive pruning must be avoided. Stone fruits suffer from 'bleeding', which weakens the tree and enables disease, especially silver leaf, to enter where cuts or wounds have been made. By government order, all pruning of plums and gages must be completed in Britain by mid-July in order to give the cuts time to 'gum' before winter, as they will not do so when the weather becomes cold.

Plums bear their fruit on both old and new wood and so crop heavily.

Training and pruning

In spring, cut back any unduly long shoots, and early in July, pinch back to half way all side shoots, which will have made new growth. Plums form their fruit buds along the entire length of the branches and a well-grown tree may be allowed to carry a greater amount of wood than any other top fruit.

The pyramid, budded on to the dwarfing St Julien A stock, is ideal for small gardens. Maiden trees are planted 240–270cm (8–9ft) apart in November. On about April 1, the trees should be cut back to 120cm (4ft) above soil level and all lateral shoots pinched back to 22cm (9in) from the main stem. In mid-July, the laterals should be shortened again, to 15cm (6in), and the following April the leader shortened by about one-third of the past season's wood. Then in July, prune back the laterals again to 15cm (6in), and in this way the tree will concentrate on making fruit buds rather than wood.

To form the fan-shaped tree, which may be planted in the open and trained against strong wires or against a wall, cut back the leader to an upwards bud and on the lower portion of the stem, about 25cm (10in) above the scion, to two buds, one on either side of the stem. Make a nick in the bark above the buds to persuade them to 'break'.

When the two buds have made 45cm (18in) of growth, cut the leader back to just above the topmost shoot. Then tie two shoots to canes at an angle of 45°. At the end of summer, cut back these side arms to a bud about 22cm (9in) from the base; then, during next summer, allow laterals on the upper part of the two arms to grow on. Cut back the arms to the laterals furthest from the base. The framework will then be established.

The only pruning necessary will be to pinch back the newly formed shoots when they have formed seven or eight leaves. Do this in early July and tie the shoots in to prevent wind damage.

Root pruning

Often fan trees and indeed all types of plum tree begin to form suckers. These are shoots which arise from the roots below the scion and they must be removed. Uncover the roots around the stem and, taking care not to damage the scion, cut away the suckers with a sharp knife before covering the roots again and treading firm.

At the same time, root pruning may be done. This is the best way of restricting growth with plums, for there will be no 'bleeding'. It is usually fan-trained trees growing against a wall that are root-pruned. Scrape away the soil to a distance

216

of 120–150cm (4–5ft) from the wall to uncover the roots and cut them back to about 1m (3ft) of the stem. This will encourage more fibrous roots to form. Scatter peat around the roots before replacing the soil and tread firmly. Then give the roots a good soaking.

The choice of rootstocks is not large. Bush and fan trees are grown on either Common plum or Brompton stock and standards on the Myrobolan stock. This is mostly used for heavy-bearing orchard trees such as Czar and Monarch. Owing to their 'gumming', plums are budded, as with roses, and not grafted. The varieties Czar, President and Marjorie's Seedling are incompatible with Common plum stock and are budded on to Myrobolan stock.

For small gardens, the Brompton stock is best, for the trees grow steadily but come quickly into bearing and make few suckers. For Victoria, however, the Common plum is used, owing to its resistance to silver leaf disease.

Plums and gages of dwarf habit for a small garden are Jefferson, Kirke's Blue, Early Laxton, Early Transparent and Greengage.

Plums enjoy best a heavy loam. They will grow well in a limestone soil provided there is plenty of humus present, but they require a moisture-retentive soil and one which receives plenty of nitrogen, preferably of an organic nature. In light soils, work in plenty of farmyard or poultry manure, shoddy or composted straw. At planting time, give a handful of bone meal to each tree, mixed well into the soil as it is placed over the roots. The trees should also be given a liberal mulch of organic manure in April each year, augmented by 28g (1oz) of sulphate of ammonia. Czar and Victoria are the most tolerant of adverse soil conditions and crop heavily in all years, established trees bearing 22–27kg (50–60lb).

Harvesting and storing

Plums must be allowed to remain on the trees until fully ripe. The best test will be to remove one when it is thought to be ripe and taste it. If it is soft and juicy and the stone readily parts from the flesh, it is ripe. Most plums will store for several weeks in a dry, airy room if removed from the plant with their stalk and placed in cotton wool in trays. Laxton's Delicious, and Coe's Golden Drop keep well.

As with apples and pears, some thought must be given to pollination.

The flowering time of plums is from eighteen to twenty-one days, so that except for the very last to bloom, e.g. Marjorie's Seedling, the flowering period of many plums will overlap. Only the very early and very late do not overlap, for plums are in bloom for only ten days and not until the early plums have finished do the late ones come into bloom.

Early	Late
Bryanston Gage	Belle de Louvain
Jefferson	Pond's Seedling
Edward	Czar
President	Marjorie's Seedling
Denniston's Superb	Late Transparent
Utility	Oullin's Gage

Victoria overlaps both groups and is a first-rate pollinator, and for early and mid-season Denniston's Superb is reliable. Czar is the best pollinator for later flowering plums and gages. These three are the best and most reliable of all varieties.

217

Plums crop on both the old and new wood, hence they crop heavily, but are more liable to frost damage than other fruits, for they are the first to bloom. In frost-prone gardens, plant those which bloom later.

Opposite: The Mirabelle gage crops heavily in a warm garden and in fertile soil. The fruit has an almost transparent skin and makes delicious eating.

Varieties
To ripen in early August

Czar One of the best plums and, though it is late-flowering and therefore misses the frosts, it is first to ripen. Compact and reliable, it does well in all soils, the purple fruit being good for cooking and dessert.

Denniston's Superb Raised in New York in 1835, it does well in all soils and is a splendid pollinator. The yellow-green fruit with its red flush has excellent flavour.

Early Transparent Gage It makes a dwarf tree and sets a heavy crop with its own pollen. The skin is so thin as to show the stone, whilst it has an apricot flavour when ripe.

To ripen in late August to early September

Late Transparent Gage It has similar characteristics to Early Transparent, though ripening a fortnight later. The bright yellow fruit, speckled red, has a peach-like flavour.

Victoria Self-fertile and frost-resistant, it is ripe late in August and crops heavily, the egg-shaped plums being crimson-red and sweet and juicy.

To ripen in mid- to late September

Belle de Louvain Flowering late, it misses the frosts and makes a large tree, the oval fruits being purple-red and excellent for culinary use.

Edward A recent American introduction making a spreading tree and flowering early. The blue-black fruit with its creamy-white flesh is sweet and juicy.

Greengage Making a compact tree, it needs Victoria as a pollinator, when it crops heavily. Its greenish-yellow fruit is juicy and sweet, and unsurpassed in flavour.

Jefferson A gage raised at Albany, New York, it makes a compact tree, blooms early and needs a pollinator. For flavour, it is outstanding. The pale green fruits have brown markings and pink flesh.

To ripen in late September to early October

Bryanston Gage It makes a large tree and bears heavily when pollinated by Victoria. The fruits ripen to pale green streaked with red and have the true gage flavour.

Laxton's Delicious Flowering late, it is at its best in late September when its deep yellow fruit, flushed red, has excellent flavour.

Marjorie's Seedling It makes a large tree and is the last to bloom. Also the latest to ripen, its large crimson-purple fruit will hang until the end of October.

Severn Cross One of the latest to bloom and ripen its fruit, it makes a tall tree and bears golden-yellow fruit spotted with pink, which is sweet and of good flavour.

Greengages make delicious eating if removed when just ripe.

219

5 Damsons and bullaces

Though amongst the hardiest of fruits and able to bear heavy crops when growing in shallow soil and rocky outcrops, these fruits remain neglected. For cold, exposed gardens they will crop more heavily than plums, to which they are closely related. Damsons and bullaces differ in that the former bears an oval fruit, the latter a round one. They may be planted as a windbreak, for they retain their foliage through autumn, or in frost-troubled gardens. Plant with them the hardiest of the plums and those which bloom late, e.g. Pond's Seedling and Marjorie's Seedling. Damsons bloom still later. Though they bear heavy crops in poor soil, where provided with moisture-retaining humus, especially of a nitrogenous nature, the size and quality of fruit will be much enhanced. Dig in farmyard or poultry manure, or composted straw and garden compost or shoddy, before planting in November or December. Damsons make new wood slowly unless provided with nitrogen, and it is advisable to scatter a handful of bone meal around the roots before replacing the soil and treading firmly. They will need almost no pruning, as they make only small twiggy growth. And with the exception of Farleigh Prolific, they will set fruit with their own pollen, and thus present no difficulties on that count. They are not suitable for dessert but make delicious preserves and pies with a unique flavour.

Plant 2.5–3m (8–10ft) apart depending on the vigour of each variety. The three best damsons for a succession are Bradley's King, Farleigh Prolific and Merryweather.

Varieties

Bradley's King Hardy and late to bloom, its crimson fruit is the largest of all damsons and the most richly flavoured. It is ready in mid-September.

Farleigh Prolific Needing Bradley's King

Damsons are untroubled by cold winds or frosts and so may be planted as a windbreak.

as its pollinator, it is the first damson to ripen. Its small, jet black, tapering fruits hang in clusters and are ready in early September. It makes a small compact tree.

Merryweather It makes a spreading tree and blooms early, so it must be planted where frosts are not troublesome. It bears heavily. The blue-black, plum-size damsons are of outstanding flavour.

Langley Bullace Hardy and prolific, it ripens its fruit in late October and will hang until late in November. It is ideal for hedgerow planting, for it is a tough thorny tree with small interwoven branches.

Shepherd's Bullace This is hardy and blooms late. It crops heavily, its bright green fruits, ready in October, are juicy but sharp, and it makes delicious pies.

6 *Cherries*

Though always in demand for dessert and culinary use, being the first of the fruits to ripen, sweet cherries are now rarely planted in the amateur's garden. They do well only as standard or half-standard trees, on which they take about ten years to bear a prolific crop. Again, there are pollination difficulties, for only cherries of certain groups will pollinate each other and several must be planted together for best results. A standard cherry needs ample space to develop and in a small garden several of the more compact apples, occupying the same amount of ground, will be a better proposition. Birds, too, are always troublesome, for even where the fruits have set well, birds can take half the crop. But early cherries are always appreciated and where space permits two or three varieties may be planted together.

The Acid or Morello cherries are grown in fan form against a north wall. They are hardy and, though they will not pollinate sweet cherries, they will set fruit with their own pollen. They may also be grown with damsons as a windbreak.

The true Morello makes a densely branched tree and its fruit ripens in late August. Flemish Red, of upright habit, ripens in July and early August, so the two together will give a long succession of fruit for tarts and jams.

Though both are stone fruits, sweet cherries require exactly the opposite condition to plums. Cherries require a dry soil, preferably a light soil over chalk or limestone. Before planting, give the ground a liberal dressing of lime or lime rubble (mortar) and some potash in the form of bonfire ash. Or give 56g (2oz) per tree of sulphate of potash. Cherries do not require nitrogen, as it encourages them to make excess growth at the expense of fruit.

Planting is done in November. Take care not to damage the bark, for that would permit bacterial canker or silver leaf disease to enter at the wound. If planting in grass, first remove a circle of 60cm (2ft) diameter, and if planting standards, allow at least 6m (20ft) between them. For a fan tree, provide a 480cm (16ft) frame of horizontally fixed wires.

Cherries are best grown as standards, and will crop in a chalk or limestone soil. They take several years before bearing heavily, and they need suitable pollinators.

Morello cherries are hardy and may be grown as a windbreak or against a north wall in the fan-trained form.

Pruning

Follow much the same pruning procedure as for plums. Fan trees are formed in the same way. Afterwards, pinch back the side shoots to about six leaves early in July; in September, pinch back to four buds. If the leader shoots are making excessive growth, bend them down as far as possible and tie in, releasing them after twelve months. Root pruning may also be done as for plums.

With standards, cut the leader shoots back to half way in April, at the same time removing any dead wood but nothing more.

Morello cherries bear their fruit on the previous year's wood, so one must stimulate the plants to produce a continuous supply of new wood. To do so, cut back the laterals half way in autumn; in spring, pinch back all side shoots to 5cm (2in). The previous season's shoots will now be bearing new wood and blossom buds, and on these the present year's fruit is borne.

Until now, cherries have been grown on wild cherry stock, which accounts for the vigour of the trees. Today, however, a gene-tic dwarfing of rootstocks obtained from crossing *Prunus avium* and *P. cerasus* is resulting in trees of dwarf habit which come sooner into bearing.

Pollinating

Cherries have a flowering period of eighteen to twenty days, twice that of plums, and except for the very earliest and latest, they overlap. Yet this plays little or no part in their pollination and only certain groups will prove fertile with each other.

Varieties

Amber Heart The best cherry in cultivation, the 'White Heart' of London's barrow boys. The handsome yellow fruits are flushed with red and are ripe by early July.

Bradbourne Black Suitable for a frost-troubled garden, it makes a large spreading tree bearing crimson-black fruits of excellent flavour.

Early Rivers The earliest, ready in mid-June when the large crimson-black fruits are sweet and juicy.

222

Emperor Francis The first to bloom (so do not plant in a frost pocket) and the last to ripen, the dark crimson fruits being ready in late August.

Governor Wood It makes a large spreading tree and bears heavy crops of sweet yellow fruits flushed with pink. It is ready in late June.

Napoleon A delicious cherry for late July, the large bright red fruits make for best dessert.

Roundel Heart Ripe in mid-July, it bears large deep purple fruits of good flavour.

Stella The first self-fertile cherry. It makes a compact tree, comes early into fruit and bears large black fruits of excellent flavour.

Waterloo Though a compact tree, it is not a regular cropper, though its dark crimson fruit extends the season until the end of July.

Variety	Pollinators
Amber Heart	Napoleon
	Roundel Heart
	Governor Wood
Napoleon	Bradbourne Black
	Roundel Heart
Bradbourne Black	Napoleon
	Roundel Heart
Roundel Heart	Amber Heart
	Napoleon
	Bradbourne Black
	Governor Wood
Governor Wood	Amber Heart
	Roundel Heart
	Early Rivers
Early Rivers	Governor Wood

At the John Innes Institute at Merton, South London, it was found that pollen of Napoleon treated with X-rays and used on Emperor Francis, produced self-fertile mutations. The variety Stella is the result of this and may be the first of self-fertile cherries which come into fruit more quickly.

Cherry trees have a flowering period twice as long as the flowering period of plums.

7 Apricots, peaches and nectarines

These are plants of the East, able to survive a cold winter but requiring a long, dry summer to ripen the fruit and the wood, without which they will bear little fruit the following year. In Britain, peaches may be grown outdoors in East Anglia, which is the ideal climate for them. Otherwise, grow them in the southern parts of England and Ireland, especially on a warm wall or at the back of a lean-to greenhouse. Apricots grow better in the west, peaches and nectarines in the dryer east.

Apricots

Apricots require a soil containing plenty of lime and so grow best in a limestone soil. Where this is not possible, give the soil a liberal dressing of hydrated lime or lime rubble (mortar) and the plants a handful of bone meal at planting time. This slow-acting nitrogenous fertiliser will encourage the formation of new wood. This is important, for apricots have a tendency to suffer from 'die back', in which established shoots, for no apparent reason, die back entirely.

Plant in autumn against a warm wall. Fan-trained trees give the best results with this fruit. Plant at least 5.5m (18ft) apart, for they make long shoots. Allow the main shoots to grow on, pinching back the side growths in summer to about 5cm (2in).

Though self-fertile, apricots will set a better crop if hand-fertilised. This is done by dusting each flower with a camel-hair brush as they open. Hand-fertilising is essential for those grown indoors. Apricots flower early and if they are grown against an outside wall, it is advisable to hang muslin over the plants as soon as the blooms begin to open.

When the fruits have set and have started to swell, thin them to three in a cluster and to about 8cm (3in) apart as they make size, removing perhaps the centre one. Allow the fruit to become fully ripe before removing it with care to trays lined with a layer of cotton wool.

Apricots fruit on the old and new wood. To prevent overcrowding, remove the old spurs after the plants have borne fruit on them for two years.

The plants will benefit from a mulch of strawy manure each season in early summer. Once the fruit has set never allow the trees to go short of moisture at the roots.

Varieties

Alfred A Canadian variety, maturing in mid-July, the fruits are large and of deep orange colouring.

Early Moorpark Ripening in late July, the large oval fruits are pale apricot and the flesh orange.

Apricots grow best in a limestone soil, as fan-trained trees against a warm wall. They set more fruit if the flowers are hand fertilised.

Above: Prune peaches by the replacement system.

Right: Peaches crop heavily without a pollinator.

Hemskerk This does well under glass and outdoors, the conical fruits being orange-yellow striped red.

Moorpark The last to ripen, in Britain it is best grown under glass, where the orange fruits spotted with red will grow to a large size.

Peaches

Outdoors, peaches are grown as fan-trained trees against a wall; in pots on a terrace or verandah; or as bush trees, like apples, when they will come into fruit two years after planting. Plant in November, allowing just over 5m (18ft) for fan trees and just under 2m (6ft) for bushes. They require a soil containing plenty of lime and a slow-acting nitrogenous fertiliser such as shoddy or bone meal. Peaches are budded on to Common plum stock, and when planting, make sure that the union is above soil level. Tread in the roots firmly and water well if the soil is dry. Each year, in May, give a liberal mulch of strawy manure to conserve moisture.

Pruning

At the beginning, give bush trees the same treatment as in the renewal system for apples, i.e. shoots that have borne fruit are grown on until they are 45cm (18in) long. Do the same for fan trees. Fasten them to the wall and pinch the tips back to a wood bud. This will produce the wood that will bear next year's crop. The wood buds are small and pointed, the blossom buds round and fat.

Pruning of established trees consists of, in May, cutting back the leaders to about one-third and, in early June, pinching back the side shoots to about 5cm (2in), to a single wood bud at the base. This is grown on as replacement for next season's crop. Those shoots that have fruited are removed at the end of summer. This continuous formation of replacement shoots on which the crop is carried will keep the trees free from old wood, which often causes 'gumming' when removed.

It should be said that with fan trees, the horizontal shoots are often less vigorous than the more vertical shoots. To correct this, bend downwards any too strong growing vertical shoots and fasten in, and train any weak horizontal shoots in an upward direction. This will serve to correct the balance of the tree.

225

Any shoots appearing next to a fruit should be pinched out from their second leaf. This is done in June and the pinching back is done over the full month. This directs the energies of the tree to the swelling of the fruits without checking plant growth.

Root pruning will also help to restrict growth and encourage fruiting. It is done about five years after planting and every three or four years hence. Remove soil to a depth of about 37cm (15in) and 90cm (3ft) around the stem, and cut away the larger roots to about half way. Then replace the soil and tread firmly.

Peaches are self-fertile and need no pollinator, but a heavier set of fruit will be obtained if the open flowers when dry are pollinated with a camel-hair brush, especially those under glass.

Do not thin the fruit until after 'stoning'. This is a natural falling of the fruits when about the size of fully grown cherries. There should be about 12cm (5in) between the fruits left to mature.

Nectarines are smooth-skinned peaches which need similar culture.

The fruit ripens from the end of July until early October, depending on variety. To determine the ripeness, place a hand beneath a fruit and lift gently upwards: it should come away easily with its stalk. Or gently press the base of a fruit: if ripe, it will be slightly soft. Place the fruits in shallow trays lined with cotton wool.

Varieties

Alexander A heavy cropper ripe by early August, when the medium-sized fruits will be golden-yellow flushed with red.

Duke of York Ready in early August, when the large yellow-skinned fruit with green flesh is sweet and juicy.

Hale's Early The first to ripen: by late July the medium-sized fruits are a deep orange.

Peregrine Its large crimson fruits are ripe by mid-August and it is a reliable and heavy cropper.

Nectarine

This is a smooth-skinned peach and requires similar culture in every way, plenty of sunshine to ripen its wood, and in spring a thick mulch to conserve moisture – without which the fruits will not swell to a good size.

Varieties

There are three main varieties worthy of planting:

Early Rivers The most reliable and the earliest, ripe in early August when the bright red fruits are of excellent flavour.

Lord Napier Good outdoors, it follows Early Rivers, its large fruits ripening to pale green flushed with orange.

Pitmaston Orange Ripe in early September, it is a heavy bearer of large orange fruits of excellent flavour.

8 Grapes

The vine is hardier than imagined and at one time was grown outdoors in most parts of England, possibly introduced by the Romans. In recent years, vineyards have been re-established and wine-making is now a flourishing business. Vines can withstand frost to a temperature of −11°C (12°F). Outdoors, fruits of the Chasselas types can remain on the plants until early December. A little frost improves their sweetness and quality.

Vines require an open, sunny situation where the fruit and also the canes can ripen. They may be grown on a stake, like runner beans, planted 120cm (4ft) apart; or three

Though vines require an open, sunny situation to ripen, they are hardier than imagined.

could be planted 90cm (3ft) apart, with the stakes tied together at the top in tent fashion; fifty will take up little space in the garden. Otherwise they may be grown horizontally against a sunny wall; in the open, training the stems along strong wires; against a wooden trellis acting as a screen; or used to clothe a garden shelter.

Planting

Vines require a deep loam, preferably over a limestone subsoil. Where this is not possible, work in plenty of lime rubble before planting. Nitrogenous manures, except for a handful of the slow-acting bone meal at planting time, must be avoided for they encourage mildew. Where planting against a wall or trellis, remove soil 60cm (2ft)

227

Grapes are usually planted outside, but grow well in a cold or slightly warm greenhouse, trained over the roof.

square and to the same depth, and at the base add a 10cm (4in) deep layer of rubble, rammed down tightly as when planting figs. Then plant the soil ball with the vine roots over a layer of soil to which has been added the bone meal and 28g (1oz) per plant of sulphate of potash. This will make the canes grow 'hard' and ripen well. Plant in October, allowing 240cm (8ft) between those vines trained horizontally.

Grapes are an excellent crop for a cold or slightly heated greenhouse with a winter temperature of 6°C (42°F) for early crops. Here the vines are trained over the roof of the greenhouse. It is usual to plant the vine outside, taking the shoots through an open-

ing in the wall. Plant as described. For indoors, either Black Alicante or Black Hamburgh are the best, as these grapes will ripen well even in a sunless summer.

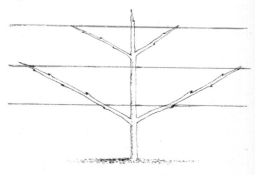

Above: A vine may be planted against a trellis in a sunny part of the garden. Tie in the rods as they make growth.

Pruning

Pruning calls for some thought. A shoot will grow 6m (20ft) in a single season, and every eye along the entire length is capable of bearing a shoot which will produce one or more bunches of grapes. In addition, a vine is able to bear fruit on the older wood, though this would prove too much for its constitution. If new shoots are encouraged, the eyes on the old wood will not be sufficiently vigorous to bear fruit, and the fruit on the new wood will be better.

There are two main methods of pruning, the long rod system and the spur system.

The long rod system This name applies when one or two new shoots or rods are allowed to grow on and all other growth is restricted.

By the long-rod system, one or two shoots only are grown on and other growth is restricted.

With vines, pruning is done in the depths of winter, the first days of January, before the sap begins to rise, being most suitable. For greenhouse plants, allow the vine to form two stems or rods; train these as far apart as possible and tie in to wires stretched across the roof. The rods will grow 6m (20ft) or more their first year. On New Year's Day, cut the weaker rod back to two buds near the base. On the other, stronger stem will be borne the next season's crop, and the stronger stem from its two buds will be grown on to produce the crop for the season after that. To prevent the formation of too much foliage, pinch back all laterals to two buds – one to bear the fruit, the other the foliage, which should be stopped at two leaves. Do this pinching back of laterals in summer over several weeks so as not to check the plant too drastically.

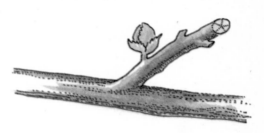

From these rods, select alternate buds on either side of the stems to produce short laterals.

During the first year, no vine should be allowed to fruit, and the following year only one bunch from each lateral should be retained.

Should it happen that buds on the lower part of the rods refuse to come into growth, lower the rod from the roof for three to four weeks before tying it in again. This will persuade the lower buds to 'break' whilst retarding the upper buds at the same time.

For vines in the open, growing vertically, follow the single rod and spur system, retaining the strongest shoot of two basal buds to bear fruit. Then, after fruiting, cut back to a single eye or bud to produce next year's rod.

The spur system From the rod which has grown away unchecked, select alternate buds on each side of the stem to produce short laterals. These bear fruit and should be stopped one leaf beyond. Then cut back each shoot to two buds in winter, one of which will form the grapes, the other the foliage. This will build up a system of spurs. Stop fruit-bearing laterals at the first joint after the bunch has formed, and pinch back non-fruiting laterals to 5cm (2in).

Vines growing horizontally against a wall should receive the same treatment as espalier pears. Cut back to the lower three buds in winter, the upper forming the extension shoot whilst the lower buds, one on either side of the stem, will form the lower arms. Train them first at an angle of 45°, tying them to canes, then gradually bring them to the horizontal position. The following year, cut back the extension shoot again to three buds, the two lower ones facing in opposite directions to form the next pair of arms, about 40cm (16in) above the lower pair and so on until the vine reaches the required height. Each arm or rod should be treated the same as for the spur system.

When the fruit has set it must be decided how many bunches the vines can mature. This depends upon age. Probably the rods will carry ten bunches in their second year, twice that number next year and so on. Should there be overcrowding, nip out a few grapes with pointed scissors, as well as any damaged fruits.

Where growing under glass, a moist atmosphere is necessary for the buds to 'break'. Syringe the vines daily to keep away red spider. This should stop when the fruits have formed and begun to show colour, otherwise they may decay. At this time, give ample ventilation so that moisture does not remain on the fruits. The grapes will be ready in late summer and early autumn.

Propagation

The easiest method of propagation is by cuttings. Canes should be removed in May and cut into 37cm (15in) pieces. Insert these 10cm (4in) deep in trenches filled with a mixture of peat and sand which is kept moist. To encourage rooting, first treat the cutting with hormone powder. By autumn they will have rooted, and should then be transferred to pots and grown on in a frame or greenhouse for another twelve

months, during which the side shoots should be pinched out. They should then be planted in their fruiting quarters and treated as described.

Varieties

Angevine Oberlin The earliest to ripen; the greenish-white grapes have exceptional flavour.

Black Alicante Best under glass, where it ripens early. The purple-black grapes have a muscat flavour.

Black Hamburgh Indoors and outside it is easy to grow, the large black grapes being sweet and juicy.

Chasselas D'Or One of the best early grapes, ripening to a rich golden colour.

Golden Queen Better under glass, it ripens early. The golden yellow grapes are treacle-sweet with a delicate flavour.

Perle de Czaba It does well indoors and out, the large white oval grapes having true muscat flavour.

Above: Grapes growing against a wall.
Right: The Black Hamburgh grape crops well in the open in a warm garden and also indoors. The fruit ripens early.
Below: White and yellow grapes have a distinct flavour. They are usually hardier than the black varieties.

9 Figs

The fig is hardier than is generally believed. Though a native of the Near East, it crops well and will ripen its fruit almost anywhere in an average summer. In the East and in the warmer parts of the USA, it bears three crops a year, being continuously in bearing.

Figs crop well close to the sea where the salt-laden atmosphere and sea mists give protection from frost. They also grow well over a chalky subsoil, for they are lime lovers. Where planting, mix plenty of mortar or crushed limestone into the soil but give no manure, for figs make plenty of leaf without it. They need a sparse diet and this means restricting the roots so that they cannot go far in search of food.

Planting

Obtain pot-grown plants and either plant the vine in the pot, burying it below soil level, or remove from the pot with the soil ball intact, and plant over a layer of stones. These should be rammed well down to make a solid base after the soil has been removed to a depth of 45cm (18in). If you are planting the figs against a wall, which is the best place for them, place pieces of slate on the other three sides of a hole made 45cm (18in) wide, to restrict the roots still further. Then when planting the soil ball, make the soil around it as compact as possible and water in.

Figs are planted in spring and require copious amounts of water through summer. They should also be given a thick mulch in May each year. They grow well in the horizontal form planted against a west wall, leaving a south-facing wall for peaches or pears.

Pruning

The fruit is carried on the previous year's wood. The replacement shoot is stopped at the fourth leaf, at the end of July – not before, as the fruits expected to mature the

Figs ripen well when planted against a warm wall.

following summer will form too quickly at the expense of new wood. Yet if the shoot is not stopped, the tiny figs will lack nourishment, turn yellow and fall off.

The fruits form at the leaf axils the previous year and begin to swell in spring. If the shoots are pinched back late in July, new fruits will form at the axil of each leaf and will be next year's crop. If the tree begins to make too much wood, some of that which carried the previous season's fruit should be thinned.

Figs under glass, growing in gentle heat, will bear two crops yearly. The fruits formed the previous year will swell early in spring and be ripe by early summer, then those formed in spring will mature by late September. The shoots formed in the last weeks of summer will bear next spring's crop.

Propagation is a simple matter. It is either by cuttings or by suckers. By the

232

tom heat is necessary; it will root in three months. Re-pot into a large pot before placing outdoors in May, in a sunny position to ripen the wood. Plant it in its permanent place the following spring. Or the plants may be moved to larger pots in which they will fruit. They should be 180cm (6ft) apart for they will soon reach that height and will grow to the same width.

The method by which plants are grown on from suckers is the easier way. These should be detached with their roots and grown on in pots.

To harvest figs, remove them before they split but not much before, and place them in trays lined with cotton wool. They may be kept for several months in a frost-free room.

Varieties

Black Ischia The hardiest variety, it crops well outdoors, bearing medium-sized purple-black fruit with crimson flesh.

Brown Turkey The best all-round fig, good under glass and outdoors, bearing heavy crops of large purple-brown fruits of excellent flavour.

Brunswick Good under glass, it needs a sheltered, sunny position outdoors. The large green figs have white flesh.

former method a well-ripened shoot 20cm (8in) long should be removed in January. The base is dipped in hormone powder to encourage rapid rooting, before being inserted in a small pot containing a gritty compost. It should be placed over a radiator or in a propagating unit, for bot-

Plant in its pot, or remove with soil ball intact and restrict roots by planting over a layer of stones.

Fruits form in the leaf axils the previous year. Pinch back the shoots in July to encourage new fruits to form.

10 Raspberries

A cane fruit to follow strawberries as the chief soft fruit of later summer. It freezes well and with its unique flavour makes excellent preserves. There are now varieties to spread the season over several months. They flower later than strawberries and are rarely troubled by frost. But if you do have problems with frost, you could plant Malling Jewel rather than Malling Promise for early fruit and then plant Glen Clova for mid-season, with Norfolk Giant for a late crop of fruit.

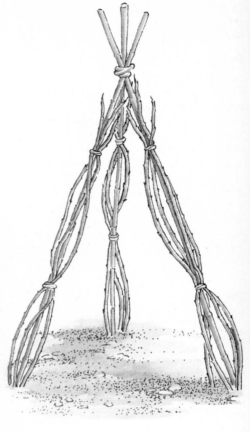

Above: Raspberries follow strawberries, fruiting on the previous year's canes.

Left: Raspberries crop well in a humus-laden soil if not planted too deep.

Raspberries require an open sunny situation. To enable the canes to receive the full amount of sunshine, plant the rows north to south. A plantation will be permanent, although raspberries fruit on the previous year's canes and it is necessary to provide the plants with nitrogenous manures to enable them to make plenty of growth. Raspberry plants also need humus in order

234

to retain summer moisture, without which there will be few new canes and the fruits will be hard and seedy.

Preparing the ground

Dig in all the humus possible, including some peat together with shoddy, farmyard manure or composted straw. Use large amounts if the soil is of a sandy nature. At planting time, rake in 30g of sulphate of potash per m (1oz per yd) of row, or of wood ash which has been stored under cover.

It is important to plant into clean ground, for it will be difficult to clean after planting without damaging the roots, as this fruit is surface-rooting. Rather than hoe too near the plants, give a mulch of peat and composted straw in early June each year. This will suppress weeds and preserve moisture in the soil.

Planting

Plant the canes in November so that they are established before the frosts, although planting can be done at any time until mid-March if the soil is in a friable condition. If not, dig a trench and spread out the roots before covering them with soil until planting can take place. As with all fruits, purchase from a reliable grower canes which are free from 'mosaic', which causes stunted canes.

Plant the canes 40–45cm (16–18in) apart, Malling Promise and Norfolk Giant needing slightly wider spacing; allow 120cm (4ft) between the rows. Do not plant too deeply, for this is the cause of failure of many plantations. Just cover the roots and tread in the soil over them. Then after a few days, cut back the canes to 15cm (6in) above ground level. There will be no fruit the first summer, though the autumn-fruiting kinds will bear a crop. This cutting back will cause the buds at the base of the canes to produce new canes on which will be borne next year's crop.

As the canes make growth, tie them to wires stretched along the rows at intervals of 45cm (18in). This will prevent the canes being broken by winds. At the end of summer, remove the tips of the canes, which will then have grown about 180cm (6ft) tall. After fruiting, cut out the old canes to about 7cm (3in) above ground and tie in the new canes for next year's crop. Burn the old canes and leave each root with six to seven new fruiting canes.

With autumn-fruiting kinds, the canes are cut back in March and the crop is borne on canes which are produced that summer. In all other respects, the culture is the same for them.

The fruit ripens quickly, and if the weather is warm it may need picking twice daily so that it will not get too ripe and become 'mushy'.

To propagate, lift a root or two in November and separate the canes, holding them near the base and pulling them away with the roots. Re-plant as soon as possible so that the roots do not dry out, treating them as described.

When planting raspberries in rows, fasten canes to wires, cut back to 15cm (6in) above ground, and grow on new canes to fruit next year.

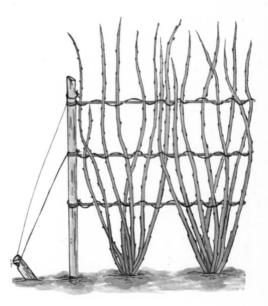

235

Varieties

Early (ready in early July)

Lloyd George An old favourite, once the only reliable raspberry. Then it lost vigour until the arrival of virus-free stock from New Zealand. It now crops well again in all soils and for flavour has no equal.

Malling Promise The first of the Malling varieties to ripen but is best grown in the warmer parts, for its canes are liable to frost damage. It bears heavily, the berries being large and brilliant red.

Mid-season (ready in late July)

Glen Clova It blooms late and so misses the frosts; it bears large crops of bright red fruits which will retain their quality after freezing.

Malling Jewel An early mid-season variety which flowers late. It bears heavy crops of large, conical, deep-red fruits.

An early variety which is widely grown in Europe, where it produces heavy crops.

Early to ripen, Malling Promise bears heavy crops.

Late (ready in mid-August)

Malling Admiral Very resistant to virus and botrytis, it is a heavy cropper whose large deep red fruits freeze and bottle well.

Norfolk Giant It blooms late, missing the frosts, and is immune to most diseases. It is the last of the summer varieties to ripen and the firm fruit freezes well.

Autumn-fruiting

Fallgold A new American variety which makes plenty of cane and bears large yellow berries from early September until November.

September An American introduction, ripening from late August until mid-October. It is tolerant of dry conditions and will crop well even when conditions are against it.

Zeva A Swiss variety, it is hardy and makes plenty of cane. It begins to fruit in mid-August and continues until late October. The large berries ripen to deep crimson and are sweet and juicy.

236

11 Blackberries

These (and their hybrid berries) are the last of the soft fruits ripening from August until November. They freeze well and make excellent tarts and preserves. They are the hardiest of all fruits and several varieties may be planted as a windbreak, trained along strong wires. They bear fruit both on the old and new canes and so crop heavily, doing well in all soils and in all climates. They do not need as much sunlight as other fruits and may be grown against a north wall or on a trellis which receives only a small amount of sunlight. Several of them have attractive fern-like foliage and may be grown against rustic poles – possibly to divide one part of the garden from another, with a central archway for access. Or plant in rows and train the stems along wires held in place by strong stakes at intervals of 240cm (8ft). Plant November to March 240cm (8ft) apart in the rows and allow 150cm (5ft) between the rows. Where possible, plant thornless varieties, which are easier to tie in and to pick the fruit. Set the roots only 7–10cm (3–4in) deep.

Another method is to grow them up 3m (10ft) poles, or posts driven well into the ground with 240cm (8ft) above ground. Tie in the shoots as they grow, and when they have made too much old wood, cut away the ties and lay all the shoots on the ground. Then cut out the older wood and tie in against the new shoots. In this way, the plants will be kept healthy for years. The time to do this is in late November after fruiting; at this time any old or dead wood is removed from those plants grown as a hedge or in rows.

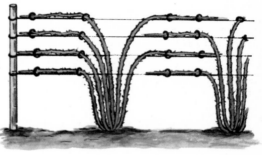

Above: Where growing on wires, space wires 45cm (18in) apart, using strong stakes to support them. Plant blackberries 240cm (8ft) apart in the rows.

Left: Blackberries may be grown against a trellis to divide up the garden, or along wires or against a north wall.

Preparation of the soil

Whilst the plants require plenty of humus to retain moisture and produce large and juicy fruits, nitrogen is not as essential as for loganberries, which fruit only on the new season's wood and must be encouraged to make as much as possible.

For blackberries, give the ground some peat and whatever humus is available. Clearings from ditches are useful, together with garden compost or old mushroom-bed manure. The plants will also benefit from a yearly mulch of lawn mowings or peat, to conserve soil moisture. In spring, 28g (1oz) of sulphate of potash should be scattered on the surface around each plant. This will improve the quality of fruit. Blackberries and all soft fruits will benefit from an occasional watering during wet weather of dilute liquid manure. This should be given from July until September and will enhance the quality of fruit and increase cane growth.

After planting, which should be done in November-December if possible, cut back the canes to 15cm (6in) above soil level. New canes will appear in spring and should be tied to wires horizontally, or vertically if growing against poles. Blackberries will fruit on the new canes in autumn and will increase in weight each year, bearing the heaviest crops of all soft fruits.

Propagation

Except for the hybrid berries, blackberries may be raised from seed sown in spring in shallow drills outdoors or in a frame. Keep well watered and by late summer they will be ready to move to the rows, where they should be planted 15cm (6in) apart. The following autumn, move to their fruiting quarters and grow on as described.

Named varieties are propagated by rooting the tips of the branches or canes. They are bent down from the wires in July and the ends inserted into the soil to a depth of about 7cm (3in). Tread firmly and keep moist. By November they will have rooted

and may then be severed from the parent plant with about 15cm (6in) of cane attached. They should then be moved to their fruiting quarters and the parent cane tied in again. Nothing could be easier.

Blackberries can be grown against poles in the same way as rambler roses, tying in the long shoots.

Varieties
Early (ready in August)

Bedford Giant   The first to ripen, it crops well in all soils and bears large firm fruits which freeze well.

Merton Early   It comes true from seed and more nearly resembles the loganberry in that it bears most of its fruit on new canes. The fruit is large and of good flavour, whilst the compact habit allows them to be spaced only 180cm (6ft) apart.

238

Mid-season (ready in September)

Ashton Cross It follows Bedford Giant and is ripe in early August. Highly resistant to virus, it crops heavily and the large berries are of good flavour.

Himalaya Giant Extremely hardy, it was first raised from seed sent from the Himalayas in 1900. It is a plant of great vigour, cropping heavily, but its large thorns make picking difficult. The fruit is large and firm and freezes and bottles well.

Oregon Thornless This American variety has ornamental foliage, and an established plant will yield up to about 6kg (14lb) of fruit in a season. The large juicy berries are ripe in late September, and it is now grown instead of the lighter-cropping Merton Thornless.

Late (ready in October)

John Innes It ripens too late for all but the warmest gardens, where it crops heavily until mid-November.

Varieties of hybrid berries

These have the blackberry or loganberry for a parent.

Boysenberry The result of a loganberry cross with Young's Dewberry, it resembles the loganberry in its habit and in the size and flavour of the large mulberry-coloured fruits, which ripen in September.

King's Acre Berry A hybrid blackberry of unknown origin, it is a plant of vigorous habit. It bears purple-black fruit of excellent flavour, which parts from its core like a raspberry.

Lowberry A loganberry cross of American origin, and like the loganberry it fruits on the new wood. The fruits measure 5cm (2in) long and are jet black with the black-berry flavour. They are ripe in October.

Young's Dewberry Known in Britain as the Youngberry, it was raised in America by a Mr Young, who crossed the loganberry with a dewberry. Like the former, it crops better in a warm, sheltered garden, when a single plant will bear up to 4.5kg (10lb) of luscious purple-black fruits. There is now a thornless variety to make picking easier. It is ripe from early August until early October.

The hybrid berries fruit in autumn and are excellent for preserves and for freezing, to use in pies during winter.

12 Loganberries

Above: Loganberries require a warm, sheltered garden.

Loganberries do not like cold winds and the canes are more frost-tender than either raspberries or blackberries. Hence they should be grown in more sheltered gardens, whilst blackberries are for colder places.

Provide the plants with a soil containing plenty of nitrogenous humus, for they fruit only on the new season's canes and as much new cane growth as possible must be produced. Farmyard manure, shoddy, poultry manure and composted straw are all valuable, or dig in some peat and garden compost and give a handful of bone meal for each plant. In April, give the rows 30g per m (1oz per yd) of sulphate of ammonia during wet weather. This will increase cane growth, on which next year's fruit will be borne.

Plant any time between November and early March, 180 cm (6ft) apart, only just covering the roots. In March, cut back the canes to 15cm (6in) above ground, and tie in the new canes as they grow. Like raspberries, this fruit will not bear a crop the first year. Should the cane tips have been caught by frost, remove them in spring when the plants are given a heavy mulch. During August, they will be laden with large crimson berries, which do not part from the core and so freeze and bottle well.

Propagation is by rooting the tips of the canes as for blackberries.

Below: Train the canes against wires like raspberries

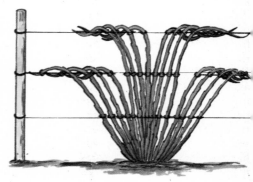

Believed to be a red-fruiting form of the Californian blackberry, or the result of a chance cross between this blackberry and a raspberry, the loganberry was discovered by Judge Logan at Santa Cruz and named in his honour. After almost a century, the canes lost vigour until the new LY59 strain recently brought about a revival in vigour and popularity. Plants of this strain will send out new canes 240cm (8ft) in length. They are quite brittle, with the arching habit of the raspberry, so that they are tied to the supporting wires in a similar way.

13 Gooseberries

Gooseberries are the hardiest of the soft fruits, cropping well where few other fruits would. They are troubled neither by frost nor by cold winds.

One of the hardiest of the soft fruits, the gooseberry prefers cool conditions to ripen. Except for Leveller and one or two dessert kinds, it does better where cool, moist conditions prevail. It crops heavily for the area of ground it occupies, and no amount of frost or cold winds will trouble it. It is one of the few soft fruits to do well in semi-shade. It may therefore be planted between apples and other top fruits, thus making the best use of the ground. It is also a very permanent plant and with the minimum of attention will continue to produce fruit for fifty years and more. In addition, the fruit will hang on the bushes for several weeks so that it may be picked when there is plenty of time to do so. But it should not be left until the fruits begin to crack and fall from the plants. The fruit is used for bottling, whilst it will freeze better than any, keeping for two years. Fresh dessert gooseberries have no equal for flavour eaten from the plant, and the culinary varieties have all manner of uses.

The first gooseberries will ripen early in June. By planting early, mid-season and late varieties, cropping will continue until the end of August. What is more, a pound of gooseberries can be picked in a few minutes and the fruit does not turn mushy, however warm the weather. It is the foolproof fruit with a distinctive flavour all of its own.

A well grown and carefully pruned gooseberry bush will yield fruit for many years.

Preparing the soil

Gooseberries, which fruit both on the old and new wood, crop so heavily that it is necessary to maintain a balance between the production of new wood and fruiting. The plants do not need as much nitrogen as do blackcurrants, but they need humus to maintain moisture in summer. Without this the fruits cannot swell and will lack both weight and flavour. So dig in plenty of peat or old mushroom bed manure or garden compost, or clearings from ditches or ponds.

If dry conditions prevail, water the plants as often as possible, preferably in the evening, giving the roots a good soaking. All soft fruits, especially the gooseberry, require plenty of moisture for the berries to grow large and juicy. If you are growing dessert kinds, an occasional application of dilute manure water given in June will help the fruits to swell and increase the flavour.

Watering should commence as soon as the fruits have formed and should continue until ripe. If left until the berries have grown large, heavy watering will then cause the skins to crack as with tomatoes.

Planting

Plant at any time between November and early March when there is no frost. But where the ground is heavy and not well drained, early spring planting is better. In any case, gooseberries do best in light soil. Where growing the more bushy varieties plant 120cm (4ft) apart in rows, with the same distance between them, for a fully grown plant will cover an area of just under a square metre (square yard). Those of a more compact, upright habit may be planted 90cm (3ft) apart. They will not crop quite so heavily but it means that more plants may be planted in the same area of ground.

During the first three or four years, little or no pruning is needed. Afterwards, begin to remove some of the old wood and thin out the shoots if there is over-crowding, so that the plants do not grow into each other. Those of spreading and somewhat drooping habit should have the shoots cut back to an upwards bud to counteract this tendency. Those of upright habit are cut back at an outwards bud in order to prevent overcrowding at the centre.

Propagation

Gooseberry cuttings are difficult to root, for the wood is relatively hard. Because of this, use only the new season's wood and insert as soon as possible after removing it from the plant. Cuttings are removed early September when about 15cm (6in) long.

Gooseberries are grown on a leg so that the lower buds are removed before the cuttings are rooted.

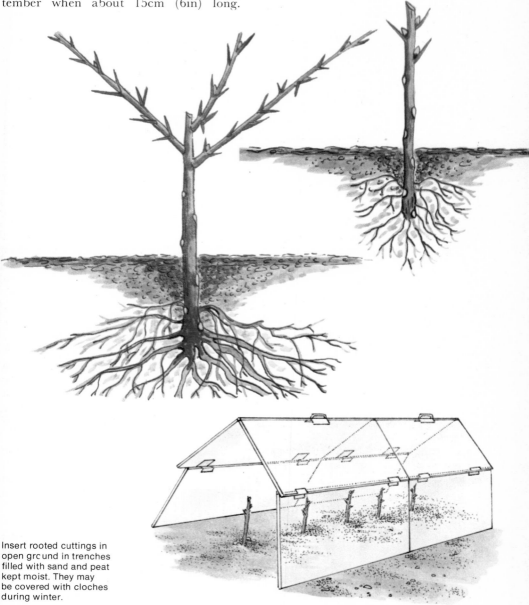

Insert rooted cuttings in open ground in trenches filled with sand and peat kept moist. They may be covered with cloches during winter.

Dessert gooseberries are delicious, and culinary varieties are excellent for the freezer.

Remove all but the top three buds so that the plant will form a 'leg' and insert the base in hormone powder to encourage quicker rooting. Then insert the lower 2cm (1in) into the soil either in trenches outdoors to which peat has been incorporated, or in a frame, the soil having been prepared in the same way. Those in trenches can be covered with cloches.

Plant the cuttings 7cm (3in) apart and make the soil firm around them. Water in and keep the soil comfortably moist. They should have rooted by early the following summer, but keep growing them on until October when they should be moved to their fruiting quarters and planted at the recommended spacing. They will begin to fruit the following year, but strawberries may be grown between the rows until such time as the gooseberries have made some growth.

Gooseberries are red, green, yellow or white when ripe, and each will have its own particular flavour. For culinary use, they can be picked green from early in June.

Varieties

Early

Bedford Red One of the first to ripen, the large round berries will be deep crimson.

Broom Girl The large berries are yellow, shaded green, and may be used for culinary purposes and later for dessert.

May Duke It can be picked green for culinary use early in June and at the month end for dessert, when crimson.

Whitesmith It makes a large upright bush and bears its big downy white fruits along the whole length of the stems.

Mid-season

Bedford Yellow Follows Broom Girl, its large golden berries having exceptional flavour.

Careless The heaviest cropper and excellent to freeze, the large greenish-white berries being of good flavour.

Gunner The large dark green berries, veined yellow, have exceptional flavour.

Late

Howard's Lancer The last to ripen and, but for a tendency to mildew, this gooseberry would be the best ever raised, for it bears large yellow fruits and crops well in all soils.

Leveller The best yellow for dessert in August, the fruits being of great size and treacle-sweet.

Whinham's Industry It makes a large spreading bush and crops heavily in late July, when the large crimson berries are used for culinary purposes and later are used for dessert.

244

14 Blackcurrants and redcurrants

Though gooseberries do well in cooler parts, blackcurrants enjoy warmth. They are intolerant of cold winds, which cause them to drop their fruit buds. No fruit is more liable to frost damage, although several varieties, for example, Wellington XXX, Westwick Triumph and Amos Black, flower late and so miss most of the frosts. But with their unique flavour, blackcurrants make a delicious conserve and may be used in tarts and pies, whilst the fruits are richer in Vitamin C than any others. The introduction of Laxton's Giant has given us the first dessert variety, to be eaten from the basket or from the plant, or served with clotted cream; for where well grown, the fruits are as large as cherries.

This continental mid-season blackcurrant bears heavily in frost-free gardens.

Preparation of the soil

Do not plant exposed to prevailing winds. Blackcurrants need a sheltered place which must also be open and sunny. Pollination of the flowers is essential if they are to set heavy crops, and if the winds are cold, there will be few insects about. Blackcurrants require plenty of humus to maintain summer moisture and need nitrogen to make plenty of new wood each year, for if the plants are allowed to carry an excess of old wood, crops will be light and the fruit small. Plants lacking moisture will produce small and seedy fruits lacking in juice.

In an average year, where frosts are not troublesome, as much as 3kg (7lb) of fruit can be expected from a four-year old plant. This will increase as the plants grow larger by means of sucker-like shoots which appear from below soil level.

Planting

It is important to plant in clean ground, for it will be difficult to clear afterwards without harming the roots. Two-year bushes are the best to plant and as the cuttings root easily, they are inexpensive. To give worthwhile pickings, two or three plants each of three varieties should be grown – an early, mid-season and late to spread the crop so there will be fruit from early July until October. Healthy plants should bear well for twenty years or more.

Plant at any time between November and March when the soil is clear of frost and is not waterlogged. Plant the more vigorous kinds, e.g. Wellington XXX 150–180cm (5–6ft) apart and the more compact 120–150cm (4–5ft) apart. For the smaller garden, plant Laxton's Giant and Amos Black for succession. These will also usually miss the frosts. They require deeper planting than other soft fruits. Insert the roots about 12–15cm (5–6in) below the surface, spread them out, add the bone meal and cover with soil, treading in the plant.

245

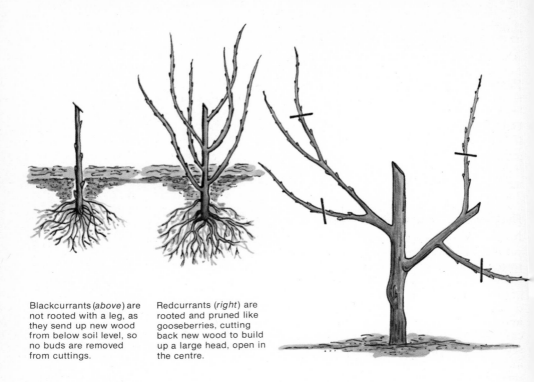

Blackcurrants (*above*) are not rooted with a leg, as they send up new wood from below soil level, so no buds are removed from cuttings.

Redcurrants (*right*) are rooted and pruned like gooseberries, cutting back new wood to build up a large head, open in the centre.

Before the end of March, cut back all shoots to about 7cm (3in) of the base. This will encourage the plants to form, during the first year, more basal shoots upon which the crop is borne the next season. For the next two or three years, no pruning is necessary. Then prune to keep the plants free of too much old wood, striking a balance between the old and new wood, for all of it will bear fruit; hence the weight of fruit increases each year.

Blackcurrants produce their new growth from base buds. To increase the stock, young shoots (one-year-old) are removed in October when the leaves have fallen and the crop has been gathered. Both young and old plants will benefit from a mulch of peat, garden compost or strawy manure given each year in April. This will suppress weeds and maintain moisture in the soil. Until the plants are about four years old, grow strawberries in rows between them to make full use of the ground.

Do not pick the fruits until they have turned black as only then will they be sweet and juicy. To pick, hold the bunches by the string (stalks) and carefully pull away the fruits with the other hand, taking care not to squash or bruise them.

Varieties
Early

Laxton's Giant The only real dessert variety, it is the first to mature. It crops heavily and is more frost and wind tolerant than other earlies, but it needs a heavy, well nourished soil to grow the large berries.

Mid-season

Wellington XXX The best all-round variety ever raised but requires plenty of room, for it makes a large, spreading bush. It blooms late, whilst the thick-skinned fruits freeze best of all.

Late

Amos Black The last to bloom and also to crop and so is valuable in a frosty garden. Ready in early October, the medium-sized fruits have good flavour and freeze well.

Baldwin The Hilltop strain is the best but this variety crops well only in a warm garden and in a light soil. It holds its large juicy berries for several weeks when fully ripe and is at its best in September.

Redcurrants and white currants

Redcurrants and white currants are two varieties of the same fruit and require completely different conditions to blackcurrants, more nearly resembling the gooseberry in their culture and habit. They do not crop so heavily as other soft fruits, and birds will take the red berries if not covered. But they make a delicious conserve to have with meats and make a pleasant sweet if allowed to grow large, being at their best served with a sprinkling of red wine.

These currants grow on a leg or as cordons and take up little space. They are not troubled by frost but are not happy in a cold windy garden. They also require a light soil but as they are shy in forming new wood, they need as much nitrogenous humus as possible. This helps to conserve soil moisture so that the fruits grow large and to produce new growth each year.

Plant between November and March when the soil is suitable, removing any growths from the 'leg' before doing so. Plant 90–120cm (3–4ft) apart, 120cm (4ft) for the vigorous Laxton's No. 1. In March, cut back the shoots to 7cm (3in) of their base, which will be above the 'leg', to form a nicely shaped head.

The fruits begin to colour mid-July, when they should be covered with muslin against birds. Remove the fruits at exactly the right moment, when fully ripe. If left on the plants too long they will become soft.

Redcurrants require a warm, sheltered garden. The fruit ripens July and August and should be covered with muslin to protect from birds.

Varieties
Early

Fay's Prolific An American introduction, it makes a compact plant and bears heavily. It blooms late to miss the frosts.

Laxton's No. 1 The earliest red and a reliable and heavy cropper in all soils with the large fruits borne in long trusses.

Mid-season

Red Lake If there is room for only one, this should be it, for it is without fault. Raised in New York, it bears large crimson berries spaced evenly about the trusses.

247

15 Strawberries

The strawberry is the most popular soft fruit, always prominent on special summer occasions, to be enjoyed with cream or sprinkled with wine. It is also popular with growers for if planted in October, it will bear a crop the following summer; autumn-fruiting varieties will crop the first year if planted in March. Yet the strawberry ripens quickly, needing constant attention with its picking, and its blossom is more liable to frost damage than other fruits. The plants are more troubled by pests and disease. The fruits may also be spoilt by heavy rain when ripening, though the introduction of new varieties to extend the season has minimised this. It is now possible to have fruit from early May (under cloches) until the year end, using cloches again in October.

Strawberries should not be grown in frosty districts, unless the resistant Cambridge Early Pine or the late flowering kinds are planted, for example Cambridge Favourite (early); Talisman (mid-season); Hampshire Maid (late). These are fairly immune to frost. In areas of high rainfall, plant those whose fruits have a glossy surface and are more readily able to shed moisture, e.g. Royal Sovereign, Cambridge Favourite and Early Pine.

For an early crop in a frame or under cloches, Cambridge Early Pine and Cambridge Premier are suitable, for they ripen quickly and do not make too much leaf. But those plants to be covered must be in the ground by early September so that they can become established before they are covered in early April. If covering with barn-type cloches, plant a double row spaced 37cm (15in) apart and 25cm (10in) in the rows. On warm days remove the cloches and give the plants a soaking before replacing the cloches late afternoon. Removal of the cloches and syringing the blooms will assist pollination. But do not uncover the plants except for a short time, if cold winds are

Strawberries are the most popular of summer fruits.

blowing. The first uncovered plants will begin to bloom towards mid-May and the first fruits will have ripened by early June. When the first fruits have formed, place straw between the rows to prevent soil splashing on to the fruit; this will help the soil to warm more quickly and the fruit to ripen sooner. From this use of straw the plant took its name. Or place 30cm- (12in-) wide strips of black polythene between the rows, held in place by large stones. Sheets of newspaper may also be used and should be kept damp. Each of these materials will also help to prevent moisture evaporation from the soil.

The plants must be kept moist if they are to make plenty of healthy foliage and the berries are to be large and juicy. So in dry weather give plenty of water, though plenty of humus in the soil before planting will hold moisture.

Preparing the soil

Strawberries grow best on light land; if heavy, it will tend to be badly drained in winter when the roots may decay because of red core, turning red at the centre and causing the plant to die back. But light land will need plenty of humus and this may be given as peat and garden compost. Unlike other fruits, strawberries crop better in a slightly acid soil and peat will encourage this. With it, mix in any other form of humus to bind the soil.

Clean land is essential, for the plants send out in all directions runners which take root, and it is impossible to clean round the plants later. Also, in weed-infested land the weeds deprive the plants of moisture and soon the strawberries begin to die back. If you are planting in newly turned turf land, treat for wireworm before planting.

Planting

Allow the ground several weeks to consolidate before planting in autumn. If planting of the summer fruiting kinds has to be delayed until spring, remove the flowers the first year so as to build up a strong plant first. Before planting, rake in 30g per m (1oz per yd) of sulphate of potash or plenty of bonfire ash.

If the land is heavy and not well drained, it will be advisable to plant on ridges or on a raised bed to allow winter rains to drain away. Also, plants on raised beds are less liable to be damaged by frost. This type of bed is made 15cm (6in) higher than the surrounding land and 150cm (5ft) across to allow for picking without treading the bed. Plant 37cm (15in) apart in rows 40–45cm (16–18in) apart.

Runners begin to form towards the end of summer, and where growing for fruit, remove them with scissors before they begin to root. This will enable the plants to concentrate on fruit production and in this way the plants may be left down for four or five years. A few plants may be allowed to form runners which are removed when they have formed roots. These are used to make a new plantation each year, to take over when the original plantings begin to bear poorer-quality berries.

When planting, use a blunt-ended trowel and make the hole large enough to take all the roots and to enable them to be spread out. Only just cover the roots, with the crown of the plant at soil level. Use a garden line to make the rows which should run north to south. Tread the plants in and do so again in spring for some may have been lifted by frost. Keep the hoe moving between the rows during April and May, but do not hoe too near the plants, for they are surface rooting.

Where the ground is not well drained, plant strawberries on ridges or on a raised bed.

Plant with a blunt-edged trowel, being careful to spread out the roots before covering.

In April, after a cold winter and to stimulate the plants into growth, give a dressing with 30g per m (1oz per yd) of sulphate of ammonia between the rows. Give this on a showery day when it will be quickly washed into the soil. If the weather is dry when the fruit has formed, water often, preferably around mid-day so that moisture dries off the blooms before night frosts.

When once the green berries have turned white, inspect them daily for they will soon turn pink and then scarlet, this taking only two days or less in warm weather. Pick them with the calyx attached if possible and place in a refrigerator to cool. Then remove the green tops, sprinkle with sugar and replace until required.

Growing in tubs

Good crops can be obtained by planting in tubs or barrels used by cider and vinegar makers. They need drilling with drainage holes at the base, and also round the side at intervals of about 37cm (15in). Make the holes large enough to take the roots with the foliage outside the hole.

The tubs and barrels can be of any size and may be placed in a courtyard where

If there is no ground available, heavy crops may be obtained from strawberries grown in tubs. Be sure to prepare the soil well before planting.

there is no garden. They need some sunshine but strawberries will grow well in semi-shade. First treat the tubs with wood preservative (though being of oak, they will usually be long lasting) and the iron bands with paint or a rust proof material. Then place a layer of crocks at the bottom, to cover the drainage holes and to permit surplus moisture to escape. Over the crocks, place a few turves, grass side downwards, then fill up to within 2.5cm (1in) of the top with prepared loam, peat and decayed manure, mixed well together. Also, give a handful of bone meal to each tub; twice that amount to each barrel.

Plant 15cm (6in) apart in a tub and put a plant in each hole in a barrel. Water from the top and, from spring, keep the plants well supplied with moisture, for they will obtain only limited amounts naturally.

Varieties
Early

Cambridge Early Pine The best early, for it is frost-resistant and moisture quickly runs off the round glossy berries. These berries turn scarlet and have a subtle pine flavour.

Cambridge Regent Resistant to frost, it crops well in heavy soil but under cloches may be troubled by mildew. The scarlet, wedge-shaped fruits freeze well.

Second early

Cambridge Favourite It is frost- and drought-resistant, and a heavy cropper in all soils, even where lacking humus, whilst the large crimson fruits continue to ripen longer than any variety.

Mid-season

Red Gauntlet Of compact habit with neat foliage, it grows well in all soils and holds its large scarlet fruits well above the ground.

Above: St Claude is one of the best of the autumn-fruiting strawberries.

Royal Sovereign The brilliant scarlet wedge-shaped berries have no equal either in appearance or in their flavour.

Late

Hampshire Maid The last of the summer varieties to ripen until those fruiting in autumn are ready. Its large conical fruits ripen deep crimson.

Talisman It crops well over a long season whilst its scarlet wedge-shaped fruits will retain their flavour and shape after freezing.

Autumn-fruiting

Popular in Europe for many years but only now becoming widely grown in Britain and America, they extend the season until almost the year end. Several are able to survive −11°C (10°F) of frost and will set and ripen their fruit.

They require a rich soil and, as they should be covered with barn cloches early in October, they are planted in rows 40cm (16in) apart and the same in the rows. If planted in spring, and the blossom is removed until early July (as it should be each year), they will fruit the same season. The plants are allowed to form runners, which are grown on to fruit, along with the parent plants so that a two-year plantation will yield heavily. Give the plants a mulch of peat and decayed manure every spring and keep them well watered in dry weather.

Fruiting begins about September 1, and continues through autumn and early winter, depending upon the amount of sunshine. If the cloches are removed towards the year end, the plants will die down completely and come to life again in April. Watering with liquid manure from early July will increase the yield and also the quality of the fruit.

Varieties

Gento It bears heavily in its first year and will form numerous runners to continue the cropping year after year. The conical, bright red fruits are large and firm.

La Sans Rivale It will often fruit at Christmas but ripens better under cloches, the conical fruits turning deep pink.

St Claude The deep crimson fruits ripen from August until November.

Rooting strawberry runners

16 Blueberries and cranberries

Blueberries crop well in acid soils and have a long life.

These plants, also called whortleberry and bilberry, are present in acid moorland soils of North America, the British Isles, and across northern Europe and Asia, growing 30cm (12in) tall and in large plantations. The wild berries are much in demand in the early autumn but they are small. It was not until Dr Colville of the US Department of Agriculture introduced *Vaccinium corymbosum*, bearing much larger fruits, into his breeding programme that the cultivated plants took on a new popularity. Modern blueberries are as large as small black grapes and begin to colour early in August, lasting until early November depending upon variety. They can be eaten raw, with clotted cream, or used in tarts and flans or for preserves. Cranberry sauce is the accepted accompaniment for turkey.

The fruits require an acid soil, like the azalea and rhododendron, so work plenty of peat about the roots at planting time which is March. The plants also require plenty of nitrogenous manures to encourage the formation of a continuous supply of new wood upon which high quality fruit is obtained. Dig in shoddy, farmyard or poultry manure or composted straw. And in spring each year scatter on the surface around each plant 28g (1oz) of sulphate of potash and the same of superphosphate of lime, mixed together. This will increase the quality of fruit. The plants will also benefit from a mulch each year.

Like blackcurrants, plant deeper than other fruits, as reproduction and new growth are by underground suckers which may be detached and replanted to increase.

Plant 10cm (4in) deep and set the plants 120cm (4ft) apart, for they grow bushy and at least 120cm (4ft) tall. Plants are expensive but have a long life and bear heavily. The plants crop better if helped with their pollination, so plant two varieties together, one to give early crops, the other later. Three plants of each will provide worthwhile pickings. Blueberries turn from green to red then pale blue before turning black.

Varieties

Early Blue   The best for cold gardens, cropping heavily and early, the large fruits appearing in short sprays.

Grover   To follow Early Blue, its large fruits are ready in September.

Jersey   The latest to mature and requiring a warm garden to ripen well. It is ready in October when it will bear a huge crop.

Cranberries

This twiggy shrub 60cm (2ft) tall grows in acid boglands. The plants will form a dense mass of long wiry stems, and in September and October, the fruits, like big red currants, ripen to brightest crimson with a delicious sharp taste.

Plant only in low ground, for during summer the cranberry plant's roots should be continually submerged in water. Plant 120cm (4ft) apart.

17 Rhubarb

Though a vegetable, rhubarb is always used as a fruit. As it can be forced during winter in warmth or in the open, it is one of the most valuable crops, and the first outdoor rhubarb always enjoys a welcome. Again, it may be grown in a shady corner where little else will grow. It will also grow well in any soil. It requires plenty of humus to maintain summer moisture and for it to make those thick, juicy sticks so much in demand for stewing or for pies and tarts. So dig in plenty of farmyard manure or shoddy or garden compost and give the roots a mulch in summer.

Rhubarb roots or thongs must contain an 'eye' which will produce a stick. Without this there will be no plant. The roots are planted any time from late October until January whilst dormant, for they begin to grow with the first warm spring sunshine. Plant 60cm (2ft) apart with the 'eye' or bud just below soil level, but make the hole deep enough to take the long root.

At planting time, give a 132g per sq m (4oz per sq yd) dressing of basic slag, which rhubarb loves for it releases its nitrogen content over a long time.

Pull no sticks the first year and only a few in the second year. By then, the roots will be established and a dozen sticks or more can be removed in the year.

After four years, the roots will have grown to 45cm (18in) across. To prevent them becoming too hard and woody, lift in

Rhubarb is a popular vegetable which is always used as a fruit.

253

winter and divide with a knife or spade, remembering that each piece of root must have at least one 'eye'. Treat the cut parts with lime or flowers of sulphur before replanting.

Producing early crops

If there are several roots, one or two can be lifted and forced in a garage or beneath the greenhouse bench. But first allow it to remain for a week or two in the open after lifting to become frosted; this will make it force all the better. Half fill a deep orange box with a friable soil (a mixture of loam, peat and decayed manure is ideal), and in it place the root with the 'eye' at soil level. Water in and place a sheet of cardboard or a sack over the top to exclude light. If planted in December, the sticks, reddish-pink in colour, will have reached to the covering by the end of January. They will be about 30–37cm (12–15in) long and are then removed as required by pulling. Use the largest first to allow the others to grow on. When cropping has finished, turn out the roots, divide them and re-plant in March or April to grow on, but do not remove any sticks that year.

Another way to obtain early sticks is to cover a mature root in the open where it is growing. This is done by placing over it a deep box or upturned bucket. The previous year's sticks will have died back during winter. Before covering, place over the root some fresh strawy manure or composted straw, which will provide some warmth.

About March 1 is the time to cover the roots, and the first sticks will be ready to pull about mid-April.

Uncovered roots outdoors will produce sticks to use in early May and they will continue until late in summer. Young sticks freeze well. Late in autumn, remove the old sticks and foliage, dig over the soil around the roots and give a strawy mulch.

Varieties
Early

Early Albert The most popular variety for more than a century, it forces well and in the open bears its crimson-red sticks before all others.

Timperley Early One of the best rhubarbs bearing large numbers of strong sticks of deepest crimson.

Mid-season

Canada Red It forces well outdoors and bears large thick red sticks right through summer.

Cawood Castle A new variety of great vigour and bearing many long red sticks through summer.

Below left: Divide long-established roots in winter before re-planting into well manured ground.

Below: Rhubarb can be forced by covering the roots in January with pots or boxes in order to draw up the sticks.

18 Pests and diseases

Apple

Aphis (greenfly) It feeds on the young shoots and leaves, causing them to curl up, and early in winter it lays on the spurs. To control, spray the trees in March with Abol-X or Sybol (but do not use on blackcurrants).

Blossom weevil It attacks the buds as they open; the grubs upon hatching eat the stamens so that they cannot pollinate. Spray in March (or earlier), with petroleum-oil emulsion, but not on Cox's Orange or Newton Wonder.

Blossom wilt Caused by the brown rot fungus, it attacks all the top fruits, causing the blossom to turn brown and die. It then works down on to the spurs and branches, also causing die-back. Wash with petroleum-oil in January but not on Cox's Orange or Newton Wonder.

Codling moth A serious pest, the tiny white grubs of which burrow into the fruits leaving a pile of brown dirt at the entrance hole. Spray with derris each month from June to September to control.

Scab Usually affecting trees deficient in potash, it attacks shoots, leaves and fruits as black blisters. Apply a 2% lime-sulphur spray in early spring. Spray Rival, Cox's Orange, Newton Wonder and Egremont Russet instead with a 1-part-in-400 solution of Murfixtan.

Winter moth They are green and feed on the blossom then on the leaves, often defoliating the trees. Late in June, they fall to the ground and pupate in winter, when the wingless females crawl up the trees to lay their eggs. Grease-banding the trees in October will prevent this.

Blackcurrant

Gall mite This pest causes big bud, the buds swelling with the pests inside and bearing no fruit. Blackcurrants are sulphur-shy but will take a 1-part-in-50 solution early in spring. For Wellington XXX and Westwick Triumph, dilute more.

Blackberry

Cane spot Attacks all cane fruits, as brown spots on canes and leaves which fall. Spray in spring, before flowers open, with Bordeaux mixture.

Raspberry beetle See raspberries.

Cherry

Rust It may attack the underside of the leaves as orange spots, causing them to fall early. Control by spraying with Bordeaux mixture early in summer and again in October after picking the fruit.

Bacterial canker It affects mostly black cherries, first as yellow leaf spots causing leaves to fall, later as brown areas on branches. Spray with Bordeaux mixture – 500g (1lb) copper sulphate and 375g (¾lb) slaked lime to 30 litres (6 gal) of water in spring before buds open.

255

Cherry

Black fly The tiny black eggs winter on the twigs; the grubs, on hatching in spring, feed on the leaves and new growth. Control by routine spraying of the trees with tar-oil in January.

Fruit moth The small green caterpillars enter the flower buds and later bore into the fruits, making them uneatable. The fruits fall, the moths emerging in spring to lay their eggs on the blossom. Dust with derris as the blossom opens.

Scale See fig.

Vine weevil The fat, creamy-white larvae burrow into the soil and attack the roots. Exterminate it by soaking the soil in March with Lindex solution, or if growing in pots, add a little Gammexane at potting time.

Winter moth See apples.

Pear

Blossom wilt See apples.

Midge The most troublesome pest, it lays eggs on the blossom buds in spring, boring into the calyx, the tiny grubs emerging to feed upon the bud, which causes it to turn brown. To control, dust with derris in spring.

Fig

Scale It also attacks vines, apricots and peaches, appearing as white scale-like insects, clustering on the stems and sucking the sap. To control, spray with Malathion in early March.

Gooseberry

Mildew It appears in summer on the shoots and fruits as a white powdery fungus. Later it turns brown, peels off and falls to the ground to winter there. Cut away and burn any affected shoots. To control, dust plants with Karathane in early May.

Grape

Mealy bug The most troublesome vine pest, it is white and produces masses of cotton-like threads on the stems. It also attacks peaches and apricots. Vine rods must be scraped each winter to prevent the beetles hiding, then the stems painted with methylated spirit.

Peach

Leaf curl The most troublesome disease, attacking the leaves and causing them to curl. Later, they take on a powdery look and die. Spraying with one-per-cent lime-sulphur at bud burst will control to some extent.

Mealy bug See grapes.
Scab Though the symptoms are similar in appearance, scab on pears takes a different form from that which attacks apples. All pears are lime-sulphur-shy but all are tolerant of Bordeaux mixture, so use this to spray them early in May and again after blossom set, early in June.

Plum and gage

Brown rot It attacks the fruit spurs, the blossom (as blossom wilt) and later the fruits, causing them to mummify on the trees. To control it, spray with a one-per-cent lime-sulphur solution in March (before the blossom opens) and with a derris spray after petal fall.

Sawfly As well as plums and gages, it attacks apples and gooseberries when in bloom, laying on the flower buds, the white caterpillars burrowing into the buds and causing them to die. As a precaution, spray with Lindex, apples at petal fall, plums ten days later; or use derris and a spreader.

Red and white currant

Clearwing moth It lays on the stems in summer. The grubs, upon hatching, burrow into the wood to feed on the sap, causing the stems to die. To control, spray with tar-oil in winter.

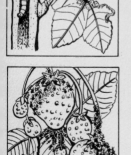

Botrytis (mildew) Both are forms of mildew, botrytis attacking the fruits, mildew the foliage as a powdery white fungus. Dust with Orthocide, containing 10% Captan, as soon as the first green fruits have set. In areas of high rainfall plant resistant varieties.

Raspberry

Raspberry beetle It also attacks blackberries and loganberries, laying its eggs on the flowers. After hatching, the white grubs eat into the fruits. To prevent, dust with derris as the flowers open and again when the fruit has set.

Raspberry moth It winters in the soil and emerges in spring as a silver-brown moth to lay its eggs on the flowers. The caterpillars eat the fruits, often entirely. To prevent, dust with derris as for raspberry beetle.

Silver leaf Its presence is shown by the leaves taking on a silver appearance and the trees soon die. It enters through cuts. For this reason, pruning should be completed by mid-July so that the cuts will 'gum' quickly. There is no known cure.

Strawberry (pages

Aphis (greenfly) Most troublesome of strawberry pests, it feeds on the sap and reduces vigour, allowing virus diseases to enter at the punctures. To control, spray with Lindex in April before the blossom opens, or with derris solution.

Red core Caused by a fungus which attacks the roots, causing them to turn red at the centre and the plants to die back. There is no cure, so, in low-lying, badly drained land, plant in raised beds or plant resistant varieties.

257

Vegetable Growing

1 Soils and digging

Before you can grow any vegetables, the soil has to be cultivated, and different soils need different treatment. The gardener has to understand and make the best of his soil, because although it can always be improved its basic character cannot be changed.

Types of soil

Heavy or clay soils These are wet and sticky in winter, drying to hard clods or a cracked surface in summer if wrongly treated.

Dig early in winter, exposing a rough surface to frost which shatters the clods into a fine tilth ready for sowing in spring. Work in bulky organic manures when digging. Never tread on the soil when it is wet. If the soil should be waterlogged when you wish to dig, try spreading some peat on top. This will make digging easier and save you getting embedded in mud.

Sandy or light soils These are easy to work, warm up quickly in spring and so are good for early crops. They dry out in summer and are often poor because plant food is quickly washed out.

Dig in moisture-holding material – manure, compost or peat. Apply compound fertilisers shortly before sowing. During the growing season top dress with fertilisers and water them in, or apply liquid fertilisers. Mulch with peat or compost.

Loams These are generally fertile soils, lighter than clays but holding moisture better than sands. A good loam has a naturally high humus content and when it derives from, for instance, old pasture-land, it crops well for several years with little manure or fertiliser. But if you are lucky enough to have such a soil you should treat it generously from the start, otherwise the initial fertility will be lost and take years to rebuild.

Chalk or alkaline soils Often greyish in colour, these dry quickly after heavy rain. This natural drainage makes for an early start in spring, but chalk soils need the same attention to watering and mulching to keep crops growing in summer.

Chalk soils rarely need lime and benefit from all the organic manure and peat that you can give them. Crops such as potatoes, which dislike an alkaline soil, do much better if plenty of peat is worked into the planting site.

Get to know your soil and the way it is affected by differing weather conditions. In a new district, learn about its peculiarities from gardening neighbours.

If certain crops fail persistently, change varieties, substituting those likely to suit the soil better: stump-rooted carrots for long varieties on clay soils, for instance, or dwarf beans for runners on dry sands.

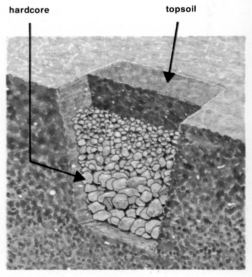

hardcore   topsoil

Drainage: to improve waterlogged soil, construct a soakaway. Dig a hole about 3ft (1m) deep, fill with hardcore topped by a layer of gravel, and replace topsoil.

1. Place one foot – left or right – on a shoulder of the blade and drive it *vertically* into the ground using just the weight of the body. If you drive it in at an angle the digging will be less deep and effective.

2. Pull the spade handle back to lever the chunk of soil loose, lift it with one hand well down the shaft at the point of balance.

3. Throw it gently forwards, twisting the spade slightly so that it slips from the blade. Repeat this in a steady rhythm, and when you reach the far side of the plot walk back and begin another row.

The why and how of digging

Digging is the first and most important part of cultivation. It breaks up the soil so that the surface weathers into a friable tilth in which seeds can be sown, it allows the penetration of water and air, both necessary for the health of soil and plants, and it permits the removal of weeds and the incorporation of manure and compost.

Digging is the hardest physical work in the gardening routine, but at the right tempo and in reasonable stints it need not be tiring. Start at a left-hand corner of the plot to be dug and work from left to right. Use a spade rather than a fork unless the soil is hard to penetrate, and dig only when the surface is fairly dry or lightly frozen.

Pick out all perennial weed roots and consign them to the bonfire. Annual weeds may be buried if completely covered, but are best taken to the compost heap.

Right: basic soil preparation. In plain digging the spade goes one spit deep and the soil is thrown forward, leaving only a narrow trench. In double digging a wider trench is first taken out and the subsoil is dug with a fork. The first trench is then filled with soil from the second, and so on, the first soil excavated being barrowed to the end of the plot and used to fill the last trench. In ridging the soil is thrown forward to form a ridge-and-furrow pattern, exposing it to frost and improving drainage.

Plain digging

Double digging

Ridging

261

2 Planning your vegetable plot

Make the most of your vegetable garden by planning ahead. The easy and obvious course is not always the best in the long run.

Give the vegetables the most open position possible, cutting back tall hedges on the south and west sides. Avoid sites overshadowed by trees. Don't plant fruit trees in the vegetable area except as espaliers or cordons on its north or east border.

Try to arrange things so that the crop rows run north-south, giving equal sunlight on both sides of a row and reducing the extent to which short crops are overshadowed by taller ones. Remember that good paths between beds and to the garden shed and compost heaps make for ease of working. The grass path is the worst, having to be mown and trimmed in the summer while in winter it becomes bare and muddy. One of the best and most quickly laid is that made of cement paving slabs with non-slip surface. Kitchen garden paths need not be more than 60cm (24in) wide.

Planning the crops

Decide at the start of the season on the crops to be grown and the space to be allotted to each, otherwise you may realise too late that some varieties you particularly wanted have been crowded out.

Crop rotation The object of 'rotating' crops is to ensure that the same crop, or a similar type of crop, does not occupy the same ground year after year, which encourages the build-up of pests and diseases and depletes the soil of particular nutrients. Divide the vegetable plot into three roughly equal areas or beds and the crops into three groups, growing each group in a different bed over a three-year period. The groups are roots (including potatoes), brassicas (all the cabbage tribe) and miscellaneous, which includes peas and beans.

The manurial treatment of the groups is different: the brassicas should receive most of the organic manure and the miscellaneous crops any left over. Root crops are not manured. All the beds get fertiliser dressings before sowing or planting. It is not, of course, possible to keep to the rotation in every detail. There is always some overlapping, and quick-growing crops such as lettuce and summer spinach may be fitted in wherever space is available.

Successional crops

Achieving maximum yields from your garden depends on making the fullest use of the ground. This does not mean cramming rows and plants closer together than the recommended distances, which often means a lower total yield, but ensuring that that group is not left unused or cluttered with the remains of a previous crop.

Wherever possible, follow a main crop with a successional one, usually quick-maturing and harvested the same season, sometimes the following spring. Clear away the old crop immediately it finishes, and lightly fork over or rotavate the surface. Most successional crops are started in the summer, when everything must be done to conserve soil moisture. Don't dig deeply, because this releases moisture and brings up intractable clods. Leave the roots of early pea and bean crops in the ground, to release the nitrogen accumulated from the atmosphere in the root nodules. Just hoe the topsoil. Work in a compound fertiliser at 50g per sq m (1½oz per sq yd), water drills thoroughly in dry weather before sowing, and keep germinating seeds and young plants watered until well established. Follow early potatoes with carrot, beetroot, turnip, leek, lettuce, radish. Follow broad beans and early peas with any of the above, or calabrese, sprouting broccoli, winter cabbage, spinach, spinach beet.

Follow dwarf and runner beans with spring cabbage, winter lettuce or salad onion.

Three-year rotation

First year

Bed A Root crops

No manure dug in. Apply compound fertiliser before sowing. Use peat freely when planting potatoes on chalk soils.

Root crops
Potato, carrot, parsnip, swede, turnip, beetroot, salsify, onion (bulb), Jerusalem artichoke, shallot.

Bed B Miscellaneous crops

Some manure if available. Fertiliser before sowing. Peas and beans fix atmospheric nitrogen in their roots and leave the soil richer in this element.

Miscellaneous crops
Pea (all varieties), bean (all varieties), spinach, sweet corn, marrow and squash, celery, leek, all salads, including salad onions, tomatoes and cucumbers.

Bed C Brassica crops

Dig in as much manure as possible during winter. Lime after digging if necessary. Fertiliser before planting.

Brassicas
Brussels sprout, cabbage, cauliflower, sprouting broccoli, calabrese, kale.

Second year

Bed A Misc. crops
Treat as Bed B, first year.

Bed B Brassica crops
Treat as Bed C, first year.

Bed C Root crops
Treat as Bed A, first year.

Third year

Bed A Brassica crops
Treat as Bed C, first year.

Bed B Root crops
Treat as Bed A, first year.

Bed C Misc. crops
Treat as Bed B, first year.

Final distance between:

	rows	plants
Potato	60cm (24in)	30cm (12in)
Carrot	23-30cm (9-12in)	10cm (4in)
Onion	30cm (12in)	10cm (4in)
Beetroot	30cm (12in)	10cm (4in)
Marrow	75cm (2½ft)	75cm (2½ft)
Broad bean	60cm (24in)	15cm (6in)
Sweet corn	45cm (18in)	30cm (12in)
Leek	45cm (18in)	23cm (9in)
Tomato	90cm (36in)	45cm (18in)
Celery (self-blanching)	22cm (9in)	22 cm (9in)
Cabbage	60cm (24in)	45cm (18in)
Broccoli	60cm (24in)	45cm (18in)
Kale	60cm (24in)	45cm (18in)

263

3 Sowing and planting

Buying seeds

Obtain catalogues and send in your seed order very early in the year. Late-comers are apt to find the varieties they want out of stock. Seedsmen usually specify an average length of row or number of plants to be expected per packet of seeds, and quantities ordered may be based on your plans for the season.

Buying plants

Some vegetables are planted out in their final quarters and not sown where they are to grow. If you intend to buy plants rather than raise them yourself it pays to get the best obtainable, preferably from a local nurseryman from whom you can order in advance. Avoid brassica plants which are leggy and drawn from crowding in the seed-bed, long-stemmed tomato plants with bluish foliage, and yellowing marrows. The best plant is not the largest, but the one in vigorous growth, short-jointed, with leaves of a healthy green.

Seeds and sowing

Seeds in sealed vacuum packs may be kept for a year after the packeting date if the packs are unopened. In ordinary packets, brassica seeds remain viable for several years but the germination of others cannot be relied on after a year. Sowing defective seed means losing irreplaceable time.

Conditions for sowing To germinate, a seed must have moisture, warmth and air. The temperature must not be too low, the soil must be in the right condition, and the seed not sown too deeply.

Recommended sowing dates are only approximate and vary from season to season. Do not begin the first sowings of the year until the soil starts to warm up and signs of growth are evident.

Soil preparation Lightly fork in a pre-sowing fertiliser dressing about a fortnight before starting to sow. If the surface, left rough after winter digging, is dry enough to walk on without soil sticking to your boots, rake it down to a fine, crumbly tilth. If still wet, wait until just before you are ready to sow.

Left: stocky, leafy cabbage plant grown in seed-bed with plenty of room.
Right: leggy plant grown in overcrowded row.

Rake the seed-bed in both directions, to ensure the soil is well broken up.

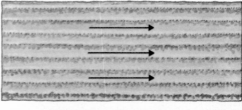

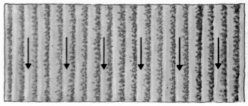

Sowing

To take out a drill, put the garden line in position and make sure it is taut. With the draw hoe, make a shallow furrow, guided by the line. For small seeds, make the drill V-shaped with the corner of the hoe blade; for large ones, such as peas and beans, take out a wide flat-bottomed drill with the full width of the blade. Measure the distance to the next row and move the line.

To sow small seeds such as lettuce or carrot, tip some from the packet into the palm of the hand and deposit them evenly and fairly thinly along the drill from between thumb and forefinger. Beans are placed individually but peas may be scattered liberally (but not touching) in a wide drill.

Pelleted seeds, which are made larger by being covered with a protective coating, are all spaced individually to facilitate thinning.

Cover the seeds by pulling the soil into the drill with the hoe or the back of the rake, leaving the surface level. Tamp it down gently with the flat of the hoe blade or by *light* pressure of the foot.

In dry weather water the drill thoroughly before sowing and continue to water until emergence of the seedlings. Moisture is absolutely vital, and pelleted seed especially may fail if the seed-bed dries out for a short period. As a general rule, early sowings are covered less deeply than those made later in the season. In the first case the soil is warmer just below the surface, in later sowings moisture is conserved better around the seeds by placing them a little deeper.

Planting out

For planting out tender subjects such as tomatoes and marrows choose a warm spell when all possible danger of late frosts is past. Unless you can protect with cloches nothing is gained by being too early.

Water pot- and box-grown plants an hour before planting. Brassica and similar plants grown in a seed-bed should be well watered the day before planting out and lifted with the trowel, ensuring that plenty of soil clings to the roots. Make planting holes with the trowel, setting all types of plant a little deeper than they had been growing previously. Firm the soil, making sure that the roots are not left in a cavity at the bottom of the hole. Water after planting and keep watered until established and growing.

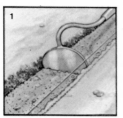

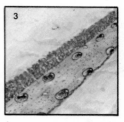
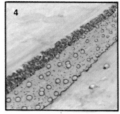

Types of drill

1. Wide drill, made with full width of draw hoe.
2. Narrow drill, made with corner of hoe blade. Used for all small seeds.
3. Beans in staggered double row in wide drill.
4. Peas scattered liberally (not too close) in wide drill.

Firm the soil with back of rake or flat of hoe blade (or light foot pressure). Water seedlings when transplanting and continue until they are established.

Use a trowel rather than a dibber and make the hole large enough to take roots easily.

Plant with the lower leaves just clear of the surface and no bare stem showing.

Plants in peat pots are planted pot and all, the top of the pot being just covered.

265

4 Caring for growing crops

Thinning

Plants growing in a row must have enough room to develop properly. If crowded together normal growth is impossible; if too far apart space is wasted and the row yields less than its potential. There is therefore an optimum distance for best results.

Plants raised in a seed-bed or under glass are planted at their final distances in the row, any thinning being done at the seedling stage in the seed-bed. Peas and beans are spaced when sowing and are not thinned. Pelleted seeds are spaced about 2·5cm (1in) apart and subsequent thinning is easy. Early and adequate thinning is most necessary in sowings of small seeds, which invariably come up too thickly.

Thin in three stages. First, as soon as the seedlings are large enough to handle, to about 2·5cm (1in) then to double this distance as the seedlings grow, and then to the final distance for the crop to mature. Never thin to the final distance in one operation; a few seedlings are always lost from pests or climatic conditions and if this happens after thinning to the full distance the row will be depleted and 'gappy'. Also, if seedlings are allowed to grow between thinning stages the thinnings in some crops will be of usable size and will not be wasted. Among root crops, small carrots and golf-ball-size turnips and beetroot are pulled as required while the rest of the crop is left to reach full size. Spinach seedlings of a fair size are usable if the roots are trimmed off and the thinnings of lettuce are a salad ingredient long before the plants have hearts.

Thin only when the soil is moist, to minimise root disturbance of the remaining plants. In dry weather give a good soaking the day before thinning: the work is easier if the tops of the seedlings are dry. Patience is needed to 'single' the crop, to reduce each clump of seedlings to one plant, but this is essential. Beetroot is especially difficult because each 'seed' is really a fruit containing several seeds, but monogerm seed producing only one plant per seed is now becoming available.

Weed control

This is a vital part of cultivation. Weeds compete with the crop for moisture and nutrients and, if allowed to get out of hand,

1. Carrots after initial thinning, still crowded.

2. After second thinning: every other one now removed for use.

3. Carrots growing on to full size after final thinning.

Types of hoe

The draw hoe (*left*) is drawn towards the operator, who moves forwards. The Dutch hoe is pushed away from the operator, who walks backwards avoiding ground already hoed.

A contact herbicide may be used on weeds between crop rows. Apply it with a can and sprinkler bar, held close to the ground to avoid splashing crop foliage.

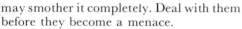

may smother it completely. Deal with them before they become a menace.

Hoeing and hand-weeding Hoe between rows regularly when the surface is dry. Do it even if no weeds are visible and you will destroy weed seedlings before they appear. Keep the hoe blade just below the surface and do not chop or jab close to the row. A rotavator may be used with the blades set very high, provided there is sufficient inter-row space and room to turn at the headlands without damage to the crop. Remove weeds to the compost heap if rain is likely or the small ones may re-root.

Weeds actually growing among crop rows must be pulled up by hand with as little disturbance to the crop as possible. Large weeds with a strong root system should be eased out of the row with a trowel. Hand weeding is essential for close set crops where other methods could damage plants and weeds alike.

Weedkillers The contact herbicide paraquat (Weedol) may be used between crop rows and is very effective on all annual and some perennial weeds. It is absorbed by the green parts of the plant and does not poison the soil. Apply it carefully, on a dry, windless day, using a shield on the sprayer and keeping it well away from the crop foliage.

To clear bramble- and weed-infested ground before cultivation, use a mixture of 2, 4, 5-T and 2, 4-D (brushwood killer). Dalapon is effective against broad-leaved perennial weeds. Care should be taken to leave the correct length of time between treatment and planting of crops. Always read the label and follow the instructions exactly.

Using weedkillers

Read makers' instructions *and follow them*.
Keep a watering-can solely for applying them, and label it plainly.
Mix only enough for immediate use and pour any surplus solution down the drain.
Store out of children's reach and *never* put surplus solution in soft-drink bottles. Weedkillers are not magic labour-savers, nor are they inherently dangerous: they are tools, and like other tools must be properly and sensibly used.

5 Watering and mulching

The soil is a reservoir in which the rains of winter are stored for use in the growing season. The better cultivated it is, the more spongy humus it contains, the greater its water-holding capacity and the more accessible is the moisture to the plant roots.

Soak drills thoroughly before sowing in dry weather. Continue to water until germination.

Conserve moisture by spreading 7·5 cm (3in) of mulch along both sides of crop row.

Water intake
1. When fully grown, the plant takes much more moisture from the soil than is lost by direct evaporation from the surface.
2. Repeated small waterings only moisten the top few cm and do not reach the feeding roots, which may be attracted upwards as a result.
3. Well-cultivated soil encourages good

root system which collects more moisture.
4. A subsoil broken up during digging permits moisture to be drawn up from deeper levels.

In the summer, moisture is lost faster than the rainfall can replace it, partly by evaporation from the surface but even more by plants transpiring from their leaves the water taken up by their roots. Crops in full growth are the ones most likely to need additional supplies of water.

How much water? It is worse than useless to give little drops in dry weather. You cannot slightly moisten the soil all the way down, for water penetrates to the dry soil below only when the upper layers are saturated. Inadequate watering causes the roots to spread upwards to the saturated layer where they are more vulnerable to the inevitable periods of drying out.

Average summer rainfall is from 5 to 7·5cm (2 to 3in) per month, and in a dry spell moisture reserves are quickly used up and the crop begins to suffer. Remember that 5cm of rain equals about 40 litres per sq m (9 gallons per sq yd) and that this is the sort of quantity needed to be effective after a few weeks of summer drought.

Crops which respond most to watering are early potatoes and carrots, lettuce, spinach, marrows, peas and runner beans. Whether you water by watering-can, hose or sprinkler, give an adequate quantity to a limited area at each watering rather than a little to every crop.

Mulches A mulch is a layer of organic material such as peat, compost or well-rotted manure applied to the soil to reduce moisture loss by evaporation. It should be spread to a depth of 5cm (2in) on both sides of the row when the crop is past the seedling stage and the soil is thoroughly moist. As an alternative, black polythene sheet may be used, which also suppresses weeds. Simplest of all is the soil mulch, the layer of loose topsoil created by regular hoeing, which prevents moisture being drawn to the surface.

268

6 Harvesting and storage

Harvesting at the right time is an important factor in the quality of vegetables and sometimes in the size of the crop. Many vegetables can be stored in the freezer, and for successful freezing they must be harvested in perfect condition and at the right stage of growth. The advice which follows is, however, concerned only with harvesting for immediate use and storing those vegetables which keep without freezing.

Potatoes
Earlies are dug as required and the shorter the time between digging and cooking the better the flavour. Dig main-crops when the tops have died down and the skin of the tubers has set and cannot be rubbed off. Avoid damage when lifting. Store in a cool but frost-free place in complete darkness. Frost destroys the tubers and light turns them green and renders them inedible.

Turnips and swedes
Lift in October or November and store in a cool place. A few degrees of frost will not hurt them. Green top turnips are very hardy and may be left in the ground for much of the winter, any not used producing edible tops when growth starts in spring.

All root crops should be stored as clean as possible, soil being rubbed off without damaging the skin.

Carrots and beetroot
Pull young roots during the growing season. Lift for storage in October, remove tops (twisting off rather than cutting beet tops), and store in boxes covered with slightly moist sand or peat.

Parsnips
Leave in the ground and dig as required, but lift remainder of crop in February before they start growing out.

Marrows and squashes
Marrows, pumpkins and winter squashes keep for several months if well ripened. Leave them on the plant until the skin is absolutely hard and sounds like wood when tapped. Store where they are safe from frost and inspect frequently for signs of deterioration.

Onions
Lift when growth finishes and dry very thoroughly spread out in shed or under cloches. Hang up in nets or tied in bunches in a dry, airy and frost-free place. The chief enemies of long storage are warmth and dampness. Shallots are stored in the same way but are usually harvested much earlier than onions.

Twist off beet tops

Potatoes spread out for drying

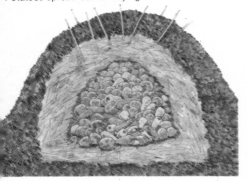

Making an onion rope

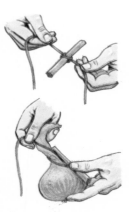

Left: clamps are used for storing beet, carrots or potatoes.

Ropes of onions are attractive, space-saving and easy to make, as the above diagrams show.

269

7 Pests and diseases

Plants have a natural resistance to their insect and fungus enemies. The more vigorous a crop the less likely it is to be attacked and the quicker it recovers from attack.

Health hints

Maintain soil fertility and keep crops growing steadily by watering and cultivation. A stunted plant is the first to suffer infection or insect damage.

Prevent overcrowding of crops by early and adequate thinning and the removal of weeds, which compete for food and moisture, and harbour pests.

Watch over garden hygiene. Trim waste and weedy corners and long grass where slugs take refuge. Clear away remains of crops, especially the stumps of Brussels sprouts and winter cabbages, which carry the cabbage aphis into a new season.

Inspect crops frequently and deal promptly with any trouble. A puff of insecticide today is worth more than a full-scale blitz next week.

Practise crop rotation, i.e. avoid growing similar crops always on the same ground.

Buying and using pesticides

Suitable pesticides may be bought in liquid form to be made up into a solution for use in a sprayer or syringe, but for the small garden the most convenient forms are the aerosol and dust in a puffer pack.

The safest preparations are those based on pyrethrum and derris, both non-toxic to humans and animals and reasonably effective against a wide range of insect pests. Dusting packs containing a combination of pyrethrum and piperonyl butoxide, or aerosols containing pyrethrum and lindane are also perfectly safe, and with one of each you are equipped to deal with most of the pests likely to be encountered.

Precautions in using pesticides Read the instructions. Note that certain plants such as marrows and cucumbers may be sensitive to the spray. *Never* use household fly-killers on plants. Keep to the recommended time between using the pesticide and harvesting the affected crop. Don't spray young seedlings or flowering crops in strong sunlight – wait until evening.

Common insect pests

Blackfly

Attacks broad beans and occasionally runner beans. Like all aphids, multiplies and spreads very rapidly. Pick out the growing points of broad beans as soon as enough pods have set and spray with garden aerosol as soon as clusters of blackfly are noticed. On runner beans they frequently appear first on the flower buds and these should be examined occasionally for any sign of them.

Cabbage aphis

Especially troublesome on cabbages and sprouts if it gets into hearts and other sheltered spots. Look for clusters of greyish insects and spray or dust immediately. In bad cases an aerosol may be ineffective and you should use a syringe and a solution of malathion to penetrate the crevices.

Cabbage caterpillars

The larvae of cabbage white butterflies, these ravenous creatures can be extremely destructive. All brassicas may be affected in summer. Use a pyrethrum dust or an aerosol containing lindane as soon as they are noticed, and repeat the treatment as more hatch out. For a consideration, the children may be persuaded to pick them off by hand and deposit them in a jar of salt water.

Pea maggot

This is the larva of the pea moth which appears in the pods. Early and late crops escape, maincrops may be affected. Spray with an aerosol ten days after flowering.

Flea beetle

Very small, punctures and seriously damages seedlings of brassicas, turnips, swedes and radishes. Keep well watered and dust frequently with pyrethrum or derris.

Cabbage root fly

The larvae particularly attack cauliflowers, eating into the roots and causing the plant to collapse. Dig up affected plants with nearby soil and burn them. As a preventive, apply 4 per cent calomel dust round each young plant.

Carrot fly

The insect is attracted by the scent of crushed foliage during thinning, where it will lay its eggs. Use pelleted seed to reduce thinning to a minimum.

Slugs

Use pellets containing metaldehyde under a slightly raised tile to keep them away from birds and pets.

Common diseases

Only two bother many gardeners.

Potato blight

Spray maincrops with Bordeaux mixture or dineb in July if the season is wet. At the end of the season cut off blighted tops and burn before lifting the tubers.

Club root

This disease of the cabbage family can become a serious nuisance. If you see any signs of swollen and distorted roots among brassicas, stop growing them on that piece of ground for two or three years and give it a heavy dose of garden lime after winter digging, followed by a lighter one the next year.

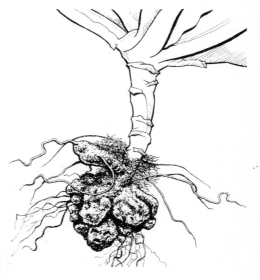

271

8 The vegetable garden month by month

January

Order seeds, seed potatoes and onion sets, keeping mainly to well-tried varieties but including a few new ones.

Continue clearing spent crops. Begin digging and manuring if the ground is workable and not too wet. Apply garden lime if a soil test shows it is necessary for the crops to be grown in that space.

Harvest winter greens such as cabbages, savoys and kale. There will also be celery, leeks, Brussels sprouts and maybe winter cauliflower. Seakale and chicory forced indoors will be ready now. Dig up Jerusalem artichokes and parsnips as required. If prolonged frost threatens, cover root crops in the ground with peat or straw so that lifting remains possible.

In a heated greenhouse you can now sow onions, leeks, and early varieties of cauliflower and French beans, and also plant a few potatoes.

Inspect autumn-sown peas and broad beans for damage by field mice and set traps if necessary.

Check over vegetables in store and throw away any that are beginning to rot.

February

Set up seed potatoes in trays in a light frost-proof place to sprout. Plant Jerusalem artichokes and shallots in all districts if soil is workable.

Sow broad beans and round-seeded peas early in the month under cloches and at the end of the month in the open. Sow Brussels sprouts, turnips and radishes in frames or under cloches. Put cloches in position two weeks beforehand to warm up the soil and keep the rain off. Seeds that lie in cold ground are slow to germinate; if it is wet as well they will rot. In a heated greenhouse sow tomatoes, cauliflower, celery and French beans.

Continue harvesting cabbages, leeks, parsnips, and celery.

If the ground was not dug last month, do so now, manuring and applying lime where necessary. Apply compound fertiliser to ground intended for planting in March, but rake it in only when the surface is dry.

At the end of winter it is important to check vegetables in store for any that may be rotting. Rub sprouts off the potatoes.

March

Use tops of Brussels sprouts and pull up brassica stalks, which harbour overwintering aphids.

Sow broad beans in late districts. In early districts, sow during the first half of the month early and second early peas, summer spinach, carrots, parsnips, turnips, onions, lettuce, radishes, parsley, and plant onion sets and early potatoes. In late districts delay these sowings and plantings until late in the month.

Sow Brussels sprouts, broccoli, summer and autumn cabbage and cauliflowers in a seed-bed for transplanting. Sow celery and leeks in the garden frame.

In a heated greenhouse, sow celery, celeriac, capsicums, cucumbers and tomatoes.

If not already done, plant Jerusalem artichokes and shallots; also plant garlic, seakale and horseradish.

Prepare compost for the mushroom bed, which may be starting to sprout after lying dormant during the winter.

Give spring cabbage a top dressing of sulphate of ammonia hoed in at the rate of 33g per m of row (1oz per yd).

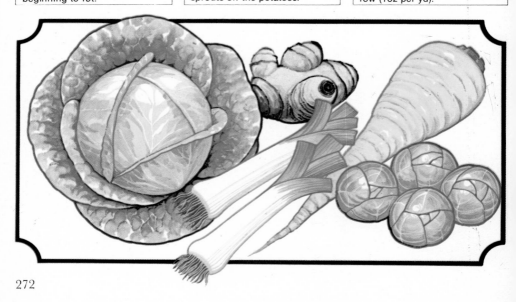

April

Keep shoots of sprouting broccoli closely picked to prevent it running to seed.

Water autumn-sown lettuce now maturing under cloches as well as any radishes and spring onions already there.

Plant maincrop potatoes and globe artichokes. Plant out Brussels sprouts, summer cabbage and cauliflower and calabrese. Prepare and plant asparagus beds.

Dig and manure the celery trench ready for planting in June.

Sow sweet corn and dwarf beans at the end of the month in the open and under cloches in mid-month. Sow maincrop peas, Windsor broad beans, beetroot and seakale beet.

At the end of the month sow marrows, courgettes, squashes and outdoor cucumbers in the frame, covering the lights with sacking on cold nights.

Begin to build the compost heap as greenstuff becomes available.

Start a regular programme of hoeing when the surface is dry even when no weeds are visible. Put down bait to combat destructive slugs.

May

Thin early crops as soon as the seedlings are large enough to handle and before they become drawn and entangled.

Sow runner and dwarf beans early in the month in early districts, second half of the month in late districts, under cloches at any time. Sow as soon as possible any crop mentioned in two preceding months if initial sowing has failed or been delayed by weather, also lettuce and radish for succession. Make first sowings of swedes and spinach beet for winter use.

Plant all varieties of autumn and winter greens, keeping well watered until established. Plant marrows and outdoor tomatoes under cloches.

Harvest asparagus from established beds, cutting all shoots including thin and deformed ones. Harvest summer cauliflowers, bending leaves over the curd to prevent discoloration by the sun.

Prepare celery trenches and manured sites for outdoor cucumbers and the marrow family ready for planting in June.

Hoe regularly and water growing crops in dry weather.

June

Regularly pick broad beans and early peas so that later pods continue to fill.

Stop cutting asparagus after Midsummer Day to allow 'fern' to develop and build up roots for next year's crop.

Plant out tomatoes, cucumbers, marrows, courgettes, squashes and sweet corn raised under glass, also plant celery and leeks. Plant dwarf tomatoes and cantaloup melons under cloches and melons and indoor cucumbers in the frame.

Make further sowings of dwarf and runner beans and stake runners before the vines become entangled.

Replace spent crops with beetroot, carrots, turnips, spinach and lettuce, watering the drills before sowing and until seedlings emerge.

Sow kale and sprouting broccoli by dropping a pinch of seed at appropriate distances, and gradually thin to one plant per station.

Mulch crops with peat, compost, grass cuttings or rotted manure when ground is moist. Give liquid fertiliser after watering crops.

July

Remove the growing points of runner beans when they reach the tops of the poles.

Stake and tie tall-growing tomatoes and rub out sideshoots as soon as they are seen.

Earth up maincrop potatoes and the stems of dwarf beans to keep the plants upright and prevent pods dragging on the ground.

Keep a close watch on maturing vegetables such as French and runner beans. Gather them while young and in top condition for immediate use or freezing. A few days too long in hot weather can make a serious difference to quality. Other vegetables ready at this time but not suitable for freezing are tomatoes, cucumbers, courgettes and marrows, globe artichokes and potatoes.

For cropping this year, sow quick-maturing endive and broad beans. Make further late sowings of summer spinach, maincrop carrots, lettuce, and summer and winter radishes.

Make final plantings of winter greens, leeks and celery, doing all you can by careful planting and watering to get the crops established quickly.

August

Bend over the tops of fully grown onions to encourage ripening of the bulbs. Harvest shallots, breaking up the clusters and storing when quite dry.

Sow spring cabbage in a seed bed for planting in October. It is still not too late to sow radishes and quick-growing lettuce for autumn use.

For an early spring crop sow winter spinach, lettuce, and onions, but only if your district is warm and you are prepared to cloche them in October.

Gather runner beans before the pods swell with developing seeds; once seeds are allowed to form the plants cease to produce. In hot weather runners may need picking every two days. Sweet corn should be tested by squeezing kernels and using before contents are solid and starchy. Use or freeze cobs as soon as possible after harvesting as conversion from sugar to starch continues. Other crops newly ready for harvest are capsicums and aubergines.

Start earthing up trench celery at the end of the month.

Lift and store unused early potatoes as the tops die down.

September

Cut off and burn potato tops infected with blight. If the skins of the tubers are set lift them immediately; if not, leave them for another week or two until the skins are too tough to be easily damaged in lifting.

Pull up tomato plants with unripe fruit if frost seems likely, hanging them under cover for ripening to continue. Or pick the fruit and keep warm indoors.

Complete harvesting of marrows, squashes, outdoor cucumbers and calabrese. Lift onions and garlic and dry thoroughly before storing. Pickling onions will be ready for harvesting.

There will also be cauliflower, the ever-present cabbages, self-blanching celery, and the first Brussels sprouts and savoys.

Transplant seedlings of spring cabbage, and transplant the lettuces, winter spinach and radishes sown last month in frames or cloches.

Cloche late-sown dwarf beans to prolong cropping. Make another radish sowing early in the month and outdoor winter lettuce in the last week.

Start earthing up celery for the second time, leeks for the first.

October

Harvest and store all root crops for the winter: carrots, beetroot, swedes, turnips, and winter radishes. Handle beetroot carefully when lifting. Left in the ground and pulled as required are Jerusalem artichokes, parsnips, celeriac, horseradish, and possibly turnips.

Sow lettuce for spring use in frames or under cloches during the first fortnight and longpod broad beans in the open during the last fortnight. Cloche autumn-sown lettuce, winter spinach, and radishes. Sow peas either out of doors or under cloches in cold gardens. Plant spring cabbage.

Complete earthing up of trench celery and leeks. Start forcing chicory and blanching endive. Cut down asparagus 'fern' when it turns yellow and lightly earth up the bed or row.

Continue picking Brussels sprouts, which will be improving in quality, and remove dead leaves from the plants. Do not on any account take out the tops. Remove dead foliage from seakale and cut down the stems of Jerusalem artichokes to keep them from being blown down.

November

Complete lifting of all root crops to be stored under cover. If very wet and dirty, spread them out in a shed to dry and rub off soil before storing.

There are still many other vegetables to take from the garden, including blanched celery, leeks, Jerusalem artichokes, cauliflower, Brussels sprouts and cabbages. The first blanched endive and forced chicory will also be ready; lift all remaining chicory roots and seakale to force as desired.

Sow longpod broad beans and early round-seeded peas under cloches. Continue to plant spring cabbage when weather is mild.

Clear away remains of spent crops. Take the yellowing leaves off Brussels sprouts, heel over cauliflowers to protect them from frost, and put a layer of straw over the crowns of globe artichokes.

Press ahead with winter digging whenever the ground is fit to work. Dot not try to dig when the soil is so wet that it clogs on your boots. That does more harm than good and makes the work harder. Manure for next year's peas, beans, onions, leeks, celery and spinach.

December

This is the month for general garden maintenance – for tidying up after the preceding year's work and preparing for the next growing season.

Continue with winter cultivations. Transplant to frames or cloches lettuce sown in frames last October. This year you will still have crops of celery, leeks, Jerusalem artichokes, cabbages, parsnips, and broccoli from the garden, as well as blanched endive and forced chicory.

There will also be many root crops stored indoors, including potatoes, onions, turnips, carrots, swedes, and beetroot. Keep them in a frost-free warm place.

Make sure overwintering crops like cauliflowers and globe artichokes are protected from frost.

Place manure and compost in convenient heaps in the digging area when soil is frozen, in preparation for digging.

Cover compost heaps with soil and, if the weather is persistently wet, with polythene sheeting held down by stones.

Order catalogues for new season unless already on their mailing lists.

9 Cabbage family (brassica crops)

Brussels sprouts

One of the hardiest and most valuable of winter greens. Two rows of sprouts, say about thirty plants, will yield good weekly pickings from October to March.

Soil

Like all the cabbage family, sprouts are fairly greedy, but only moderate amounts of manure or compost should be dug in during the winter. Over-feeding tends to produce lush, leafy growth which suffers in severe weather, and too many 'blown' or open sprouts. The crop often does well on land manured the previous season, provided any lime deficiency is corrected and digging is done early to allow the soil to settle. Loose ground produces poor sprouts. Rake in 100g per sq m (3oz per sq yd) of a general fertiliser when levelling the site for planting.

Right: Tight, medium-sized sprouts of the type preferred for kitchen and freezer. Loose, 'blown' sprouts often result from loose, over-manured soil.

When to sow and plant

As early as possible – a long growing season pays dividends. Sow in February or March. Plant in April to June.

Above: Well-filled stem of brussels sprouts. Pick them from the base so that the upper sprouts will develop.

Below: Plant seedlings out at 60cm (24in) intervals.

How to sow and plant

If you are going to buy plants, get them as soon as they are available and your planting site is ready. Alternatively, sow in a seed-bed in the open in March or in the frame or under cloches in February. Do not prick out the seedlings; sow thinly in drills 2cm (½–¾in) deep and 15cm (6in) apart, and thin to about 2·5cm (1in) apart as soon as possible. When about 7·5cm (3in) high, lift carefully with a trowel after watering and plant out 60cm (24in) each way. Water in and keep watered until established.

Time to germination

10–14 days. Germination is good, and if pelleted seed is used, it may be safely spaced at almost the final seed-bed distance.

Season of use

October to March.

Good varieties

Peer Gynt, Early Half Tall, Indra, Siltrex. All are compact varieties suitable for the smaller garden. Siltrex is good on light soils.

Special note

Avoid those commercial varieties in which all the sprouts develop simultaneously. Pick systematically, taking the larger sprouts from the lower part of the stem and removing the top only when crop is finishing.

276

Cauliflowers, summer

Cauliflowers cut in June are the finest of all for quality. They grow quickly, filling an awkward gap before the bulk of summer vegetables becomes available.

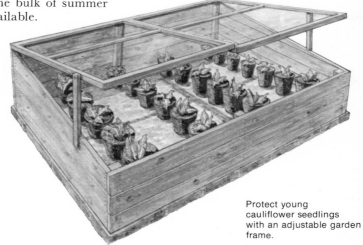

Soil
The better the soil, the better the cauliflower. Dig in as much organic material as possible, spent mushroom compost and hop manure being as good as anything. Before planting, rake in the standard dose of general fertiliser, 100g per sq m (3oz per sq yd). If summer cauliflowers are cleared by July, there is plenty of residual fertility in the site for late crops of beetroot, turnips or carrots.

Protect young cauliflower seedlings with an adjustable garden frame.

When to sow
If you have no facilities for raising seedlings, order plants for delivery in April. A small number of plants is, however, easily produced if you have a little space on a windowsill, or in a greenhouse, a frame or a few cloches. Start in February or early March.

How to sow and plant
Sow a small quantity of seed very thinly in a pan, using seed compost, covering the seed lightly and keeping moist until germination. A minimum temperature of 10°C (50°F) is required. Prick out the seedlings 5cm (2in) apart in trays of potting compost as soon as the first true leaves develop. Better still, prick out singly into peat pots. Seedlings may be put in the frame or under cloches in early March. In early April harden off by leaving uncovered except on very cold nights, and plant out from mid-April, 37·5cm (15in) between plants and 45cm (18in) between rows.

Time to germination
7–10 days.

Season of use
Late May to July. The small, tender heads of these cauliflowers may be frozen whole. Freezer life: 6 months.

Good varieties
Early Snowball, Suttons Classic.

Special note
Quality in summer cauliflowers depends upon quick growth. The avoidance of checks in planting out, and of night frosts through planting too early, is important as they can cause the plants to 'button', or form small premature heads.

Summer cauliflower Early Snowball. These cauliflowers are of the highest quality, but need generous treatment.

Cabbages for summer and autumn

The cabbage addict can have this vegetable all the year round. Here we deal with those sown from January to May and cut from May to November.

Soil
Dig well and incorporate some organic manure. Dried poultry manure, which has a fairly high nitrogen content, is a good choice. Before planting, rake in 100g per sq m (3oz per sq yd) of general fertiliser. If at any time the plants seem to be 'standing still', top dress with 33g per sq m (1oz per sq yd) of sulphate of ammonia, hoed and, if necessary, watered in.

When to sow and plant
Varieties listed as summer-maturing should be sown as early in spring as possible, preferably in February under glass. Autumn varieties are sown in April or May. Plant from early April to June. Plants are usually easy to buy during that period.

How to sow and plant
The early summer cabbages are sown in seed trays in the frame in February if no greenhouse is available. Prick out, harden off, and plant out in April. Or sow in shallow drills, 15cm (6in) apart, under cloches in March and thin out early. Decloche a week before planting out. The larger and later summer varieties and the autumn types are sown in a prepared seed-bed in April or May in drills 2cm (½–¾in) deep and 15cm apart and thinned to at least 2·5cm (1in). Many varieties are obtainable as pelleted seed and this is one way of ensuring well-spaced seedlings. Plant out when about 7·5cm (3in) tall. Planting distances are: early small-headed varieties, 45cm (18in) either way; larger and later ones, 45cm (18in) in the rows and 60cm (24in) between rows.

Time to germination
7–14 days. Cabbage seed, like that of other brassicas, remains viable for several years and a surplus should not be thrown away.

Season of use
June to August for the earlies, August to November for the later varieties.

Good varieties
For the first sowings, Hispi, Primata, Greyhound. The pointed Hispi is outstanding. Later sowing, Primo, Winnigstadt, Golden Acre, Autumn Monarch. The last is reputed to stand a long time without splitting.

Above: Small cabbages will form on the stump of a cut spring-maturing cabbage.

Left: Fine summer cabbages of the Primo type. They need good soil and adequate watering.

Below: A fine specimen of a spring-maturing cabbage.

Calabrese

Calabrese is a green sprouting broccoli, differing from the white and purple forms in being too tender to survive the winter. It is used in late summer and autumn, when new additions to the menu are welcome.

Soil
Any reasonably good soil will do, but the best quality calabrese is produced on soil treated as advised for summer cauliflowers. If planted in succession to early peas or potatoes, a dressing of 100g per sq m (3oz per sq yd) of compound fertiliser should be hoed in before planting.

When to sow and plant
Sow in a seed-bed in April or early May and plant out in June. Or sow direct where it is to grow in June.

How to sow and plant
Sow in the seed-bed as advised for other brassicas, planting out 45cm (18in) between plants and between rows. Or sow where the plants are to grow in early June in a drill 2cm (½–¾in) deep in groups of seeds 45cm apart. Thin by stages to one plant per group. Water the drill thoroughly before sowing in dry weather.

Brassica seedlings frequently need protection from birds, and where this is the case, protection by nylon net is more easily given when the plants are grouped closely in a seed-bed than when strung out sparsely in a long row. Where bird damage is likely, the seed-bed/transplanting method may be preferable to direct sowing for seedlings liable to attack soon after sowing.

Time to germination
7–14 days, according to time of year.

Season of use
August to November and possibly later in a mild autumn. Calabrese freezes well, the sprigs having a freezer life of six months.

Good varieties
Green Comet, a very early single-headed type with

The tender autumn-maturing green sprouting broccoli is becoming increasingly popular. The picture shows the central head, harvested first, and the smaller sprouts which follow it.

few side shoots. Late Corona, similar to Green Comet but matures later.

Atlantic, producing a central head followed by a large crop of side-shoots.

Special note
The plant normally forms a central cluster of buds like a rough green cauliflower. Earlier types produce many lateral shoots when the central head is cut, and such varieties still give the longest-lasting crop. Recent hybrids, however, have been bred to form a larger head at the expense of the side-shoots, and these varieties do not furnish pickings over a long period.

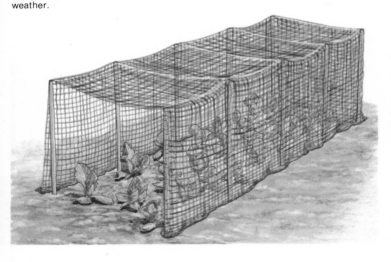

Protect young seedlings by grouping them closely in a seed-bed and covering with nylon net.

279

Kale

Because of its extreme hardiness kale is regarded as a 'coarse' vegetable. In fact, when harvested at the correct stage of growth, it is one of the best of winter greens.

Soil
Dig deeply and leave the soil in a condition to ensure good drainage. This should have been done for the crop preceding kale, which is usually sown or planted after early potatoes or peas. A light dressing of compound fertiliser, raked in when clearing and lightly cultivating the ground, is advisable to give the kale a good start, but the crop needs no other feeding.

When to sow and plant
Only two varieties matter, Green Curled and Hungry Cap. Green Curled may be sown in the seed-bed in April and planted out in June, or sown where it is to grow in June or early July. Hungry Gap is sown direct in July and not transplanted.

How to sow and plant
In the seed-bed, sow thinly in shallow drills 15cm (6in) apart, thinning to give plenty of space to the seedlings. Plant out 45cm (18in) apart with rows 60cm (24in) apart. When direct sowing, take out a drill 2cm (½–¾in) deep, flood it if the weather is at all dry, and drop groups of seeds at 45cm (18in) intervals, thinning the seedlings by stages to one at each station. Gaps may be filled by transplanting. There must be no lack of moisture during or after germination; if the July sowing fails it may be too late to try again.

Time to germination
5–10 days. Very rapid in summer – watch for bird attacks on emerging seedlings.

Season of use
Curled, January to April. Hungry Gap, April and May.

Good varieties
Only those already mentioned. Choose the Dwarf rather than the Tall Curled.

Dwarf curled kale. Like all kales, this will do well in colder areas where winter cabbage and sprouting broccoli are not very successful.

Cabbages for winter and spring

From the gardener's point of view the main difference between these cabbages and the sorts grown for summer and autumn consumption is in the matter of hardiness. A wrong choice of variety can be disastrous.

Soil
Good, but not too good. On sandy and chalky soils dig in some manure or compost and apply a light dressing of compound fertiliser. On stronger land, especially when the cabbages follow a well-treated previous crop, additional manuring is probably unnecessary. Spring cabbage, for instance, may be planted after runner beans with no preparation other than clearing and hoeing the site.

When to sow and plant
Sow winter varieties in May and transplant in June and July. Sow spring varieties at the end of July in cold districts and by mid-August in mild ones. Transplant between mid-September and mid-October.

How to sow and plant
Sow in a prepared seedbed as advised for late summer and autumn varieties, moving to permanent quarters when about 7·5cm (3in) tall, taking care that the roots are damp before lifting. Winter varieties are spaced at 45cm (18in) in the row and 60cm (24in) between rows. Spring cabbages are spaced at 23cm (9in) in the row and 45cm (18in) between rows. The close spacing allows every other cabbage to be pulled for 'spring greens' as soon as a fair amount of leaf has developed, leaving the remainder to reach full size and heart up.

Time to germination
7–10 days.

Season of use
Winter varieties, December to March. Spring varieties, March to June. Solid hearts may be frozen, keeping for six months.

Good varieties
Winter cabbages, Christmas Drumhead, Winter Monarch, January King. Savoys (hardy winter

Savoy cabbage. Very hardy and succeeds on poor soil.

cabbage succeeding on poorer soils), Ormskirk, Ormskirk Late. Spring-hearting varieties, Flower of Spring, Ellam's Early, Harbinger.

Special note
In addition to the main cabbage crops listed here, some others are worth growing. There is the red pickling cabbage such as Ruby Ball, useful for purposes other than pickling. And there is Winter White, sown in late spring and producing large solid hearts which may be cut from December onwards and will store perfectly for weeks in a cool shed.

January King, probably the best all-round mid-winter cabbage.

10 Peas and beans

Broad beans

An easy vegetable to grow, not a universal favourite but rich in proteins and giving back more to the soil than it takes out.

Broadbean seedling, with its white flower. Check the growing points for black aphis when the plant blooms.

Soil
Preferably a cool, moist, rather heavy one, deeply dug well before sowing. On light sands and chalks dig in some well-rotted manure or garden compost. Fertiliser is unnecessary.

When to sow
Spring sowings should be made as soon as the soil is dry enough to be raked down to a reasonable condition. The first sowings, which get established in the cool, damp conditions of early spring, are usually the most prolific and even quite sharp frosts will not harm the young plants. Sow under cloches in February and in the open in February and March, with successional sowings in April. Autumn sowings are made in October or early November and have a better chance if protected by cloches.

How to sow
In drills at least 15cm (6in) wide, 5 to 7·5cm (2 to 3in) deep and 60cm (24in) apart. Sow two rows in the drill, both the rows and the seeds in each row being 15cm (6in) apart in staggered formation. Make the soil firm after covering the drill.

Time to germination
14–21 days.

Season of use
June to August. Freezer life: 1 year.

Good varieties
For autumn sowing, Giant Seville (also listed as Claudia Aquadulce). This variety is useless for spring sowing. Early spring sowing, White or Green Longpod. Later sowing, White or Green Windsor. Dwarf types for the small garden, The Sutton, Dwarf Fan.

Special note
The broad bean has one serious insect pest, the black aphis. It starts in the growing point when the plant is in bloom and may spread down over the pods. Pick out all growing points when a fair number of pods have set. This checks the aphis and speeds up the growth of pods.

Below: A prolific crop of Longpod broad beans. Plants as loaded as this must sometimes be supported by running a length of string along both sides of the row.

Dwarf beans

The dwarf or French bean may be regarded as an alternative to the runner bean. It often succeeds better than the runner on light sandy soils; may be sown a little earlier in the open; is very suitable for starting under cloches; and is a better proposition in cold and windy districts.

Use branching twigs to prop up the pod clusters of dwarf beans, which get dirty and suffer slug damage if allowed to rest on the ground.

Soil
No compost or manure is needed if the soil is in good heart after being manured the previous season. It should be dug early in the winter, left rough and broken down to a fine tilth when dry enough to work easily. It is a good idea to rake in a dressing of sulphate of ammonia or other nitrogenous fertiliser at a rate of 33g per sq m (1oz per sq yd) shortly before sowing, dwarf beans being one of the few pod-bearers to respond to nitrogen.

When to sow
Early districts, first week of May. Late districts, mid-May. For succession, three weeks later. Under cloches, late April.

How to sow
In drills 5cm (2in) deep. The seeds should be 10cm (4in) apart and may be sown as a single row in a narrow drill with rows 45cm (18in) apart; or as a double row in a wide drill as described for broad beans, the double rows being 60cm (24in) apart. Sow a group of extra seeds at the end of the row and use the seedlings to fill up possible gaps.

Time to germination
14 days. If no emergence in 21 days, dig up some seeds to discover if seed has rotted owing to low soil temperature.

Season of use
July to September. Freezer life: 1 year.

Good varieties
Masterpiece, The Prince. For northern or cold districts Glamis. For freezing, Tendergreen.

Special note
Germination is sometimes erratic owing to sowing too early or too deep. Sowing at 5cm (2in) is the maximum depth, though the later sowings in light soils dry out rapidly at this depth and should be kept watered until the beans are well up and properly established.

Peas

Garden peas, so called to distinguish them from the very different asparagus and sugar peas, are a most important summer crop, both for immediate consumption and freezing.

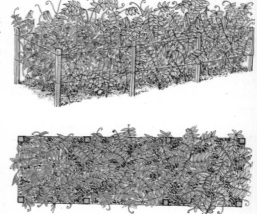

Soil
A medium or heavy moisture-holding soil is preferred, but peas do quite well on lighter land if some manure or compost is dug in during the winter. They do not like acid conditions, and if there is any doubt on this score lime should be applied after digging. Fertiliser is not necessary where manure or compost has been used.

When to sow
Early varieties, February to March under cloches, March and April in the open and again in June for the latest crop. Maincrops, March to May.

How to sow
In drills 15cm (6in) wide, 5 to 7·5cm (2 to 3in) deep and 60cm (24in) apart. Early sowings are made in the shallower drills, late ones in the deeper. The seeds need not be spaced individually but should be scattered evenly and generously in the drill so that a good plant population is obtained. Make sure that the soil of the drill is moist for the late sowings, if necessary by a thorough watering before sowing.

Time to germination
10–21 days. Be prepared to protect from birds which often discover the emerging seedlings before they are visible to the human eye.

Season of use
June to September from successional sowings. Year-round when frozen.

Early peas Kelvedon Wonder, one of the best for the earliest sowing of the year, under cloches or in the open.

Peas supported by strings along both sides of the row. The crop may be damaged if allowed to lie flat on the ground in a wet season.

Good varieties
For cloches, Histon Mini, Feltham First, Hurst Beagle. Early outdoor sowings, Pioneer, Kelvedon Wonder. Maincrops, Early Onward, Onward, Hurst Green Shaft. Latest sowing, one of the first three earlies given above.

Special note
Only dwarf varieties are recommended but even these need some support. Short, twiggy peasticks are excellent but are now rarely obtainable. A neat alternative is to drive in wooden stakes or canes at intervals of 2m (6–7ft) along both sides of the row and close to it, running two or three strands of stout garden twine tightly from stake to stake and enclosing the row in a string fence to prevent it flopping sideways.

Asparagus peas and sugar peas

The asparagus pea is not a true pea but a relative of the lotus. It is half-hardy and must not be exposed to frost. It does not grow in a thickly sown row but as separate bushy plants with attractive pinkish flowers. The sugar pea or mangetout is grown like the garden pea, but the edible parts are the pod and the seeds. The same applies to the asparagus pea.

Season of use
July to September.
Freezer life: 1 year.

Good varieties
Sugar pea Dwarf Sweetgreen is a new and improved variety. There are no named varieties of asparagus pea.

Special note
Edible podded peas must be harvested at the cor-rect stage or they are simply uneatable. Sugar peas must be picked when well grown and fleshy but before the seeds have developed. Asparagus peas are gathered when the pods are about 2·5cm (1in) long.

Sugar peas picked at exactly the right stage. The pods must not be left until visibly swollen.

Soils
No special preparation is needed for soils in good average condition, but any lime deficiency should be remedied by a dressing of garden lime after winter digging.

When to sow
Sugar peas are sown from late March to May. Asparagus peas may be started in pots in the frame in April and planted out in May when frost is no longer expected, or sown in the open in early May.

How to sow
Sugar peas are sown in drills 5cm (2in) deep exactly as advised for garden peas. Asparagus peas may be sown in seed compost in small peat pots, three seeds to a pot and 2·5cm (1in) deep, and started in the frame or on the windowsill. Reduce the seedlings to one per pot and plant out in late May. Alternatively, they may be sown in small groups in a narrow drill and reduced to one seedling at each station by thinning in stages. Whether planted out or direct-sown the plants should stand finally at 45cm (18in) apart.

Time to germination
10–21 days. Asparagus peas are rather erratic in germination outdoors though more consistent in pots.

Runner beans

One of the most productive late summer vegetables, the runner bean is also excellent for freezing. It will produce a worthwhile crop in the smallest garden and even has some decorative value. It was grown for many years as an ornamental climber before it was realised that the pods were edible.

Soil
Some organic manure should be dug in during the winter, if at all possible, and supplemented with 100g per sq m (3oz per sq yd) of a general fertiliser, raked in 14 days before sowing. Fortnightly feeds of liquid manure from the time the plants start to bloom, watering and overhead spraying in hot weather, and a peat or compost mulch, are as important as the initial state of the soil. So is a situation sheltered from strong winds.

Good varieties
Enorma, Streamline, Achievement. The dwarf variety, Hammond's Dwarf Scarlet, may be sown under cloches and kept there until in bloom. The variety Kelvedon Marvel is suitable for growing without poles if sown in a double row as described for broad beans and grown with its stems continually pinched back to produce bushy growth. All varieties may be frozen if gathered in the right conditions.

Above: how to stake a continuous row.
Left: 'wigwam' staking for small groups. Use bamboo canes, which last for many years.

When to sow
Early districts, mid-May. Late districts, late May. Under cloches, late April. A few degrees of frost are fatal to runners.

How to sow
In narrow drills 5cm (2in) deep, with the seeds 10cm (4in) apart. For growing up poles, sow two rows 30cm (12in) apart, placing a row of poles along the outside of both rows of beans and tying the poles together at the top to form a stable inverted V-shaped structure. Sow a few extra beans to provide transplants for gaps.

Time for germination
14 days.

Season of use
July to October if a successional sowing is made in June. Freezer life: 1 year.

Special note
Runner beans, like all leguminous plants, should not be pulled after cropping. Tops should be cleared away and the roots left in the ground to release their accumulated nitrogen.

Prizewinner, a heavy-cropping runner bean of high quality. Beans like this are produced by good soil, watering and mulching.

11 Permanent crops

Asparagus

This semi-luxury crop is not difficult to grow and an established bed remains in production for up to twenty years. It is now usually grown on the flat and not on raised beds.

During the season all shoots should be cut – thin and deformed ones as well as fine sticks like these.

Soil
Asparagus may be grown in any type of soil, though the crop is easier on light land. Eliminate all perennial weeds by thorough cultivation, as it is impossible to do so after planting without damaging the asparagus roots. Dig deeply and if necessary break up the subsoil to ensure good drainage. Work in some manure or compost and about a month before planting fork the soil over and break up any clods.

When to plant
Mid-March to mid-April.

How to plant
Order one-year-old plants early in the season from a good nurseryman. Do not unpack the roots until you are ready to start planting and never leave them exposed, even for an hour, to sun and wind. Take out a trench 30cm (12in) wide and 20cm (8in) deep. Plant the roots 45cm (18in) apart in the trench, sitting each clump on a small heap of soil so that the fleshy roots have a downward slant. Cover carefully with fine soil and fill the trench in.

Cut no shoots the first year but encourage growth by watering freely and giving an occasional feed of liquid manure.

Season of use
April to June. Sticks may be cut for a short period in the second season after planting and a full crop cut the following year. All cutting should cease about Midsummer Day (24 June) to allow strong growth of the 'fern' and strengthening of the plant for next year's crop. Freshly-cut asparagus freezes well. Freezer life: 9 months.

Good varieties
Connover's Colossal, Martha Washington. Strain is more important than variety. Order from a specialist nurseryman.

Special note
When hoeing near an asparagus row draw the soil towards it, gradually creating a low ridge. Cover with a layer of compost or rotted manure or compost in winter, top dress with 100g per sq m (3oz per sq yd) of compound fertiliser in February or March.

Newly-planted asparagus crown, arranged on a little mound of soil at the bottom of the trench so the roots spread downwards.

287

Globe artichokes

The globe artichoke requires a lot of space to produce its edible flower buds and so is not an economical crop for the small garden. It is, however, an impressive plant, and individual specimens may be dotted about and look quite decorative if a row is out of the question.

Left: Cut off suckers as close as possible to where they start growing.

Soil
It must be well drained and the site open and free from tree-drip. Plants which die in the winter are usually killed by a combination of cold and wet. Work in manure, compost and any available bonfire ashes during winter digging. Before planting rake in a dressing of general fertiliser.

When to plant
Plant in April, ordering the plants in advance from the nursery. They may be grown from seed but it is a long business.

How to plant
Globe artichokes are often planted much too closely. Allow 1 to 1·2m (3 to 4ft) between plants in the row and between rows. Plant very firmly and water after planting in dry weather.

Season of use
Late summer. In the first season there will not be many heads worth using and the plants will be getting established and making growth. Normally, the large terminal buds form first and should be picked before the scales on them begin to turn purple. They are followed by smaller buds on lateral shoots. The artichokes deteriorate rapidly when cut and should be used or frozen as soon as possible after harvesting. Freezer life: 1 year.

Good varieties
Try to obtain Vert de Laon.

Special note
The plants remain profitable for three years and must then be replaced. Propagate by taking suckers or offsets from the base of adult plants and establishing a new row in April of the third year. Protect plants in winter by covering with straw after removing dead foliage. Better still, cover them with cloches.

Below: Harvest heads of artichoke before the scales begin to turn purple.

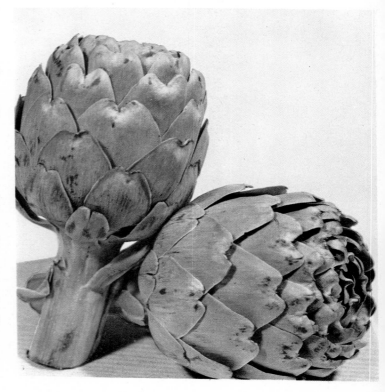

12 Salad crops

Celery

Blanching or trenching celery is grown in a trench and earthed up to blanch the stems and render them eatable. Self-blanching types are grown on the flat and not earthed up. They are mild in flavour and of good quality, but cannot be left in the ground after the beginning of winter frosts.

Above: Plant celery in the bottom of a trench leaving the excavated soil on either side for earthing up to blanch later.

Below: Blanched or trenching celery. Self-blanching are usually shorter and sometimes green or yellow.

Soil

Dig in plenty of moisture-holding organic matter, compost, manure or peat, during the winter. For blanching varieties the trench should be prepared at this time and manure dug into the bottom of it. Make it 45cm (18in) wide and 30cm (12in) deep and leave the excavated soil in a ridge beside it for earthing up.

When to sow and plant

Seed may be sown under cloches in April. Plants are available from the nurseryman in May and June.

How to sow and plant

It is much simpler to buy plants than to raise them, especially as only a limited number are required. If, however, it proves difficult to order the variety you want, sow seed *very* thinly in a shallow drill under a cloche in April. Keep the ends of the cloche closed. Water daily from a rosed can. Prick out the seedlings 5cm (2in) apart as soon as you can handle them, using more cloches to cover them for a few weeks. Plant out when 7·5cm (3in) tall, one row down the centre of the trench, 22·5cm (9in) apart, and the self-blanching varieties the same distance, both in and between the rows.

Season of use

Self-blanching, August to

December. Trenching, November to February. Celery can only be frozen cooked and used as a vegetable. Freezer life: 1 year.

Good varieties

Trench-grown, White Ice, Prizewinner. Self-blanching, Avon Pearl, Golden Self-blanching.

Special note

Lots of water is needed during the plants' growing life. Start earthing up trench varieties in mid-August, tying the stems of each plant loosely together just below the leaves and packing soil carefully round to half its height. Repeat monthly until the trench has become a ridge with only the tips of the plants showing.

Chicory

This valuable winter salad is generally neglected by the amateur gardener although it is an interesting crop to grow. The home-grown product will not equal the solid white heads of imported chicory in appearance but it will be fresh and crisp.

Chicory is a biennial plant, making growth and a substantial root one year, dying down and shooting up to flower the following year. The part eaten is the beginning of the second year's growth, grown in darkness so that it is blanched and cut before the leaves unfold.

Special note
The chicory roots should be lifted very carefully when the tops die down in autumn, placed in a shallow trench and covered with soil or peat so that they may be withdrawn a few at a time for blanching. Remove dead leaves but take care not to damage the crown.

To blanch, place a number of roots close together in a deep pot or plastic bucket, fill with soil-less compost or a mixture of soil, sand and peat to the level of the crowns, and place in a *completely dark* cupboard or cellar. Keep the compost uniformly moist and so long as the temperature is over 10°C (50°F) the heads will develop.

Fine heads of Witloof chicory, showing the type of root necessary to produce them.

Soil
Any good garden soil, well dug to allow good root development and easy lifting. Wild chicory is a chalkland plant and a dressing of lime should be given if the soil is at all acid.

When to sow
May or June. The latter month is best as a number of plants from early sowings usually bolt and send up premature flower stems.

How to sow
In shallow drills 30cm (12in) apart. Sow thinly and thin the seedlings to a final distance of 23cm (9in). This distance is a minimum for the development of good plants, as overcrowding and shortage of moisture are two more causes of bolting. So thin rigorously and water freely in dry weather.

Time to germination
10–14 days. The seedlings are too bitter to suffer much from birds or insect pests.

Season of use
December to March.

Good varieties
Brussels or Witloof (virtually no difference).

290

Cucumbers

Here we are concerned with cucumbers that can be grown outdoors with or without some cloche protection.

Bottom: One of the improved types of outdoor cucumber, seedless and of excellent quality.

Below: Prepare continuous mounds of soil and compost on which to plant out rows of cucumber.

Soil
Outdoor cucumbers were formerly known as ridge cucumbers because they were grown on raised beds of manure topped with soil. That much manure is no longer available but some compost should be mixed with the soil for each plant and the planting site formed into a low mound. This is because cucumbers need a lot of water but also good drainage to prevent stem rot.

When to sow and plant
Plants may be bought locally and planted out in early June with some cloche protection or a fortnight later in the open. Seed may be sown in May in a greenhouse or on a warm windowsill and planted out after hardening off in the frame.

How to sow and plant
Sow two or three seeds to a small pot, reducing to one seedling if more than one germinates. Sow in seed compost and preferably in peat pots so that there is no root disturbance in planting out. If the plants are to trail on the ground the planting mounds should be 90cm (3ft) apart, but if they are to be trained up a trellis or other support only 45cm (18in) apart. Water in when planting and do everything possible to shelter uncloched plants from cold winds.

Time to germination
Cucumber seeds germinate quickly, but only if a temperature of about 18°C (64°F) can be maintained. A propagator is useful. Sow 2cm (½in) deep, placing the seeds on edge.

Season of use
July to October.

Good varieties
Bedfordshire Ridge, Burpless (not indigestible), Burpee's Hybrid, Chinese Long Green.

Special note
When grown as ground trailers the plants should be stopped at six leaves to encourage the growth of laterals. In climbers, the main stem is tied to the supports and stopped when it reaches the top. The laterals are also tied and only they are allowed to fruit.

291

Endive

Endive is a useful substitute for inferior lettuce in autumn and early winter. It is difficult to grow on heavy, wet soils as it has to be covered up and blanched and is then liable to decay under wet conditions.

Soil
The ideal is a light one with plenty of old manure, mushroom compost or the like dug in well before sowing. The subsoil should be broken up to facilitate drainage. Fertilisers are not used.

When to sow
July is the best month if only one sowing is to be made.

How to sow
In narrow drills 2cm (½–¾in) deep. As this sowing takes place at the hottest time of the year the drill should be thoroughly soaked beforehand and kept damp until germination. The seedlings will also need watering in dry weather. If more than one row is grown they should be 30cm (12in) apart, and that should also be the final spacing of the plants after thinning. The plants must not be allowed to overlap or the dense, curly foliage will start to rot. Seed may be sown thinly as there are usually few losses of seedlings from birds or other causes.

Time to germination
10–14 days.

Season of use
Autumn and winter.

Good varieties
Curled, Batavian Broad Leaved, Sutton's Winter Lettuce – Leaved. The first is the hardest to grow but by far the best to eat.

Special note
The blanching of endive is essential; the leaves are bitter and inedible until they have lost their green colour. About three months after sowing, start covering the plants with buckets, flower pots with the drainage holes covered, or anything to keep them warm and dry and completely in the dark. Get them all covered well before Christmas and the advent of severe weather. If you have cloches to spare, begin to cloche over the plants in October and cover the cloches with strips of black polythene sheeting firmly anchored down with stones.

Curled endive before blanching. The delicate leaves are liable to decay under damp conditions.

Lettuce

One of the most important ingredients of the salad bowl, lettuce are easy to grow but less easy to grow well. The secrets are a fairly good soil, adequate moisture in summer, and frequent small sowings.

Soil

Choose a site that received some manure or compost during the winter or one following peas or beans for the later-sown crops. Try to get a good tilth, and a week or so before sowing rake in 100g per sq m (3oz per sq yd) of a general fertiliser.

When to sow

For spring use, sow varieties to overwinter without protection in early September, and those needing protection in early October. For summer use, sow outdoors in March as soon as the soil is dry and workable and make small sowings every fortnight until July.

How to sow

In drills 2cm (½–¾in) deep and 30cm (12in) apart. Start thinning summer crops when they reach the first true leaf stage. Autumn-sown crops should be thinned only lightly in autumn and more drastically in spring, when you may transplant the thinnings if you wish. The later thinnings may be used and the final distance apart for most varieties should be about 23cm (9in). Pelleted seed is advisable for summer crops, being sown 2·5cm (1in) apart. Protect uncloched seedlings from birds.

Time to germination

10 days for summer and cloche sowings, over 14 days when soil is cooler. Summer sowings of pelleted seed must be kept consistently moist or the seedlings will not emerge.

Season of use

Autumn sowings, April to June. Spring and summer sowings, June to November.

Good varieties

Lettuce come in three types: round or cabbage, cos or long, and curly. The last two are slightly more difficult to grow well. For autumn sowing in the open, Winter Crop (cabbage), Winter Density (cos); autumn sowing under cloches, May King (cabbage), Little Gem (cos); spring and summer sowing, Hilde, Unrivalled (cabbage), Webbs Wonderful (curly). Little Gem, Lobjoits Green (cos). Tom Thumb is the smallest and fastest-growing cabbage lettuce.

Special note

A new development has been the advent of the leaf lettuce, a non-hearting type from which leaves are taken as required without cutting the whole plant. A good variety is Salad Bowl.

Cos lettuce Lobjoit's Green. One of the best types for summer, but less easy to grow than the cabbage or round varieties.

Large round cabbage or butternut lettuce.

Radishes and salad onions

These two salad crops are useful short-term fillers of the odd space as well as being essential to the complete salad list. They sometimes disappoint for want of a little care.

Radishes and spring or salad onions. Grow them as catch crops on any small area available.

Soil
Any soil in reasonably good heart, as one manured for a previous crop, will do for these crops, which make no great demands on it. The worst soils, especially for radishes, are very poor, dry ones. A little garden compost forked in before the ground is levelled for sowing is a help, but do not use large quantities of organic manures or fertilisers.

When to sow
Radishes, under cloches in February; in the open, March to September, with a final cloched sowing at the end of that month. Onions, March to July, remembering that if you are growing onions for storage there should be plenty of thinnings for a time in May or June. A final sowing of onions for spring use may be made in September, wintering unprotected in mild districts and protected by cloches in colder ones.

How to sow
Both crops are sown in drills 2cm (½–¾in) deep and 15cm (6in) apart. Sow thinly and thin the radishes further if the seedlings are at all crowded. The commonest cause of failure with radishes is not giving the roots room to develop. Salad onions may be left fairly thick and withdrawn for use as soon as large enough.

Time to germination
Radishes, 5–10 days.
Onions, 14–21 days.

Season of use
Spring to autumn.

Above: Oval radish French Breakfast. An old variety, unbeatable for quality.

Good varieties
Radish, Scarlet Globe, Sparkler, Cherry Belle (globe-shaped), French Breakfast, Twenty Days (oval). The last is a faster-growing version of French Breakfast, itself unequalled for quality. Onions, White Lisbon. The pickling onion, Silver Skin, is grown like salad onions, sown in July, and lifted when the roots are as big as marbles.

Below: unthinned radishes, roots unusable. (*left*): properly thinned or sown very thinly (*right*).

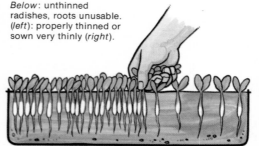

Special note
It is far better to sow salad onions than to rely entirely on the main onion bed for the supply of 'spring' onions. This leads to onions too large for the salad and too crowded, owing to delayed thinning to make good storage bulbs.

294

Tomatoes

Outdoor tomatoes are a worthwhile crop in a warm and sunny season, and fairly reliable under cloches in not-so-good years. A sunny, sheltered site makes a lot of difference to the yield, especially if it is sunny from September onwards, when much of the crop is ripening and the sun is much lower in the sky than at midsummer.

Miniature tomatoes, Sugar Lump variety. Some top-quality varieties, such as Tiny Tim or Gardener's Delight, make decorative pot plants.

Soil
If possible, select a position on the south side of a wall or fence and dig thoroughly. Rake in 100g per sq m (3oz per sq yd) of general fertiliser before planting. When plants are fruiting, feed regularly with a high-potash liquid fertiliser.

When to sow and plant
Order plants from a local nursery and plant out in early June. Alternatively sow seed in early April, harden off and plant out. Plant under cloches in mid-May.

How to sow and plant
Sow in seed compost in trays in the greenhouse, on a light windowsill or anywhere maintaining a temperature of 6°C (60°F), prick out seedlings into small pots of potting compost before the first true leaves appear, grow

Good full-size tomato specimens.

on in a good light to ensure sturdy growth, and harden off in the frame before planting out. Tall varieties are planted 45cm (18in) apart, and each is tied to a stout cane. Bush or dwarf varieties, the only ones suitable for growing under cloches, are planted 60cm (24in) apart.

Time to germination
10–14 days in the right temperature. Very early pricking out of the small seedlings is essential to get sturdy plants.

Season of use
July to November. The last of the crop is ripened indoors. Tomatoes for cooking may be frozen; storage life, 1 year.

Good varieties
Tall varieties, Outdoor Girl, Ronaclave, Ailsa Craig. Bush varieties, Sleaford Abundance, The Amateur. Small-fruited, Gardener's Delight.

Special note
Tall varieties are grown as a single stem. Nip out all side-shoots as soon as they show in the leaf axils. Remove the growing point after the third or fourth truss has set and not later than mid-August. Restrict the number of branches on bush varieties to three or four.

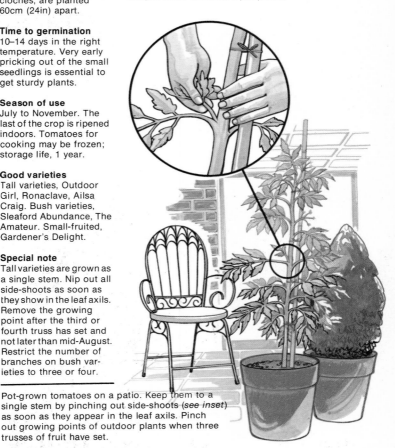

Pot-grown tomatoes on a patio. Keep them to a single stem by pinching out side-shoots (*see inset*) as soon as they appear in the leaf axils. Pinch out growing points of outdoor plants when three trusses of fruit have set.

13 Root crops

Beetroot

Beet succeeds on most soils provided its growth is not checked by cold or drought, which may cause it to bolt instead of forming a proper root or to produce roots which are tough and woody. Do not sow it too early in spring and be prepared to water it on light, dry soils.

Certain varieties of beet are grown for their edible leaves and stems instead of for their roots (see perpetual spinach).

Soil
No manure is used and the crop is better without it. A compound fertiliser may be raked in well before sowing at the rate of 100g per sq m (3oz per sq yd) but on land in good heart after manuring for a previous crop this may not be necessary.

When to sow
Round beet from late March outdoors in early districts. Mid-April onwards in late districts. Mid-March onwards under cloches in all districts, but put cloches in position for a fortnight before sowing to warm the ground. Long beet for storing, May and June in all districts. Last sowing of round beet for small roots in autumn and freezer storage, late June or early July.

How to sow
In drills 2·5cm (1in) deep and 30cm (12in) apart. For midsummer sowings in dry weather, water the drills before sowing and keep watered until seedlings emerge. Protect from birds with netting or black cotton if necessary.

Time to germination
10–21 days according to season and soil temperature.

Season of use
Fresh and stored, late June to late February. Freezer life: good condition for six months.

Good varieties
Round, for early sowing, Boltardy, Avonearly; for late sowing, Little Ball. Long, Cheltenham. Recommended for freezing, Housewives' Choice.

Special note
Start thinning beet as soon as the first true leaves appear. Thin in stages to 2·5, 5, and 10cm (1, 2 and 4in), using sizeable roots from the last stage. At the first thinning, take care to reduce to one seedling the little clumps that often emerge from each seed.

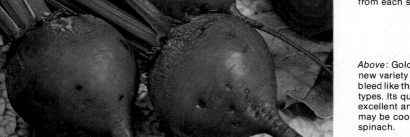

Above: Golden Beet. This new variety does not bleed like the ordinary red types. Its quality is excellent and the leaves may be cooked like spinach.

Left: Globe beet, best for winter storage. Semi-flat early-maturing beet.

296

Carrots

The carrot is one of the most useful of root vegetables, pulled young and tender from successional sowings in summer, kept in that condition in the freezer, or stored naturally when mature for use throughout the winter.

Soil

Light land produces the finest long carrots, but the stump-rooted and cylindrical varieties do well on heavy land well dug and left rough to weather through the winter. The crop responds to the standard fertiliser dressing of 100g per sq m (3oz per sq yd) raked in about a fortnight before sowing. No organic manure is needed.

When to sow

In early districts and under cloches, March. Otherwise, April to the end of June, choosing a short, quick-growing variety for the latest sowings. Carrots are a useful crop to succeed early peas or potatoes.

How to sow

In drills 2cm (½–¾in) deep and 23 to 30cm (9 to 12in) apart. Monthly sowings from March to June

Below: Forked carrots are caused by manuring the ground with fresh manure just before sowing.

will ensure young roots for immediate consumption and freezing over a long period and plenty of full-sized ones for winter storage. Thin by stages to a distance of 10cm (3in), using the later thinnings.

Time to germination

14–21 days.

Season of use

Freshly pulled and naturally stored, June to March. Freezer life: 1 year.

Good varieties

On deep soils, New Red Intermediate. On all types of soil, Amsterdam Forcing, Early Scarlet Horn. Recommended for freezing, Sweetheart, Nantes.

Special note

The major pest of the carrot is the carrot fly, whose larvae scar and distort the roots. It is controlled more by management than by pesticides. Choose an open and exposed site for the carrot bed as the fly prefers a sheltered habitat. It is attracted to the crop for egg-laying by the smell of the carrots, frequently when they are disturbed during thinning. Thin on a dull day or after sunset, firm and water the seedlings after thinning and, best of all, use pelleted seed sown 2cm (½–¾in) apart and reduce thinning to a minimum.

Above: Carrot Chantenay. An intermediate variety, red-cored, early and fine for freezing.

Right: The long, cylindrical type of carrot which gives its best performance on deep, well-cultivated soils.

(12in) apart in the row with 45cm (18in) between rows. Water before lifting and plant so that the roots are covered but the small swelling at the base of the stem rests on the surface. Water from a rosed can after planting to settle the plants in.

Time to germination
14–21 days.

Season of use
October to March from the ground and from store. Not much point in freezing.

Good varieties
The variety Globus appears to be outstanding.

Left and below: Improved types of celeriac. Modern varieties have better-shaped roots than the older forms.

Celeriac

Also known as turnip-rooted celery, this rather unattractive-looking root serves a useful purpose. It is a celery-flavoured vegetable and may be used in cooking as a celery substitute, although useless for salads. It will grow where celery consistently fails, is less trouble to cultivate and may be lifted and stored for winter like other root vegetables.

Soil
Well-manured soil that will hold moisture is essential for succulent roots. If manure is short, dig in plenty of peat on the site of the row and rake in a dressing of general fertiliser before planting out.

When to sow
Under cloches in early April, in the open a month later. Celeriac plants, unlike celery plants, are difficult to buy.

How to sow and plant
Sow thinly in very shallow drills 15cm (6in) apart, lightly covering the seed with fine soil. Sowings under cloches need daily watering from a rosed can and outdoor sowings must also be watered in dry weather. The seedlings, like those of celery, are apt to look crowded and fragile, and if you do not want the trouble of pricking out, they may be thinned and left to grow on. In this case you must sow a sufficient length of drill to give the required number of plants when thinned to 5cm (2in) apart.

Plant out when the young plants are big enough to handle, 30cm

Jerusalem artichokes

The Jerusalem artichoke has no associations with Jerusalem; its name derives from the Italian *girasole*, a sunflower. Its knobbly tubers are not universal culinary favourites but it has the advantage of being extremely easy to grow.

Soil
Neither manure nor fertiliser are normally used. The ground should be well dug in the winter and forked over again before planting to leave it loose and open.

When to plant
February to April as soon as the soil is workable.

How to plant
In separate holes or a continuous trench 15cm (6in) deep, spacing the tubers 30cm (12in) apart. Planting tubers may be bought from the seedsman or you can use those bought from the greengrocer for culinary purposes. It is unlikely that more than one row will be required, and as the plants grow a good 2m (6–7ft) tall this should be sited where it will least overshadow other crops. In a windy situation it may be necessary to support the tall stems by running a strand of wire or twine, attached to poles or stout canes, along the row.

Time to emergence
Shoots will appear 3–4 weeks after planting.

Season of use
November to March, the tubers being lifted as required, or stored in a cool place covered with peat if hard frost seems likely to make lifting impossible. The tubers may be frozen but the high-quality storage time is only 3 months, so freezing in the autumn is pointless. The season of use may, however, be prolonged a few months by freezing in February before growth restarts.

Varieties
There are no distinct varieties of Jerusalem artichokes.

Special note
This is a difficult plant to eliminate from the garden

Jerusalem artichokes make a good screen for less attractive items – such as a compost heap.

once you introduce it since every small and broken tuber left in the ground proliferates like a weed. It is better to leave it out of the rotation and confine it to some corner of the plot where it may be grown for several years running.

Jerusalem artichoke tubers bear no resemblance to the globe variety and are cooked quite differently. They take up less planting space than the globes and are a much underrated vegetable – the globe variety being considered a glamorous starter to a luxurious dinner.

Onions

This concerns bulb onions for storage. Salad onions are dealt with under that heading.

Soil
Choose an open, sunny site and dig it deeply during the winter. If the onions form part of the root-crop section in the rotation, no manure or compost need be used, but some may be dug in if a special bed is prepared. Onions are one of the few crops which may be grown on the same ground for years if free from disease. Compound fertiliser should be raked in at the rate of 100g per sq m (3oz per sq yd) as soon as the soil dries in early spring. Then tread it until quite firm and rake it again to a fine, level tilth.

When to sow or plant
Sow seed as soon as the soil is workable in late February or March. Plant sets in April.

How to sow or plant
Seed is sown in drills 2cm (½–¾in) deep and 30cm (12in) apart. After covering the seed, firm the soil by lightly treading the drills. Thin the seedlings by stages to a final distance of 10cm (4in). Use the later thinning for salads but do not be tempted to delay thinning

to ensure a supply of 'spring' onions.

Onion sets are small bulbs whose growth was checked the previous season. When planted they start growing again and mature more quickly than seed-grown plants. Take out drills the same distance apart as for seeds, press the sets into the bottom of the drill 10cm (4in) apart, and fill in the drill so that only the necks are visible.

Time to germination
14–21 days. Sets begin to root in 14 days.

Season of use
July to March. Chopped or sliced onions may be frozen for two months.

Good varieties
Seed, Bedfordshire Champion, Best of All. Sets, Ailsa Craig, Rijnsburger.

Special note
Onion seedlings are small and fragile and should be carefully hand weeded from the time of emergence. If weeds are allowed to get established they can soon smother the young crop.

Flat onion. The Stuttgartner variety shown here is one of the best to grow from sets.

Globe onion, the most popular type for growing from seed.

Onion sets

300

Parsnips

The parsnip is a hardy and undemanding vegetable, but perfect long specimens are only grown on deep loams or similar soils. For heavy clay soils choose short or stump-rooted varieties.

Perfect long-rooted parsnips. On heavy clays stump-rooted varieties give better results.

Soil
Dig deeply, breaking up the subsoil if possible, though without bringing any of it to the surface. Try to complete digging early in the winter, leaving the ground rough. If it was manured for the previous crop no fertiliser need be used when preparing to sow. Rake the surface down to a fine tilth.

When to sow
March or April in all districts, when the soil is in workable condition. This crop is not expected to mature until autumn so there is no point in wasting cloches to give it a start.

How to sow
Sow in narrow drills 1·25cm (½in) deep and 30cm (12in) apart. The seed is large enough to be sown quite thinly, but is also very light, and when sowing in a strong wind the hand should be held close to the drill. Thin seedlings by stages to 15cm (6in) apart.

Time to germination
14–21 days, but in early spring you should allow 4 weeks before assuming a failure.

Season of use
October to March. Parsnips are left in the ground and lifted as required during the winter. They should not be stored in the freezer.

Good varieties
Short, Avonresister. Intermediate and long, Hollow Crown, Tender and True.

Special note
Parsnips do not store well out of the ground and so are better dug only when needed. This becomes difficult during prolonged hard frost, and it pays to keep the row covered with a thick layer of peat to reduce the depth to which the ground is frozen. Lift all unused roots when they begin to grow out in late February or March and store in a cool shed in a box of peat.

Potatoes

Early potatoes are a semi-luxury and should be grown if room can be found. Second early and maincrop varieties are only worth growing in the larger garden

Seed potatoes set up to sprout.

Soil
Potatoes prefer a slightly acid soil rich in humus. Compost or well rotted manure may be used in the trench when planting but a combination of peat and fertiliser is almost equally good, especially on light sandy or chalk soils. The ground should be dug in winter and forked over again before planting. Potatoes do not need a fine tilth but do best in a loose soil not settled and compacted.

When to plant
Earlies, late March to mid-April. Maincrops, April and early May. Much depends on the frequency of late frosts in your district and nothing is gained by early planting if the growth is cut off. Gain time by getting the 'seed' tubers at least a month before planting and setting them up in trays in a light, frost-proof place to develop sturdy green shoots.

How to plant
Take out a trench 12·5cm (5in) deep with the spade. Space the potatoes in it 30cm (12in) apart, with the rows 60cm (24in) apart for earlies and a little more for maincrops. Cover each tuber with a double handful of peat or compost. Sprinkle compound fertiliser along the trench at the rate of 66g per metre of row (2oz per yd). Fill in the trench with the rake or draw hoe.

Time to emergence
2–4 weeks according to soil temperature. Watch for the shoots and draw soil over them if frost threatens at night.

Season of use
June to the following May. Apart from normal storage of the mature crop, new potatoes may be frozen partially cooked and will keep for up to a year.

Good varieties
Earlies, Foremost, Arran Pilot, Home Guard. Maincrops, King Edward, Pentland Crown, Desiree.

Special note
Potatoes should be earthed up to encourage tuber formation and prevent tubers greening from exposure to light. Draw the soil up to the stems to form a ridge when the plants are about 20cm (8in) tall. If growth seems to have been slow a further light dressing of fertiliser may be scattered near the plants before earthing up.

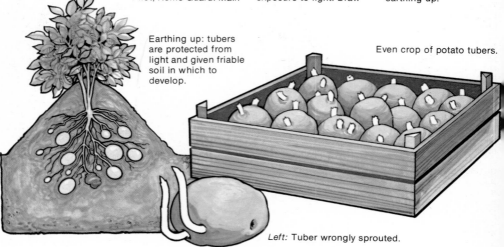

Earthing up: tubers are protected from light and given friable soil in which to develop.

Even crop of potato tubers.

Left: Tuber wrongly sprouted.

Swedes

The garden swede is a useful vegetable and although related to the turnip is different and distinctive in flavour and texture.

Soil
Heavy and loamy soils grow better swedes than light and chalky ones. As with most crops in the root section of the rotation, the ground should not be manured when dug in the winter, but 100g per sq m (3oz per sq yd) of general fertiliser should be raked in before sowing. Swedes are an excellent crop to follow early peas, beans or potatoes.

When to sow
Any time from April to mid-July.

How to sow
In drills 2cm (½–¾in) deep and 45cm (18in) apart. Sow thinly and start thinning as soon as the seedlings get their first true leaves. Continue thinning in stages to a final distance of 15cm (6in). The thinnings are of no culinary use as swedes do not develop their proper flavour until nearing maturity.

Time to germination
7–10 days. Germination of the later sowings is very rapid.

Season of use
October to March from store. Swede purée keeps for a year in the freezer.

Good varieties
Western Perfection, Best of All. The latter is recommended for its keeping qualities and mildness of flavour.

Special note
It is a mistake to sow swedes too early. The roots are not wanted in the summer and early crops are often badly affected by mildew. Sown in June or early July following the clearance of early peas or potatoes, the crop has plenty of time to mature and is usually healthy. In dry weather, water the drills before sowing and keep the seedlings watered until well established.

Right and below: Purple-topped swede. This unjustly neglected vegetable does best sown in late spring or early summer.

Turnips

Turnips flourish in most gardens, given a consistent supply of moisture. Drought and erratic watering may cause them to bolt and form no root at all or to produce roots strong in flavour and stringy in texture.

Red-top Milan turnip

Soil
Try to give them a site manured the previous season. Rake in 100g per sq m (3oz per sq yd) of compound fertiliser well before the early crop is sown. The late crop should follow early potatoes, peas or broad beans and for this a dressing of 50g per sq m (1½oz per sq yd) should be hoed in.

When to sow
Not too early. The first week of April is soon enough in all districts, and although an earlier start may be made under cloches the crop is not usually thought worth cloche space. A final and quite important sowing is made during the first half of July.

How to sow
In drills 2cm (½–¾in) deep and 37·5cm (15in) apart. Turnips should not be crowded at any stage of growth and the leaves need plenty of room to spread. Start thinning when the first rough leaves appear and thin by stages to a final distance apart of 10cm (4in), using the small roots from the later thinnings.

Time to germination
5–14 days. June and July sowings, if kept moist, may emerge in 4 days and careful watch must be kept to see that the small seedlings are not being pulled up by birds. Pro-

tect with netting or black cotton if necessary.

Season of use
From the ground or store, June onwards and for most of the winter. Freezer life: 1 year.

Good varieties
Early sowing, Early Snowball. Later sowings, Golden Ball, Green Top Milan.

Special note
A productive late crop may be obtained from a broadcast sowing. Select a strip about 60cm (24in) wide, hoe up weeds and incorporate fertiliser. Rake level, and in dry summer weather water thoroughly. Scatter seed thinly over whole area and cover lightly with fine soil, keeping watered. Thin where crowded and pull when large enough. Such a bed will go on producing for much of a mild winter.

Milan turnip, a flat variety. Globe varieties are usually better for earliest sowings.

14 Miscellaneous crops

Leeks

The leek is not only one of the hardiest of the onion family but also the most delicately flavoured. Nothing quite replaces it as a winter vegetable.

Soil
Good soil produces large, plump leeks. Dig deeply in winter, working in some manure or compost. Before planting, apply 100g per sq m (3oz per sq yd) of a general fertiliser, forking it well into the topsoil.

When to sow and plant
Sow in a seed-bed from early March to mid-April. Plant out from May to July. Give leeks the longest growing season possible.

How to sow and plant
Sow in the seed-bed in shallow drills 15cm (6in) apart. Thin the seedlings to 5cm (2in) and plant out when about 20cm (8in) tall. Well-grown plants are easier to transplant than thin, grassy ones, and for that reason it pays to allow them plenty of space.

Water before lifting, and trim back the longest leaves of the seedlings by about one-quarter of their length before planting. Plant 23cm (9in) apart in rows 45cm (18in) apart. Make a hole with a dibber, not quite as deep as the leek plant is long, drop the plant in it, and fill the hole with water. Do not fill it with soil, either then or subsequently. Enough soil is washed down to cover the roots and the stem is left with room for expansion.

Time to germination
14–21 days. May be rather slow. Seedlings are practically immune to insect and bird damage.

Season of use
Autumn to spring. Plants are kept in the ground and lifted as required. Leeks may be frozen for use in summer.

Good varieties
The Lyon, Musselburgh, Marble Pillar.

Special note
Although leeks survive hard frost, they are almost impossible to lift without damage when the ground is frozen. One solution is to surround the stems with dry peat and cover with cloches.

Well-grown specimens of this delicious winter vegetable are frequently underrated. Provided they are well cleaned they are delicious separately or combined with chicken or sea food soups.

Far left: Leek seedlings planted. The holes are filled with water after planting but are not filled up with soil.

Marrows and squashes

This is a large and varied family which also includes courgettes and pumpkins. They all need basically the same treatment and the same humus-rich soil. They are all tender and must not be exposed to frost.

Soil

These vegetables cannot be grown without some organic manure or compost. They do not respond well to inorganic fertilisers, which need not be used. Use the manure or compost to prepare stations for the plants, digging the manure into the soil at each site and raising it into a low mound. Do not leave manure and soil in separate layers. A barrowload of manure is enough for three plants.

When to sow and plant

Sow in the garden frame in early May, planting out in the first half of June.

How to sow and plant

Sow in seed compost, preferably in peat pots. Marrows dislike root disturbance in planting out. Sow two or three seeds per pot at a depth of 2cm (½–¾in.) keeping only the strongest seedling. Do not sow earlier than suggested or the plants will be starved and pot-bound before it is safe to plant them out. Alternatively, sow in the same way on each prepared mound in the first week of June, placing the seeds in little pockets of compost or sifted soil and watering daily if necessary. The prepared sites should be spaced as follows. For bush marrows and courgettes, 75cm (2½ft). Most squashes, 90cm (3ft). Trailing marrows and pumpkins, 1·2m (4ft).

Time to germination

10–14 days, provided a night temperature of 10°–13°C (50°–55°F) is maintained. In tempera-

Right: Marrow zucchini, a productive bush type which may be cut as courgettes or left to grow to full size.

Below: Summer squash Baby Crookneck.

Below: Squash Vegetable Spaghetti. One of the best of the marrow family, with flesh of a distinctive texture.

tures below this seed is likely to rot.

Season of use

Marrows, courgettes and summer squashes, July to October. Ripened marrows, pumpkins and winter squashes, October to January.

Good varieties

Trailing marrows, Long White Trailing, Table Dainty. Bush Marrows, Zucchini, Zephyr. Courgette, Green Bush. Summer Squashes, Vegetable Spaghetti, Baby Crookneck. Winter squash, Hubbard. Pumpkin, Hundredweight. Ornamental gourds are sometimes quoted in vegetables but are in fact inedible.

Melons

Although melons are generally thought of as a greenhouse crop, the smaller cantaloup varieties may be grown in the frame, under cloches, and, in most summers in the warmer districts, without any protection.

Soil
Like marrows and cucumbers the melon must be grown on a prepared site. For each plant mix a good pailful of rotted manure, spent mushroom compost or garden compost with the soil taken from a hole about 30cm (12in) square. Loosen the soil at the bottom of the hole to promote good drainage and replace the mixture, shaping it into a small mound. The same procedure applies whether the plants are in the open, under cloches or in a frame. Distance between planting sites should be 60cm (24in).

When to sow and plant
Seed requires a temperature of 16°–21°C (60°–70°F) for germination, and the plants cannot be transplanted to the frame or cloches until late May or to the open ground until early June. Therefore, even if you have a heated propagator you should not sow until the beginning of May.

How to sow and plant
Raise seedlings as described for cucumbers, remembering that melons are a little more tender.

Plant out with the least possible root disturbance, choosing the sunniest, most sheltered site you can find for the unprotected plants. Never allow the plants to suffer from lack of water, using it tepid for young seedlings and watering newly-planted outdoor and cloche plants before sunset.

Time to germination
7–10 days in the right temperature. If too low the seeds will rot.

Season of use
August to October. Freezer life: 1 year.

Good varieties
In the open, Sweetheart. Frame or cloches, Unwins No Name.

Special note
The trailing shoots are stopped after the fifth leaf and the laterals they produce are stopped at the third leaf. The fruits are borne on these laterals. Rest the fruit on pieces of tile or polythene as they ripen and cut when they develop the characteristic melon scent.

Top and left: Cantaloup melon. Several varieties may be grown in frames, under cloches or even in the open.

Seakale beet

This rather neglected vegetable is another leaf beet, related to perpetual spinach. The edible part is the broad leaf stalk and midrib, pure white in the seakale beet and pink in the variety Ruby Chard. This is a delicious vegetable and should be better known.

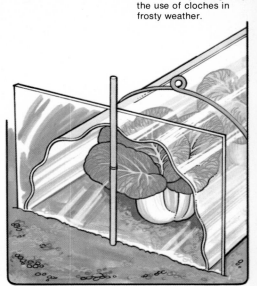

The production of seakale beet can be prolonged by the use of cloches in frosty weather.

Soil
Treat it as for the growing of spinach. The only difference is that seakale beet is slower in reaching maturity and has time to respond to weekly feeding with liquid fertiliser in addition to regular watering. In well grown plants the edible stems should be 5cm (2in) wide.

When to sow
April. This is a late summer and autumn crop and too tender to carry on into winter.

How to sow
In drills 2·5cm (1in) deep and 45cm (18in) apart. Thin the seedlings to 10cm (4in) apart as soon as they can be handled. A week or so later remove every other plant and leave the remainder at twice this distance. Seakale beet, in both white and pink forms, is quite a decorative plant, and clumps of it may be grown in the shrub or herbaceous borders if kitchen garden space is limited.

Time to germination.
14 days.

Season of use
July to October.

Good varieties
No named varieties. Listed as Seakale Beet, Silver Beet, Swiss Chard, Ruby Chard.

Special note
The outer leaves are cut at ground level when large enough and the plant continues to produce more from the centre. The leaf is stripped from the midrib and may be cooked like spinach if there is enough of it. Leaf stalks and midribs, the main part of the crop, are cooked separately.

Below: Ruby Chard, the red form of seakale beet A valuable addition to the menu and so decorative that it may be grown in the flower border.

308

Summer spinach

Summer or round-seeded spinach is one of the fastest vegetables to mature. A March sowing is often ready for cutting in late May and sowings at intervals of three weeks will maintain a continuous supply.

Soil
Spinach is a leaf crop and must have plenty of moisture and adequate nitrogen to produce abundant foliage. Its worst feature is a tendency to run to seed, and the poorer and drier the soil the quicker it does so. On heavy clays and very light soils dig in all the humus-forming material you can spare, even if it be only peat. Then, before sowing, rake in 33g per sq m (1oz per sq yd) of sulphate of ammonia.

When to sow
Any time from March to September. Early sowings may be cloched if desired.

How to sow
The largest crop from a given area is obtained by sowing in a drill about 15cm (6in) wide and rather less than 2·5cm (1in) deep. Sprinkle the seed thinly and evenly over the bottom of the drill, first soaking it with water if the soil is dry. Fill in and firm the soil. If more than one row is sown the drills should be 30cm (12in) apart. Allow the seedlings to grow to about 10cm (4in) and then thin for the first time. The thinnings are large enough to use, it being only necessary to snip off the roots. After a few days, the row will have filled up again and more thinnings may be used, the rest of the plants then being spaced widely enough to grow to full size for cutting.

Time to germination
10–14 days.

Season of use
May to October. After that date perpetual spinach comes into use. Young spinach with a minimum of stalk may be frozen. Freezer life: 1 year.

Good varieties
Longstanding Round. The variety Longstanding Prickly (the description applies to the seed, not the leaves) is often used for the latest sowing and is referred to as 'winter spinach', but although useful in autumn it is not truly winter-hardy.

Special note
Spinach is one of the few vegetables to succeed in shade – though not in competition with tree roots.

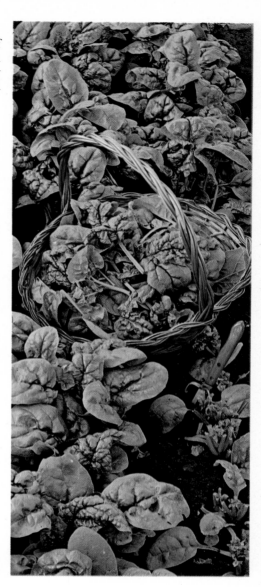

Above: Summer spinach Bloomsdale Longstanding.

Left: Sowing seed for summer spinach.

Perpetual spinach

Also known as spinach beet, the plant is unrelated to summer spinach. It is a leaf beet, a biennial with a strong tap-root that may live for several years, though in practice it should be sown annually. It produces a succession of edible leaves in autumn and spring and, if cloched, throughout the winter.

Soil
Any soil in reasonably good heart if well cultivated. The crop is a good follow-up to early potatoes, which leave the soil in the right condition so that it only needs to be raked level before sowing. A light dressing of general fertiliser raked in at that stage helps to get the seedlings away quickly, but more important is to have the soil in good physical condition to encourage a strong root system.

When to sow
Mid-June to mid-July. It may, of course, be sown earlier but is not usually wanted as a summer vegetable.

How to sow
In drills 2·5cm (1in) deep and 45cm (18in) apart. Thin by stages to 15cm (6in). Protect from birds if necessary, as the seedlings are sweet and an unprotected row can disappear in 24 hours.

Time to germination
Ten days if the soil is moist. Germination is hastened if the seed is soaked for 12 hours before sowing, but in this case the soil must be moist when sowing and kept so until germination, otherwise the seed may start to shoot and then dry out and die.

Season of use
Autumn, spring and early summer. In mild districts and under cloches some pickings are possible throughout the winter.

Good varieties
No named varieties. Listed as Perpetual Spinach, Spinach Beet or Leaf Beet.

Perpetual spinach

Special note
Keep picking young and tender leaves for use. Pick the old and tough ones too to encourage more leaves. When flower stems begin to appear in spring it is time to discard the row and prepare for a new one.

Sweet corn

Sweet corn likes a sunny, sheltered position. It is quite decorative and may be grown in groups in the shrub or herbaceous border if no other space is available.

Soil
Compost or manure during winter digging if possible. Compound fertiliser at the rate of 100g per sq m (3oz per sq yd) raked in 14 days before sowing or planting.

When to sow or plant
Sowing outdoors: early districts, May; late districts, first week of June. Under cloches: mid-April. In pots in the frame: mid-April, for planting out in May or June.

How to sow
In drills 3cm (1in) deep. Distance between rows: 45cm (18in). Final distance between plants 30cm (12in). Sow in groups of three seeds close together every 30cm and reduce each group to one good seedling. Sow in the frame in seed compost in small peat pots, two or three seeds per pot, and reduce to one. Grow in several short rows rather than one long one to improve

fertilisation by air-borne pollen which falls from the 'tassel' to be caught on the sticky 'silk' of the cobs.

Time to germination
14–21 days. Be prepared to protect seedlings from birds with black cotton or nylon netting as soon as they emerge.

Harvest at the correct time, when juice squeezed out of the kernels is the consistency of thin cream and before it becomes solid and starchy.

Special note
In dry weather keep plants well watered and mulched with peat or

compost in the weeks before formation of cobs.

Season of use
Fresh, August to October. Freezer life: good condition for a year.

Good varieties
Earliking, Northern Belle, John Innes Hybrid F$_1$, Extra Early Sweet.

Well-filled cobs of sweet corn. The crop is easily spoiled by harvesting too late, when sugar in the kernels has been turned to starch.

Herb growing

1 What is a herb?

In spite of its general use in describing a plant which is grown for its scent or flavour, the term 'herb' actually has more than one meaning. Botanically, it is a plant which, unlike a tree, has a stem or stems which die back at the end of its season. Thus, the name 'herb' refers, botanically, to thousands of annual, biennial and perennial plants which are by no means aromatic or wholesome. In the non-botanical sense, herbs are the leafy or soft flowering parts of certain plants. These can be used in the preparation of food or for medicine, for cosmetic purposes, for potpourris, insect repellents and scented toilet waters. Some may even be used in wines and liqueurs.

Spices, often used with herbs in certain dishes, are sometimes confused with them. Spices are not leafy. Usually they are the seeds of a plant. Sometimes, as in the case of the nutmeg, they are the fruit of a tree. Mace, also from the nutmeg tree, is the dried membrane which surrounds the nut when it is growing. Cloves are flower buds, cinnamon is the bark of a tree. Some plants, for instance perennial fennel, provide both spice and herb, but this is not general. It should not be assumed that every part of every culinary herb is good to eat.

The spices used in potpourris are a little more varied and exotic. Orris root is the dried, ground root of the Florentine iris. Angelica root can be dried and used for the same purpose as orris. Calamus is powdered palm root. Khus-khus is fragrant grass. Some plant resins are fragrant. These include gum benzoin and gum olibanum or frankincense. Balsam is an oil-resinous sap tapped from certain trees.

Fennel (above) is an attractive herb to grow in a flower border and is tall enough to act as a background for other plants. Fresh parsley (left) can be used as a garnishing as well as lending its own special flavour to a wide variety of dishes.

To carry the distinction even further, culinary herbs are always added to a dish. Except for tisanes or herb teas, they do not form the basis of a dish itself. Thus, while garlic is a herb, onion, a close relative, is a vegetable.

In spite of the true botanical meaning of the term, to most people's minds, herbs are not necessarily plants which die back at the end of the season. Some – the herbaceous kinds – do, but there are also some herbs which are trees, such as the bay, and others which are shrubs, albeit very small ones, such as thyme, sage and rosemary.

Most of the plants we grow as culinary herbs are 'cut-and-come-again' kinds. Fortunately, some of these are evergreens and last for years. These include sage, thyme, rosemary, winter savory and lavender.

The long stem-like leaves of chive (above) have a delicate flavour and, when chopped, are a culinary delight. Sage (left) is used in Italian cuisine. Its purple flowers are ideal in borders.

Constant clipping keeps these plants neat and compact. Although they have a summer flowering season, at which time they are best gathered for drying, they are available all the year round. Obviously, growth is greater in summer, but the leaves are also there to be gathered fresh in mid-winter. Where the climate is cold, these plants can either be grown in a sheltered place or they can be given winter protection. The less exposed they are to the cold, the more shoots they will produce. Some of these evergreen herbs are such handsome plants that they deserve to be grown in some decorative manner, a subject which is discussed in chapter 3.

Most people prefer to have plants which come up year after year; fortunately, there are many herbs which are herbaceous perennials. These include chives, bergamot, tarragon, marjoram, fennel and mint. Usually, the more these are picked the more shoots they will produce. It is often an advantage to keep picking the tips of the stems so that the plant does not flower. For instance, once mint has bloomed, it begins to die down and so from late summer is of little use; yet if the shoot tips are taken as they are ready, more will be produced down the stem, and fresh mint can be picked right on into the autumn. Fennel, a truly handsome plant, can also be

315

something of a nuisance if it is allowed to drop its seed because seedlings will then sprout up all over the garden. Further, if allowed to flower, the sweet young succulent shoots do not form and only the large, tough leaves are available. If fennel seed is required, it is best to allow just a few stems to seed and to keep taking the young shoots from the others. Once chives have flowered, the plants begin to die down. Where a row of chives is grown as an edging alternate plants could be allowed to flower, while the others are constantly cut, to provide a decorative effect. Like many other perennials, chives are kept rejuvenated if the plants are lifted and divided every three or four years.

The handsome angelica is a biennial, yet if it is prevented from flowering it will come up again the following year, and again the year after that and so on if the same method of removing the flower buds is followed. Otherwise, once it has flowered and set seed it will die.

Parsley is also a biennial, but since we do not cultivate it for its seed, which is produced the year after sowing, it is treated as an annual and therefore sown afresh each year.

There are many annuals among the herbs. Those which are grown for their

All parts of lovage (top) except the roots have value in cooking. The leaves and stems have a celery-like flavour. The delicate flowers of coriander (above) make a delightful bouquet but it is the seeds that are used in cooking. This particular variety of thyme (right) has a pungent lemon-like scent.

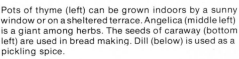

Pots of thyme (left) can be grown indoors by a sunny window or on a sheltered terrace. Angelica (middle left) is a giant among herbs. The seeds of caraway (bottom left) are used in bread making. Dill (below) is used as a pickling spice.

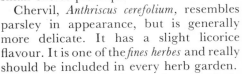

leaves should be sown in succession to provide a constant supply.

It is an interesting fact that the main herbs are from just a few plant families. Those which are most versatile and offer the greatest range of flavours come from the parsley family or *Umbelliferae*. The flowers of these plants grow in flat or rounded umbels. Parsley, *Petroselinum crispum*, has a swollen-rooted form known as Hamburg parsley which produces both edible leaves and roots, the latter looking and tasting like small choice parsnips.

Chervil, *Anthriscus cerefolium*, resembles parsley in appearance, but is generally more delicate. It has a slight licorice flavour. It is one of the *fines herbes* and really should be included in every herb garden.

Carrying a similar flavour is sweet cicely or Spanish chervil, *Myrrhis odorata*. Like the Hamburg parsley, its roots can be cooked and its leaves used like chervil or parsley.

Fennel, *Foeniculum vulgare*, comes in two forms. The first is used in the same way as any green herb, as a garnish or in soups and sauces, while the second, *F.vulgare* var.

317

flowers are attractive as well as excellent examples of this characteristic. Sage, *Salvia officinalis*, is a small shrub. There are other attractive forms of this useful plant that are described more fully on page 332.

Thyme has many species which differ from each other slightly in habit. There are also some variegated forms and varieties. The common thyme most used in cooking is *Thymus vulgaris*. The lemon-scented thyme is *T.x. citriodorus*.

Mint also is more varied than is usually realised. There are many species and only a few are cultivated. *Mentha spicata* is the common spearmint. *M. rotundifolia* with more rounded, woolly leaves is known as the apple mint. *M.x alopecuroides*, a cross between *M. longifolia* and *M. rotundifolia* is not common but well worth growing if it can be found. Peppermint is *M. piperita*. Pennyroyal is *M. pulegium*. These are the most commonly cultivated mints although there are many more which can also be used. All are perennials.

Fast-growing chervil (left) matures from seed in a mere two months. Apple mint (below) has woolly leaves and dense spikes of pinkish flowers.

dulce, known as sweet or Florence fennel, is a variety with swollen stem bases which form a 'bulb'. It is grown as an annual and used as a salad, much in the same way as celery.

Dill, *Anethum graveolens*, provides both leaves and seeds and is an annual. The same remarks apply to anise, *Pimpinella anisum*. Caraway, *Carum carvi*, a biennial and treated as such, is grown for its seeds alone, as are coriander, *Coriandrum sativum*, and cumin, *Cuminum cyminum*.

Lovage, *Ligusticum officinale*, the last herb in this umbelliferae list, is a hardy perennial. It has a strong characteristic celery flavour, which is the reason its leaves are used in soups and bouillon when celery itself is not available.

The next largest group of herbs is to be found in the sage family or *Labiatae*, the plants with 'lipped' flowers – the sage

Marjoram (left) grows well in a sunny site but does require some winter protection in cold climates.

Rosemary (below left) is a handsome shrub that can be wintered out of doors in a mild climate but elsewhere must be grown as a pot or tub plant that can be moved inside during cold weather.

There are several varieties of mint. One of the most popular for flavouring iced tea is peppermint (below).

319

smothered with these pretty, lipped flowers. The flowers can be used in salads and they can be candied. The plant is a shrub. Only the tips should be picked and this has the effect of keeping the plants neat and bushy. There are many varieties including one with white flowers, and one variety that grows much taller and more erect than the others. Rosemary and its varieties are grown outdoors all year round in mild climates. Elsewhere they are grown in pots or tubs. One variety, *R. humilis* is of low and spreading habit.

Marjoram or origanum comes in several species. *Origanum majorana* is a tender sub-shrub usually treated as a half-hardy annual and known as sweet or knotted marjoram. *O. onites* is the perennial pot marjoram. *O. heracleoticum* is winter marjoram and not quite so hardy as pot marjoram. *O. dictamnus* is Dittany of Crete, and *O. vulgare* is the native European species of which there are other forms to be mentioned later.

While the individual flowers of mints and thymes are very small, forming in a mass a pretty inflorescence all the same, those of the rosemary, *Rosmarinus officinalis*, are larger and differently distributed on the stem. They are an attractive blue and when the plant blooms in late spring, its stems are

Balm (above left) is a hardy perennial that will grow well even in shade. The aromatic leaves are most refreshing in tisanes. Laurel or bay (above) is the only herb to grow to tree size. It is winter-hardy in mild climates. Basil (left) is easy to grow from seed and can be raised both outdoors and indoors in pots and trays.

'Cosmetic and potpourri herbs', page 356.

The Liliaceae or lily family gives us the essential garlic, *Allium sativum*, and the shallot, *A. ascalonicum*, both of which are bulbous plants which are raised annually from 'seed' bulbs or individual cloves in the case of garlic. From this group also come chives or *A. schoenoprasum*, a hardy perennial which is easily grown from seed although plants can also be increased by division.

The splendid bay, *Laurus nobilis*, is the only true laurel, even though there are other, non-edible plants known by this name. It is also the only tree among the

Garlic (left) is a pungent herb that comes in familiar clustered bulb shape, each section of which is called a clove. French tarragon (below) is much more flavourful than the Russian variety. It is widely used in sauces and vinegars.

Two kinds of basil are grown, sweet basil, *Ocimum basilicum*, and bush basil or *O. minimum*. Both are half-hardy annuals and are discussed more fully in the section 'Herbs from seed', page 340.

Balm, sometimes called lemon balm and even lemon mint, is *Melissa officinalis*, a hardy perennial with insignificant lipped flowers. It forms a large dense mass of roots and must be kept under control.

Bergamot, *Monarda didyma*, is the source of Oswego tea and is used mainly for this tisane, although the leaves and flowers are also good in salads. This is a decorative plant and is discussed more fully in 'Colour in the herb garden', page 330.

The daisy family, or *Compositae*, provides us with a few important herbs such as tarragon, *Artemisia dracunculus*, a hardy perennial. French tarragon is a variety with dark green smooth leaves, while Russian tarragon has less smooth leaves which have a milder taste. Other species of artemisia are grown for potpourris and other household uses and are dealt with in

herbs. Its great advantage, apart from its highly individual flavour, is that where it is not possible to let it grow to its full height and width it will still grow well confined in a tub or some other large container. Here it is best constantly trimmed to shape.

There are a few other solitary herbs which may appear to have only little culinary value, yet all the same come into their own on occasions and so are well worth growing. These are discussed more fully later.

2 Herb gardens

Most people imagine a herb garden as a place apart, a special plot set aside for special plants, although not necessarily specially designed. A herb patch is often to be found at the edge of a vegetable patch, down the end of a path, in some odd corner – a horticultural afterthought. Yet no matter how small, a herb garden can be both attractive and interesting.

However, before radically changing an existing garden to accommodate a special herb plot, it is as well to realise that all herbs are basically garden plants. They can be scattered about the garden or grown at different sites, just like any other garden plant. Annuals can go in annual borders or among bedding plants, just as they can be sown in rows among the other vegetables in the kitchen garden. Perennials can go in the herbaceous border; indeed some are grown more for their appearance than for their flavour by some gardeners. The shrubby herbs can be planted in shrub borders or in mixed borders. Some of the sprawling kinds can be introduced into the patio or on to any paved area, where they will revel in the warmth of the sun held by the stones. Some can be grown in tubs and other kinds of containers.

So much depends upon how important a role the herbs are to play. Obviously, if herbs are used daily it is essential to maintain a constant and adequate supply. The greater the variety of herbs at one's disposal, the less one is likely to depend upon one particular herb, and so it might be helpful to make changes with this in mind. For instance, where chervil and fennel are grown these can be used in place of parsley for certain dishes. They can also be mixed with it. If it is decided to grow the herbs among the other garden plants, it might be necessary to grow those herbs which are most frequently gathered, parsley and chives for instance, in some other place – as a vegetable row, or as a path edging, for example.

Culinary herbs can be planted in the same bed or border as the cosmetic or fragrant herbs, and where a special herb garden is being designed this has great advantages. One kind of plant can be used to separate a group of another kind.

For convenience, it is useful to site a herb

Herb gardens range from tiny corner plots to magnificent formal gardens laid out amid stately paths and set off by elaborately trimmed shrubbery (right).

The massed spikes of flowering thyme and the pretty tufted heads of chive add a delightful splash of colour to an informally arranged herb border (left).

plot near the house although, of course, this is not essential. However, where fresh herbs are preferred to dried ones, even in winter, it is helpful to have them near at hand. Also, a bed near a house is often more protected than one in the open.

A patch of earth as small as 1m (3ft) square should prove adequate for a small family. It is also important in this case to realise that a great many herbs can be grown in containers, which means that the small plot can be extended in an attractive manner. Before deciding which plants to grow in the open soil, it is worth learning which will grow well in containers. There are more details in chapter 5, 'Herbs in limited spaces', page 348. Ideally, the thing to do would be to design a little bed near the house and among paving, so that this could

be complemented and supplemented by, for instance, a pair of clipped bays placed one on each side of the doorway, rosemary trained against the house wall, thyme at the very edge of the bed and encouraged to sprawl over the paving, and winter savory in wide, low tubs or giant saucers placed on the paving.

As you would expect, the taller a plant grows the more space it will require at ground level, usually because its lower leaves are so large. This means that tall plants such as angelica are really not suitable for a very small plot. On the other hand, fennel, which is also tall although not so bulky, can be kept fairly well under control simply by gathering it often and keeping the tips of the shoots from flowering.

The few herbs which grow in a small plot

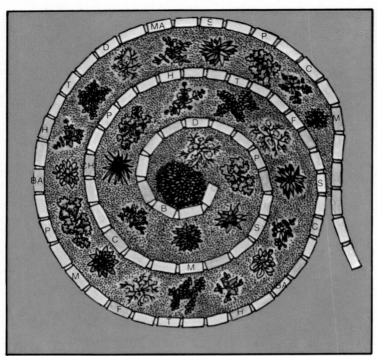

A corner of a small garden can be transformed into a compact and colourful herb area by building a snail garden. From a short distance away it will resemble a small island set off by the surrounding lawn. Here, the following herbs have been grown:

B – bay
BA – basil
C – chervil
CH – chives
D – dill
F –fennel
H – hyssop
M – mint
MA – marjoram
P – parsley
S – sorrel
T – thyme

are likely to be cut often, which is a good thing, for this means that the plants remain neat and compact. This is another reason for increasing the variety of plants grown rather than to grow several of only one kind. These several may not all be cut often enough.

Incidentally, it should be borne in mind that while annual kinds, or those treated as annuals, can be cut as soon as the leaves are large enough, it may take perennials and shrubs two or three years to become established. These should not be cut heavily during the first year; indeed it is best to leave them alone during this time. Later, when at least some of them are large enough to be divided, it is best to lift only one and to leave the other one or two as a supply. When the divided plant is ready for cutting, the other can be lifted and discarded or divided as the case may be.

Some herbs are inclined to dominate the rest, usually because they have invasive roots. Mint is an example. Where a very small herb plot is being planned, it is best to grow the mint separately in a deep container, preferably in shade or partial shade. If this cannot be done, the roots should be isolated in some way.

Fortunately, herbs lend themselves to both formal and informal planting and to both modern and traditional designs of beds and borders. There are some charming traditional patterns which fit well into small modern gardens. For instance, a square or rectangular plot will take a snail-shell herb garden. The 'snail' is made by making a paved path which goes round inside the rectangle in ever decreasing circles until the centre is reached. The soil on each side of the continuous curving path is planted with herbs.

Snail gardens can be very attractive, but success depends upon what herbs are grown and how they are planted. If the plants are very tall and straggly the effect is

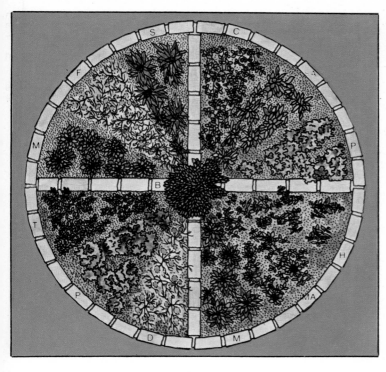

A cartwheel shape is another compact and useful way to grow herbs. Here, a number of different varieties radiate out from an imposing bay tree at the 'hub' of the garden.

B – bay
C – chervil
D – dill
F – fennel
H – hyssop
MA – marjoram
M – mint
P – parsley
SA — sage
S — sorrel
T — thyme

lost. Tall plants can be grown in the corners of the rectangle left by the curving path. These can be in groups either of one kind or mixed. The latter will probably be more attractive, but much will depend upon the area available. The smallest and most compact herbs should be planted or sown close to the edge of the paving so that they follow the lines of the curve. The slightly taller ones can go behind these. It is best to work from the shortest plants at the very beginning of the snail path, gradually going upwards, until the centre is reached.

. Another favourite is the cartwheel pattern, in which a circular plot is divided into wedge-shaped sections radiating out from a central ring, thus imitating the spokes and hub of a wheel. Usually, a different kind of herb is planted in each section, although the imaginative gardener may devise attractive bedding schemes, with contrasting colours and textures mingling together in alternate beds with the plain greens be-

tween them. Alternatively, beds can be reserved for the annual kinds, such as parsley and chervil, or for those herbs which are constantly clipped, such as chives.

If the area is large enough the sections should be divided by narrow paths, otherwise they are divided by a band of low-growing herbs, possibly and preferably all of one kind. Paths can be paved, simply trodden down or – and this is more in the spirit of a herb garden – be carpeted with low-growing and spreading herbs such as some varieties of thymes and pennyroyal. Camomile can also be used for this purpose, but this has to be clipped more frequently or it will not form a mat. The other two herbs should be clipped after flowering.

The garden looks better, also, if a path is made round its perimeter. This can be both prettily and usefully edged by a border of those plants which are frequently cut, such as chives, parsley, marjoram and basil, so that these are conveniently placed even in

325

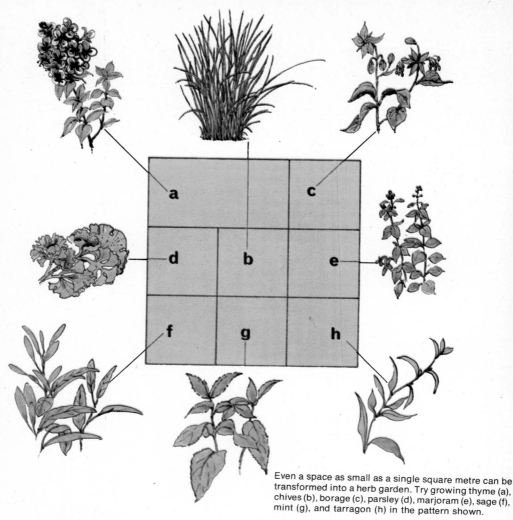

Even a space as small as a single square metre can be transformed into a herb garden. Try growing thyme (a), chives (b), borage (c), parsley (d), marjoram (e), sage (f), mint (g), and tarragon (h) in the pattern shown.

very wet weather. These in turn can be alternated with shallots which are attractively spiky and a pleasant bright green while growing. Their fading leaves at the end of summer will be well masked by the herbs. For the little space these plants occupy, the rewards are great.

Where the garden suits its setting, in an old cottage garden for instance, or as part of a garden of a house built two or three centuries ago, a knot garden made after the Elizabethan style can look delightful. In this case, each bed, carefully hedged apart from the other beds, contains just one kind of herb, is geometrically shaped and forms

part of an overall pattern. Usually, there is a gravel or shell walk between each bed.

Most of the evergreen herbs stand clipping; indeed, this is often the only means of keeping some in good condition. Where culinary herbs and others are grown in the same garden, dwarf lavenders can be used as hedging. Hyssop is also attractive.

Some herbs make good edgings to beds and borders of other kinds of plants, even rows of vegetables. The side of a vegetable plot, with the vegetable rows at right angles to it, will be improved in appearance as well as made more productive if it is planted with a variety of herbs. Obviously, the tallest kinds will have to be thoughtfully placed. Usually, these are best at the ends of the border. A useful border can be made to follow the edge of any garden path. Herbs fill the area both attractively and economically and it is always helpful to have herbs growing where they can be easily reached and cut in wet weather and in winter. Obviously, the shortest, most compact plants are best for this purpose. These include both perennials and annuals, for instance thymes, chives, parsley, savory, basil, marjoram, sage; the latter should be kept short. Some evergreen kinds should be included so that the border is still well defined and attractive in winter.

In a border, the herbs are planted in much the same way as other plants in a herbaceous border. However, it is wise to site the most used in a convenient place. If you have to cross a wide border to reach a

Herbs can be raised in rampant borders (right) or in compact bunches (below) against a warming wall.

Keep lavender neatly shaped (right) by trimming the flowers and rapidly growing young shoots.

A luxuriant bay (left) surrounded by an informal arrangement of rosemary, sage, hyssop and thyme can create a wild but natural look in a suitably large garden.

plant, add a few paving stones to step on.

It is not essential that a wide herb border, as opposed to an edging border, be straight. 'Island' beds can also be used for herbs. In this case, the very tallest plants should go to the centre. In a 'backed' border they should be planted at the back. If plants are too strictly zoned into tall, medium and short, the border can look dull. A better effect is gained if some of the plants of medium height are placed in front.

Fortunately, very few herbs need staking. Dill is an exception. Fairly tall twiggy sticks – pea-sticks – are best for dill. These should be pushed into the ground round the plants while they are young so that they can grow against and through the twigs. They will then be held quite fast and the supports will be hidden. Tall fennel and angelica are usually sturdy enough to stand unaided, but sweet cicely sometimes needs support. Much depends upon the frequency and strength of the prevailing wind.

When planning a mixed border, put the evergreens in place first, leaving plenty of space around them. Most of these are fairly

short, which means that they will not smother any of the annual kinds planted between them. If there seems danger of this happening, keep the evergreens frequently clipped. Clippings can always be dried.

Most herbs prefer a well drained soil. This does not need to be specially rich, but it should be light. Heavy soil has an effect upon the pungency of plants. If a plant appears not to be doing as well as it should, it can always be given plant food in a soluble form and this should act as a tonic. Where soil is heavy it can be made lighter by adding humus, peat and some sand.

Most herbs originate in hot, sunny countries, but not all grow best in full sun. Some prefer shade or partial shade, at least in summer. Mint will grow best where the soil is slightly moist and there is some shade. In summer, both chervil and parsley will grow lusher in shade, although chervil will germinate quickly in a sunny warm spot early in the year.

Where the border is sited in a sunny place, shade can often be provided, at least for part of the day, by some taller plant.

Where an island bed is made, or where a border runs from east to west, there is always a shady or shadier side.

A good way to use a herb border is as a link between the utility and decorative sections of a garden. Where the existing soil is neither light nor warm, there is an advantage in making a raised border or a bank. A raised border need be no more than one brick high, or it can be stepped so that one level, wide enough for short herbs, is one brick high, with another level two bricks high above. The bed can be made higher than this if required. This method is particularly effective if you wish to hide the utility garden from the decorative part, because the raised bed holding tall plants higher from the ground acts as a screen in summer. In winter, although the tall plants are cut down, the raised bed provides protection for the vegetable area.

A long mound does not entail so much preliminary labour, and it can be gradually raised as the years go by. Annual mulching with peat, well-rotted manure and compost will keep the plants in good health as the mound increases in height. The soil will certainly be well drained. Many of the herbs will help to bind the banked soil and hold it in place.

This formal herb garden demonstrates the elaborate layout and colour that can be achieved in a well-planned garden.

329

3 Colour in the herb garden

Many culinary herbs are extremely handsome, with foliage ranging through many hues of green as well as grey, silver, bronze and purple. Some have leaves which are variegated in yellow, cream or white, and some have multi-coloured variegation. When these plants flower, they add colour and beauty to the garden. Some have lacy umbels of white; others have thick yellow umbrella-like flowers borne aloft on tall stems. There are leafy stems studded with lipped flowers of rose red and carmine. There are fascinating whorls, tufts and spikes of these same colours as well as blue, violet and soft mauves.

All this means that a herb garden can be decorative, an important point where the main garden is small and there are no far corners in which the less flamboyant plants can be hidden away. However, the herb garden can be made even more colourful, for apart from those herbs used mainly for their leaves, there are a few others whose flowers and seeds are also edible. These plants are colourful and pretty and because they are annuals are easily grown. They are borage, pot marigold, *Papaver somniferum*, the dusky mauve, grey-leaved poppy whose seeds are used to garnish bread, and the bright nasturtium. Marigolds and nasturtiums grow well in containers, so where there is not much space in the actual herb bed or border, these can often be grown in raised pots of some kind and placed near the other herbs.

To these herbs roses can always be added, not simply as the odd isolated bush, but also as a hedge or screen.

If potpourri plants are to be included, then the herb plot can be as colourful as any herbaceous border at certain times of the year. Lavender makes a wonderful mass of colour and the flowers last for many weeks. The evergreen, or rather ever-grey, plants remain decorative throughout the year, becoming smudged with the flower colour a few weeks before the flowers actually open and continuing to be pretty in a quiet way as they fade.

Apart from its self colour, lavender (*Lavandula officinalis*) varies. There are some varieties with deep violet flowers, *Lavandula* 'Munstead Dwarf', a popular example that grows about 45cm (18in) tall. There is a white dwarf variety, and a soft and pretty pink-flowered variety. If these are not to be found in a local nurseryman's list or at a garden centre, they are sometimes offered by mail-order specialists. It is always well worth keeping an eye open for them, especially for those which seem to vary even a little more from the usual.

Fortunately, lavender, like most of the other shrubby herbs, is easily propagated by cuttings. Take unflowered shoots from the old wood of a plant. Pull each shoot downwards so that it comes away with a little tail of the skin of the wood. This is known as a 'heel'. It is usual when taking cuttings to trim the heel, but lavender cuttings should be handled as little as possible, so do not trim the heel in this case. Prepare a little good soil in a frame or in some protected place in the open garden; a cloche can be used if necessary. Top the soil with a little clean horticultural sand, water it and make a little hole to take about one-third the length of each cutting. Put them 5–7cm (2–3in) apart, and firm the cuttings in well by treading the soil against them. Water the cuttings once more and leave them to root.

The cuttings should be taken in late summer or autumn. If they are taken in summer, they should go into frames or under cloches. The older the wood from which the shoots are taken, the colder should the cuttings be grown. So it follows that if the cuttings are not taken until the autumn, they have been taken from older wood, and in this case they are best taken and inserted into the open ground in some

A banked herb border can be used as a dividing wall to separate one section of a garden from another.

sheltered place.

It is possible to raise some types of lavender from seed but not all seedsmen carry stocks.

Like lavender, hyssop, *Hyssopus officinalis*, has also given rise to varieties. The species has lipped flowers of a fine rich violet blue. The varieties have white, pink and purple blooms.

This plant, but not the varieties, can be raised from seed. It and the varieties can also be propagated by cuttings, which should be taken in April or May and placed outdoors in some shady spot. The plants can also be divided in spring or in autumn.

One of the mints whose leaves are used in the preparation of potpourris – although also delicious in salads, they are infrequently used this way – is a particularly attractive variegated plant, *Mentha rotundifolia variegata*. The broad, slightly hairy leaves are splashed with creamy-white and when the shoots are young there may be no trace of green on them at all. Sometimes these shoots are a beautiful, delicate tint of magenta.

A hardy geranium or crane's-bill, *Geranium macrorrhizum*, has strongly scented roots and leaves, both of which are used. Apart from this it is a fine garden plant and a splendid ground cover. Its large, attractively shaped leaves soon cover a wide area if required and they turn beautiful colours as autumn approaches. The flowers are borne well above the leaves and are a dusky rose colour.

This plant is a perennial and is very easily propagated by division.

Bergamot, *Monarda didyma,* already referred to as being the herb from which Oswego tea is prepared, has attractive flowers which grow in whorls and are a pleasant dusky rose hue. There are now many cultivars, varieties of this plant whose flowers are in other colours ranging from soft pink to purple – useful if one is planning a full range of colours in a herb border.

For the full impact of colour, it is important to group and site the plants carefully. For instance, both the green-leaved and the

The rose pink colours of flowering bergamot can be used to lend a splash of colour to a herb border.

handsome bronze-leaved varieties of fennel grow between 120–180cm (4–6ft) tall, so it follows that they will look best at the back of a border. Usually, when an ordinary herbaceous border is being made, the gardener is recommended to plant in groups of three so that they make a greater impact, but it is not necessary to follow this rule – nor might

it be practical – when planning a herb plot or garden. Fennel is a very well furnished plant and after the first year, soil and other conditions being suitable, it will grow rapidly and fill a space some 60cm (2ft) square. However, fennel is not winter-hardy in most northern regions and so is treated as an annual.

As it grows taller and comes into flower, the base of the plant becomes slightly bare as the first leaves fade. For this reason it is best to plant some dense-growing plant, possibly an evergreen, in front of it. One of the best plants for this purpose is sage. The grey-leaved common sage is quite handsome, but handsomer by far is the so-called red or purple sage. The new shoots are a rich red-purple. The leaves can be used for cooking in exactly the same way as the common sage.

Another charming umbellifer, though much shorter, about 35–45cm (14–18in), is the pretty coriander. Its flowers, which grow in loose, lacy umbels, are soft lavender-mauve. It needs to be grown near the front of the border, and looks good flanked by the variegated 'silver' thymes. These come into flower a little earlier than the coriander, but the flower heads are retained, misty-mauve, for some time.

Thymes make lovely mats of colour and since all are pungent and can be used, one could supplement the common thyme with others. These are discussed more fully in the following chapters.

It is well worth studying seed catalogues in the hopes of finding unusual herbs. Quite recently the seedsmen introduced a handsome form of basil with dark bronze leaves which are just as pungent as the green. Known as 'Dark Opal', it brings a rare colour to the border – imagine leaves the colour of copper beech.

It is best to raise the plants in boxes and to plant them out at the beginning of summer. They need careful watching over for the first two weeks or so, and watering. Beware of slugs, which seem to like this variety above all others.

To see this plant at its best, grow it next to or near the golden-leaved marjoram. This is an ideal plant to grow right at the edge of a bed or border if it is flanked by a paved path, because the stems will trail over it and soften the edges attractively. The plant is best increased by division in spring or autumn.

The apple-green balm also sports a variegated form whose leaves are blotched with a bright yellow. The colours and their variegation are stronger when the shoots are young, and at this time they are very

Bronze fennel is a variety with burnished foliage and makes an excellent foil to the predominant green of a herb garden.

vivid indeed. Like the green form, this plant is invasive and should be kept under control. The best way of doing this is to lift the entire plant when it has occupied its given space, then to chop off a good portion from the whole mass, using a spade. Enrich the soil a little from which the plant was taken and replant the piece. Do this in spring or autumn.

Chives have pretty little rosy-purple pompom flowers borne on slim stems which take the flowers above the leaves. The flowers can be used in salads. The only drawback to allowing the plants to bloom is that once this happens they begin to die down. If they do not flower, the 'grass'

continues to grow. For this reason, flower buds are usually picked off. If the flowers are wanted for colour, it is best to grow plenty of plants and to remove the flowers from some and not others.

The tall, graceful poppy, *Papaver somniferum*, mentioned earlier, has beautiful glaucous leaves, stems, buds and seed capsules and grows to 70–85cm (2½–3ft). Altogether it is a very handsome plant. As one would expect, the foliage and the rest harmonise delightfully with the dusky mauve, sometimes dusky pink, flowers. Fortunately, they also harmonise beautifully with many herbs, especially those with silver, grey or purple in their foliage.

This poppy is easily grown from seed. It will also seed itself. There are 20,000 to 30,000 seeds in each capsule. It is these rich oily seeds which are used in cooking, in bread, confectionery and some desserts. The plants grow best if they are given plenty of space and it is well worth while thinning out seedlings to leave roughly a space from 30–50cm (1–2ft) square for each plant. One plant treated this way will give a better show and very much larger flowers than a mass of inferior plants. This goes for most annuals, incidentally.

The quality of the seeds of the species and the beautiful cultivars seems not to differ and can be used in just the same way. There are lovely double-flowered varieties which are listed in the seed catalogues as 'Peony' or 'Carnation-flowered'. They vary a little in colour from the species, having a slightly wider range. They will also seed themselves, but if they are allowed to do this, after a time they will revert to the species and all will be single-flowered.

Sow the seed of the species or the varieties in September if you want the plants to bloom early, i.e. late spring the following year. Sow the seed in early spring for summer flowering. Like most hardy annuals, this poppy's season is short and so, to ensure a long period of bloom, it is best to make the two sowings. The seed is viable and so long as the opened packet is not kept in an airtight container – although it should be kept out of the way of mice – the seed bought for autumn sowing should keep for the spring and *vice versa*.

Try grouping this poppy next to bronze-leaved fennel with purple and grey sage before it. Try it behind the soft feathery foliage of *Artemisia abrotanum*, southernwood or lad's love. Mild-climate gardeners who have a rosemary hedge, can sow a row of these poppies parallel with it, but should keep a good distance between them because the lush poppies soon smother plants which are too close to them.

A cluster of tall, stately poppies (left) is a colourful and unusual addition to a herb garden. The seeds of this plant are delicious when baked in confectionery. Silvery cotton lavender (right) erupts into brilliant yellow flower balls. Ranked growths of lavender and looming fennel (below) form a wall of contrasting colours.

For those who enjoy a vivid display of floral colour, pot marigolds, poppies and nasturtiums – simple, bright annuals – can be used here and there among the more permanent plants. Alternatively they can be sown in rows in an edging mixture.

Special effects can be achieved by allowing herbs to play special roles. Some herbs are ideal for hedges and often one needs only a low boundary hedge to separate one part of a garden from another – perhaps to limit the area in which herbs are cultivated. Lavender, rosemary (where hardy) and santolina are the best but in climates which are colder germander, *Teucrium chamaedrys*, is a safer choice if the hedge need not be too tall. Germander, which takes well to clipping, will grow about 30cm (12in) high.

Santolina chamaecyparissus, lavender cot-

335

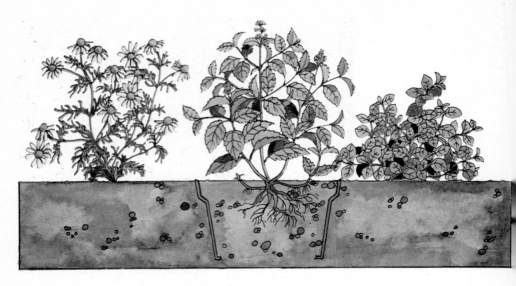

tons, used as a potpourri component, is an attractive, light silver plant which looks well in association with stone. It softens the edge of a paved area particularly prettily. All santolina hedges as well as those of other plants should be clipped back immediately after flowering to keep them compact. Some gardeners do not allow them to flower but aim to keep them as silver as possible all the time. When they bloom, the flowers are yellow.

The common rosemary's erect form, already described, is the best hedging variety, but any rosemary except the sprawling type will do for this purpose. This, incidentally, is a fine plant for seaside gardens but it cannot safely be recommended for most northern gardens because it is not reliably winter hardy in a colder climate.

Earlier reference was made to the invasive nature of mints and balm. These must be thinned out rigorously or planted in separate bottomless containers if they are grown with other plants to prevent the roots wandering over the soil surface. On the other hand, this particular invasiveness can be·used to advantage, for these plants will cover a bank and hold the soil in place. If the plain green forms are used they will be neat rather than decorative, but there

Bottomless pots (above) can be used in the garden to restrain the growth of mint plants. They keep the root mass within a closely confined space and stop it from spreading rampantly.The flowers of camomile (below) form attractive daisy-like heads. When dried they are used to make an extremely refreshing tea.

Spearmint (right) has pointed spearhead-like leaves and purplish flowers that appear in autumn. This is the best known variety of all the mints and is widely used in sauces.

Camomile lawns (below right) are soft and fragrant. They are formed by keeping the creeping stems of the plant cut short but allowing them to spread out and form a living carpet.

are sufficient varieties of these plants which are variegated or coloured in some way to make a covered bank quite interesting. The bergamot mint, *Mentha citrata*, becomes beautifully coloured at the end of summer before it dies down and, of course, a certain amount of colour will be provided by the mint's flowers.

Some mints, the little pennyroyal in particular, can be used to carpet the ground, like the creeping thymes. These plants are tough enough to take a certain amount of walking upon. Camomile also can be used as a lawn, just as it can be used to carpet a path. It has to be clipped or mown occasionally, unlike the mint or thyme. It can also be mixed with grass, in which case it makes a really hardy lawn.

Finally, one should not forget the roses. If potpourri is to be made, then some of the highly scented old-fashioned varieties and

species are essential. Further, these are culinary plants, once highly regarded as a source of health-giving salads, or for special jams and preserves and wines and vinegars. This being the case, they will not look out of place in a herb garden where there is adequate room to display them. Indeed, they make a delightful backing for a non-island

Common thyme (left) grows to form a low bush-like shape. It spreads rapidly and, when flowering, becomes covered in a mass of strong scented tiny purple petals.

A border pf Pink Parfait roses and lanky growing lavender (right) forms a beautiful wall of colour when in flower. This particular variety of rose has a deliciously fragrant scent.

A highly productive and colourful herb garden (below) can be established even in a limited space, provided it is a sunny, well-drained location.

border. Roses also look well combined with lavender, and, for a vivid effect, dwarf varieties can be grown alongside them.

How they are grown will depend upon what space is available. Roses can be grown among other plants, but they should not be so crowded that they are smothered. It should be a simple matter to ensure that low plants, such as thyme, grow at their feet rather than tall kinds, such as fennel. However, there are some roses which can be grown as a formal hedge, such as the species *Rosa eglanteria,* the sweet briar. This is an ideal herb garden rose because it has fragrant foliage. It will grow to 180cm (72in) unless trimmed each spring so that it remains compact and under control. The clippings, which are scented, of course, can be dried and used in potpourri.

Do not expect the same long period of flowering from species and varieties of old-fashioned roses generally as from the modern varieties. Most bloom only once, in early summer. Some are followed by decorative fruits, some of which are worth preserving as syrups or as jam; some can be dried and the largest can be cooked like any other fruit in pies.

339

4 Herbs from seed

Some herbs must be grown from seed. Others can be but it might not prove practical to do so. Annuals and biennials, many of which are sown where they are to mature, grow quickly and are soon ready for cutting, but perennials take much longer. It may be as long as three years from the time that the seed was sown to the time that the plants have made sufficient growth to be cut. This being the case, it is often best to begin with a selection of mature plants. Most nurserymen sell a basic collection and there are also specialist herb growers. Obviously, the larger the plants, the better. If these are canister-grown, they can be bought and planted at any time of the year when the soil is suitable. Planting should not be carried out when the soil is frozen. Drought is not a great drawback. Water the plants well in the canister an hour or so before planting, and again when they have been taken out of the canister and planted in the ground. Keep an eye on them and keep the soil round them moist.

Seed is so cheap that it may be thought that this is an expensive way of stocking the garden, but it could well prove to be more economical in the long run. A compromise can be reached which may be helpful for

Annual herbs such as chervil, dill, borage, and summer savory (left) are quick-growing and can be cut for use within weeks of being planted. Where herbs are frequently used, grow them in convenient rows (right).

those who budget carefully. Just one mature plant of each herb can be bought as a beginning. While this is becoming established and ready for cutting, more of the same kind can be raised from seed gradually filling the border as they come along.

Where a large quantity of certain herbs is to be used, it is often more convenient to grow them in rows like vegetables. Most herbs treated this way are annuals, with some biennials such as chervil, basil, summer savory, sweet marjoram, parsley, shallots and garlic. Plants grown for spices – anise, caraway, coriander, cumin and dill – can also be raised this way.

Some of these, chervil for example, should be sown where they are to mature, simply because they will not transplant well. Most of the others are best sown in boxes or in short nursery rows and lifted and transplanted when they are large enough to handle. This method is usually safer, in as much as the young plants, individually spaced, are not so likely to be eaten by insect pests or slugs; nor are they so

likely to be influenced by bad weather or by drought. Also, germination is usually better when planted this way.

In countries where there is a short season, there is much to be gained by sowing the more tender kinds, and those which will transplant, indoors under fluorescent lights or in a sunny window in the early part of the year. The seedlings germinate very quickly and grow apace. As soon as these are large enough to handle they can be 'pricked off', a term which means lifted, separated and transplanted – either spaced out about 5cm

(2in) in boxes, or, better still, into small individual pots. Pot plants are best because they suffer little check when they are transplanted and they are not so liable to become starved while they are awaiting planting outdoors. Usually these little plants are kept indoors until the weather is good. They are then introduced to it slowly, a process known as 'hardening off', by being stood outdoors on good days and brought in at night, or by being transferred to a garden frame or placed under a cloche. When all fear of frost is gone, by which time

Prick out chervil seedlings
to a distance of 30cm (12in)

30 cm
(12in)

they should be well acclimatised to out-doors, they can be planted in their perma-nent places – permanent, that is, for that year.

Plants usually treated this way include summer savory, sweet marjoram, and basil, both green and ornamental.

It is also possible to steal a march on time and to raise a few kinds of herbs from seed sown in pots and grown on a sunny win-dowsill or in a greenhouse. These are cut while they are quite young, the plants then being considered expendable. Details are given in chapter 6.

Some seed, especially from certain plants of the umbelliferae, is not long-lived. If a packet has been stored unopened for some months under the wrong conditions, the seed might never germinate. Indeed, once a herb garden has been established, it is a good plan to allow just a few kinds, those with the least viable seeds, to seed them-selves. These are chervil, parsley and angelica.

On the other hand, chervil and parsley are often sown in succession so that a con-tinuous supply is available, which means that one cannot wait for the self-sown plants alone. Self-sown chervil is ready only in early spring. Again, a compromise works best; let some plants seed themselves but sow more from time to time.

Parsley is notoriously slow in its germi-nation, sometimes taking as long as six weeks. Although it is usually sown where it ·is to mature and then thinned out to give the plants adequate space, it is often quicker and more convenient to sow the seed in boxes and to transplant from these.

When seed has to be sown in straight rows it is simple to draw a shallow drill using a garden line as a guide. Generally speaking, a drill should be as deep as twice the depth of the seeds that go in it. Sow the seed as thinly as possible. If the seeds are to be sown in spaces among existing plants, it helps to define the area in which the plants are to grow. Press a large upturned flower pot on to the raked soil. Sow the seeds thinly in the circular drill thus made. Always cover the drill with soil and always tread the soil down lightly to prevent it and the seeds from being blown away by the wind or washed out by the rain.

Even when you sow thinly it will still be necessary to thin out the seedlings to give each little plant its own living space. It is best to make two or three thinnings rather

Prick out young herbs (left) when they are large enough to handle, being careful to grasp them by the stem and not the delicate leaves.

Summer savory (right) is a small bushy annual somewhat like a long-leaved form of thyme.

Miniature herb gardens can be created in trays (below) if the soil is deep enough to protect the roots.

343

The outer flowers of calendula or pot marigold (left) and not the leaves are used in cooking. Of the two varieties of tarragon, the French (above) has the best flavour. It grows to a spindly mature height of 1 metre (2–3ft).

than to take away the plants in one go. Should disaster strike, there will still be some plants to carry on. Thin out after a shower, or after watering the rows an hour or so beforehand.

Remember, it is not always possible to buy seeds of all herbs. Many plants are propagated by cuttings or by division. Here is a list of the most common herbs which can be raised from seed. Plants grown for their seeds (spices) are also included.

Angelica archangelica, **angelica** Sow packeted seed in March, in deep moist soil in a shady place. Alternatively – and this is likely to be more successful – sow seed when ripe, as soon as it is taken from the plant, in August or September.

Allium schoenoprasum, **chives** Sow seed in boxes in March or April; prick off and transplant outdoors in May. Alternatively, sow thinly in pots and begin cutting the 'grass' when seedlings are large enough.

Anthemis nobilis, **camomile** Sow seed outdoors in shallow drills in April where the plants are to flower.

Anthriscus cerefolium, **chervil** Sow at intervals from February to October for succession in boxes, under cloches, in frames or in the open ground according to the time of the year. Crop matures in 6–8 weeks.

Artemisia dracunculus, **tarragon** Seed can be sown in spring but it is much more usual – and faster – to buy plants.

Borago officinalis, **borage** Sow seed where the plants are to flower, in March for summer flowers, in September for May flowers.

Calendula officinalis, **pot marigold** Sow seeds where the plants are to flower in March or April.

Carum carvi, **caraway** Best sown as soon as ripe in the autumn. Autumn-sown plants flower the following summer. Plants from packeted seed sown in spring do not flower until the summer of the following year.

Coriandrum sativum, **coriander** Sow seeds in shallow drills, 0.5cm (¼in) deep, 30cm (12in) apart in April in rich, light soil where the plants are to flower.

Cuminum cyminum, **cumin** Sow seeds in shallow drills, in May, where the plants are to flower.

Foeniculum vulgare, **fennel** Sow outdoors in shallow drills in March, transplant when the seedlings are large enough to handle in ordinary soil in a sunny position.

Melissa officinalis, **balm** Sow seeds indoors in May. Plant out when seedlings are 7–10cm (3–4in) high in ordinary soil in a warm sunny place. Or buy young plants.

Monarda didyma, **bergamot** Sow seed in boxes in March. Keep in cold frame or greenhouse. Plant outdoors in late May.

Myrrhis odorata, **sweet cicely** Sow seeds in shallow drills in ordinary soil outdoors in April or September. The latter time with newly ripened seeds gives best results.

Ocimum basilicum, **sweet basil** Sow seed indoors from March to April. Plant outdoors in late May or early June.

Ocimum minimum, **bush basil** As above.

Origanum majorana, **sweet or knotted marjoram** Sow seed indoors in March; plant outdoors in April in rich soil in a sunny place. Or buy plants.

Origanum onites, **pot marjoram** Sow seed outdoors in March or April in ordinary soil in a sunny position.

Petroselinum crispum, **parsley** Sow in February under cloches or indoors in boxes for early crop, outdoors in shallow drills. Sow in April or May for summer crop, in July to August for late autumn crop, in ordinary but non-acid soil in a sunny position.

Peucedanum graveolens, **dill** Sow in shallow drills, in rich, ordinary soil, in a sunny, open position in spring where the plants are to grow and flower.

Pimpinella anisum, **anise** Sow seeds in shallow drills in well drained, ordinary soil, in spring where the plants are to flower.

Salvia officinalis, **sage** Sow seed indoors in March in boxes. Plant outdoors in May or June in rich but light ordinary soil in a sunny position.

Sanguisorba minor, **salad burnet** Sow seed in boxes indoors in February to March; plant outdoors in April or May in light but moist ordinary soil in sun or light shade.

Satureia hortensis, **summer savory** Sow seed in shallow drills in ordinary soil in a sunny place in April where the plants are to

Borage is a hardy annual that thrives even in poor soil. Its leaves are used fresh to make infusions.

flower. Alternatively, sow indoors in boxes and transplant later.

Once the perennial herbs are well grown, most can be divided should you wish to increase their numbers. Chives grow better if, once they are three years old, they are lifted and divided each spring. Do this when the plants show above ground again. Some of the surplus divisions can be potted for forcing the following spring.

Shallots and garlic are grown from small bulbs known as 'seed', which in fact they

The little golden bulbs of shallots (right) have a milder flavour than onions and are widely used for pickling. Parsley and chervil (below) can be grown in pots along a sunny window ledge. As these are frequently used herbs, growing several pots at once is a good idea.

are not. One small clove of garlic will grow into a tight cluster of several large bulbs. Once you have harvested a good crop of garlic you can save your own seed. Garlic 'seed' is usually bought from the seed merchant, but that sold for cooking can also be used. So can any cloves which begin sprouting in the kitchen, even though it may not seem the correct season for this.

Plant garlic 5cm (2in) deep and 10–14cm (4–6in) apart any time from late winter to early summer. Lift the bulbs when the tall green tops have faded. First spread them out on the ground to let them dry in the air a

Salad burnet (above) is a perennial whose leaves have a delightful cucumber flavour. White-flowered sweet cicely and woolly-leaved apple mint (below right) are tall plants that look attractive growing at the back of a herb border.

weather is moist, spread them out under a cloche or in some dry airy place. When the skins rustle and the bulbs are dry, they can be made into ropes or hung in net bags.

Bulbs can be set aside for seed. If there are any very small bulbs, too small for pickling or cooking, set these aside and plant them in early winter. They will provide good-sized fresh shallots for the following summer.

Formerly, the traditional method was to plant shallots on the shortest day and to harvest them on the longest. Certainly they are very hardy and with garlic are among the first which can be planted in a vegetable patch. However, this is not a rule to be strictly observed. Bulbs can be planted, so long as they are obtainable, until late May or early June. Usually, sound bulbs will last from one season to another.

Some gardeners save some of the newly lifted garlic bulbs and plant the bulbs in autumn, for early crops the following year.

little, and then hang them to finish drying in a cool, dry place, by their fading tops. Later they can be made into ropes or simply stored in net bags.

Shallots should be planted 14cm (6in) apart but not deeply. Some people simply push the bulb into the soil, but the trouble with this method is that because the bulb is not firmly anchored it is moved out of position during the night by foraging earth worms. It is best to make a small depression in the soil with a trowel and bury the bulb up to its 'nose' in the earth. Once it begins to grow roots it will pull itself upwards. Wait until all the leaves die right down before lifting the bulbs for storing, unless, of course, using them fresh, which can be done throughout the summer. The green tops can be used like chives or cooked in soups.

To harvest the shallots, first lift the clutch of bulbs with a fork and so allow any remaining roots to dry in the air. Spread them out in the sun for a while. If the

347

5 Herbs in limited spaces

Where open garden space is limited, it is possible to grow herbs on patios and in containers of all kinds. These need not look strictly utilitarian. Properly planned and grown in good soil, they can be quite attractive, and since many of the best plants for containers are also evergreen these captive gardens can be of interest, and use, the year round.

The possibility of standing a bay tree or two by the door has already been mentioned; indeed, these are ideal plants. If there is room, the bay trees can be accompanied by shrubs such as rosemary, winter savory, sage, thyme and perennial marjoram, either planted in their own contain-

ers or growing in company. It is important, of course, to begin with good plants if it is hoped to cut herb snippets from them soon after planting. It is also important to realise that the containers should be emptied from time to time, say every two or three years, and replanted. Usually, the existing plants can be divided. Parts not used can be potted and used while the larger ones are recovering and growing. In cold climates, the bays must be tubbed so they can be moved inside in winter.

It is easy to become over-romantic about growing herbs and to forget that one is likely to take all the leaves from one plant, say parsley or chives, for just one dish. It

Annual and perennial herbs may be raised in dense clusters in window boxes (right) provided only that the soil is deep enough to retain moisture and keep the roots from becoming parched in the hot sun.

Where climates are not suitable for herbs to be grown outdoors all year round, they can be raised in containers and tubs (left) that are moved indoors or to more sheltered locations during cold weather. Such compact herb gardens are also ideal for limited spaces. Here, chives, parsley, thyme, basil and marjoram are being grown with a selection of colourful lilies.

follows that unless there are more plants to take the shorn one's place, the cook will have to wait a very long time for her next supply. For this reason, it is important to think in terms of growing more than one plant of most herbs and, so far as herbs raised from seed are concerned, to think of growing several pots of each kind – a container row in fact. These can be grown outside for part of the time, and for part of the year brought indoors to mature on a sunny windowsill. Among these fast-growing herbs are chives, chervil, parsley, basil and mint, the later being increased by roots, not seed. Even though these are annuals or treated as such, and are therefore short-lived, usually they can be cut quite severely and then nursed a while, that is, fed with a little liquid plant food and grown outdoors where they will begin shooting up again. Meanwhile other plants which are fuller, will be taking their place.

As always, much depends upon the space available, but it is often possible to erect some shelves on which pots can stand while they are holding seeds and seedlings. They need to be in good light when they have germinated, otherwise the plants become drawn and of little value. Herbs grow well under fluorescent lights at all stages of growth.

It is not necessary to use large pots for these successional sowings. Pots with roughly 0.5 litre (1pt) capacity will do, although, as one would expect, the larger the pot, the better a plant usually does. What is most important is that the soil should be good. It is possible to buy specially mixed soils, confusingly called composts, which have been scientifically designed for seed sowing and for transplanted seedlings – for the latter they are known as potting soils. Seedlings need a slightly different food than older plants and

349

also be fed with a soluble plant food once it is growing well.

To save time and space, it is also possible to fill a pot almost to the top with plant soil mixture and then to add a shallow top layer of seed soil mixture. This means that seed can be sown thinly in the top layer. The seedlings need not be transplanted although they are almost certain to need thinning out. Their roots will grow down into the richer soil when they need it. Usually, with the quick-growing herbs, allow three to five plants in each 7cm (5in) pot.

Do remember that contained plants of all kinds need water, and in hot, dry weather, they may need watering two or three times a day. Usually, the smaller the pot, the more likely it is to dry out quickly, even disastrously – because sometimes it is not possible to revive a plant which has become dehydrated. If the surface soil is damp to the touch, the plants' roots are probably moist enough. A pot in which the soil is too dry will give an empty ringing sound when rapped. One way to prevent too rapid loss of water is to plunge each pot up to its rim in a bed of peat which is kept constantly moist, though not sodden. Rows of pots can be plunged in troughs or boxes. As you would expect, pots in shade do not dry out so quickly as those in the sun, but not all herbs like deep shade.

Pot-grown herbs (top) can be raised in a thin layer of seed compost over a coarser potting compost. Seeds must be sparsely sown then thinned out to give the young plants space (above). Parsley and mixed herbs (right) can be grown in terracotta 'strawberry pots'.

they do not need it quite so rich, which is why there is a difference in most soil mixtures. However, those mixtures which are known as 'soilless' are sometimes suitable for all purposes, so one should read carefully the descriptions on the wrappings.

It is possible to use the same soil in the pot after the old plant has been removed, so long as this has not been diseased in any way. Where this is done, the old soil should be topped with new, and the plant should

Parsley is a herb which seems in demand and, fortunately, it is very easy to grow this plant in a variety of ways. It can, for instance, be grown in one of the specially designed terra-cotta pots known as 'strawberry' or 'crocus' pots which have pockets set all over the surface. These have one disadvantage, in that the water, poured in at the top, courses down and out through every hole, which means that the soil at the core does not get properly soaked. Once the plants grow well they block the holes and the water loss is not so great. It is best, in the early days, to stand the jar in a low bowl or deep saucer and to keep this filled with water when the weather conditions are dry. When the water no longer courses out of the holes immediately, the pot can be taken from the saucer and stood on its own, when it should be watered from the top.

Parsley also grows well in a hanging basket. Line this with moss, plant the parsley by pushing the seedlings through the moss from the outside of the basket. Begin at the bottom of the basket and cover the parsley roots as you go. Once the lower portion is planted, stand the basket in an empty buc-

Light plastic troughs (above) are ideal for raising miniature gardens in the kitchen. Even hanging baskets can be pressed into service as herb gardens. Below, a parsley basket is shown.

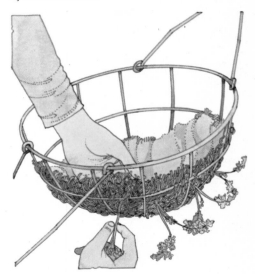

ket while the upper sides and the top area are planted. Water the plants carefully. Hang the basket in partial shade and be sure to water it regularly.

351

Individual paving stones can be lifted from a terrace or patio and the space used to raise herbs. Here, a gangly fennel plant basks in the reflected warmth of the sun-heated concrete tiles.

Constant watering, which is so essential for most contained plants, tends to leach out the soluble plant foods from the soil, and when this happens plants will become starved and spindly. For this reason it is wise to feed plants regularly with a soluble plant food.

It is possible to raise a good supply of herbs in window boxes and tubs so long as the soil is rich and is kept well watered and fed. As we have seen, some herbs prefer sun and some shade, so this should be taken into account when planning what herbs are to be grown and where. Window boxes need to be fairly deep – not less than 15cm (6in), but deeper if possible.

Where a paved patio or backyard exists, it is sometimes possible to lift an occasional paving stone and to make this area into a tiny herb patch. Where it is possible to lift more than one stone, try to make this appear planned rather than haphazard. Three linked stones might look better than three isolated ones. On the other hand, it might be best to lift a stone from each of the four corners, or in such a way that you leave a square or a diamond-shaped bed in the centre. If there is a shady corner, this could take a large and handsome angelica or a stand of feathery fennel.

One good way of making the most of a little space is to build a raised wall along one or more sides of a yard or patio, two or three bricks high. This, like the area from which a paving stone is lifted, should be filled with good soil. Thyme (or rosemary in mild climates) could be trained to cover some areas of the wall. This would look well alternated with any other good climbing plant such as roses or nasturtiums.

6 Herbs in winter

There is no doubt that fresh herbs are best and are certainly more versatile. It is possible to flavour dishes with dried herbs, and later on we discuss ways of drying, but these are not really suitable for mixing in salads or for garnishing. Part of the herb's value is its visual appeal – and fresh green leaves, no matter how finely chopped, always look better than dried flakes or powder. Of course, herb-flavoured vinegars help to impart herb flavours to salad dressings, but ideally one needs fresh green herbs the year through. Fortunately, there are some which will provide leaves in winter. Naturally, supplies depend upon the weather or the season and on the district or locality in which the garden is situated. In a mild season or in an area where severe frosts are rare, it should be possible to gather fresh herbs of some kind or other right through from the end of summer to spring when larger supplies again become available.

In some cases it is simply a matter of protecting the plant with cloches; parsley, for example, responds to this treatment. It is worth pointing out that all herbs will grow best in winter and come to less harm if they are on well-drained soil and in a sunny, well-sheltered position. In gardens where the soil and conditions vary considerably, it is worth setting aside an area for winter herbs. Parsley can also be grown in a cold frame. Some people simply lift the plants in early autumn and transplant these in the frame. As a rule this is a quicker method of supplying leaves than making a late sowing in the frame, but much depends upon the amount of space that is available.

Some other herbs can be lifted and these are usually transplanted into pots or boxes and grown on in more warmth than can be provided by a cold frame, in a greenhouse for example, or even indoors under lights. These include basil, fennel, mint and tarragon. Rosemary can be pot grown entirely, brought indoors and stood in good light, and taken out again in spring. This should be necessary only in cold regions because rosemary is hardy enough for most gardens so long as it is given a sunny and sheltered spot. It is also a good plant for the seaside.

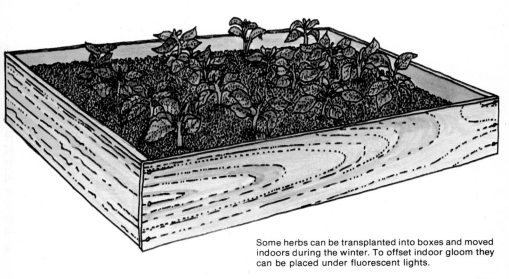

Some herbs can be transplanted into boxes and moved indoors during the winter. To offset indoor gloom they can be placed under fluorescent lights.

The soil is usually moist in autumn and as a rule plants can be lifted easily enough, but should the season be dry, water the plants well for an hour or two before lifting so that the roots come up in a moist mass. Select a flower pot which will take the root ball comfortably. If necessary, place a little good soil at the bottom of the pot. The crown of the plant should be kept above soil level, just as it was when it grew in the garden, yet there should be a space left between the soil surface and the rim of the pot to take water. Fill any space between the root ball and the sides of the pot with good potting soil. Make sure that this is firm, as firm as the soil in the root ball. Pour in a little soil to begin with and then ram it down with the fingers or a stick. Add a little more and so on until the top level is reached. Water the plant in and let it drain. Leave it out of doors in a shady place for a few days to let it become settled in the pot before bringing it indoors. Spray the foliage over with clean water from time to time but do not keep the soil wet. Let this dry out a little so that the roots are activated into working properly to search for moisture. Do not let the soil become too dry, however.

Though unusual for herbs, plastic cloches can be used to give them an early start outdoors.

When you water next time, pour in the water so that the space between soil and pot, rim is filled. The water should course through the soil.

Mint can be grown in a deep seed box. Almost fill this with soil. Spread the mint roots all over the surface, cover them with more soil and water them in well. Bring the box indoors. Incidentally, remember that mint will go on producing shoots well into early winter if you keep cutting the plants and prevent the stems running to flower.

As with all other herbs, it is more helpful to fill more than one box of mint so that boxes can be brought in in succession. If you grow mint in a pot on a sunny window-sill, keep it standing in a saucer of water. When growing mint in pots, see that one-third of the pot is filled with drainage material, e.g. shingle, pebbles, broken flower

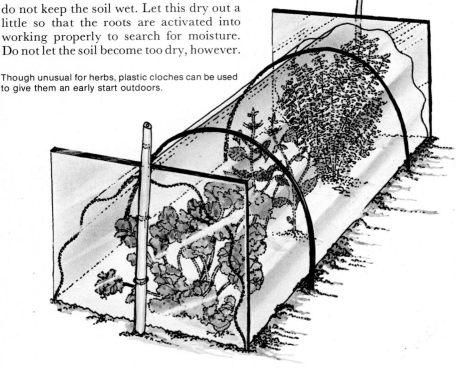

Herbs raised indoors in pots must be given an adequate growing medium. Drainage material should be laid in the bottom of the pot. Bits of pebble and broken pot fragments, coarse gravel and charcoal pieces are all suitable for this purpose. They should be topped with a good potting compost in which the plants' roots can flourish and grow.

clay pot

charcoal nuggets

pebbles

broken pot shards

crushed brick

potting compost

pots (remember, though, that clay pots are becoming rarer) and crushed brick, topped with a few nuggets of charcoal. This will ensure that the soil stays moist but does not become water-logged and sour.

If space is available, it is possible to raise a succession of batches of marjoram, basil and chives, simply by sowing a pinch in small pots, then snipping the entire growth off as soon as it is large enough to be of use. Onion seed can also be grown this way and the pungent 'grass' is excellent in winter and early spring salads.

It is important to understand that potted herbs are not house plants and will not tolerate the low light intensity indoors for long. Even a sunny windowsill does not give as well-lit a home as a place outdoors. If plants soon become drawn and spindly they are not getting enough light. Sometimes plant foods help to correct this weak growth a little. It helps to turn the container a quarter turn each day so that all parts of the plant face the light on a regular basis at some time.

It is also important that the air in which the plants are growing is unpolluted. Domestic gas and oil fumes both take their toll of many plants grown indoors and herbs are no exception.

355

7 Cosmetic and potpourri herbs

Borage (left), with its brilliant blue flowers, makes a refreshing hot or cold tea. Both its furry leaves and bright flowers are used for this purpose.

Honeysuckle (right) twines itself decoratively along walls, fences and arches. Its flowers add a delightful perfume to potpourris.

Lavender flowers (far right) are used to make scented water and lavender bags and to lend fragrance to potpourris. The flowers can also be candied.

Many herbs are grown for their sweetly scented leaves and flowers or even for their roots. From them are made potpourris, scented waters, scented sugars and other confections, tisanes or teas, conserves and syrups, shampoos and soaps, to mention only a few of the most important products. Besides adding to the spice of life, in more ways than one, these same plants add greatly to the interest, attraction and charm of a herb garden.

We have already seen that in some cases, such as with roses and lavenders, plants can be used as boundaries. Carnations and pinks can be prettily grouped among evergreen thymes in a border and since the grey-green foliage of these plants is handsome and also evergreen – although perhaps not so profuse in winter – the plants furnish a border for most of the year.

Hyssop will produce purple and pink flowers that look pretty among green parsley or feathery dill. Bergamot adds height as well as colour to a border.

Honeysuckle can be grown up poles, over archways or trained to cover a wall or a bank. Where there is space for climbers and the climate is mild, the sweetly scented jasmine, *Jasminum officinale* can be grown. The white flowers go in potpourri and they can be used for jasmine tea. The yellow winter jasmine is not scented.

In a well protected garden or in mild areas, the lemon-scented verbena, *Lippia citriodora,* deserves to be grown. This is a shrub which sometimes makes a small tree and is deciduous. The fragrance of the leaves is very strong. Another, smaller shrub, the sun rose, *Cistus ladaniferus,* which needs a sheltered place and light well drained soil, has aromatic leaves. So does the neat, shrubby St John's wort, *Hypericum patulum,* which smells of resin and tangerine when the leaves are bruised. Its handsome variety *Henryi* is also scented. Mock orange or *Philadelphus coronarius* and any of the other fragrant species of the same genera are ideal for scented gardens. If these are to be screened or divided from the rest, it is possible to make a border from scented

shrubs, including roses and lavender, thyme, rosemary and, of course, bay.

As one would expect, the roses used for potpourri and scented toilet waters or other items, should be highly scented. Usually, the red-petalled roses are most highly favoured since these usually have the sweetest perfume, sometimes with a hint of lemon in it, but this is not a hard and fast rule. Both modern and old-fashioned varieties and some species can be used. Among the most scented species are *Rosa centifolia*, the cabbage or Provence rose; *R. damascena*, the damask rose; *R. gallica officinalis*, the French rose; and all of the many varieties of moss roses.

It should be understood that these are not roses for small gardens. Often they are called 'shrub' roses because they are not pruned back hard each year like the modern hybrid teas and floribundas. In time each bush occupies an area of ground over half a metre square (several square feet). One should remember also that if the roses are to be gathered when they are at their

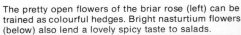

The pretty open flowers of the briar rose (left) can be trained as colourful hedges. Bright nasturtium flowers (below) also lend a lovely spicy taste to salads.

The delicate pink moss rose (above) has a ravishing scent. Though brief-flowering, it is ideal for potpourris.

best they will not add much to the colour in the garden.

The scented-leaved sweet briar, which has already been described, is sometimes sold under its synonym, *R. rubiginosa* instead of *R. eglanteria*. It has a double vari-

ety, *duplex*. Although the natural habit is to grow 150–200cm (5–7ft) tall, this rose makes a good low hedge if it is clipped back each spring just before growth begins. If later, the leafy shoots are clipped for drying, this also tends to keep the plants neat and compact.

Of course, not all of the plants used for potpourri, for liqueurs, for candying or for any of the other uses, need be grown in a herb garden proper. Some can be set about the garden as isolated plants – shrubs are often best grown this way. Some can take their place in the usual type of border or bed. Some can be used as ground covers. This term is given to plants which grow so thickly that in time they cover a large area of soil with a thick cover of foliage. This discourages the growth of weeds because it prevents their seeds from germinating freely. Ground covers also help to keep the soil moist round the base of shrubs and taller plants.

One of the best plants for this purpose is a little woodland plant, the woodruff or *Asperula odorata*. The scented dried flowers can also be used as a tea. They are sometimes mixed with China tea to make it go a

Recipe for a herb potpourri

Flowers	Leaves (dried)
borage	angelica
camomile	basil
elder	bay
lavender	bergamot
marigold petals	borage
nasturtium	lemon balm
rose petals	lovage
violet	marjoram

mint
rosemary
sage
sweet cicely
tarragon

Spices

cinnamon
cloves
nutmeg

Place a selection of leaves, flowers and spices from the above lists in a wide bowl. Put them in layers, using the flowers which are the most attractive for the layer which is topmost (visible).

little further as well as to enhance its own fragrance.

Another good ground cover, with larger leaves than the woodruff, is *Geranium macrorrhizum*. Bruise the leaves, either by accident or on purpose, and their powdery fragrance fills the air. Thymes also can be used as carpeting plants, as we have already learned, but these need not necessarily spread themselves on stone or pathways. They will also help to clothe a bank.

Pinks are extremely hardy plants. They will grow in ordinary soil and will flower freely so long as this is rich. Prepare the soil well before planting and feed the plants with a liquid plant food in spring and autumn. Pinks like the sun. They can be grown in beds where their attractive grey-green tufted shoots will soon smother the ground. They also look good grown in a

Choose the ingredients for a potpourri with care. A well-made one will remain scented for years.

wide band to edge a path. And they also look attractive this way sprawled out before lavender. They will even carpet the ground below apple trees or some similar plants; so long as they are not in deep shade a little partial shade during the day will do them no harm.

There are annual, biennial and perennial kinds of pinks, but naturally, those with the most petals are the best for potpourri. There are some highly scented double varieties of *Dianthus plumarius,* some of which possess a strong clove fragrance. Consult catalogues for varieties and descriptions.

It is possible to make an attractive border of all scented plants, concentrating on those whose flowers are used, but alternating them with some of the more attractive of the scented-leaved kinds. Fortunately, many of these are a soft grey-green and so are the perfect foil and buffer alike for any vividly coloured blooms near them.

A few members of the daisy family can be grown. Costmary, *Chrysanthemum balsamita,* has attractive grey-green leaves, and tiny yellow button-like flowers borne in clusters on straight stems. Camomile, besides being used for tea, can add to the attractive appearance of potpourri and contribute a little of its own particular scent into the bargain. The dried petals of the pot marigold, *Calendula officinalis*, also add colour and pungency to potpourri.

A few sage leaves can be used in flower mixtures and more of the sages can be grown to provide colour. The annual clary, *Salvia sclarea*, nowadays comes in several prettily coloured varieties, whose bracts decorating the stem ends are ruby, magenta, purple and violet. These give more colour than scent to potpourri, but like some other herbs, their scent is stronger when the flowers are dried.

Artemisias – of which family tarragon is the best known herb, although some of the others are used in the preparation of liqueurs – are more scented than pungent. These include lad's love or southernwood, mentioned earlier. *A. absinthium* is common wormwood, *A. vulgaris* is mugwort, *A. pontica* is Roman wormwood, *A. tridentata* is the

sage bush (a confusing name since this is not a sage). This species grows really tall, 2–2·5m (6–8ft), and is silvery and fragrant.

All parts of the handsome angelica – roots, stems and leaves – are fragrant. Besides being used for confectionery, it plays an important role in potpourri. The roots should be cleaned, dried and powdered for culinary use.

Other culinary herbs which are used in potpourris are marjoram, balm, mints and borage. The latter is used for the flower's colour, not perfume, and marjoram, balm and mints can be candied.

Of the annuals, possibly mignonette is the most delightfully scented. Where there

Vivid floral arrangements can be made from herbs. Roses, camomile, borage and calendula (pot marigold) spill colourfully from a vase (left). Wallflowers (right) are a vibrantly colourful addition to any herb garden. Purple-leaved basil (below) is an ornamental variety well suited to herb borders.

is little garden space for it, the plant will grow well in all kinds of containers outdoors and as a pot plant in a greenhouse or on a sunny windowsill. Wallflowers are often overlooked, yet these are an excellent way of adding colour to the herb garden in the spring, so long as one takes care to see that they do not smother the perennial herbs. They also grow well in tubs and other containers. They could occupy the area set aside for herbs that will be planted out in late spring, basil for example. When the wallflowers are pulled up after flowering, enrich the soil with a little plant food.

361

8 Drying herbs

Obviously, all the herbs used in potpourris dry well and the same methods are used for these as for the culinary kinds. Some of the latter dry much better than others. Generally speaking it is the shrubby labiates, the kinds with lipped flowers, which dry best – sage, thyme, marjoram and rosemary for instance. These all retain their essential oils and are strongly flavoured even when dry or powdered. The same is true of bay. Some of the soft-leaved kinds dry well enough but are likely to be disappointing when used, parsley and mint being examples. Chives, balm, borage, chervil and fennel are really not worth drying. Fortunately these are available – or can be made so – in winter and the cook does not have to depend upon dried supplies.

Usually just the tips of stems are taken. They should be cut and not picked or pulled, so that they come away cleanly from the plant with no faded stem ends, or portions of root with soil still clinging to them. By picking the tips the plant is encouraged to make more growth. The time to gather herbs is when the plants are ready to come into flower, for it is at this time that their flavours are strongest. However, this is not a hard and fast rule, and many people harvest the herbs two or three times a year.

If many herbs are to be dried, it is best to make the shoots into small bunches of one kind so that once these are hung up, the air can circulate round each shoot.

There are various methods of drying the bunches. If the weather is warm they can be dried by hanging them upside down outdoors in the shade. They should not be put out until the warmest, dryest part of the day and they should not be left outside overnight in case of heavy dews moistening them again. They should not, of course, be hung in any place where they are likely to become dusty.

If there is no suitable place outdoors, or in damp weather, the bunches can be hung

indoors in a warm kitchen, away from steam, or in an airing cupboard.

If only small amounts are to be dried, the simplest method is to spread them out on paper or on a sieve and turn them from time to time so that all parts are exposed to the air. Another easy way to dry small quantities is to place them, in their individual kinds, in small net bags and then to hang these in some dry, clean and airy place. Herbs simply laid on a sunny windowsill indoors will dry very quickly, but one should bear in mind that those which are dried away from sunlight keep their colour best. Also, the faster herbs dry, the better their colour.

When herbs are dusty, or thought to be

Herbs can be dried in a warm kitchen by hanging them in small bunches before grinding them fine for cooking.

bag to keep them dust-free. Alternatively, they can be cleaned from their stalks and stored in air-tight jars. Some can be mixed and put into small muslin or cheesecloth squares to make a bouquet garni. The dry leaves are easily stripped from their stalks; let them fall on to clean paper and then lightly rub them between the hands to reduce them to crumbs. To make a really fine powder, bay leaf powder for instance, grind the herbs in an electric grinder. Traces of herb flavour can be removed by wiping the grinder round with lemon juice.

Potpourri petals and leaves are not usually rubbed or crumbled. Incidentally, one of the best and least troublesome ways of drying petals is to use the string bag method. Pack the petals in loosely and use a large mesh netting. When the petals seem dry, spread them out in some airy place indoors to let them finish off.

If cut herbs are to be kept for a day or two it is best to treat them as cut flowers and to stand them in water out of direct sunshine. If they are to be kept in a refrigerator, store them in an airtight container but not too near the freezer compartment.

Herbs will deep-freeze but the longer they are left frozen, the more will they lose their flavour. (There really is nothing so good as growing fresh supplies the year round.) Chives will not keep their texture or their flavour, yet vichyssoise soup flavoured with chives will freeze well. This soup should of course have the chives added at the last moment.

Mint is best made into mint sauce and frozen in small quantities.

Parsley should not be chopped if it is to be deep-frozen or it will lose most of its flavour. Wash and dry the sprigs after the main stem has been cut off. Press these down into a container and freeze. When ready to use, in soups or sauces and not as a garnish, turn out the complete block and either grate or shave it.

A good way to store mixed dried herbs so that they are conveniently assembled and ready to use is to make them into a wrapped

so, make them into bunches, draw them through clean water agitating them so that any dust is removed and then shake or swish them in the air until all the surplus moisture is thrown off. After this, make them into smaller bunches or spread them out, depending upon what method is used to dry them.

Take care when using an oven to dry herbs, because too much heat dries out the essential oils.

It is possible from this point to store them as they are in their bunches. They can, for instance, be enclosed in a paper or plastic bouquet garni, briefly referred to earlier. The basic herbs which should always be included are parsley, thyme and bay although stronger and more aromatic herbs are often needed, especially for marinades. It is a good plan to prepare a few bouquets for special dishes in which different herbs are allowed to predominate. Thus, for boiling fowls or chicken the bouquets should be mostly tarragon whereas for beef stews extra marjoram should be included. For a court-bouillon (fish stock), one could make a bouquet that includes parsley roots, celery, fennel, thyme, bay, coriander seeds and a few pepper corns.

Herbs make attractive gifts when wrapped as bouquets. These can be packed into air-tight glass jars so that they will not lose their flavour quite so rapidly. If you are certain that the recipient will be quick to store the herbs, you could even assemble

A Cordon Bleu garland (above) is a splendid wreath of intertwined herb sachets, shallots and bay leaves.

Dried herbs (left) must be stored in air-tight jars.

them in a Cordon Bleu garland. Begin by preparing the little bouquet bags. First, cut three or four-inch squares of muslin and have ready several lengths of fine twine. For a small bouquet garni use a level teaspoonful of the mixed, crushed herbs. Gather up the four corners and tie the little bundle lightly using the twine, leaving a long end so that the bag can easily be pulled out.

Take a strip of plastic-covered wire netting, roll it up and shape it into a circle. Cover this with blue crepe paper. Transform the bouquet garni bags into 'apples' by pushing a clove into the centre of each. Back each 'apple' with two bay leaves. You can join these with some wire-spined twists used to close bags. Use the thread on the muslin bag to fasten the bay leaves to the 'apple' and to tie the entire bunch to a cocktail stick. Push the stick down through the plastic covered wire netting. Alternate the 'apples' with shallots, also mounted on false cocktail stick stems.

9 Wild herbs

Some of our garden herbs have been domesticated from the wild. Others have escaped from cultivation and become native. Nowadays, most of the wild herbs that are gathered are used to make wines and preserves although some still continue to be valued for their old uses. One of these is the elder blossom. The dried blossoms can be added to tea, to gooseberry jams and to pies and dishes of all kinds. They can also be pounded into lard to make a soothing ointment for burns and can be mixed with dried peppermint to make a tisane against influenza. Freshly picked, elder blossoms can be dipped in batter and fried then drained, sugared and eaten as a dessert. The fragrant flowers of broom also make a good wine and the buds can be pickled as

Hundreds of different varieties of wild rose (above) brighten countryside fields. The leaves of dandelions (left), one of the most common of herbs, make delicious salads and teas. The delicate white-flowered elder (below left) grows wild in hedges and fields. Elder blossoms make a refreshing tea.

false capers. Dandelion leaves are good in salads and their flowers make a delicious wine as do those of white clover. Red clover can be made into a tea to ease whooping cough. The small white flowers of feverfew, make a tonic tea. Wild thyme, marjoram and mints can be used to flavour meat dishes. They can also be blended into potpourris along with lime flowers, meadowsweet, camomile, hawthorn, meliot, sweet cicely, sweet flag leaves, tansy, woodruff and others.

10 Uses of herbs

To many people, herbs are simply plants which are used, usually in a dried state, to flavour meats and stuffings or to give zest to soups or sauces. Yet herbs can play a much more important role than this. Before the introduction of modern chemical drugs, herbs were the source of a wide array of medicines, salves and ointments of all kinds. The word 'drug' comes from the Anglo-Saxon 'drigan' – to dry – and is a reference to the manner in which medicinal plants were preserved for use.

In former times, such plants, most of which are now neglected, were grown in special plots or were gathered in fields or forests. People believed that there was always a plant somewhere which could be used to cure, or at least counteract, the ill effects of every disease or pain.

It seems that some plants were chosen simply because they appeared to have some obvious affinity with a disease. Thus, the bright, yellow-flowered greater celandine with its acrid juice was considered a herb to be used against jaundice. Herbs were also widely used to staunch wounds and to knit broken bones as well as to make fomenta-

White wine vinegar can be given a delicious and subtle herbal flavour by allowing sprigs of thyme to marinate in it.

tions and poultices for swellings and for wounds that had turned septic. The pretty little centaury is said to have been so named because a Greek centaur used the plant to heal the wounds made by a poisoned arrow.

To this day, many herbs are still used as a prophylactic against colds or as a febrifuge. Others are to be recommended as gargles for sore throats.

A great many herbs, particularly the

refreshing drinks, but some are particularly noted for their medicinal and soothing qualities. Most are brewed in the same manner as ordinary tea and are taken either hot or cold with perhaps a little sugar or honey. Camomile is a very popular tea and is deliciously fragrant. Woodruff tea, although it can be drunk on its own, is also blended with Indian or China teas to make these go a little further and to enhance their flavours. At one time mugwort, *Artemisia vulgaris*, was used as a tea substitute even though its original use was in the brewing of beers. Lime-flower tea is considered by some people to be the most refreshing of all.

In the past, many more herbs were used in salads than are today, and this included the flowers as well as the leaves, as the vegetables we now know as salad were not so intensively cultivated then. The memory lingers on, however, in the name of Salad Burnet, a plant which has a hint of cucumber in its scent and is still to be recommended for salads.

Herb teas (above) are some of the most refreshing hot drinks. They are renowned for their restorative and soothing properties. Tarragon (right) will impart a delicate flavour to olive oil.

aromatic artemisia group (such as mugwort and wormwood), are used to flavour liqueurs. Juniper berries are also used to flavour gin and like so many other herbs also are used in cooking, especially to flavour sauerkraut and many meat dishes, such as veal. Sorrel was highly valued in the days when only salt-preserved meat was available in the depths of winter because it is a natural tenderiser. Leaves wrapped round a joint before it is cooked render the meat more palatable.

Few people consider Indian or China tea to be made from a herb yet the *Camellia sinensis* leaves which are infused or brewed are but one of the many different kinds of teas or tisanes made from the leaves or flowers of plants. In many countries teas are also made from plants other than the camellia. For instance, in North America a brew made from bergamot is known as Oswego tea. Most teas are intended as

Savoury dishes

ANGELICA
Angelica archangelica

In salads, use raw stems and thick leaf midribs.

BALM, LEMON BALM
Melissa officinalis

Use chopped finely in sauces and salads, in stuffings or forcemeats for veal and poultry.

BASIL
Ocimum basilicum and
O. minimum

Use fresh or dried with tomatoes, white fish, ham and in many Italian dishes. Makes a splendid garnish for beans of all kinds, squash, courgettes and other marrows.

BAY
Laurus nobilis

Essential in bouquets garnis. Use fresh or dried to flavour savoury dishes. (Dried leaves can be ground to a powder, which should always be stored in an air-tight container.)

BERGAMOT, OSWEGO TEA
Monarda didyma

Use fresh leaves and flowers in salads, but in moderation because of their pungency.

BORAGE
Borago officinalis

Use very young leaves in salads.

CAMOMILE
Anthemis nobilis

CARAWAY
Carum carvi

The leaves and stems are not eaten. The seeds are used as a spice.

CHERVIL
Anthriscus cerefolium

As an essential ingredient of *fines herbes*, with parsley and tarragon, it is used in omelettes and other egg dishes, salads and salad dressings, poultry and some white fish. Use as a delicate garnish for vegetable purées, or with shell fish and with cream soups.

CHIVES
Allium schoenoprasum

Cook only by adding to a dish at the last moment or as a garnish or condiment. Cut 'grass' finely with scissors. Blend with butter for garnishing grilled meats and fish.

Sweet dishes	Drinks	Potpourris, etc.	Other uses
Cook stalks as a sweet or as a conserve mixed with rhubarb. Candy them for confectionery.	Use leaves as a tisane. Use roots in liqueurs.	Dry roots for potpourri.	
		Dry and mix in potpourri.	
Use fresh or dried in milk puddings.		Mix leaves or powder in potpourri.	
	Use fresh or dried as a tisane or mix dried leaves with Indian tea to make it go further and add to its flavour.	Mix dried flowers and leaves in potpourri.	
Cook young leaves in batter, with the flowers, as fritters. Flowers can also be candied.	Add sprigs of fresh flowers and leaves to fruit cups and iced drinks.	Use dried flowers for colour in potpourri.	
	Main use, fresh or dry as a soothing tisane. Gather daisy heads when the outer ray petals begin to turn back but while centres are still bright.	Mix dried flowers in potpourri.	Boil flowers in rain water as a hair rinse for blondes.
The leaves and stems are not eaten. The seeds are used as a flavouring in confectionery.			

Savoury dishes

CORIANDER
Coriandrum sativum

The aromatic seeds are used as flavouring, and are an important ingredient in curries. Coriander is always included in mixed spice.

CUMIN
Cuminum cyminum

Use as a spice in curries and in sauces for fish.

DILL
Peucedanum graveolens

Cook young shoots, like mint, with new potatoes and add moderately to potato dishes. Garnish peas with the finely chopped leaves. Excellent with cucumber. Use flower heads and seeds to flavour cucumber pickles. Use seeds (very pungent) in heavy white sauces.

FENNEL
Foeniculum vulgare

Cook young leaves or shoots with fish, veal and offal. Use raw with tinned fish, chopped finely like parsley. Blend in curries. Seeds are very pungent and good in sauces and fish mousse. Fennel dries well, but becomes strongly flavoured and must be used with care.

GARLIC
Allium sativum

An essential ingredient in many dishes. The individual bulbs, known as 'cloves', are either crushed or chopped. Leaves can also be used.

LAVENDER
Lavendula officinalis

Not often used in cooking, but can be used like rosemary with poultry.

LOVAGE
Ligusticum officinale

Good substitute for celery flavour. Use stem in stocks and bouillon. Use young leaves, ribs and stems finely sliced in salads or soups. Use moderately when dried.

MARIGOLD
Calendula officinalis

Pot marigold can be used to flavour soups and also to make an attractive garnish for a salad. Fresh or dried petals can be used.

MARJORAM
Origanum dictamnus,
O. marjorana,
O. onites

An essential bouquet garni herb for marinades. Use sweet or knotted marjoram in casseroles, stews, soups and terrines. Dries well, but use discreetly. Suits lamb, pork and beef. Pot marjoram is best for salads and egg dishes. Mix with thyme and parsley for scrambled eggs and omelettes.

MINT
Mentha piperita,
M. pulegium,
M. rotundifolia,
M. spicata

Cook pennyroyal with new potatoes, spearmint with peas. The round,woolly-leaved apple mint is best for mint sauce. Mint leaves can be used in salads and sauces, or chopped and sprinkled on lamb and mutton for roasts. Does not dry well because aroma becomes too strong.

Sweet dishes	Drinks	Potpourris, etc.	Other uses
Coriander is used in sweets and for flavouring liquor, especially gin.			
			Use in veterinary medicine as a carminative.
Use the seeds, which are very pungent, like caraway, to flavour bread and cakes.			
Sprigs in a jar of sugar will scent and flavour it.		Used mainly in toilet waters, sweet-smelling bags and potpourri.	
Seeds are used in confectionery.			
Can be used to flavour custards.		Pot marigold is best known as an ingredient of potpourri.	
		Mix dried leaves and flowers in potpourri.	
Use mint leaves in sorbets. Leaves can be crystallised.	Use mint leaves in iced drinks, fruit cups and tisanes.	Use pineapple mint leaves in potpourri.	

Savoury dishes

NASTURTIUM
Tropaeolum majus

Once known as Indian Cress because of the cress-like taste of its flowers, leaves and seeds. All can be used in salads, and the seeds can be used as a substitute for horse radish.

PARSLEY
Petroselinum crispum

An essential bouquet garni herb. Very versatile: seems to suit eggs, all meats and fish. Used widely as a garnish. Can be fried and used this way. As a condiment, chop finely and add to the dish at the last moment to keep the colour bright. Best used fresh, but will dry.

POPPY
Papaver somniferum

ROSEMARY
Rosmarinus officinalis

Good cooked with all meats and poultry. Chop finely and sprinkle on roasts. Mix with chopped garlic for lamb and kid. Use sprig to flavour pea, pulse, spinach and minestrone soups and add to old boiled potatoes. Will dry, but becomes very pungent.

SAGE
Salvia officinalis

One of the most popular of herbs, in its dried form it is used mostly in stuffing or forcemeat. Good fresh and well chopped – in cream and cottage cheese or sprinkled on meats to be roasted or grilled.

SAVORY, WINTER AND SUMMER
Satureia hortensis,
S. montana

Summer savory considered to have the finer flavour of the two, similar to thyme. Excellent in forcemeats for goose, turkey, chicken, veal and pork. Mix with chives and parsley for duck. Use for trout and other freshwater fish. Include in bouquet garni for all marinades and when poaching fish. Cook with broad beans and peas.

SHALLOT
Allium ascalonicum

Has a distinct flavour midway between garlic and onion. Can be used young or allowed to ripen and be stored for winter use. Leaves can be used like chives.

TARRAGON
Artemisia dracunculus

An essential ingredient of *fines herbes*. Cook with chicken boiled or roasted. Use for stuffing and pâté, white fish, rabbit, veal and all egg dishes. Used in hollandaise, béarnaise and tartare sauces. Serve in tarragon butter with shell fish. Dries well, but becomes very pungent.

THYME
Thymus vulgaris,
T x citriodorus

Common thyme is an essential bouquet garni herb. Very pungent when fresh, so use discreetly. Use with all kinds of meats, poultry, fish, soups, forcemeats, marinades. Use in onion, marrow family, aubergine and salsify dishes. Add lemon thyme to any savoury dish for a slight lemon flavour. Blend with butter for grills.

WOODRUFF
Asperula odorata

372

Sweet dishes	Drinks	Potpourris, etc.	Other uses
The dark grey oily seeds are used in confectionery.			The seeds are used in bread-making.
Flowers can be candied.	Makes a good tisane, fresh or dried.		When boiled in water resulting liquid makes excellent hair rinse.
Use lemon thyme in milk puddings.		Mix dried thymes of any species in potpourri.	
	Can be used as a tisane or tea. It is often blended with fine teas – China or Indian – to make them go further and to enhance their flavour.	Can be used as an ingredient in potpourri or alone in scent bags to be laid among linen.	

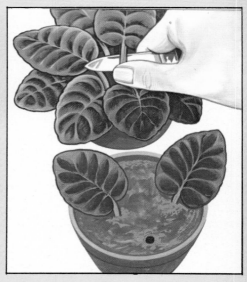

Indoor gardening

1 Indoor plants

Plant requirements

Our personal needs and those of the plants we try to grow indoors are remarkably similar. We both need food and water, light and air and a degree of cleanliness, warmth and shelter. Some of us like or enjoy more of one than of another and we flourish when we get what we want. Plants are exactly the same and this is one of several reasons why it is impossible to lay down hard and fast rules about how many times a certain plant should be fed or watered. They differ, just as humans do.

But there is more to it than this. If two identical plants were bought on the same day in the same city and taken home to almost identical houses, one could be dead in a week or two while the other flourished in spite of the fact that each owner followed the same directions for the plant's care according to his own interpretation. For one thing, conditions in the two homes may be entirely different, one being warmer, lighter, cleaner and more humid. And again, what does the recommendation 'water lightly' mean to you? Once a day? Once a week? How much? A tablespoonful? A cup?

But although the best guide is undoubtedly experience, it is possible to get a rough idea of the cultural requirements of most plants simply by looking at them and perhaps by knowing something of their families. As far as recognition goes, nearly all cacti, for example, are unmistakable; we know that cacti like as much sun as they can get and that although they need plenty of water in summer they should go almost completely dry in winter. So if we are given a plant that looks like a cactus we treat it as

Note that the flowering plants, mainly cyclamen, in this group are nearest to the window light.

we have learned to do and the probability is that it will thrive.

This is a particularly simple example, but there are other guide lines we can follow with every probability that we will be right. All flowering plants and all with variegated foliage must have good light to retain their vivid colours. The darker green the leaf the less light the plant will need. Only cacti and certain other succulents can be allowed to bask in full summer sun. Only cyperus and certain other bog plants can be allowed to paddle, their roots actually wet rather than merely moist.

Detailed instructions for the care of indoor plants will appear in subsequent sections, but for convenience most plants can be divided into groups with similar tastes or requirements. There is the group which we have already noted as being particularly easy to care for, the cacti. Cacti are plants which grow in the open, not under trees, in meadows or in forests, and consequently they are accustomed to the full

Nearly all rebutias are spherical like these and all are among the 'easier' cacti in terms of flowering.

Agave leaves are sharply pointed and saw-edged, so plants should be given plenty of space indoors. *Agave franzosinii* 'Aurea' is easy to grow and long-lived if kept in light, warm conditions.

light of the sun. Therefore if we glance through a list of indoor plants and pick out those which normally grow in the open the chances are that these plants too will require full sun. Pelargoniums, or pot geraniums, love the sun and so do nearly all the succulents such as echeverias, kalanchoes, sansevieria, aloes, agaves, crassulas, sempervivums and the like. These may not be so readily recognisable as cacti, but practically without exception they have thick, fleshy leaves which are capable of absorbing and storing quantities of moisture on which they can live during their dry season. All these plants need generous supplies of water in the summer and when they are in flower, but if they continue to receive the same quantities in the cooler months when they are inactive, their roots will tend to rot, leaves or swollen stems will yellow and fall, or turn soft and slimy. In the cold months some of these plants will actually appear to shrink, the skin tissue shrivelling

Like many succulents, *Aloe spinossissima*, with its prickly leaves, is more interesting than beautiful.

and wrinkling. They look badly in need of water – and so they are – but they should not be watered until there is hot sun again.

The only real exceptions in this group, the succulents, are the epiphyllums, the zygocactus and the schlumbergeras. These include the so-called Christmas cactus and the Easter cactus. They are epiphytes, which grow in their native lands high on forest trees. As such they do not demand full sun nor complete winter drought. They can stand full sun for periods and they can stand drought for periods, but neither should be too extreme.

Apart from the special cases of cacti and other succulents, most indoor plants need good light but not full sun, and they need dryer conditions in winter than summer – though not complete drought.

As a general rule, if we know the requirements of one plant in a genus, we can be fairly sure that those of others in the same genus will tend to be similar. Some of the most useful, most tolerant and easily available of all indoor plants are the hederas or ivies, the ficuses and the philodendrons. All the hederas, whether green or variegated, whether derived from *Hedera helix* or *H. canariensis* require much the same treatment, although the variegated kinds keep their colour best when they are in good light. There are a great many varieties of ivy, some with very little difference and some which because of leaf colour or size vary widely. All are excellent, all are easy to grow indoors.

The fig or ficus family is also widely spread. Its most famous example is probably *Ficus elastica*, the rubber plant, and this again is found today in many versions, some with different colourings and some merely tougher and easier to grow examples of the old species. *F. benjamina*, the weeping fig, will grow just as tall as the rubber plant but it has smaller and daintier leaves and a rather engaging and elegant drooping habit of growth. More like the rubber plant is the fiddle-leaf fig, *F. lyrata*, with large and somewhat crinkled leaves

Ficus benjamina is a graceful, tree-like member of the decorative and useful fig family.

collectively known as room pines or bromeliads. The pineapple itself is generally grown indoors in a more colourful and decorative form than that which appears on our tables, striped with green and gold with pink tinges and heavily toothed. It is known as *Ananas bracteatus striatus*. But most of the bromeliads are epiphytes, growing on the bark of trees rather than in the soil. They grow in the form of long, slim leaves, all radiating from an open centre which forms a cup or vase. In the jungle, this cup is filled with rain water, and the clinging roots gain their sustenance from falling leaves which get caught up as they drop. It therefore follows that when we grow bromeliads indoors they will be happy in surprisingly small pots of any soil so long as it is well drained. The plants are watered merely by keeping the central vase or cup filled with water at all times. From the centre of this cup in many species will arise a flower, sometimes at the end of a long, arching spike. Some of these flowers are strikingly beautiful and others are very long-lasting.

The best known of these bromeliads is probably *Aechmea rhodocyanea*, or the Greek vase plant. It has grey-green glaucous foliage and produces a long flowering stem bearing a spiky series of bracts of soft pink from which grow a multitude of tiny flowers – pink, blue and violet. These soon fade, but the pink inflorescence lasts for about two or three months.

Other bromeliads normally grown indoors include neoregelia, nidularium, vriesia, billbergia and cryptanthus.

A plant which was once so familiar that it became derided and unfashionable is the aspidistra, parlour palm or cast-iron plant. It was in its heyday in Victorian England largely because it was one of the very few plants that could grow in dark rooms lit by gaslight and warmed by smoky coal fires. Today *Aspidistra elatior* and the more attractive gold-striped form, *A. e. variegata*, have achieved respectability once again. Obviously they are easy to grow and make no particular demands on the grower.

shaped much like the body of a fiddle or violin. Equally large is *F. benghalensis*, the banyan tree, with leaves much like those of the rubber plant.

Quite different are two creeping or trailing plants, *F. pumila*, the creeping fig, with small leaves on wiry stems and *F. radicans variegata*, similar but with a golden variegation in the foliage. Both of these need a little more water than the larger, tree-like examples of the same family.

Curiously enough one of the most useful groups of indoor plants comes from a family which used to be known only for the fruit it provided for our dining tables. This is the pineapple, and plants from this family are

Plant shapes

It is difficult to explain the shape of an aspidistra plant. To say that the leaves are spear-shaped, about 70cm (2ft) long and grow arching out from the rhizomatous base on short stems gives little impression of what the plant looks like. If it were necessary to classify the general shape or appearance of the plant one would probably say that it was bushy rather than tree-like, trailing or climbing.

It is probably true to say that the majority of indoor plants have to be classified as being of bushy shape because they will fit into no other category. There is little one can do to a plant that has a bushy shape or habit of growth to stop it growing this way. It is possible to train some plants to grow up a wall or along a shelf, but a bushy plant merely stands and occupies a certain space, the outline of the tips of its leaves probably

Sedums or stonecrops (*Sedum pachyphyllum* and *Sedum rubrotinctum* are shown here) are of compact shape, like a light, chalky soil and sunlight. Easy to grow, they can be propagated from the small leaves.

being more or less round in appearance.

It is much easier to describe a tree-like plant, yet not so easy to find them indoors, for real indoor trees are very few in number. Probably the best known is the familiar India rubber plant, *Ficus elastica*, with some of its relatives. Less well known but still a genuine tree in appearance as well as fact is the Norfolk Island pine, *Araucaria excelsa*, a miniature conifer and relative of the monkey puzzle tree a familiar feature of so many lawns. The araucaria is an easy plant to grow indoors, making no particular demands for warmth, light or humidity.

Much more difficult to grow for long periods is *Dizygotheca elegantissima*, sometimes known as *Aralia elegantissima*. It is tall, slim and elegant indeed, with stems standing out along the single main trunk, each bearing a compound leaf composed of eight to ten narrow, toothed segments. It likes a moderately warm atmosphere (about 20°C, 68°F) and protection from all draughts. It is almost impossible to prevent the lower leaves gradually falling and so leaving a portion of bare stem at the base, and for this reason it is worthwhile growing some other plant at the floor level to hide this naked and unattractive portion.

Schefflera actinophylla is a little tongue-twisting tree with palmate green leaves growing at the ends of reaching stems or stalks. It grows well and will make a large plant. It is sometimes known as the umbrella tree, which is a pity – because it is not nearly so like an umbrella as *Hepta-pleurum arboricola*, which is itself sometimes called a schefflera. The foliage here is smaller, more arching, and not in fact unlike the ribs of an umbrella. It will also make a fairly large specimen if required.

It is a rare thing in the world of botany to find a bigeneric cross, which is to say a plant derived from two separate genera. But there is a first-class example in the indoor plant world in *Fatshedera lizei*, which is a cross between a fatsia and a hedera or ivy. The fatsia is a shrub which will grow quite large and the hedera is a climber, so as one might imagine, the fatshedera can be either climber or tree-like, depending on how you treat it. It is generally sold as a specimen tree, its one or more main stems clipped or tied to a central stake. If this stake is elongated from time to time the plant can quite well be induced to grow up and up into a tall, slim tree. It is easy and accommodating with no particular preference for either sun or shade, warm or cool conditions, moist or dry soil.

There are other indoor plants which can be trained to grow tall, but most of them are hardly tree-like. And of the few genuinely tree-like plants mentioned here, all can be grown as shorter, rounder shrubs by the simple process of pinching out the main growing shoot or tip and allowing the side

growth to develop. Some plants look quite attractive grown this way, largely because they are a little different from most other plants of the species.

All indoor plants depend to some extent for their charm on the way in which they fit or suit their environment. It is possible to bring home a plant and place it in a particular part of the home for which it is eminently suited and then to find after some months that it has lost its charm, although

Most indoor plants suffer from overwatering, but the graceful, tall and feathery *Cyperus alternifolius gracilis* is a bog plant and its roots can be allowed to paddle.

in no way misshapen or unhealthy. The reason is probably only that it has grown too large for its position, and this is a further cause for limiting most strictly the amount of food or fertiliser given to any plant. All plants must be kept growing if they are to be healthy and natural in appearance, but if they are over-fed they will grow too large too quickly, and by out-growing their strength they will render themselves liable to attack by insects and disease. For these reasons it is always helpful to keep indoor plants growing slowly, with health and vigour.

It is probably true to say, however, that most indoor plants are left too much to their own resources and not trained to do what the owner requires. A plant is brought home and placed in position and so long as it grows and gives an appearance of health, so long as it fulfils its function of looking decorative, it is left alone. Yet it might look

Ivies indoors can be trained to trail, climb, spread or become a tree or a bush. The picture on the right shows a climbing *Hedera canariensis*.

Many indoor plants grow differently in their natural surroundings. This bushy palm, *Neanthe bella* (1), would normally be a tall tree. *Pilea cadierei nana* (2) should have its growing tips pinched out regularly in order to keep it attractive and bushy. Tradescantias and zebrinas (3) are excellent trailers for the home if their stems are not allowed to grow too long. Philodendrons (4) vary widely, but many are climbers and some will cling with their roots to a nearby wall. The thick, fleshy, spear-like leaves of *Sansevieria trifasciata* (5) have given it the popular name of mother-in-law's tongue.

much more attractive if it were pinched, pruned or trained to fit more pleasingly into its particular position in the home, if pointed in another direction, trailed over a nearby picture or encouraged to climb over the wall behind it. It is too easy to regard indoor plants as pieces of furniture, to grow accustomed to them and allow them to develop by themselves instead of adapting them to our own needs or purposes.

To take one example we have only to look at the popular *Chlorophytum comosum variegatum*, the easy, grass-like plant with arching green and cream leaves which is seen in so many homes and which has unfortunately received the common name of spider plant. This is usually bought or brought home when it is a small plant, a mere tuft growing from the centre of a small pot and no more than about 15cm (6in) tall. It grows quickly and in a matter of only a few weeks the little tuft of leaves will have become a central mass with several arching stems growing out of it, each of which bears a few little white and insignificant flowers. Subsequently, each small flower may become a miniature plant itself, a little tuft of leaves with rudimentary roots. The plant will by now have draped itself completely over its original pot and covered the surface on which it stands and in a few more weeks it will be hanging down over the shelf or table, a cascade of plant life.

It may look highly decorative like this, but it will certainly be occupying more space than was originally envisaged and allotted to it.

If you want a big, blowsy, tumbling mass of green and cream plant material then by all means have it, but give it space where it

383

Indoor plants need discipline and training if they are to grow attractively. Pruning and pinching will eliminate overcrowding, let in light and air and encourage attractive and bushy new growth.

Ivies, shown below, are probably the best-known trailers. They are easy to reproduce by layering. One trail is led to a nearby pot filled with soil and a few cm (inch or two) of the stem are buried. New roots grow here.

will look its best: not where it will be cramped and confined, its arching stems bent by obstructions and its grass-like foliage acting only as a dust trap. If there is space and the plant is in good health then it can look magnificent, but if the plant is cramped and consequently looking unhealthy or unhappy, then rest one or more of the little plantlets at the end of the arching stems on a small pot of soil and let it take root, which it will do quickly and easily (see chapter 5). As soon as you have one or two small young plants growing away well, move, discard or give away the parent plant and keep only the small baby which will fit more comfortably and happily into the space available.

Several of the bromeliads will begin to die after they have flowered. This process may take several months or even years and in the meantime they will produce a young plant from the soil in which they grow. It is quite possible to allow both plants to grow in the same pot until the elder has become unpleasant in appearance, but it is better before this stage to discard the old plant and repot the new in fresh soil so that it can replace its parent with credit.

Some plants, particularly climbers, such as ivies, cissus and rhoicissus, grow so rampantly that in a year or so they will form a fat column of foliage from floor to ceiling or will cover a wall or make a thick hedge. It is

possible merely to take the scissors or secateurs and cut away some of the long trails in order to thin the plant and make it more decorative again, but this nearly always disfigures the plant. It is better to take a cutting or two and grow these to maturity,

discarding the old and overgrown plant. It is an easy matter to take cuttings of such plants, for all that is needed is to take one of the trails and remove the foliage from a portion several cm/in from one end. This bare stem portion should be buried in a pot of soil nearby. In a few weeks it will be obvious from the new growth that it has

Plant trails can be made to cover a wall or form a partition. Fix the string or canes in position, then tie or clip each trail along the most convenient.

taken root, in which case it should be severed from the parent and you will have a new young plant.

On the other hand it could be highly decorative to have a plant with a dozen or more trails up to 3m (10ft) or so long. They can be attached to a central pillar, cane or string easily enough or they can be trained to cover a wall surface by tying the trails to guide string or something similar. Ivy plants can be induced to cling to a wall surface with their aerial roots and pull themselves up by these just as they would on an outdoor wall or a tree. The lightest of sprays of water on the wall surface where

the ivy grows will be sufficient to encourage the roots to take hold. It should be said, however, that these aerial roots are strong. They will do no real damage to the structure of the wall but they will certainly grow into wallpaper or other surfaces, and if taken down at any time will leave traces of their earlier activities.

By rather more artificial means it is possible to take advantage of both these and less advanced forms of aerial roots to grow certain climbers up special supports. Suitable plants are ivies, some philodendrons, scindapsus and one or two other similar plants. The method is to tie a fat skin of sphagnum moss or some similar material around a central cane or stick, or alternatively to stuff a hollow cane of small mesh wire netting with the same material. The small and immature plant has a trail tied to this moist material and will quickly send roots growing into it. Subsequently the plant will pull itself up with its own roots so long as the moss is kept moist and attractive to these roots.

Many plants will climb a cane covered with moist sphagnum moss using their aerial roots. A cylinder of wire mesh stuffed with moss can be equally effective.

Flowering plants

One of the main reasons why indoor plants make such excellent home decoration is that the majority of them depend for their effect on their foliage, and this changes but little over the seasons. Flowering plants are a different matter. They are, almost without exception, grown only for their flowers and when these have passed the plant itself may have lost its interest and attraction. For this reason we classify some flowering plants as temporary decoration, to be used and enjoyed while they come into flower and while they actually bloom, but to be discarded once this process has ended. But there are some flowering plants such as the dainty African violet, *Saintpaulia ionantha*, which can be kept flowering for almost the entire year; some like cinerarias and calceolarias which we can grow from seed; a few from which we can constantly propa-

gate, like the familiar and rightly popular busy lizzie, called patient lucy in America. There are herbaceous pot plants such as chrysanthemums which can be bought in flower or in bud, or can be raised from seed. And there are many, many special plants such as azaleas, cyclamen, poinsettias and the like which are usually grown for special seasons or festivals and which are only seldom retained for another year.

Among favourite indoor flowering plants are those grown from bulbs. Apart from their obvious beauty and the fact that so many of them are a herald of spring, a major reason for their popularity is that one is involved with them from their original purchase as plain, brown-skinned bulbs to their final flowering in the home.

Among the best spring-flowering bulbs to grow indoors are narcissi, tulips, hyacinths and crocuses. Some of these can

Narcissus Cragford will thrive in pebbles.

Flowering plants must have good light (*see left*) for good results.

Special crocus pots show off the vivid flowers to best advantage.

Hyacinths grow well in bulb fibre.

be bought 'prepared', which means that they have been specially treated so that they will flower earlier than usual.

The actual treatment of bulbs can differ according to varieties grown, so read instructions carefully when you buy your bulbs. In general the principle of growing bulbs indoors is that they should be planted up as soon as they are received or bought, usually in late summer or early autumn. They should then be placed outdoors or in a cold shed, suitably protected from mice and other predators, until their roots have grown deep and strong and shoots are beginning to burst from their blunt noses. They can then be brought indoors into a cool atmosphere and gradually introduced to normal living conditions, where they will soon come into flower.

One needs to be a little careful when buying a flowering plant for the home. Obviously the plant which is smothered with bloom, vivid with colour, will have the strongest appeal. But if it is at its peak there is only one way it can go – downwards. You have bought a plant with only half its life remaining. Look instead for a plant with a future, one with buds just beginning to open, with strong, green foliage, with the soil in the pot just moist. Never buy a plant with yellowing, drooping, limp or diseased foliage.

Some plants are grown in the home for many years and they flower only occasionally, or sometimes they never come into bloom at all. Cacti and epiphyllums are examples. Without knowing the conditions under which these plants are grown, it is difficult to be too dogmatic and give firm reasons why they have not flowered and firm directions to bring them to bloom. If the plants are strong and healthy and if they are mature enough to bloom, there is every probability that a change of treatment will induce them to flower.

One thing to bear in mind is that plants become accustomed to their surroundings and they do not generally like to be moved about from one position to another. Find a good spot for your plant and leave it there. If on second thoughts you think it should

have more light or some other comfort, move it to what you think is a better place; but try not to shift plants around as though they were furniture. You may find that flower buds tend to appear on a plant where the light is strongest, that is, on the window side of the plant. In this case do not turn the pot around completely, but move it just a quarter turn a day so that all sides of the plant get a chance at the light.

One of the main reasons why a flowering plant may be unproductive is that it has been hurried along too much. All plants of all kinds have a dormant or resting season and during this period they should be given every assistance to rest by cutting down the amount of food and water they are given, perhaps even cutting down the amount of light they receive.

If the season is winter and the weather is cold or frosty, make sure that the plant is well wrapped when you bring it home. The wrapping paper should cover not only the pot but the entire plant. At home place the pot in a bucket of water, submerging it completely. Watch for the bubbles to rise and when these have ceased remove the pot and stand it to drain.

As the plant develops the buds will gradually open into flowers and these will gradually fade. Once they have passed their best make sure that they are cut away and removed. Fading flowers give plants a shabby appearance and in addition there is a constant risk that they may become diseased. They consume a certain proportion of the available food and moisture in the soil without giving anything in return. Far better that this nourishment should go to the developing buds.

All flowering plants of whatever type need good light if they are to develop well, so stand your plant close to a window where it will not get direct sunlight for more than a few minutes a day but where the average of the light is good. Never stand it over a radiator or any other source of heat, and if possible find a fairly cool spot but without draughts.

Neoregelia carolinae tricolor, a bromeliad, turns a vivid scarlet at the centre when its small blue and insignificant flowers appear in the characteristic cup, which should always be kept filled with water.

During the warmer months leaf cacti, orchid cacti or forest cacti enjoy periods in sun and rain.

Zygocactus truncatus, the Christmas cactus, has several varieties and can have flowers of several colours. These appear at the tops of the long, flattened stems, which resemble leaves.

Euphorbia splendens (crown of thorns) treated well, will flower continuously throughout its long life. *E.s.* 'Bojeri' is shown below.

In general cacti and all other succulents will rest during the winter months and at this time their soil should be kept almost bone dry. If the atmosphere in the home is too warm and dry some of the plants may begin to suffer from this treatment of deprivation, in which case a little more water will do no harm. But on the whole the plants will give a better performance in the summer months if they have been allowed to suspend their activities almost completely during the winter. When the warmer and longer days arrive, watering can be stepped up until in mid-summer the plants get as much water as non-succulents. They will swell and grow and if the light is good there is every chance that strange and beautiful flowers will appear on mature plants.

The one exception to this method of treating cacti in order to get them to flower is with the leaf or epiphytic cacti. These include the popular Christmas cactus, *Zygocactus truncatus*, the Easter or Whitsun cactus, *Schlumbergera gaertneri*, the epiphyllums and the rhipsalis, all of which can produce such large, such vivid and such beautiful flowers that they have been called orchid cacti. In their native habitat these plants grow high on jungle trees instead of in rocky, parched and desert soil, like most cacti, and for this reason they require a different kind of treatment.

The Christmas cactus obviously flowers in midwinter in the northern hemisphere, so it will require good light and plenty of water at this time instead of being starved. Its resting period is in mid-summer, when it can well be stood outdoors for the sun, the fresh air and the rain (not too much of this) to help the flat, leaf-like stems to ripen. Although the Easter cactus flowers in the spring instead of in winter, its treatment should be much the same, including the period outdoors in the heat of the summer.

There are hundreds of varieties of epiphyllum mainly in various tints of white, pink and red. They produce a good many flowers, sometimes of very large size. It is wise, though not essential, to prune away old stems after they have produced their flowers, because once a bloom has appeared at one spot no flower will ever again come from here. Try to encourage strong new growth each year as this will aid flower production. Re-pot plants if they grow too large for their containers.

Epiphyllums have been the subject of much hybridisation, as a result of which huge, magnificent and flamboyant flowers of many colours have been produced (with the exception of yellow). Where space is limited, the plants can be pruned back.

Rhipsalis are like smaller, daintier versions of epiphyllums and they require much the same kind of treatment. A light shade suits them better than strong sunlight and even in the winter their roots should receive a little water to keep them from becoming too dry. In recent years greater interest has been shown to rhipsalis, possibly because some of the epiphyllums grow so very large.

A succulent which is not a cactus but is a member of an extraordinarily wide-ranging family is the so-called crown of thorns, *Euphorbia splendens* or *E. millii*. This plant gets its name from the vicious thorns growing up its stems and from the many vivid, tiny red flowers like drops of blood. There is also a version with yellow flowers. This is an easy and rewarding plant to grow, liking full sun and plenty of water most of the time and appearing to need no resting period. One specimen in my possession is more than twenty years old, some 1·5m (4½ft) tall and constantly covered with flowers, summer and winter.

It is unfortunate in a way that some of our most colourful flowering house plants

391

The popular cyclamen (*right*) is available in many colours. Cool conditions are necessary indoors for the plant to last and to continue producing its flowers.

come normally at a time when our homes are least suited to receiving them. These are what are known in the northern hemisphere as Christmas gift plants, and they include *Euphorbia pulcherrima*, poinsettia, *Cyclamen persicum* and *Azalea indica*. All need cooler and more airy conditions than they generally find in our homes at this time of year, and consequently too many of them either fail to give of their best or they die prematurely.

Poinsettia is grown mainly for the colourful bracts it produces, red, pink or white, rather than its flowers, which are the comparatively insignificant berry-like objects at the top of the vivid bracts. As a result of a great deal of hybridising, new varieties are now available which will last in the home for months instead of days. They are bred under artificial conditions of daylight and darkness and with chemical treatment which keeps them dwarf, bushy and well-coloured. The roots of these plants should always be kept moist but not wet and a cool part of the room (about 15°C, 60°F) in good light will suit them best. It is possible to keep the plants after they have dropped their leaves and bring them into condition for the following season, but this can be a tricky exercise best left to the expert.

Cyclamen can be beautiful flowers and almost always are when they are first brought into the house. But the conditions they find there are so disagreeable to them that they quickly lose their beauty. Cyclamen should be kept cool, given plenty of fresh air and never allowed to get dry.

Azalea indica, a member of the rhododendron family, has also been grown under highly artificial conditions for the Christmas trade. Its roots have usually been heavily pruned so they will fit into a comparatively small pot and this makes the plant highly sensitive to any shortage of water. The roots must be kept moist at all times.

The safest way to water a dry azalea plant is to place the pot in a bucket of water, keeping the blooms dry. Wait until bubbles cease to rise from the soil surface, then drain and replace.

392

Care of house plants

A selection of the most popular house plants is given below. From this you can tell at a glance what watering, light, temperature and atmospheric moisture conditions your plants need for healthy growth. However, iron cross begonias, cyclamens and poinsettias need different conditions during their dormant periods. Consult your florist about this when you buy the plants.

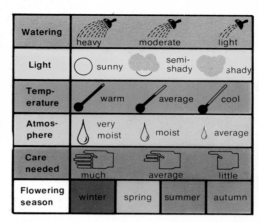

Watering	heavy	moderate	light
Light	sunny	semi-shady	shady
Temperature	warm	average	cool
Atmosphere	very moist	moist	average
Care needed	much	average	little
Flowering season	winter / spring	summer	autumn

Plant	Watering	Light	Temperature	Atmosphere	Care needed	Flowering season
Azalea						
Begonia masoniana (iron cross begonia)						
Cacti						
Chlorophytum (spider comosum plant)						
Chrysanthemums						
Cissus antarctica (kangaroo vine)						
Coleus blumei						
Cyclamen persicum						
Euphorbia pulcherrima (poinsettia)						
Epiphyllum						
Ficus elastica (rubber tree)						
Hedera helix (English ivy)						
Monstera deliciosa (Swiss cheese plant)						
Philodendron scandens (sweetheart plant)						
Saintpaulia (African violet)						
Sansevieria trifasciata (snake plant)						
Tradescantia (wandering jew)						

Exotics

When one writes of exotics one tends to think in terms of glamorous plants such as orchids, yet some of these are comparatively easy to grow under home conditions, while other and apparently less 'exotic' plants are very much more difficult.

The many caladium hybrids, for example, have what is possibly the most beautiful foliage of any plant, at least 30cm (1ft) long, so fine and thin as to be almost translucent, in pale greens and creams or more vivid tints and shades. The main veins are usually picked out in contrasting colours. These plants need to be kept warm, though not uncomfortably so (about 20°C, 68°F) and in conditions which are as humid as can conveniently be arranged. They grow from tubers which come into leaf in spring, display their beautiful leaves until midsummer and then begin to fade. The tubers should then be put away in their pots in a place which is warm and dry and completely forgotten until early spring, when they can be potted up in a peaty soil mixture and placed in a warm, moist atmosphere for the foliage to begin growing.

Smaller, thicker and more sturdy leaves appear on the dieffenbachias, and although less ethereal and longer lasting the foliage can also be very beautiful – streaked, spotted, blotched and marbled, usually in various tints of cream and green. *Dieffenbachia picta* and *D. amoena* are a little difficult to grow, liking warmth, humidity and consequently a rich, peaty soil mixture. But stronger varieties and hybrids are being produced which are less demanding, one of the best of these being *D. arvida* 'Exotica'.

The dieffenbachias are collectively known as dumb canes, the reason being that their sap contains a poisonous element which causes the tongue to swell in conditions of intense pain if it is taken into the

The dignified beauty of *Dieffenbachia amoena* (*above*) fits well into the clean lines of modern decor.

Caladium hybrids develop in spring and must be kept in a warm and humid atmosphere to give of their best.

Dieffenbachia leaves, which can grow to a considerable size, are strikingly marked. Keep them warm, out of draughts, in moist soil.

Philodendren scandens will cling to a wall or a mossed cane with its aerial roots.

If kept out of full sun and intense heat, caladiums should remain attractive until mid- to late summer.

mouth. Plants can be handled perfectly safely: it is only the sap which is poisonous. So if a fading leaf is cut away, for example, it is well to take precautions and wash the hands thoroughly immediately after the operation.

Most members of the large and useful philodendron family, mentioned earlier, are easy to grow and quite dependable as well as being comparatively ordinary. *P. melanochryson* has the same heart-shaped leaves as *P. scandens*, the well-known sweetheart plant of America. But although they are about the same shape and about the same size, their colour and texture are completely different, being a rich green-bronze-gold-copper in colour and having a velvety texture on the upper surface. High humidity, warm temperatures, rich soils and no draughts are the main demands of this plant.

Several of the foliage begonias could be called exotics because of the extraordinary and vivid colours or textures in their leaves.

395

Begonia masoniana, popularly known, for obvious reasons, as the iron cross begonia, is named after Maurice Mason, a Norfolk farmer and distinguished plantsman. Its crinkled, patterned and hairy leaves make it instantly recognisable.

Coleus plants in the widest variations of vivid colours are easy to grow from seed or cuttings. They grow indoors and, in warm areas, in the garden. They like moist soil and plenty of food.

B. rex and *B. masoniana* are examples which come immediately to mind. Both will bear flowers but these are insignificant compared to the leaves – which in the former can vary widely across a range of tints, shades, tones and patterns of greens and reds, purples and silvers and whites, some almost furry and others so metallic as to demand a touch. *B. masoniana* is known as the iron cross begonia because of the distinctive pattern on the soft and crinkled leaves. All begonias, flowering or foliage, have the same lopsided heart shape in their foliage. Some people find them difficult, others say they are easy, and there appears also to be argument on how they should be handled. A rich, peaty soil, some warmth, some light and no particular concessions to

humidity seem to summarise the general opinion.

Two other beautiful plants with vividly coloured foliage are *Codiaeum variegatum*, usually called croton or Joseph's coat, and *Coleus blumei*. The first has handsome spotted, streaked and mottled leaves, glossy surfaced and in several shapes. The colours are green, gold, cream, red, pink, purple and white. Crotons used to be very difficult to grow in the home, but hybridists have now produced types which have just as much colour and excitement as before but are very much less demanding. Coleus plants can be just as colourful as crotons but their texture is soft and sappy instead of hard and glossy. Plants can be grown quite easily from seed, or if you like a particular plant you will find it a simple matter to grow a cutting from it.

Three further plants with gorgeous foliage but which are admittedly difficult to grow until one finds the perfect position or the accepted technique, are the marantas, the calatheas and the fittonias. The most distinctive maranta is *M. leuconeura erythrophylla*, which has soft leaves of brownish green, with the veins picked out in scarlet edged with cream. Somewhat easier but less beautiful is *M.l. kerchoveana*, sometimes called 'rabbits' tracks' because of the brown-on-green marking of the leaves, and known also as the prayer plant because it folds its leaves as if in prayer at night-time.

Calathea mackoyana is sometimes known as *Maranta mackoyana*, and in fact the difference between the two consists only of the number of cells in the ovary. It is generally known as the peacock plant because of the sheer flamboyance of its leaf colour and pattern: the colours are silver, green, red, purple, according to the way the light strikes it, for the upper and lower sides of the leaves differ and the white part is almost translucent except for the dark green veins. Humidity, careful watering, some warmth and a little shade are needed to keep this plant looking its best.

And finally in this little trio is the snake-skin plant, *Fittonia argyroneura*, small, delicate and beautifully patterned, as the common name suggests. Too much water will kill the plant as will too little. Cold will kill it and so will heat. A plant in the sun will curl up and die almost as you watch it. Somewhat easier is *F. verschaffeltii*, with rather larger leaves, more velvety, a basic green with red veins.

All these difficult and delicate plants are worth trying more than once, for the sensitive plant-grower will suddenly find that he has discovered the conditions or the treatment enjoyed by a certain plant and then he need never look back.

But if one enters the world of orchids through the right door, once again there is no need to look back, for it is possible to

The peacock plant, *Calathea mackoyana*, is often called *Maranta mackoyana*. With reasonable care this plant will keep its looks for long periods.

grow orchids as easily as one can bring a hyacinth into bloom in the house. Begin with the simplest and progress to the more difficult, not a hard thing to do when one realises that there must be something like 25,000 orchid species in the world, that something like ten per cent of all flowering plants in the world are orchids, that they grow wild in jungles, on mountains and in roadside verges in many of our most industrialised nations. Orchids were treated with awe when the only examples we saw were those in museums or in the orchid houses of the rich. Those days are over. New methods of propagation, which involve growing tiny slivers of stem in flasks containing a jelly-like sterile substance, mean that a thousand young plants can be easily and inexpen-

sively produced where only a single plant existed before. It is still possible to pay very heavily for an orchid, but it is equally possible to buy fully grown and established plants at prices within the reach of anyone.

So easy is a pleione to grow that bulbs can be bought for a matter of pennies and ready-planted specimens can sometimes be picked up complete in their pots, awaiting merely the addition of water to start them off into growth. The easiest one to find is *Pleione formosana*, available as little bulbs in winter. They are pressed into a bulb-fibre type of compost, watered lightly, and the beautiful pink or white flowers will appear with no further attention. A light windowsill in a warm room is all that is required. The pseudo-bulbs can be retained after the flowers have faded and grown again another year.

Another similar orchid is the bletia or bletilla, also grown from pseudo-bulbs and probably sold either as *Bletia striata* or *Bletilla hyacinthina*. Planted in March, several to a bowl, they will grow and flourish for several weeks in about May or June.

All orchids have three petals and three sepals, but one of these petals is usually grown in another form, looking perhaps like a pouch or a slipper, and is frequently different coloured or patterned. Just above this curiously shaped petal, known sometimes as the labellum or lip, is the column. This single organ takes the place of the more usual male and female parts, the stamens and pistil.

Probably the best known of the slipper orchids is the species still known as cypripediums, although they are more correctly paphiopedilums. *P. insigne* is one of the easiest to grow as well as one of the most popular, easily recognised and longest lasting. The blooms, from 7–15cm (3–6in) long, are generally a greenish-gold with brownish spots; they last from three to six weeks during their winter season. A great deal of work has been done on breeding paphiopedilums and there is a large number of hybrids available. The best known of these is probably *P. i. sanderae*, having a white dorsal sepal and the more familiar greenish-gold base. Plants can usually be bought quite inexpensively.

There are a considerable number of paphiopedilums, the flowers of which come from almost every colour of the spectrum. Some are comparatively large, both as plants and as flowers, while others are less than 10cm (4in) tall. Most species have only a single flower to a stem, but some have two, three or four.

The paphiopedilums do not require high

398

temperatures or strong light, which is one reason why they grow well indoors. But needless to say they like as much humidity as they can get, and their compost or potting medium should always be kept moist. Any orchid nursery will sell special orchid compost, usually made of a mixture of osmunda fibre, sphagnum or peat moss and perhaps some granular peat. They will also be able to supply other types of composts and the various sundries such as special pots or baskets, which are used by orchid growers as they become more interested and enthusiastic.

Only one or two of the paphiopedilums have any fragrance, but most of the cattleyas are scented. Instead of a slipper or pouch, cattleyas have a more open, bell-shaped lip, frequently prettily frilled and divided. The cattleyas come in two types, the labiate or unifoliate with only one leaf growing from each pseudo-bulb, and the bifoliates with two leaves. Once again, there are many hybrids in each type, some large and some dwarf, some with flowers up to 25cm (10in) wide and others with blooms no larger than 5cm (2in). Cattleyas like it fairly warm and humid and they need a significant drop of temperature during the night hours. As they flower in the winter this is not a difficult matter to arrange.

Cattleyas grow to nearly 1m (about 3ft) in height, and this is too large for some homes, although some of the cymbidiums will grow to nearly 2m (over 6ft). However, there is a useful and attractive group of hybrid dwarf cymbidiums which grow no more than about 25cm (10in) tall. Although these are sometimes difficult to grow indoors, the range of the flowers is so magnificent that it might be worth trying. Easier and similar in many ways are the laelias, small, epiphytic and with up to twenty flowers on a stem.

One of the easiest groups to grow indoors is the odontoglossum, with many species and even more hybrids. It is also one of the most rewarding, having many flowers per stem – from about five to thirty-five – and many colours – whites, yellows, reds, pinks, purples. The flowers appear in spring and last from three to six weeks. Plants dislike too much heat in both winter and summer, and prefer to be well ventilated although never in a draught. The roots should be kept moist at all times.

399

Pip plants and herbs

There is a curious fascination in growing a plant from a discarded portion of one's food. To plant an orange pip and watch the little plant growing a few weeks later is always satisfying, and there is an enormous number of plants that can be grown this way. Few will live for very long indoors and even fewer are attractive after the first few weeks, but so powerful is the appeal that even knowledge of this fact will not stop people doing it.

The miniature orange trees that one can buy, complete with little oranges, are no more than an acknowledgement of the fascination of growing a plant from a pip. Do not expect to produce oranges from your own home-grown tree, however, for the flower- and fruit-covered plant you buy is a special kind, specially grown. It is known as the calamondin orange or *Citrus mitis*. The white flowers are sweetly scented and they appear on the little tree at the same time as the fruits, which, by the way, are so bitter as to be quite inedible. Keep the plant on the cool side, out of direct sun, well fed and slightly humid.

An avocado pear stone is easy to grow either in soil or in water. Plant it only half into the soil and watch it split into two as the shoot begins to appear. Or grow it in a hyacinth glass or a jam jar, its blunt base just touching the water, and the more pointed end upwards. Sometimes you will get a single shoot which grows very quickly and quite tall before it puts out its first leaf.

Left: Citrus mitis, the calamondin orange, produces fragrant flowers at the same time as its fruits. Grow in strong light and keep the roots moist.

In this case, after it has produced several leaves pinch out the growing tip to induce the plant to become bushy and attractive.

Mustard and cress, mung beans, alfalfa and several other sprouting foods can be grown easily enough indoors and actually used in salads and as garnishes. Techniques for growing mustard and cress are too well known to need repeating here. Seeds of the other crops, available from most good seed stores, usually require a different sort of treatment.

Some herbs can be grown in the kitchen for use as flavouring or for garnishes. Mint, chives, chervil, tarragon, savory, fennel, parsley, garlic and shallots can all be pot grown, preferably grown outdoors and brought in to a light and warm window sill only to force them into tender growth just before they are used. Do bear in mind the fact that if you really wish to grow herbs indoors for kitchen use, you will have to have a considerable number all potted up and ready to come indoors as they are needed. A single pot of chives, for example, can be used for a single dish. If you have

Plant grown from an avocado pear stone.

facilities and space the best thing is to keep a cold frame stocked with potted herbs, replacing each pot as it is used.

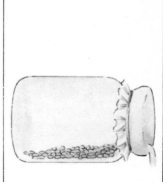

The easiest way to grow seeds is to put a spoonful into a clear glass jam (or other) jar and cover the neck tightly with muslin.

Pour in a little tepid water through the muslin, shake the seeds around, leave for a few minutes, then stand the jar on its side so the water runs out again.

Repeat this process for three or four days. It then will be evident that the seeds have begun to grow. Remove them when they are large enough to eat.

401

2 Environment

Light

The simple statement that giving a plant light is more important than giving it water will come as a surprise to most indoor gardeners until they begin to examine the proposition in greater depth. In the first place, to deprive a plant of light is a total deprivation. It carries no sources of light within itself. But to deprive a plant of water is less important because the soil in which it is growing is almost certainly moderately moist, and every root, branch, stem and leaf also contains moisture.

As humans we can recognise the importance of moisture much more easily than we can recognise the importance of light. We can tell if a plant has been watered by the colour of the surface soil, by the feel of it on our fingers and by the weight of the pot. But we would find it difficult to measure the difference in the quality of light at a south-facing window and in the centre of a room. Only by using the mechanical aid of a photo-electric meter can we recognise the vast difference, a difference of minor importance to us but vital to plants. After all, the reason why plants are grown in greenhouses is not only to give them warmth or protection but also to give them the maximum possible quantity of light.

The quantity of light a plant receives will depend upon the length of day and hence the season, unless one wishes to go into the question of artificial light. Actually the quantity of light is more important than is generally realised, for some plants such as chrysanthemums are short-day plants, which is to say that they will flower only when they receive a certain limited amount of daylight. This can be critical, and commercial growers have learned to extend the season by growing chrysanthemums for a period each day under the artificial but total shade of black plastic sheets. Other plants are grown under artificial light to lengthen their day and so hasten their flowering.

Normally in the home we accept the seasons as they come and we are more concerned about the quality than the quantity of the light our plants receive. This quality of light can vary surprisingly. Light in an industrial city, for example, is considerably weaker than light in the cleaner air of the countryside. Light in a room with a wall or even a tree immediately outside is much less than in one without. Light from a south-facing window is stronger than from a window facing north. Light from a grimy window can equal that from a clean window half its actual size. And above all, light loses its intensity or quality in inverse proportion to the square of the distance from the light source.

Light is vital to plants. Those which flower or have variegated foliage need most light, though not direct sunlight.

Never allow any plants to spend a wintry night between curtain and window pane, where they can easily become frosted.

Cacti and some other succulents are the only plants which can tolerate direct sun on them for long periods.

Plants with dark green, fleshy leaves can generally tolerate poorly lit locations better than brighter plants.

This means, then, that in general terms plants should be placed as near to the windows as possible. But this advice must be qualified in some ways. Only cacti and some other succulents can be grown directly in a south facing window in summer. No plants should ever be placed directly in a window that is loose, cracked, or allows draughts to pierce through. No plant should be placed between a window and a curtain during times of intense cold or frost.

Knowing these facts, it is possible to divide our plant residents into sections: those that demand the most light, those that need good light, those that like a steady and modest light, and finally, those that will grow further away from light. In the same order, choose a south window, an east

or west window, a north window and the centre of a room or a position away from the light. Follow these rules: all cacti and succulents in strong light, even sunlight; all flowering plants and those with variegated foliage in good light but no sun; all others in the less favoured positions, remembering that the darker green and fleshier the leaf the more unfavourable light a plant will accept. It is also worth bearing in mind the fact that any plant growing away from good

Top left: plants with variegated foliage tend to lose their attractive colouring if they do not get a regular quota of good light.

light will not grow so quickly nor so well as one in a window. So to slow down a rate of growth it may be possible to bring a plant into the centre of a room, although it is probably best to know your plant fairly well before doing so. Also, it might be wise to place the plant in good light for brief periods at regular intervals.

Top right: try to place plants in positions where they will each receive the amount of light they need. They will look better and grow better as a result.

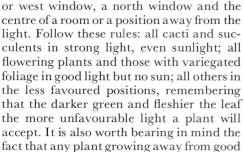

Cacti and succulents react favourably both to strong light and to warmth. Give plenty of water in summer but keep their roots almost dry in colder months.

Warmth

A certain amount of warmth is necessary for nearly all indoor plants, but less than is generally believed. Some, all ivies for example, are quite hardy and will grow in most temperate climes as well in the garden as in the house, although possibly with a change in characteristics. Many plants such as cyclamen will remain fresh and immaculate for weeks longer in a cool room with a temperature of about 10°C (50°F) than in one heated to the more normal 20°C (70°F). In other words, cyclamen plants in flower (and many other flowering plants) should not be kept in the living-room but either in a cool bedroom or possibly in a bathroom.

One trouble with our living habits is that we tend to gather together in social or family groups in certain rooms at certain times.

The rooms are heated and often filled with cigarette smoke and the like, which suits their human occupants – but causes the plants to suffer. After a period of time, and during the colder and darker hours, the room is vacated and as often as not windows are opened to clear the air. The air is certainly cleared, but simultaneously the temperature is lowered – to a dangerous degree for many plants.

There is a common fallacy that indoor plants are hot-house plants, but this is not so. Some, it is true, have been bred from plants which originally grew in heated and humid greenhouses, but without exception these have been educated to accept more realistic living conditions. So long as the home is heated sufficiently to keep out frosts, many indoor plants will grow there quite happily. They will prefer slightly

Too often plants given as gifts are displayed in the living-rooms of homes where the temperature rises in the evenings and the air is polluted with tobacco fumes.

The buds of cyclamen will develop and open and the flowers will remain fresh-looking for long periods if the plants are kept in a well-lit but cool and airy location.

If a plant must be placed over a source of heat, protect it by standing it in a tray filled with gravel or sand kept just moist. The warmth will cause the water to evaporate and keep the plant cool.

higher temperatures, but given a choice between cooler conditions with clean air and some humidity, and warmer conditions with a stuffy atmosphere and dry air, they will do better in the first.

Most indoor plants, especially those which rely for their interest and attraction on their foliage, have their resting period in the colder months. They remain semi-dormant for some weeks. Their watering should be cut down during this period and they should be fed hardly at all. Yet if they are in too warm an atmosphere the moisture in the soil around their roots will be baked away and either the plants will wilt or they will require more water. This will tend to activate the plants into renewed growth again before their rest period has been completed. One useful answer to this and other problems is described in the sec-tion on humidity, beginning on page 407.

No plant should be placed too near a source of heat of whatever type. Even the sun can be too hot for some plants at some parts of the day, particularly if it shines through glass. If for some special reason a plant must be placed, say, over a radiator, then it is usually possible to deflect the rising warm air away from the leaves of the plant. Another means of providing some protection is to stand the plant on a gravel tray with a little water in it. The rising hot air will by this means produce a moist atmosphere and so do little harm.

Try to avoid great differences of temper-ature at different times. Some rooms, for example, are heated only in the evenings; during the night they cool off and in the mornings they can be quite cold. Most plants dislike violent changes although they will adapt to gradual ones. There are, however, a few plants such as some orchids which definitely need a temperature drop of several degrees at night-time to conform with the cooler nights they found in their normal habitat.

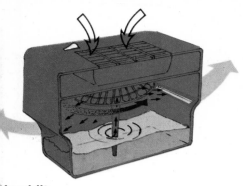

Humidity

We have become accustomed to associating humidity with high temperatures, whereas this need not be so. For example, in a centrally heated room in winter with the temperature at, say, 20°C (70°F) we will find that the relative humidity reading on a hygrometer may fall to 50° or perhaps even less. With a window or two open, the temperature drops but the relative humidity rises. This is simply because the moisture in the room has been evaporated by the heat, and when the windows were closed the outer air with its inherent moisture could not enter.

When we consider that all plants either grow or originally grew out of doors it should be apparent to us that they will require a greater degree of humidity than is generally found in our homes. It is more comfortable for us to live in dry air than in moist, although this can be a matter of degree. We tend today to live in too dry an atmosphere in our homes and public places, to the detriment of our skins and our furnishings. Fortunately, only the slightest increase in humidity is sufficient to improve the health of our skins, the condition of our furniture and the comfort of our plants. In most areas of the temperate world relative humidities out of doors probably range for most of the time between about 60° and 80°. The first figure is sufficient for most of our plants indoors, but is a higher figure than is generally found indoors today.

The most efficient humidifiers send a gentle current of moist air into the room from a reservoir of warmed water (*top left*). One type widely available is shown above.

A significant rise in relative humidity can be gained by placing small bowls of water about the house. They can be made to look decorative with flowers, shells or stones.

Using a plunge pot lessens the risk of overwatering, keeps the flower pot cool and moist, and sends a constant current of humid air up around the plant foliage.

So if humidity is low we should do something about it; fortunately this is a simple matter. There is a large range of humidifiers on the market, from complex and expensive electric machines to the simple and inexpensive provision of a pan of water. The mere provision of one or two saucers or dishes of water in a room can significantly raise the humidity level. If the saucer cannot be discreetly hidden, then use a more decorative vessel of some kind and pour into it a collection of sea shells, marbles, pebbles, or even make a flower arrangement. It is possible to buy quite inexpensive pottery or china vessels to hang on a radiator which when filled with water gradually increases humidity by releasing water vapour to the room.

Plants can be given their own local humidity without much trouble by standing their pots on a tray holding a layer of constantly moist shingle or sand, or by making use of what are commonly known as plunge pots.

This last aid is important for several reasons. The vast majority of indoor plants are grown in the traditional pot, either terracotta or plastic, with a hole or several holes in the base for drainage purposes. This means that indoors this pot must be stood in a saucer or some other receptacle to avoid staining or marking the furniture. It is very easy when a plant is watered for the water to come through the drainage hole, fill the saucer and spill on to the furniture. Or even if this does not happen we may find that the saucer is filled with water and, unknown to its owner, the plant stands in this perhaps for a day or two while it steadily drowns.

The plunge pot is a means of overcoming this problem, of providing a localised humidity and of increasing the decorative value of the plant all at the same time. This is a vessel of some kind which has no drainage hole and is a little larger than the flower pot. It can be a purpose-made pot, a flower vase, a bucket, a salad bowl, a sauce boat, almost anything that is decorative. It should be selected for its suitability and its appearance so that it blends or contrasts with the plant colour, texture, size and shape. This vessel should have a good layer of peat or some other moisture-retentive material placed at the base and the flower pot should be stood on this, while the space between the pot and its cover should also be filled with peat.

Now when the plant is watered any excess will be absorbed by the peat without doing any damage. The peat will also serve to insulate the flower pot from extremes of temperature. The moist peat inside will gradually release its moisture to the air and waft a slightly humid breeze upwards around the leaves of the plant.

Nearly all plants enjoy an occasional bath such as they might get during a summer shower, and when conditions allow it is a good thing to put most plants out into a light rain for an hour or two, allowing them to drain and dry out before they are replaced in position. Many plants in the home can be given their own artificial rain occasionally with a spray of clean tepid water. This seldom marks furnishings if done with discretion. It should not be given to plants with furry foliage or those which are in flower.

There is one plant with furry foliage which benefits greatly by an occasional humidity bath and this is the beautiful and tender saintpaulia, or African violet. One way of helping it is to give it a steam bath. In the centre of a large bowl or basin make a little island of, say, an upturned saucer. On this stand the saintpaulia in a waterproof container. Pour boiling water into the bowl, which should fall just short of the level of the pot of the saintpaulia. The steam will rise up around the plant and do it the world of good. Leave the plant there until the water has cooled.

Pressure sprayers such as these produce a fine film of moisture so fine that there is no risk of damage to furnishings.

A steam bath takes time and trouble but is a great help to sensitive plants such as African violets when the atmosphere is too hot and dry. Many other types of plant will benefit from this treatment too.

409

3 Decorative uses

As furnishings

Nothing furnishes a home more quickly than a few indoor plants. They soften sharp corners, drape bare walls, fill empty space and give an immediate imprint of your personality to a previously anonymous area. A young couple setting up home for the first time can save significant sums by filling their empty spaces with plants until they can gradually fill them with furniture, and when they have acquired furniture the plants will still give useful decoration.

For the more established home, plants can be employed as stage props to bring about certain required effects. If, for example, a certain piece of your furniture has in the past been damaged or soiled by a cigarette burn, a glass ring or even by the careless scuffing of feet, you can put this

A wide spreading trailer will make a room appear wider than it is.

A climbing monstera will take the eye up to its tip and make a room appear higher than it really is.

piece behind the safety barrier of a tall plant. You can hide a stained wall or disguise the unpleasant view from a window. You can even change the apparent shape or size of a room to a certain degree by using your plants intelligently.

If your room is long and narrow, for example, and you wish to give the impression that it is wider, spread a long trailer horizontally along a shelf, mantelpiece or

article of furniture along the narrow wall. This will have the effect of making the eyes move horizontally and thus apparently widen the room. In the same way, if you want to make a room look taller, grow one or two pillar plants from floor to ceiling.

Alternatively you can achieve much the same kind of results by using colour, although you may have to resort to flowers on this occasion at certain times of the year. Dark or deep colours are said to be recessive, that is, they seem to recede from you. So if you wish to extend a room, place against the wall you wish to recede a group of dark-leaved plants or a flower arrangement of dark blue, dark green or dark red flowers. Light and bright colours are advancing, so use these to obtain the opposite effect.

You can also use colours, shapes and textures to draw attention to a picture or piece of furniture, or perhaps to emphasise a colour or pattern. For example, you may have on your walls a reproduction of a famous picture which might appear to be somewhat hackneyed although a favourite of yours. Try dressing it up by curving a trail of ivy around the frame, pointing to it with the exclamation mark of a sansevieria spear, or picking out its main colours in a plant arrangement by its side.

A screen of plants need not be dense and overpowering. A single plant such as a cissus can be woven through canes to look almost like a hedge or, as here, several different plants can play a more decorative role.

411

Climbers

Ivies, cissus and rhoicissus, *Philodendron scandens*, fatshedera, hoya and the ivy-like Cape ivy and German ivy, *Senecio macroglossus variegatus* and *S. mikanoides*, are all easy and popular climbers which can be used to great advantage decoratively in the home. Train them to climb a pole, to cover a wall, to act as a soft green frame to a doorway or interior arch. Most can be tied or clipped to a cane, or even to stout string fixed from floor to ceiling, which is easily hidden. Several climbers can be made to climb up a mossed pole as described on page 385.

A climbing plant suited to larger homes, offices or showrooms is the fascinating *Monstera deliciosa*, known popularly as the Swiss cheese plant because of the holes, perforations and slashes in the large leaves.

Cissus antarctica, or kangaroo vine, a natural climber, is easy to cultivate and quick to respond to care. It is best grown up a string or cane support.

This will grow up a wall and grow right around the room if allowed to, a decorative feature which can be most useful. This, and certain other plants, present a problem because of the production of aerial roots, long, thong-like shoots which appear on branches and trail downwards. In their native state these aerial roots serve a useful purpose in drawing sustenance from the

Opposite: Monstera deliciosa, the Swiss cheese plant, will grow very large, so for limited spaces it is better to choose the smaller *M. pertusa* or *M.d. borsigiana*.
Below left: the popular *Hedera helix* 'Chicago'.
Below right: the so-called Cape ivy, *Senecio macroglossus variegatus*.

soil to higher portions of the plant, but in the home they are apt sometimes to be an embarrassment, for they are not particularly attractive. It will be obvious that in theory the best thing to do with these aerial roots is to lead them down into the original container of soil, or if this is too far away, into a secondary or subsidiary pot, for this way they will help to feed and encourage the plant growth. On the other hand, if you have no objection to the plant growing perhaps a little less speedily, a little less lushly and a little less large, then there is no reason why these roots should not be cut neatly from the plant and thrown away.

413

Trailers

All climbers can, of course, also be trailers. In this case one does not train them up a cane or string but allows them to hang downwards. But there are a few plants which actually look better hanging downwards ·than they do climbing. They are excellent inhabitants of indoor hanging baskets, and look well tumbling from a torchère, a bracket or a shelf. Two of the best of these are the familiar tradescantias and zebrinas. Yet these and most other trailers need careful grooming to look constantly at their best. Many are apt to brown and shrivel at their tips and so trails should not be allowed to grow too long except in the case of stronger plants such as a scindapsus or a *Ficus pumila*.

Other useful trailers include *Peperomia scandens* and *P. glabella* and the delightful, easy, eager and decorative *Plectranthus fruticosus*, which grows so well and so easily that it is almost impossible to buy and can be propagated only by begging a cutting from a friend. But it is so prolific and puts

Contrast in shape, size and texture. The monstera on the floor reaches up to the plectranthus growing above and tumbling downwards. Both are easy to grow.

This little trailing fig, *Ficus pumila*, needs moist and humid conditions to give of its best. It grows well twining among other plants in a mixed bowl.

414

Philodendron scandens, the sweetheart plant, has better foliage and will cling to walls, but the hoya annually produces delicate waxy flowers.

out roots so quickly that this is a simple matter. It has almost round leaves 3–5cm (1–2in) across, dark green with a purple fuzz. It produces clouds of dainty white flowers through the summer.

A first-class, easy and strikingly attractive fern that grows well as a trailer is the stagshorn fern, *Platycerium alicorne*. This grows dramatic fronds or leaves very similar to a stag's horns, glaucous blue and slightly furry, from a central ball. The plant can be knocked from its pot and nailed or tied to a board or a piece of cork bark and placed high on a wall. It can be left there safely until the fronds appear to be thirsty and then the entire plant plus its board or cork mount can be immersed in water until bubbles cease to rise from the centre. Then leave it to drain and replace.

And perhaps the most charming trailer of them all is the little hearts entwined, *Ceropegia woodii,* with its trails studded with little grey-green heart-shaped leaves at intervals, looking almost as though they were moving about on feet.

415

Trees or shrubs

Probably the greatest number of indoor plants can be said to fall in this group, yet this is the most diverse of collections. The plants may be tree-like or shrub-like, but they can differ widely in the size, shape, colour and texture of their individual leaves. The familiar *Ficus elastica* and the tough little *Araucaria excelsa* are both trees but they are entirely different in appearance from each other.

Most trees and shrubs are at their best when they are comparatively mature and large, for then they have a dignity, a presence and a definite function as a part of the furniture. And this they most certainly can

In the foreground the soft, luxuriant trails of a plectranthus make a solid but lightweight wall of colour, while behind it the larger glossy green leaves of a *Philodendron bipinnatifidum* reach out on long, arching stems.

be, for they fill significant space and can therefore act as a barrier to guide the steps in a certain direction or as a screen to give just a little added privacy to the corner of a room or an office.

Because they are large, trees and shrubs can be used effectively in groups, for their individual shapes can be contrasted attractively one with another, and the shapes, textures and colours of their foliage can be compared in an exercise of careful and subtle choice.

416

Trees and shrubs useful as indoor plants can include: *Schefflera actinophylla*, many of the larger palms, the tree-like *Pittosporum undulatum*, several of the larger philodendrons, some of the larger dieffenbachias, *Fatsia japonica*, the elegant *Dizygotheca elegantissima* and *Grevillea robusta*, and for limited periods and at certain seasons such splendid flowering shrubs such as hydrangeas, azaleas, poinsettias and fuchsias.

Unfortunately many people believe that bonsai, or dwarfed Japanese trees, are suitable for indoor gardening. This is not so. Bonsai trees are meant to be grown out of doors, not necessarily completely in the open, for most have the shelter of some kind of light roofing and shading, but in the atmosphere of the open. Most can be brought indoors for a few days at a time and then taken out again, and if a number of bonsai trees are grown it is possible to have a succession of them on display indoors.

Cocos weddeliana is a pretty little palm tree with dainty foliage which sometimes tends to go brown at the tips.

Several varieties of rubber plant have been hybridised. This all-green form is *Ficus elastica* 'Decora'.

Ficus lyrata has large, slightly waisted leaves which have given it the popular name of fiddle-leaf fig.

417

4 Treatment

Watering

More indoor plants are killed by overwatering than anything else. This warning has been given countless times, yet it is still ignored. The reason is probably that the basic function of watering is not properly understood. Water is needed by plants for two main and related reasons: (i) to keep the stems and leaves turgid so that (ii) they can be fed with a constant stream of liquid foods from roots to leaf tips.

Plant roots require both air and water and when a pot is overwatered all the air is expelled and the roots drown, rot and gradually kill the plant. Correct watering is a means of feeding the roots with both the moisture and the air that they need.

It is impossible to lay down hard and fast rules about watering, for much depends on circumstances, weather and season. But it is safe to advise most strongly that no plant should be watered if the soil surface in the pot is moist. Let it get almost bone dry first. Plenty and seldom should be the aim.

With a new plant, for the first few times pour in water to the top of the pot and see if

Left: the leaves of most bromeliads form a vase or cup which should always be kept filled with water.

it gradually trickles out of the drainage holes in the base. If it does not, give it a little more until it does, and try to bear in mind roughly how much water you gave it. Let the pot stand in the puddle it has made for about an hour. The soil may reabsorb this water, but if it does not, then empty it out. Never let any plants stand in water.

What you are doing by watering in this manner is moistening the whole of the root ball, not just a part of it, and bringing in air at the same time. The water in the top of the pot courses down through the spaces in the soil, pushing downwards the air that was lying in these spaces. At the same time, as

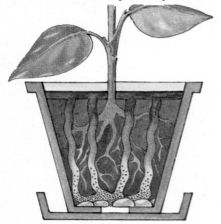

An underwatered plant (*left*) will eventually die because some of its roots are dry and cannot absorb food or moisture. Stale air accumulates to poison these roots and the soil cracks away from the pot sides. When a

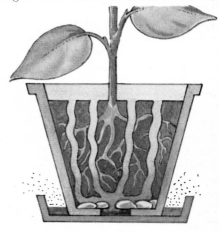

plant is given too much water (*right*) all the air spaces are filled and the plant cannot breathe. The roots become slimy, rot and fail to feed the plant with food or moisture.

418

An overwatered plant. Whether overwatered or underwatered, a plant will respond by drooping and, eventually, shedding its leaves.

the water rushes downwards it drags after it fresh air. So the watering pushes out the foul and used air and brings in new.

Remember always that it is a simple matter to add more water to a plant pot when it is needed, but it is an almost impossible task to take away water once it has been added. A human being or an animal can make a choice whether or not to take another drink, but a plant can only accept.

Unfortunately the symptoms of overwatering and underwatering are almost the same. Leaves will droop and turn yellow and eventually fall. So if you notice this, never give more water unless you are certain that the plant needs it, perhaps because you have been away, for example.

We know that plants require very much more water in summer than in winter, but watch the weather closely. A hot day might also be dark, overcast and humid, in which case the plant is likely to lose but little water through transpiration. A hot, sunny day may cause some plants to wilt, yet their soil is still moist. The answer to this is that transpiration is taking place more quickly than the plant can absorb moisture through its roots and the addition of water will make no difference. Instead give the plant a light spray of clean and tepid water all over its foliage. If this is impossible, move the plant to a cooler or darker place, or draw the curtains for a little while.

419

Feeding

Once again, those people who take their indoor plants seriously almost always over-feed them. This is bad for the plants and also bad for the owners, because if the plants survive this treatment they will grow large too quickly, outgrow their strength and become prone to disease.

Every plant newly bought should have enough food in its soil to last at least two or three months and will not require feeding during this time. After this, feed the plant regularly according to season, but very lightly. Never for any reason exceed the quantities recommended on the bottle or packet. It is, if anything, far better to reduce the dosage slightly.

What kind of food or fertiliser you apply will depend on your personal preferences and their general availability. Fertilisers come as liquids, powders or pills. Plants can absorb foods only in the form of liquids in solution with the moisture around their roots, so obviously feeding should take place simultaneously with watering.

In winter feeding should either be suspended entirely or the frequency should be greatly reduced, depending to some extent on conditions of warmth, light and weather. In summer a very light feed once a week is preferable to a heavier dose fortnightly. Make the change from winter treatment to summer as a gradual process rather than a sudden one.

There are various foliar feeds available on the market which may prove to be quite

Fertilisers in pelleted form are pressed into the soil and gradually dissolve each time the plant is watered.

Spraying plants with a foliar feed has certain special advantages, for it helps to keep the leaves clean and gives a welcome humidity as well as providing food compounds accepted by leaves as well as roots.

useful for many plants. However, since they are sprayed all over a plant, it may not always be convenient to use them owing to possible damage to furnishings. If a plant cannot be taken out of doors for this treatment, remember that it is by no means essential; other methods of feeding also exist.

On the other hand, even foliar feeds can be absorbed by the roots of a plant, so if you cannot spray over the leaves of an entire plant, consider using the foliar feed as a normal fertiliser applied to the roots of the plant through the soil.

Not all plants need feeding through the soil, although this is normally where their roots and therefore their feed source is to be found. The room pines or bromeliads, for example, have a shallow and comparatively unimportant root system. If they are fed consistently through their roots, or even watered through their roots, they would suffer root rot and die. Most of them are epiphytes, which means that they grow on trees in the jungle, using the trees not as food but as a means of support. They make their food from the leaves and other debris that might fall and be collected by the obstruction of their roots. Bromeliads, therefore, can be fed as they are watered, by filling their central cups or vases with a dilute liquid feed. Depending on the fertiliser used, this can stain or encrust the central vase – a disfiguration which is unnecessary. Fortunately, the very occasional feed that is advisable for bromeliads can very well and quite safely be given through the soil instead of through the central cup.

With feeding, as with many other aspects of growing indoor plants, a measure of common sense is necessary. If a problem arises and a certain answer seems the most sensible, then it is probably the correct one, although it might sometimes be prudent to check to make quite sure.

421

Group therapy

There is a double advantage to be gained in growing two or more plants together, or making a plant arrangement. The obvious advantage is decorative, for opportunities are presented to create an artistic effect by blending and contrasting colours, shapes, textures and forms. Less obvious is the advantage to be gained by the plants.

Most plants benefit from close association with other plants just as they do in the wild. One plant helps to protect the other. In addition, because all plants transpire moisture from their leaves, this moisture

the cyperus is a bog plant which needs to have its roots constantly moist. There are two ways of making plant arrangements, in pot or out. In other words, the plants can be grouped together in their individual pots, placed in a large bowl or other vessel with the pots concealed with moss, peat or pebbles. Or the plants can be knocked from their pots and all planted together in a common soil inside the large container. Both ways have certain virtues. If plants retain their pots they can far more easily be taken out and replaced. The greatest benefit from knocking plants from their

helps to create humidity and manufacture a micro-climate around the group which is of mutual benefit.

What plants can successfully be grouped together is more a matter of taste than technique so long as certain basic rules are obeyed. Plants to be grouped together must have an affinity in moisture requirement. It would be impossible to grow cacti and cyperus, for example, in the same bowl, because the cacti normally need little or, at some time of the year, no water, whereas

Plants grouped together in a mass can look effective if the collection has been selected with skill and taste and the plants have similar food and water requirements.

pots for planting is probably when comparatively small plants are used, for there will then be no problem about hiding the container.

A compromise method giving the best of both worlds is to knock the plants from their plastic or terracotta pots and slip the root ball into a black polythene sleeve. The sleeve, being of negligible thickness and

422

completely pliable, allows the plants to be grouped more closely together and yet remain quite easily removable.

Which ever method is used, special care will have to be taken with drainage in the large container that holds all the plants. If the plants are in their pots it will be possible to some extent to control watering so that some plants get more than others, but there is always the danger that excess water from one might damage the roots of its neighbour. Plants out of their pots and in a common soil will obviously need some special provision for drainage, because in both cases the communal container will have no drainage holes itself. So for all types of plant arrangements it is essential to fill the bottom inch or so of the container with some draining material such as pebbles or pea gravel. At the same time, be sure to water with care, in the knowledge that any excess moisture cannot run away but will be contained in that basic drainage layer. If water does, in fact, collect in this area and stay there for some time, there is always the danger that it will begin to smell, so a few nuggets of charcoal among the drainage pebbles will help to absorb this smell and keep the water sweet.

It is quite easy to plant a bowl or dish garden and to make a terrarium, and so long as the advice above is followed no real problems should be encountered. Rather more difficult is the creation of a bottle

To make a bottle garden, first ensure that you have everything to hand. Check that the bottle is spotlessly clean and dry, for once work has started it will be too late to go back. Put a good drainage layer at the base of the bottle. Use a light, open soil – a sterilised sort, so that no weed seeds will germinate. Grouping plants in a bottle garden demands an artist's talent. Look for contrasts in shape, colour and texture but not of type, for all must live together under the same conditions.

garden, where the opening or neck is too narrow to permit entry of the hands. The following suggestions will probably be helpful to those who wish to try.

First make sure that the interior of the bottle is scrupulously clean before you begin and that it is completely dry. Pour in just a little peat through an improvised chute or funnel. This is mainly to break the fall of the next layer, the drainage material, and avoid shattering the glass. This drainage layer should be fairly deep, preferably at least 5cm (2in). On top of this should go the soil, which must be sterilised to prevent weeds growing and must be sufficiently rich in plant foods to sustain gentle growth over a long period. When inserting the soil down your chute try to make sure that it does not soil the sides of the bottle, yet try also to slope it somewhat or make one or two hills rather than keep it dead level.

The plants to choose for a bottle garden will obviously have to be small enough to enter the neck, so they will generally be immature. But the thing to remember is that they will grow. Never choose a subject which will grow either too large or too

Attach any improvised tools securely to a slim cane.

Dig a small hole for the plant roots, being careful not to go too deep. Gently tease away most of the soil from the plant roots.

quickly, for in both these cases the plant will have to be severely cut down or removed completely to avoid damage to other plants. Do not, for example, use creeping or trailing plants such as ivy or *Ficus pumila* unless you are prepared to prune them at regular intervals.

The following plants are all suitable for a bottle garden: *Acorus gramineus* (grass), small-leaved varieties of *Begonia rex*, *Carex japonica* (grass or rush), *Codiaeum variegatum pictum* (croton), *Cryptanthus acaulis* (earth star), *Dryopteris erythrosa* (fern), *Fittonia argyroneura* (snakeskin plant), *Maranta makoyana* (peacock plant), *Neanthe bella* (palm), *Pellionia pulchra*, *Peperomia caperate*, *Pilea cadierei nana* (aluminium plant) and *Pteris biaurita argyraea* (fern).

With a spoon tied securely to a long cane dig a little hole for the plant. Knock the plant from its pot and very gently tease away some of the soil in the root ball, then, holding the plant by the tip of its foliage insert the root through the neck of the bottle and lean the bottle so that the roots hang directly over the hole. Let it drop, use your spoon to move it to an upright position and then cover the roots with soil and firm. Repeat the process for the remainder of the plants. If you wish you can add an occa-

In order that the finished bottle garden can be seen clearly and enjoyed, the sides must be clean, clear and free from condensation. Water with great care and at long intervals for healthy and attractive plants – removal of unsightly elements is by no means easy.

Below: two unusual and attractive containers for similar gardens.

sional rock or piece of driftwood to dramatise the picture.

Add no more than a cupful of water, preferably sprayed gently on to the plants and soil and also on to the inner sides of the glass bottle to remove any traces of dust or

424

Holding the plant by the tips of the leaves position it and the bottle so that the roots will drop neatly into the prepared planting hole.

Spread soil over the roots and firm down.

soil that may have been added as work progressed. Theoretically you can then seal the top and the plants will grow for months without any further need to water. In practice, to seal the top nearly always leads to damping off, mainly because the balance of moisture to plant life must be exact. But watering should be minimal, certainly no more than once a month and in the smallest quantities. Keep the carboy or bottle out of direct sunlight and not in too warm a situation, to avoid excess evaporation.

425

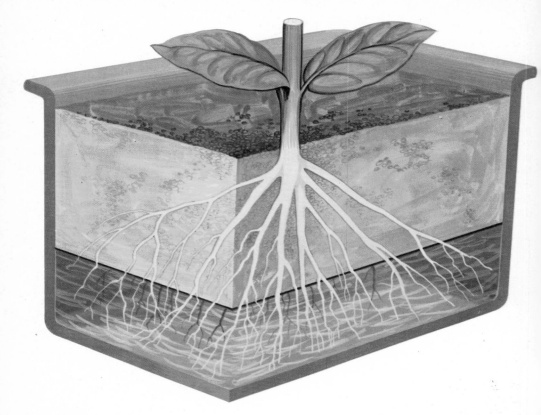

Hydroponics

In view of the dangers of overwatering indoor plants, it seems paradoxical to say that if you grow your plants in water alone this risk vanishes. Plant roots need air as well as water, so surely the plant will drown if grown in water alone? The answer is that the roots are not merely submerged in water, but grow in a special medium which is kept moist from the water below. Thus they get both moisture and air.

The latest method registered under the name 'hydroculture' makes use of inert clay granules as the growing medium. The plant's roots, washed of all soil, are grown in this medium, which extends down to a water reservoir that is kept always at a specific level as shown on a clearly seen indicator. The fertiliser used is a specially prepared material with a long life, which

The growing medium of inert clay granules exists merely to anchor the plant through its roots, which serve also to absorb and distribute moisture, food and air.

gradually releases its properties into the water and so lasts for some six months.

There is no doubt that this hydroculture method is an excellent and problem-free way of growing indoor plants. But it is only a somewhat expensive refinement of simpler means of growing plants hydroponically which have been used for many years. Without special containers, special clay granules, special water-level indicators and special slow release fertilisers, it is still perfectly possible to grow many types of indoor plants for months or even years at a time so long as one basic rule is observed.

The plant must rest in the neck of the container so that its roots can go down into the water and the upper portions of the plant grow upwards. This can be easily enough organised with a little grid of wire mesh or something similar. The container itself should preferably be of glass so that the water level can easily and quickly be checked. The roots should be carefully washed clean of all soil and inserted in the vessel so that the plant is securely held in position. Water should then be poured in so that it covers all the roots. A touch of liquid fertiliser is added. The important point to remember is that to prevent the plant from drowning, the water level must now be allowed to drop, through absorption by the plant and by evaporation. This will mean that the roots are totally submerged in water only for a day or so and then are gradually exposed more and more to the air, only the longer roots remaining below the water level. So long as these deeper roots still touch the water, the plant will receive sufficient moisture for its requirements, and so long as some of the roots are above water level they will receive sufficient air to keep them alive. Fertiliser applications should be light but regular, to avoid excessive build-up in the water.

Water should be topped up to cover the whole root system only at moderate intervals, allowing the water level to drop considerably so that some roots touch water and some are in air. In the right-hand jar, the water level has been allowed to drop rather too far: half-way down is enough.

427

5 Propagation

Half the fun of indoor plants is growing your own, and with many plants this is indeed a simple thing to do. Some plants even produce their own young.

Although some indoor plants can be raised from seed this is not generally a satisfactory means of growing them, partly because of the excessive time involved and partly because high temperatures and high humidity are often necessary. Without the assistance of a propagating case and a greenhouse, the best means of growing seeds is to make use of a translucent plastic bag and a warm situation such as an airing cupboard.

Sow the seed in the normal way in a pot or box and then place this inside the plastic bag. Blow into it so that the film stands clear of the soil surface and then securely tie up the opening so that the bag is virtually sealed. Place the package in some warm

A seed pan or pot in a sealed plastic bag is protected from cold and draughts. The seeds germinate safely and can then be gradually exposed to a normal environment.

situation and watch carefully for the first signs of growth. If during this period so much condensation takes place that water lies in puddles inside the bag, open it, remove the pot or box, turn the bag inside out and replace. As soon as growth is noticed open the bag slightly, leaving the pot still inside. Remove the package from the warm location for a few hours each day, gradually lengthening this period and gradually opening the bag more and more until it can be removed entirely. When the little plants are large enough to be handled, prick them out into individual pots.

Apart from growing plants from seed they can be propagated by division, from cuttings, by layering and air layering.

428

Division Many of the exceedingly useful and decorative plants known collectively as bromeliads or room pines will produce a young plant growing up from the soil beside the parent after it has flowered. By knocking the plant from its pot it is a simple matter to cut away this young plant with a portion of root and plant it separately.

Some plants such as aspidistras and sansevierias will produce more and more spiky leaves as they grow older and eventually these so overcrowd the pot that they should be divided. Again, merely knock the plant from its pot and divide the roots into portions, giving each a separate pot.

After having been grown in the home for some time the little *Saintpaulia ionantha* or African violet will produce so many leaves that they choke the pot. Many of these are from separate plants, so once again knock the plant from its pot and very gently and carefully tease the tiny roots apart so that you get several individual plants. Pot these up separately.

Cuttings There are several types of cuttings, and to begin with the simplest we need mention only the ubiquitous tradescantia. We all know how easy it is to pinch out the growing tip of a long trail and stick the end in a pot of soil. It will take growth almost immediately. Many indoor plants can be propagated easily enough with this type of stem cutting.

Leaf cuttings can be divided into several kinds. An African violet leaf, for example, with a portion of its little stem, can be inserted in a pot of peat and sand and will quickly take root. A long, spear-like sansevieria leaf can be cut into portions, each portion planted in soil, and rooting will take place with each portion. Begonias and *B. rex* can be propagated in much the same way. It is possible to take a leaf and cut it into portions, planting each one and gaining many new plants. Or a leaf may merely be pegged to a soil surface so that it lies flat, and if the major leaf veins are cut through, new plants will grow from these places.

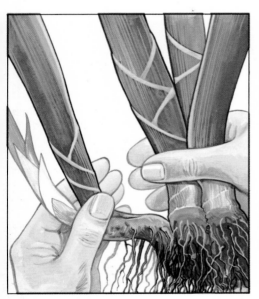

When dividing the roots of a plant always make sure that each portion includes some good root hairs.

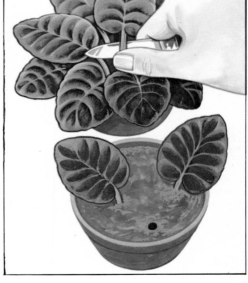

Bury the petiole right up to the leaf when taking leaf cuttings of saintpaulias.

429

Part of the attraction of a chlorophytum is the long, arching stems bearing miniature plants at the tips.

To propagate a chlorophytum by layering, rest the plantlet on another pot of soil, if necessary holding it down with a hairpin, weight or toothpick.

Layering One of the reasons for the popularity of the familiar *Chlorophytum comosum variegatum* is its habit of sending out long arching stems which carry first the little white flowers and then miniature plants. If these plants are allowed to rest on the soil surface of another pot they will quickly take root and can then have the original stem cut away.

Most climbers can easily be propagated by layering. Take one of the stems or trails and a few cm from the growing tip gently bend or twist the stem so that it is fractured but not broken off. Bury this portion in a pot of soil and after a period you will notice new growth, which indicates that new roots have been formed. Then cut the new plant away from its parent.

430

Air layering It is obviously impossible to bend the growing tip of a rubber plant, say, to layer it in the way described above. So we resort to another type of layering. In just the same way, choose your spot a few centimetres from the growing tip and in this case cut a little nick or sliver. Cover this with a good ball of moist sphagnum moss, tying it securely in position around the stem to cover the wound. So that the moss will not dry out too quickly, cover it with a piece of plastic sheeting and again tie this securely in place. After a while it will be evi-

Collect together stem cuttings from ivies, rhoicissus and cissus, tradescantia, *Philodendron scandens*, impatiens or busy lizzie, coleus, peperomia or *Saxifraga sarmentosa* (there are many others), and insert these in the vessel, using more pebbles to secure them in place. Arrange the cuttings so that they contrast decoratively one with the other. Pour in water with just a trace of liquid fertiliser. Very shortly the cuttings will put out roots into the water and the little plants will grow. As time goes by, the arrangement will become more and more

Plant cuttings of many types will quickly take root if they are held by pebbles in a water solution. Make sure that the water level never drops too much for too long, or the plants will suffer.

Many plants, such as tradescantia, can be induced to grow roots if cuttings are merely placed in plain water. When the roots are well developed, remove the cutting and pot it up in a good soil.

dent that roots have grown into the moss and when this happens cut away the top under these roots, remove the plastic sheeting and pot up the young plant in the normal manner.

A surprising number of plants will send out roots if cuttings are merely placed in water. It is possible to make use of this fact to make a long-lasting home decoration and to grow a number of new plants at the same time. Take a fairly large waterproof vessel and cover the base with pebbles.

beautiful and significant.

Eventually the plants will grow too large to be collected together in this fashion. They can then be removed and potted up individually. This 'puddle-pot' method, as it is called, is a particularly easy and useful means of propagating several plants at the same time. Make sure that the water level does not drop too low at any time, but on the other hand do not always keep it filled to maximum level. Allow the roots to get some air occasionally.

431

6 Pests and diseases

So long as indoor plants are given the minimal attention that they require there is no real reason why they should suffer from any but the most superficial damage from pests or diseases. If they are kept clean, examined at regular intervals, maintained in conditions which are suitable for them, and not over-watered or over-fed, most plants will live for years without trouble.

Examination is the real answer. Though one cannot subject every plant in the home to a minute appraisal every day, after a time even a casual glance will suggest when something is wrong: a twisted leaf, a yellowing, reddening or browning, a drooping – these are the first indications of trouble.

Pests are far more likely than disease and these are more likely to occur in summer than in winter. There is always the threat of attack from aphis coming in from the garden, normally quickly seen and as quickly settled. Red spider mite will attack only where the atmosphere is over-dry and arid. Less frequently, a tuft of white cotton will appear, indicating mealy bug, or a grey protuberance, which suggests scale.

Caterpillars, ants, earwigs, worms, slugs, thrips, white flies and other insects may also cause trouble, but none of these is likely to escape the preliminary examination, when a plant is first brought home.

Everything mentioned so far can be dealt with and eradicated by a programme of spraying with an insecticide such as malathion. This is a poison and as such it should never be used inside the home.

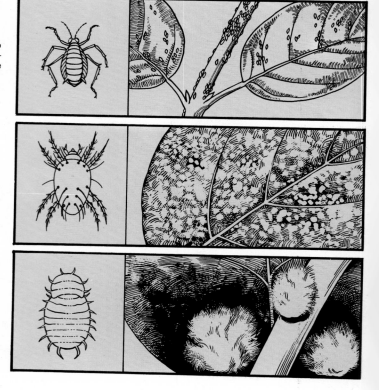

Aphids, usually greenfly or blackfly, can be brought into the home on garden flowers – or they may fly in through the window. They can be easily controlled by spraying with one of several proprietary insecticides.

The almost invisible red spider mite attacks only when the atmosphere is dry and arid. Good humidity or an occasional spray will ensure that your plants are kept clear of this pest.

Mealy bugs are again almost invisible, but give themselves away by the white woolly substance with which they surround themselves. A drop of methylated spirits will kill them.

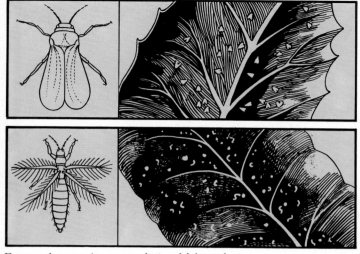

White flies can sometimes be difficult to eradicate, but a regular spraying with a systemic insecticide will do the trick. This is absorbed by the sap and then sucked by the insects.

Systemic insecticides are the answer to an attack by thrips – small black-winged insects which cause tiny pale spots on leaves where they suck the sap from the plant.

Every plant to be treated should be taken out of doors and given a thorough spray, or even turned upside down and dipped in a bucket of the mixture as recommended on the label. There are other sprays that can be used indoors, but these will kill only mild infestations of aphis or similar pests.

Mealy bugs can be cleared safely and with little trouble by dipping a matchstick in methylated spirit and touching the white, woolly surround to the bug, which will then disappear to reveal the little brown insect within. Scale can actually be scraped off the leaf with a knife or some other similar object.

Red spider is a little different. It will appear only when the plant or plants concerned suffer from too dry and arid an atmosphere. It will be noted by a twisting, curling and drying of leaves and on examination it will be found that leaves are covered with a fine web in which move a great number of minute red-brown insects. Red spider mite can be cleared with careful and thorough application of most insecticides, such as malathion, but the best way of preventing a further attack is to increase the humidity by spraying the plant which has been attacked.

There are very few diseases which attack indoor plants, and those which might appear are caused almost without exception by lack of care in the treatment of those plants. If subjected to over-watering, for example, many plants can suffer from root rot, damping off, mildew or botrytis. Viruses and rusts can begin when a plant is sick through being too wet or too cold or both. If plants are kept in the dark or in too shaded a position for too long they will tend to become lank, drawn and weak, and disease is then liable to enter the tissues.

Pests are on the whole a simple matter to clear, but diseases are a more complex matter, for they arise only after the plant has been seriously weakened. On the whole it is advisable to treat pest attack but to throw the plant away if disease appears. You may waste considerable time and effort attempting to treat it and there is also every possibility that other plants will be affected.

If, on the other hand, a plant is so admired or so much a member of the family that every attempt must be made to cure it, a fungicide spray may help, plus if possible a period of recuperation in a greenhouse under ideal conditions.

On the whole, however, it is better not to be too sentimental about indoor plants. Keep them while they are attractive and giving their best. When they grow too old or become ill, throw them away.

433

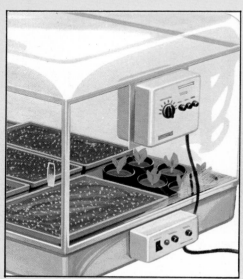

Greenhouse gardening

1 Why grow plants under glass?

Nowadays, a greenhouse is essential for the complete gardener. One of its most important assets is that it makes possible substantial economies in household budgets: ordinary fruits and vegetables can be grown both in and out of season, and more exotic items – usually expensive in the shops – can also be produced at low cost. Seedlings and cuttings can be raised by the gardener himself, reducing annual expenditure on garden plants, and giving him the satisfaction of creating something more or less from nothing. What is more, the protection given by greenhouses against outdoor weather conditions allows many tender decorative plants to be grown, which will give enthusiasts increased pleasure.

Right: Greenhouse gardening provides an opportunity to grow a wide variety of colourful plants, such as the orange-flowered *Streptosolen jamesonii* shown here.

Below: The pendulous flowers of fuchsias provide beautiful summer flower displays in greenhouses.

2 Types of greenhouse

Before buying a greenhouse, look at several types and decide what sort suits your purposes best. They are usually classified according to use – and by size, shape or construction materials. The temperature and degree of humidity at which the greenhouse is to be maintained determine the type of plants which can be grown in it and also, in a general sense, the purpose for which it will be used. Experts usually refer to greenhouses in the following ways.

Cold greenhouse This type depends entirely on the heat of the sun for warmth, and it is therefore most valuable in the spring, summer and autumn. Its great disadvantage is that it affords little protection against severe frost and is therefore not able to protect tender plants in winter unless the season is exceptionally mild.

Cool greenhouse In many ways a cool greenhouse is the most useful type for most gardeners. During the summer, when unheated, it fulfils the function of a cold greenhouse. During the spring, autumn and winter it is heated enough to maintain a regular temperature of 7°C (45°F). This is sufficient to keep out the frost and so allows many tender plants to be overwintered, together with, for example, dahlias and begonia tubers. A cool greenhouse can also be used for raising plants from seed. Tomatoes given an early start in growth by greenhouse conditions will be certain to ripen no matter what sort of summer weather prevails outside.

Intermediate or warm greenhouse This is the type that true gardening enthusiasts, eager to extend the interest and scope of their hobby, will wish to acquire. With all the many very valuable practical aspects listed above, the warm greenhouse combines the advantage of enabling such commodities as tomatoes and cucumbers to be grown all the year round, together with some of the more exotic fruits and vegetables – such as aubergines, figs, avocado pears, peaches and nectarines. Warm greenhouses are heated to a minimum temperature of 13°C (55°F), which makes it possible to grow decorative houseplants and to carry out propagation.

Stove or hot house This type is more for the connoisseur than the ordinary gardener. Heated to a regular temperature of at least 18°C (65°F), it can be used for growing certain kinds of orchids; among the other plants that flourish under such conditions are aechmea, the painter's palette (*Anthurium scherzerianum*), the zebra plant (*Aphelandra squarrosa*), dieffenbachia, peperomia and strelitzia. Like the warm greenhouse, the hot house is useful for propagation, especially when a high temperature is essential.

Dieffenbachia needs a warm, humid atmosphere and so is best grown in a stove or hot house.

Greenhouse shapes

Physically, greenhouses are classified by their shape, which to some extent determines their function. The common ones are listed below.

Span or ridge This is the most popular type. It has a roof in the form of an inverted shallow V and the more conventional type has vertical glass sides, although there is now a tendency to produce this type with glass panels set at an angle of about 10° to the vertical. It is claimed that this provides greater resistance to crosswinds and a greater stability; greenhouses built in this way require less bracing, and there is better light transmission.

If mainly ground crops (such as lettuce, chrysanthemums and tomatoes) are to be grown, span greenhouses, in common with some other types, are glazed to the ground. If pot plants are to be the speciality, the glazing is usually supported on a bench-high wall of brick, concrete, wood or metal.

Three-quarter span This type of greenhouse is built against a wall. It has an inverted V-shaped roof, but the span on the wall side is shorter than the other, which is of normal length. This type has an advantage over a standard lean-to (see below) in that it gives more light and headroom, but

it is more costly. One of the best uses of this greenhouse is to grow fruit on the wall side and display plants on the opposite side.

Lean-to The lean-to has a single sloping roof and is built against a wall. It is the least expensive to buy and heat, and indeed, can often be heated from the domestic system. Its disadvantage is that plants grown in it tend to bend towards the light.

Circular This is among the latest ideas in greenhouses. Of very attractive design, the circular type is excellent for pot plants and cultivation. However, extractor fans usually need to be installed to prevent overheating in hot weather.

Above: A three-quarter span greenhouse has the virtues of the lean-to type but has the advantage of giving more light and height.

Left: This span, or ridge, greenhouse is glazed to the base, making it valuable for growing ground crops such as chrysanthemums, lettuce and tomatoes.

Right: A lean-to greenhouse can be very useful, especially where space is restricted. As it is built against a wall, it is suitable for fruit.

Mini For gardeners with only a very small space to spare, a miniature greenhouse could be the answer. Among the designs available some are free-standing, while others 'lean-to' against a wall. This type of greenhouse, though small, can fulfil many of the functions of a full-size greenhouse.

Conservatory This is essentially a greenhouse which is accessible from a living-room, to which it can be a pleasing adjunct. Filled with exotic plants, it makes a restful extra room in both summer and winter, combining the atmosphere of the garden with the comfort of light and heat from the domestic supply.

Above: Both the ridge and lean-to types of miniature greenhouse are invaluable to those with little space.

Below: The attractive design of this circular greenhouse allows it to be positioned anywhere.

Above: A conservatory makes an excellent and very useful extension to a living-room.

439

Construction materials

The merits of the various materials used in constructing greenhouses are listed below.

Wood This is warm and relatively easy to work. The strongest is teak, and redwood is very popular. Both need oiling, and the latter is more easily worked. The cheaper whitewood must be regularly painted.

Metal (steel and aluminium) Steel needs painting, but aluminium does not. Aluminium alloys are strong, and although light they stand firm provided the greenhouse itself is firmly sited. The metal frame must be rigid and include provision for expansion and contraction to avoid glass breakage and air leakage.

Concrete Reinforced concrete is usually used for greenhouses, and although not as attractive as some other materials, concrete does provide a very durable structure.

Downpipes and guttering These essentials are best made of plastic – as are water

A greenhouse constructed of red cedar requires treatment with linseed oil annually.

butts, another useful addition to the greenhouse.

Glazing: glass v. plastic Glass has long proved to be a very satisfactory material for glazing, but recently plastic-glazed greenhouses have been introduced. Although not ideal, they are very cheap and functional.

The principal disadvantages of plastic as opposed to glass are:
(a) it is weathered by sun and torn by wind, and its life span is only about two years;
(b) a plastic-glazed greenhouse cools down more quickly;
(c) plastic becomes opaque and dirty because it attracts dust and cannot be satisfactorily cleaned in the way that glass can;
(d) condensation is greater: powered fans can be installed to combat it, but this will offset to some extent the saving made originally by choosing plastic instead of glass.

3 Choosing a greenhouse

Buying a greenhouse is an investment, so before you purchase one decide on the way you intend to use it. This, of course, depends entirely on the type of crops that are to be grown. For ground crops, such as chrysanthemums and lettuces, the greenhouse will need glazing right down to the base. Flowering pot plants and propagation call for benches, in which case the glazing can be fixed to basal walls 60–100 cm (2–3 ft) high, and heat loss will be reduced. If both types are to be cultivated, a greenhouse glazed to the ground on one side, with a bench and wall on the other, will fit the bill. With restricted space, or if wall-fruits are to be grown, a lean-to is the best proposition.

If it is the gardener's intention to cultivate plants that need heat, the most economic construction in this respect should be chosen. It is also as well to visualise the possibility of any future expansion.

Size

Although the choice of greenhouse will depend upon the gardener's pocket, it is a great mistake to buy one that is too small.

Above: This greenhouse is only 2.5m (8ft) by 2m (6ft) yet has ample headroom and good space for staging.

Left: A greenhouse must have a door wide enough to take a wheelbarrow comfortably.

In any case, a small greenhouse is difficult to manage – it warms up too quickly in summer and cools too fast in winter. A greenhouse must have adequate headroom and, ideally, be wide enough to allow for a wheelbarrow to pass through the door. (It is important to ensure that the door opens inwards, or slides easily backwards and forwards.) Another inconvenience of too narrow a house is that it will not allow for a wide enough path, or adequate depth to the benches. A good minimum size is about 2·5m (8 ft) wide by 2 m (6 ft) long.

4 Installing a greenhouse

Siting

Careful attention should be paid to choice of location. The site should be level; if it is not, it should be levelled. It should be well-drained, sheltered from strong and cold winds and should receive plenty of sunshine. The position chosen will of course be influenced, particularly in a small garden, by miscellaneous factors such as existing paths, boundary fences, the situation of the house, etc., but the above criteria are ideal, and will also determine the direction in which the greenhouse should run. The best position is running north and south, to afford the maximum amount of light throughout the year. However, if the greenhouse is to be used largely for raising seedlings and propagating plants in winter, an east-to-west direction will give maximum light at that time of year. A lean-to should preferably be erected facing south. A conservatory is best positioned so that it forms an extension to the living room and has direct access from it.

It is also important to position the greenhouse where water, gas and electricity supplies are available, or where they can easily be made so.

Note Greenhouses above a certain size, stipulated by the local authority in each area, will require planning permission. Before committing yourself to buying and erecting a greenhouse, it is as well to check this point, and also to consult with neighbours regarding the proposed position of the greenhouse.

Laying foundations and paths

A path of concrete slabs or ashes should be laid through the centre of the greenhouse. It is also advantageous to lay a path giving access from the house.

Good foundations are essential to eradicate the risk of movement, and consequent glass breakage. Solid foundations also provide good anchorage. Greenhouse makers always provide a foundation plan prior to delivery, and some also sell suitable ready-made foundations.

In aluminium greenhouses the weight to be supported is fairly low, so the foundations need not be as heavily constructed, but must still provide a firm base.

A suitable foundation for a greenhouse glazed to the ground can be provided by digging a trench 25cm (10in) deep by 30cm

Left: A modern conservatory with direct access from a living-room is ideal for house plants.

Right: Erecting a greenhouse.
(1) These two drawings show typical foundations, the first for a greenhouse glazed to the ground, the second for one with a bench-high base wall, supporting a glazed super-structure.
(2) Positioning the sides.
(3) Putting on the roof.
(4) When glazing, use putty for wood frames and plastic sealing compound for metal frames.

(1ft) wide with vertical sides. In this, a brick or concrete footing should be built. If the superstructure is to be supported on brick or concrete block walls, the top of the foundation, which in this case might be a filling of concrete, should be 15cm (6in) below ground level. Do not forget to lay the services before the concrete is put in.

Erection

Greenhouse manufacturers always supply very complete directions for the erection of their products. The work usually consists of bolting prefabricated parts together, and calls for few tools other than spanners, screwdrivers, and perhaps a masonry drill. For glazing, use putty in a wooden greenhouse, elastic sealing compound in a metal one. Manufacturers will also erect greenhouses themselves.

Maintenance of the fabric

The most important tasks are as follows.
(1) Occasionally treat teak and oak by wiping it with a rag dipped in linseed oil.
(2) Unless allowing it to weather, treat red cedar with a cedar preservative.
(3) Regularly paint softwood and steel. (Aluminium needs no painting.)
(4) Wash glass regularly, removing moss, etc., by scraping and hosing down.
(5) Scrub and whitewash walls annually.
(6) Paint heating pipes with aluminium paint. Do not, however, use creosote on the staging, etc., inside the greenhouse; it emits fumes which are toxic to plants.

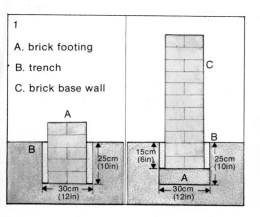

1

A. brick footing

B. trench

C. brick base wall

5 Running a greenhouse

Ventilation

No matter what the type of greenhouse – cold, cool, warm or stove – ventilation is most important because it enables heat and humidity to be controlled, and such disorders as 'damping off', which can have a disastrous effect, to be avoided. In a well-designed greenhouse there are ventilators, i.e. fan-lights that open, on either side of the roof, and one in each side panel. Normally, one set is provided for each 3 m (10 ft) run of length. Some greenhouses are fitted with louvre ventilators in the sides. These provide ventilation which can be very finely controlled. Ventilators on the leeward side can be opened when it is windy without there being any cold draughts. In warm weather they may be opened on both sides to reduce the temperature, control humidity and admit fresh air to the plants.

Ventilation in greenhouses demands considerable attention, and for this reason automatic methods of control have been developed. One of them is a simple device which is fitted on to each ventilator to open and shut it automatically. It does this by

virtue of a cylinder filled with a mineral substance that expands or contracts with variations in temperature. The device is very sensitive, easy to fit and comparatively inexpensive.

A second method of automatic ventilation control is to use an electic fan controlled by a thermostat. Fans are normally fitted in the gable end of the greenhouse.

Above: Careful attention must be paid to ventilating a greenhouse. An automatic ventilating fan, which is thermostatically controlled, can be fitted in the gable end of the greenhouse. Sometimes a fan is operated in conjunction with a louvre fitted on the outside of the mounting panel.

Left: A method of ventilation is a mechanical system that automatically opens or shuts as necessary.

Shading

Shading is another way of effectively cutting down the heat in a greenhouse, and is used in conjunction with ventilation. It is particularly valuable for certain pot plants, early propagation and tomatoes suffering from verticillium wilt. Shading can be done in the following ways.

(1) The glass on the outside can be painted with well-diluted emulsion paint, a lime and water mixture or a proprietary shading.

Such shading is effective during the summer but should be progressively washed off by winter, when all the available light is needed.

(2) Blinds, either of the venetian or the roller type, can be fitted either inside or outside; the outside type of blind is better because the sun's rays should ideally be checked before they reach the glass. There is one type of blind made from unplasticised PVC tubes, which, if they are rolled down at nightfall during winter, minimise fuel consumption in a heated greenhouse.

Shading from the hot sun is important for keeping down the temperature in a greenhouse and these external blinds made from unplasticised PVC tubes can also reduce heat loss in winter.

In some cases roller blinds fitted inside can be automatically controlled by means of a thermostat or photoelectric cell.

(3) Sun visors, in which the blinds are held rigid at the correct slope for the roof of the greenhouse, can be used. They can be controlled by an electronic eye, and are among the most efficient types of shading.

PVC blinds are excellent for shading from the sun.

Heating

Heating a greenhouse is by no means cheap, and in the long run the final decision will depend on which fuel is cheapest and how easily a supply can be provided for the greenhouse. The choice must remain an individual one, but if, for example, the rate for the domestic gas supply is cheaper than other forms of power, then quite obviously this is the one that should be given the first consideration. The various alternatives are considered below.

Hot-water pipes This is the traditional method of heating a greenhouse, but it necessitates the installation of a boiler and hot-water pipes, which are usually placed under the staging. Formerly, such a boiler was fired with solid fuel, usually coke, but today gas, oil or electricity are more usual. The advantage of these is that any system

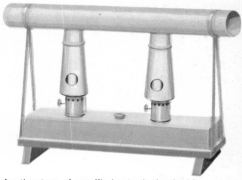

Another type of paraffin heater is the double-burner heater illustrated above.

using them can be fully automatic. Two advantages of hot-water pipes are that they distribute the heat uniformly and retain their heat for some time.

If the domestic system has enough spare capacity it may be possible to heat the greenhouse from that.

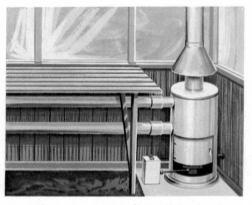

Above: Hot-water pipes are a long-established method of heating greenhouses.

Left: A paraffin heater, such as the single-burner heater illustrated here, is a useful source of heat.

Paraffin heaters Although these are quite effective, the less sophisticated ones have to be regulated by hand, which can be an onerous task when temperatures are fluctuating. Paraffin heaters are good for protection during short periods of frost, but not so good for prolonged heating of greenhouses because the amount of water resulting from combustion creates heavy condensation, which in turn necessitates some form of constant ventilation. Although the relatively high carbon dioxide production from the combustion is beneficial to plants, other gases produced interfere with growth. It is also a comparatively cheap form of heating.

Electric heaters Although heating by electricity is costly, it has a number of advantages in greenhouses. It is clean and always reliable unless there are power cuts. With thermostats of a correct and trustworthy design, control of the greenhouse temperature can be more precise than with any other form of heating. However, once the power is cut off cooling down will take place, except where night storage heaters are used – but with these there are problems of temperature control, therefore they are not highly recommended.

The types of electrical equipment more usually installed for greenhouse heating are fan heaters, tubular heaters, mineral-insulated cables and soil-warming cables.

Fan heaters are extremely efficient electric heaters for a greenhouse. They are usually light, 2–2·5 kg (4–5 lbs), and are quite portable, so that they can be positioned anywhere – however, they are most usually placed in the centre of the floor. Their great asset is that they maintain a gentle movement of air, which is appreciated by plants and encourages growth. Fan heaters work on the principle of sucking in cold air at one end, warming it and blowing it out at the other one. This heated air rises naturally by convection, circulates, cools and

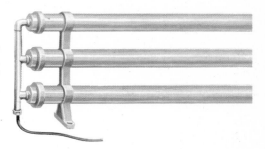

A bank of electric tubular heaters provides a clean, controllable, reliable and flexible form of heating.

then falls to the ground again, where it is reheated. Fan heaters are thermostatically controlled, but even when the heating elements are switched off, the fan keeps the air gently circulating.

The great qualities of tubular heaters are their long life, almost negligible mainte-nance costs, their comparatively low initial cost and their adaptability. They come in lengths ranging from 60 cm (2 ft) to 3·75 m (12 ft) with power ratings from 120 units to 720 units respectively. They are best fitted singly or in banks against the wall of the greenhouse.

Tubular heaters can, however, get very hot and scorch plants close to them unless they are thermostatically controlled. This also ensures, of course, that current is used only when necessary, and at the same time automatically maintains the required minimum temperature.

For safety reasons, it is a wise precaution to mount tubular heaters on wooden supports when installing them in a metal greenhouse.

Mineral-insulated cables are another system of heating a greenhouse. These copper-sheathed heating cables are fixed round the base wall by means of plastic brackets. They are most useful when the demand for heat is not great, and are in fact best used for protection against frost. They can be purchased in kits of different loading. Be sure to acquire a cable of the appropriate power rating for frost-protection. Cables are usually controlled

Electric fan heaters can be wall-mounted (*top*) or floor-standing (*above*). With or without thermostatic control, they are very convenient.

447

by an air thermostat, which for the latter purpose is usually set at 7°C (47°F).

Cables are usually slow to warm up – appreciably slower than warm-air fan heaters. Their surface temperature is high, and they can cause burns if touched.

Soil-warming cables are a form of local heating. This is discussed in more detail on page 451

Gas heaters When burned, gas derived from coal gives off chemicals that are detrimental to plants, but the products of natural-gas combustion are beneficial, especially the carbon dioxide that enters the air. Natural-gas burning apparatus is now available for greenhouse heating. Such apparatus is easily placed below the staging and connected to the gas pipe by means of a flexible pipe. Burners can have thermostatic control and be fitted with a flame-failure device as a safety precaution.

For the running of a gas burner there must be adequate air to burn the fuel. Usually this requirement is adequately met by

A thermostat is invaluable for controlling the temperature in an electrically heated greenhouse.

the normal leakage in a greenhouse. If there is any problem, an air brick in the foundation wall above ground level will solve it. Lastly, note that a gas heater may be unsuitable for a plastic greenhouse because of the condensation caused, which is heavier than that brought about by electrical heaters.

Heat conservation

No doubt double glazing would reduce the heat losses in a greenhouse. However, the cost of hermetically sealing together two sheets of glass is high, and it would be prohibitively expensive to double glaze an ordinary domestic greenhouse.

Heat losses and draughts can, however, be reduced by lining the greenhouse inside with thin polythene, leaving the vents, of course, uncovered. Lining will increase the humidity, so careful attention to ventilation will be needed afterwards.

448

6 Fitments and equipment

Benches and shelves

Staging is an important and valuable part of greenhouse equipment. Benches are essential when a greenhouse is to be used primarily for growing flowering pot and house plants, especially when they are displayed for their beauty. Benches are also very valuable for raising plants from seeds or rooting cuttings in boxes or pots; ideally, the benches should be slatted, to allow warm air to rise up through them from the heaters below and thus provide bottom heat. The dark place under the benches in a greenhouse with basal walls can be used for storage or for such purposes as blanching endives and forcing rhubarb.

Often made of red cedar or softwood, benches or staging in a greenhouse gives more space.

Benches are usually fitted 75–86 cm (30–34 in) above floor level – a comfortable working height. If possible, they should be 90–105 cm (3–3½ ft) wide. Whether slatted or solid, they should be fitted away from the wall, to allow for air circulation. The materials most commonly used are wood (hard- or softwood), particularly when the benches are slatted, and aluminium. Sometimes slatted benches are supplied with timber slats and aluminium framing.

Shelves are of great value in a greenhouse, and should be of similar construction. They are very useful for keeping plants near the light, especially in winter.

Aluminium shelves, fixed above the staging to the greenhouse structure, are a great asset.

They are particularly valuable for displaying pendulous plants, such as cascade chrysanthemums. If of softwood, benches and shelves must be kept regularly painted.

Watering

Systematic watering is essential to all kinds of plants grown in a greenhouse.

Watering by hand For this task it is important to have a watering-can with a fine rose that delivers a gentle stream of water, particularly when seeds, seedlings and small cuttings are being handled. The best type for this purpose is a Haws watering-can, which has a long spout with a fine rose fitted so that the perforations are almost in a horizontal plane; this ensures a gentle delivery of water.

When watering by hand it is of great value to use a moisture indicator, which takes much of the guesswork out of the task.

Automatic watering Watering by hand can be a hard and inconvenient chore, yet to fail to water, even once, might result in disaster. Fortunately, automatic watering systems, not too expensive and quite easy to install, are now available.

A very good type is a capillary system, which allows plants in pots to keep themselves automatically supplied with their requirements of water. The pots, which should not be crocked, are stood on a water-absorbent substance, usually sand, which is contained in a specially constructed fibreglass tray on the bench, or on a capillary fibre mat laid out on a plastic sheet directly on the staging. In either case, there is a supply trough which overhangs the front edge of the staging and is kept filled with water. The water is absorbed continuously by the absorbent substance. In the case of the sand tray, this absorption is achieved by means of a fibreglass wick partially buried in the sand with its ends in the water. The capillary mat, on the other hand, is cut to shape so that a tongue can be inserted in the trough.

With automatic watering equipment, water is transferred from a tank to the absorbent sand on which the plants are standing.

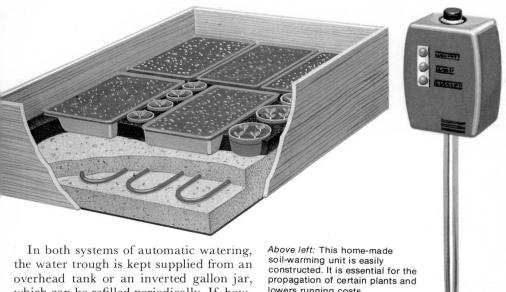

In both systems of automatic watering, the water trough is kept supplied from an overhead tank or an inverted gallon jar, which can be refilled periodically. If, however, mains water is laid on, the system can be made fully automatic by means of a ball valve and float.

Soil warming

Soil warming is a very useful and inexpensive modern greenhouse technique. By warming the soil in the borders or on the benches, it is possible to increase the range of heat-loving plants that can be grown. It is also of the greatest use in seed germination, rooting cuttings and producing out-of-season vegetables and fruits. This can all be done without raising the temperature of the whole greenhouse.

Warming cables can be bought in lengths ranging from 6m (20ft), carrying 75 watts, which will heat 0·9–1·1 sq m (10–12 sq ft) to 82m (267ft), carrying 1000 watts, suitable for a surface of 12·5–15 sq m (133–166 sq ft). The soil-warming system is quite easy to install. However, if you are inexperienced in such matters, you should seek the help of a qualified electrician for connection of the cables to the mains supply. First, place a sheet of asbestos or roofing felt on the bench and erect 22·5cm (9in) wooden walls around it. In the bot-

Above left: This home-made soil-warming unit is easily constructed. It is essential for the propagation of certain plants and lowers running costs.

Above right: A moisture indicator minimises the risk of plant fatalities caused by drying out or overwatering.

tom of this enclosure, put a 5cm (2in) layer of coarse washed river sand. The warming cable is laid on this base, running evenly backwards and forwards. It is then covered with a further 5–7·5 cm (2–3 in) of sand. The seed pans or boxes are stood on this sand. To ensure a uniform temperature throughout the bed, pack granulated peat in the spaces between the seed containers. If desired, part or the whole of the sand bed can be covered with a mixture of peat and sand and the cuttings to be rooted can be inserted directly into it.

If it is necessary to warm the air around the plants, a similar warming cable can be run round the walls, and the bed covered with a sheet of glass or plastic.

Generally, if the power is switched on for ten to twelve hours each night, all the heat needed is given. If completely automatic control is desired, a soil-warming thermostat should be fitted. Ready-wired units can be purchased.

Propagation units

Propagation units are useful devices, particularly for rooting cuttings. To succeed in getting roots to grow on a short length of stem it is necessary to keep the stem perfectly healthy and the tissues active; if it flags in any way, rooting is not likely to take place. If, however, the process is allowed to take place in a propagation case, the temperature and humidity will be higher than if it occurs out in the open greenhouse. In consequence, the tissues of the leaves and stems remain moist and the rooting process is accelerated.

Two very simple forms of propagating case are, firstly, a seed-box covered with a sheet of glass or a polythene bag enveloping a seed pan or a pot. The more highly developed propagation units are in fact based on the elementary principle embodied in these two devices.

A propagating case has numerous uses. In the first place, it allows a cold

Right: This miniature propagator has dimensions of about 32·5cm (13½in) long and 20cm (8in) wide.

greenhouse to be used for raising seeds and rooting cuttings with little extra expenditure on fuel. It also enables an earlier start to be made with raising seeds, which results in earlier crops in the greenhouse – for example, tomatoes. Flowers, normally produced from seeds planted during the summer for the following year, need not be exposed to severe winter weather. They can be sown in January in a propagator to produce better summer results. If a propagation unit is used in a heated greenhouse, the greenhouse can be satisfactorily run at

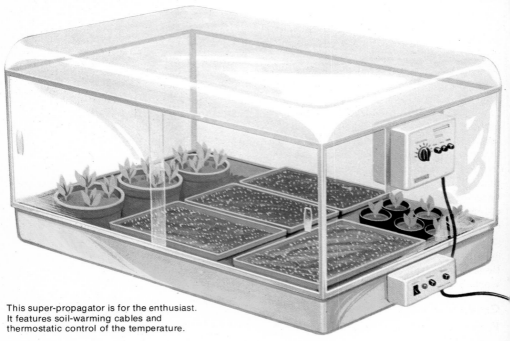

This super-propagator is for the enthusiast.
It features soil-warming cables and
thermostatic control of the temperature.

5–10°C (10–20°F) lower than otherwise.

Among the more sophisticated propagation cases that can be purchased, the simplest and smallest consists of a heating panel on which stands a plastic standard seed tray containing sown seeds and covered with a ventilated plastic cover. It can also be used to provide bottom heat for small pot plants and cuttings. They should be stood on *moist* gravel that almost fills the tray. There are more elaborate models, such as a multi-top unit that has four seed trays with covers, and a larger one, thermostatically controlled, with greater headroom to allow young plants to grow to maturity. This is in effect a miniature heated greenhouse that can be housed in a cooler one.

Above: Mist propagation is useful for rooting cuttings.
Below: By controlling greenhouse lighting, the gardener can make chrysanthemums bloom any time of year that he wishes.

Mist propagation Mention has already been made of the failure to root when a cutting dries off. While it is not a system that many amateurs are likely to employ, mist propagation is one that has been designed to lessen this risk. By this method, cuttings will root better and more quickly.

Fundamentally the equipment consists of mist nozzles which are mounted on standpipes and connected to a water-feed pipe, placed at intervals of 1–1·25 m (3–4 ft) along the bench (from which the drainage must be perfect), a control box, a solenoid valve and a detector, which is placed amongst the cuttings. The latter works on the balance principle and has two arms, one with an absorbent pad, the other being a low-voltage electrical contact. While the cuttings are being sprayed, the pad absorbs moisture and eventually becomes heavy enough to break the electrical contact of the other arm. As moisture evaporates from the pad (and the cuttings get drier), it lightens, contact is made again, and through the solenoid valve and the control box the mist is turned on. This works in conjunction with soil warming.

Greenhouse lighting

For the enthusiast, lighting in the greenhouse is essential. For general lighting, ordinary light bulbs are quite suitable; however, waterproof fittings are essential.

Another interesting aspect of greenhouse lighting is its use in extending the duration of daylight. Chrysanthemums, in particular, respond to this, because in natural conditions they form their buds during the long summer days, and flower when they shorten. By artificially lengthening and shortening the day by means of lighting, they can be made to bloom at any time.

453

7 Greenhouse culture

Fertilising greenhouse plants

Greenhouse plants, like outdoor ones, need certain plant foods. The main ones are nitrogen, potassium, phosphorus, magnesium and a small number of others known as trace elements, in which iron and manganese are normally included, that are consumed in small quantities.

The functions of the main plant foods are as follows.

Nitrogen This element assists in leaf production, but an excess of nitrogen leads to lush growth, prone to disease. It is also an important ingredient in the synthesis of many essential plant chemicals.

Potassium This plays an important role in the plant's manufacture and utilisation of starch. It also assists in the development of roots, tubers, seeds and flowers, particularly enhancing the colour, and helps to ripen young wood, reducing its vulnerability to disease and early frosts.

Phosphorus This element plays a very important role in the formation of tissue cells and in plant growth. Without it, plants will become stunted.

Magnesium, iron, manganese These three are either essential ingredients of, or essential to the production of, chlorophyl, which enables plants to manufacture starch.

Greenhouse plants get their essential foods in the same way as outdoor plants – from fertiliser. The main sources of fertilisers are the composts that are used for potting, which normally contain balanced mixtures. Others are the liquid manures which are subsequently applied.

Composts

Two growing media are used in amateur greenhouses: the traditional John Innes potting composts, and the newer soilless composts which have to a large extent superseded the former. Though most gardeners now buy their composts, it is as well to know how they are made up.

John Innes potting composts These are composed of loam, peat and sand, plus a fertiliser mixture (John Innes base fertiliser). The best loam for this purpose is a friable, fibrous loam prepared by allowing turves to rot in a stack. (This is becoming very hard to obtain, and hence soilless

Useful data for greenhouse gardeners:

32 litres (1 bushel) of potting compost is sufficient for:

6 standard seed boxes, 7·5cm (3in) deep

90 rooted cuttings in 7·5cm (3in) pots

50 larger plants in 11·25cm (4½in) pots

16 mature plants in 20c (8in) pots

454

composts are replacing John Innes compost.) The peat (or leaf-mould) should be sedge peat, and the sand should be washed sharp sand, graded from very fine up to 3mm (⅛in) grains.

The formula of John Innes base fertiliser is two parts (by weight) hoof and horn meal, two parts superphosphate of lime, one part sulphate of potash and one part ground chalk or limestone.

John Innes potting compost consists of a basic mixture of seven seed trays of loam, three of peat (moist) and two of sand, making two bushels (36 litres) in all. (The bushel is the traditional measure for John Innes composts.)

To this quantity is added John Innes base fertiliser in varying amounts to produce the different composts which are used as plants develop from seedlings and cuttings to mature plants.

Soilless composts Soilless composts for sowing, cutting and potting are based on selected grades of peat to which have been added plant nutrients. When using them, it is important not to compact them. After six weeks, plants growing in them should be fed with liquid manure.

Propagation

There are a number of ways in which to propagate plants. It must, however, be remembered that only with species is it possible to obtain true reproduction by sowing seeds; cultivars must be propagated vegetatively – for example, by means of cuttings.

Seed propagation Most seeds will germinate readily if given some heat, ideally by placing them in a propagator.

Seeds should be sown thinly and as shallowly as possible in trays, pans or boxes. If they are very fine, mix them with sand for better distribution. Water them and place them in the propagator. Cover them with brown paper to exclude the light and close the transparent dome. As soon as germination takes place, remove the paper and lift the cover to allow the air to circulate.

When the seedlings are large enough to handle, prick them out. Use a cleft stick to lift them, and firm them into prepared holes in moist compost in another box. Shade the seedlings for a short while until they are established. Finally, when they are large enough, put each plant in a pot containing compost.

Stem cuttings Different types of stem cutting are used for propagating softwoods and hardwoods. For softwood plants, nodal cuttings are usually taken. They should be about 5cm (2in) long, cut from a shoot and trimmed off with a sharp knife just below a node (leaf joint). The lower leaves should be removed. The prepared cuttings should be inserted in moist cutting compost in a box, or around the edge of a pot, and kept in a moist warm atmosphere until growth commences – evidence that roots have formed.

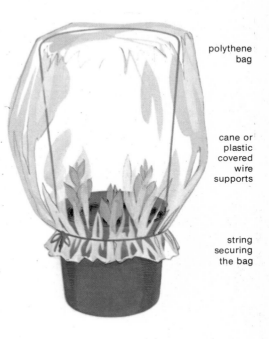

polythene bag

cane or plastic covered wire supports

string securing the bag

An improvised propagator will provide a moist, warm atmosphere for a small number of cuttings.

When a good root ball is formed, they should be re-potted into larger pots.

Nodal cuttings of hardwood plants are taken and prepared in much the same way, usually at the end of the growing season. They are usually about 25cm (10in) long. They should be inserted into moist compost, and should initially be shaded. When they are growing they should be potted on.

Another type of cutting, often taken from

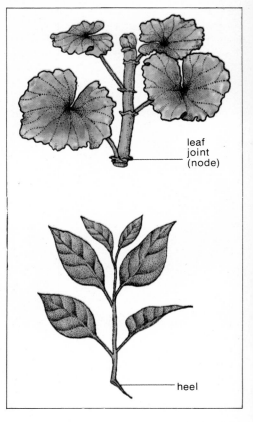

leaf joint (node)

heel

plants that are more difficult to root, consists of side shoots, of about the same length, torn away from the stem with a heel of the more mature wood. This end should be inserted in moist compost and then be allowed to root.

Stem sections Certain plants, such as ficus and dracaena, can be propagated by cutting a thin section of a stem containing a bud. When planted just below the surface in cutting compost a good plant will develop.

Leaf-bud cuttings This form of propagation is especially suited to aphelandra, pilea, ficus and camellia. A centrally situated dormant bud is cut out from a

Above left: A bud cutting. The drawing on the left shows the bud being taken, and on the right it is planted.

Top: a nodal cutting of a softwood plant
Above: a heel cutting of a hardwood plant

Below: Crocks at the bottom of a seed box will ensure that the box has good drainage.

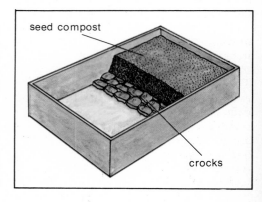

seed compost

crocks

456

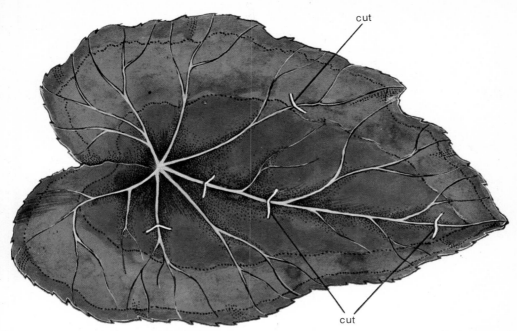

cut

cut

semi-ripe wood stem, with a leaf intact. The length of the portion of stem removed should be about 2cm (¾in) long. This is planted in a vertical position in cutting compost, with the leaf and bud just above the soil surface. It should be given some gentle bottom heat until the roots form.

Division and root cuttings Some plants can be propagated by division. This means that the root of an established plant is cut into several viable portions with a sharp knife, and planted in compost. In every case the portion used should have at least one healthy eye or shoot and some healthy roots. This form of propagation can be practised with chlorophytum, maranta, iris and dahlia. There is also another form of division, applicable to bulbs and corms. These have attached to them smaller bulbs and corms, known as offsets, which can be detached and planted in pots.

Allied to division are root cuttings. These are sections of roots cut into pieces, some 5–7·5cm (2–3in) long. They are inserted into compost in boxes, with the upper end just below the soil surface.

Above: Propagate fleshy-leaved plants by snipping the main veins and laying their leaves flat on compost.
Below: Streptocarpus are propagated by dividing a leaf and planting each part upright in compost to root.

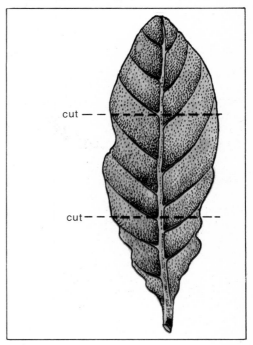

cut – –

cut – –

8 Growing plants under glass

At the beginning of each of the descriptions that follow is a recommendation pertaining to the type of greenhouse needed for successful cultivation of the plant in question. Sometimes alternatives are suggested: for example, 'cool or warm'. Generally, while a specific plant can be grown under the cooler conditions, it is normally better when cultivated at the higher temperature.

Anthurium scherzerianum (flamingo plant, painter's palette)

Stove. This is a most colourful plant with a bold, bright scarlet, wax-like spathe about 7·5cm (3in) wide and long, enclosing a spiral orange-red spike (spadix). Its leaves are long, shiny, lance-shaped and light green.

It is propagated by dividing the rootstock in February. The divisions are planted in potting compost in such a way that the roots are high in the pot on a slight mound. Half-fill the pot, which should be 15cm (6in) across if the size warrants it, with crocks. This plant needs humidity.

Anthurium scherzerianum is a colourful, fascinating and very exotic plant.

Aphelandra squarrosa 'Louisae' (zebra plant)

Stove. This is a very popular, beautiful, showy plant. It has 25 cm- (10 in-)long pointed dark green leaves with veins that are boldly cream in colour. During summer and autumn it produces yellow flowers, which should be removed as they fade. Two other attractive varieties are *A. squarrosa* 'Brockfield' and *A. squarrosa* 'Silver Beauty'.

Aphelandra are propagated from cuttings taken during the spring and summer and rooted in sowing compost at 21°C (70°F) in a propagator. They should be potted on in potting compost. Feed while they are in flower.

Aspidistra elatior (cast-iron plant, parlour palm)

Cool. This foliage plant was a great favourite of the Victorians and Edwardians. It has beautiful long, wide, shiny green leaves.

Aphelandra squarrosa is beautiful but difficult to grow.

A. elatior 'Variegata' has cream variegated leaves.

This plant needs little attention, although it is beneficial to sponge its leaves from time to time. It is best to re-pot it in the spring, but this should be carried out only after several years.

Propagate by dividing the rhizome in March so that each piece has some leaf and roots. Plant in potting compost.

Begonia

Cool or warm. *Begonia rex* is grown entirely for the beauty of its leaves, which include silver, dark green, pink and darkest purple colours. It is propagated by means of the leaves, which are cut across the back of the main veins and pinned down flat on a surface of cutting compost in a tray. They are then placed in a propagator at 18–21°C (64–70°F). Another interesting foliage begonia is *B. masoniana* (iron cross begonia).

B. semperflorens is fibrous-rooted and has red, pink or white flowers; these begonias make lovely greenhouse plants for the later autumn. Seeds are sown in late June. They should be put into a propagator at 18°C (64°F) and then potted on. They like humid conditions.

Begonia 'Gloire de Lorraine' (Christmas begonia) is winter-flowering, with clusters

Few greenhouse plants are more beautiful than *Begonia rex*, with its colourful, almost triangular leaves.

Aspidistra elatior 'Variegata' is grown for its foliage.

of delicate rose-pink flowers. It is propagated from cuttings and basal shoots taken in spring and ultimately potted on in 15 cm (6 in) pots. It likes a moist and semi-shady warm position when potted. Its stems must be supported. Remove all flower buds until October, when they should be allowed to develop, and then give weekly doses of liquid manure. After flowering, cut the plants down by half and keep them, watering little, until early spring when they will provide more cuttings.

Beloperone guttata
(shrimp plant)

Warm. This plant's common name results from its pinkish-brown bracts that resemble shrimps. It prefers a warm house and should be grown in well-drained potting compost. It should be given plenty of water during the summer, but little in the winter.

Cuttings should be taken in early summer and inserted in soilless sowing compost

Beloperone guttata has become a favourite exotic pot plant. It seldom exceeds 30cm (1 ft) in height.

at 18°C (64°F), and then potted on into 7·5cm (3in) pots and afterwards 13cm (5in) pots. Bushiness should be induced by regular pinching back of the shoots. When established, give liquid manure regularly during the summer.

Bouvardia x domestica

Warm. Nowadays it is usual to grow varieties, of which 'President Cleveland, with its terminal clusters of bright crimson-scarlet tubular flowers, is representative. They flower from August to September.

After flowering, rest the plants with little watering until late February. Then water the soil and spray the stems to start fresh growth. Also prune, if necessary. Pinch back during the summer to encourage late flowering.

Propagate from cuttings from young shoots placed in a propagator at 19°C (66°F), or from root cuttings.

Brunfelsia calycina
(Franciscea calycina)

Stove. Has fragrant, salvia-shaped violet-purple flowers with a long tube, which fade to almost white from April to August. The variety 'Macrantha' has 7·5cm (3in) wide flowers.

After flowering, shorten the stalks by half and encourage new growth by spraying with water. Provide a moist atmosphere.

Propagate from cuttings taken between February and August. Insert in soilless cutting compost and give bottom heat at about 21°C (70°F).

Bulbs
(spring)

Most bulbs are easy to grow, and do not need any great heat. They provide a magnificent display in the greenhouse. A few planted successively from late summer onwards will bloom from Christmas until May. As they spend much of their growing time in plunge beds outdoors, they do not

460

take up space in the greenhouse for long.

The most popular bulbs are daffodils, narcissi, hyacinths and tulips. Daffodils, hyacinths and narcissi should be planted so that their noses are just visible through the surface of the soil, tulips should be just covered, and small bulbs such as crocuses and snowdrops buried by 6–12mm (¼–½in).

The following description of the cultivation of narcissi bulbs is fairly typical, despite small modifications for other bulbs.

Narcissi bulbs should be planted in John Innes potting compost no. 2 or a soilless potting mixture. A 15cm (6in) pot will accommodate three or four bulbs.

After planting, place the pot in the soil in a cool plunge bed outdoors for about eight weeks, when the young, pale green leaves appear. Then bring them into the greenhouse and stand them in a dim light until

the leaves turn green, when the pot should be given more light and warmth – a day temperature of 10°C (50°F) – until the plants flower. Water and feed with liquid manure about every three weeks.

After it has flowered, put the plant outside. When the leaves are dead, harvest and dry the bulbs, and use them *outdoors* the following year.

Narcissi bulbs which are planted in August or September will flower from December to January.

Daffodil bulbs planted in August-October flower from January to April.

Tulip bulbs planted in September-October flower from January to April. These will stand rather more heat, up to 15°C (60°F).

Hyacinth bulbs planted in September-October flower from January to March. These usually take about seven weeks to produce growth when plunged.

Trumpet daffodils brighten the dark days of winter.

Calceolaria
(slipper flower)
Cool. It is the herbaceous calceolaria that is grown most frequently in a greenhouse. This has large clusters of red-orange and red flowers with distinctive markings and ovate mid-green leaves. Many fine hybrids are obtainable.

461

The seeds are sown thinly in seed compost and germinated at 18°C(64°F) during June, with shading when needed. Prick off the seedlings singly into pots in July and keep in a cold frame. In September pot on into 10cm (4in) pots and take inside. Keep warm and moist at night at a steady temperature. In February pot on again in 20cm (8in) pots using growing compost. Keep near the glass, shading from strong sun. Stake securely and water modestly. Feed with liquid manure fortnightly when buds appear.

Camellia
Cool. These popular plants are much appreciated for their shapely white, pink and red flowers and their rich green, shiny, bold foliage. They need comparatively little attention other than regular, fairly modest watering and occasional feeding. They might need re-potting every three or four years.

They can be propagated by taking leaf bud cuttings.

Campanula isophylla
(bellflower)
Cool. *Campanula isophylla* is a prostrate plant, which overhangs the rim of its pot and has star-shaped blue flowers in abundance during August and September. Its cultivar *Campanula isophylla* 'Alba', with white blooms, is even more charming. It is useful for hanging baskets.

It should be watered and fed regularly while flowering and dead-headed regularly. Keep comparatively dry in winter.

Propagate from cuttings from sturdy basal shoots taken in spring. Insert these in cutting compost and provide some warmth.

Carnations
Cool. Carnations will produce flowers continuously throughout the year, with some peak periods, in a cool, well-ventilated greenhouse with plenty of headroom.

New carnations are usually supplied in spring in 7·5cm (3in) pots. On arrival they

Campanula isophylla is excellent for a hanging basket.

can be transplanted into 15cm (6in) pots, or to a raised (22·5cm- (9in-)high) bed on the ground, of either John Innes potting compost no. 4 or a soilless compost. Place the plants 20cm (8in) apart each way in the bed.

When the plants are growing well, pinch their tips out to encourage the growth of side-shoots. When these are about 15cm (6in) long, they in turn can have all the buds removed, except one, so that each stem only bears one good bloom.

Regular watering is very important: water quite copiously during the summer, with much less in winter when growth slows up. A night temperature of up to 10°C (50°F) is suitable; during the summer a little light shading might be needed to lower the daytime temperature.

Carnations should be supported with canes and wire rings when in pots, and with large-mesh netting, about 15cm (6in), strung from four corner posts when growing in a bed. After the first blooms are cut, the carnations should then be fed with a fertiliser which is suitable for carnations.

Carnations last two years, so new stocks should be raised by taking side cuttings in early spring. Plant them in cutting compost and place them in a propagator at 16–18°C (61–64°F), admitting air when the tips begin to grow and lowering the temperature to 10°C (50°F) over the course of a week. Then pot into 7·5cm (3in) pots. When they are 22·5cm (9in) tall, remove the growing tip; repeat if desired when the resultant side shoots are long enough. Pot on when needed.

Chlorophytum
(spider plant)

Cool or warm. *Chlorophytum elatum* 'Variegatum' is the variety most grown, solely for its long, grass-like leaves, which are green with a broad streak of white running down their centre. These plants are excellent for hanging baskets.

The spider plant is very easy to grow. Apart from reasonable watering during the summer, and a regular feed with liquid manure, little more is needed.

Inconspicuous flowers develop in the ends of long slender stems, weighing them down. Chlorophytum can be propagated by planting the plantlets that are formed as the flowers fade. Otherwise, root divisions can be taken in spring or summer.

Chrysanthemum
(late-flowering)

Cool. Start with disease-free, rooted cuttings. Subsequently new plants can be raised by taking cuttings from the old plants.

To do this, cut selected healthy plants down to 15–22·5cm (6–9in) *immediately* after flowering, still keeping them in their pots. Give them an initial watering, and keep them in a light airy position in the greenhouse at a temperature no higher than 10°C (50°F) without much further watering.

After a time basal shoots will appear. Choose healthy shoots about 3 mm (⅛ in) thick, with four or five fresh leaves closely spaced along the stem, for cuttings. Guard

Chlorophytum elatum 'Variegatum' (spider plant) is very easy to grow and propagate.

against greenfly by spraying them with malathion. Propagate by cutting the shoots just below a node.

If necessary, trim off any lower leaves to facilitate planting. Wet the lower ends of the stems and insert in a rooting compound. Shake off the surplus powder, and insert in John Innes potting compost no. 1 or soilless cutting compost, 5cm (2in) apart, in a seed-box. Place the cuttings in a moist atmosphere and provide bottom heat up to about 15°C (60°F) for about a week or ten days, preferably in a propagator. When they show signs of growth shade them with paper on bright days, and when they become robust give the cuttings both ventilation and a temperature which is no higher than 7°C (45°F).

When they are well rooted, transplant the cuttings into John Innes potting compost no. 2 or soilless potting compost in 7·5cm (3in) pots and place them in a cold frame. About the end of May, when the root ball is well-formed, pot on into John Innes potting compost no. 4 or soilless potting compost in 22·5 cm (9 in) pots. At the same time, insert two stakes, at least 1m (3ft) tall, in the compost either side of the plant. Tie each stem securely but not tightly to these.

Stand the potted chrysanthemums outdoors in rows on boards or another hard surface for the summer. To prevent them from blowing over, tie the stakes to horizontal wires running along the rows. In late September bring the pots into the greenhouse, giving them good ventilation and a little heat.

Chrysanthemums first form a terminal bud on the main stem. As soon as the side shoots appear at the leaf joints, remove this bud, for it will either die or give poor flowers. Allow the side shoots to develop buds. The centre large one, known as the first crown bud, produces the best decorative blooms. All the other buds on each side shoot that is retained should be removed,

Clivia miniata blooms best when it is pot-bound. It is as tough and durable as the aspidistra.

leaving one bloom to a stem. All further side shoots should also be pinched out as they form.

Clivia miniata

Cool. This plant has strap-shaped leaves and lily-like clusters of flowers of orange-

Chrysanthemums are first 'stopped' by pinching out the 'break bud', which either dies or flowers poorly, appearing on the main stem when shoots first appear in the leaf axils (*left*). The latter are eventually 'disbudded' to leave the centre bud or 'first crown bud', which usually produces the best blooms. It is then 'secured' by removing any further axil shoots that appear (*right*).

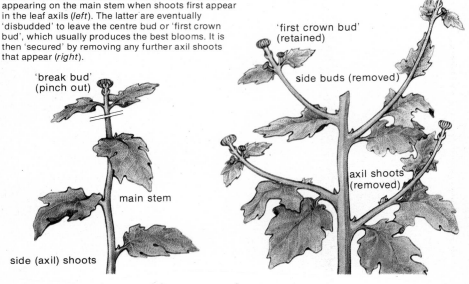

'break bud' (pinch out)

main stem

side (axil) shoots

'first crown bud' (retained)

side buds (removed)

axil shoots (removed)

464

red. Young plants need re-potting every year into 20cm (8in) pots. Mature plants may remain undisturbed for several years if they are top-dressed with fresh rich soil annually, and fed occasionally with liquid manure. After they have flowered keep them warm and moist. Then give them a resting period, which can be induced by minimising watering.

Propagation is best achieved by division after flowering or from offsets.

Codiaeum
(croton)
Stove. Various crotons are grown for their leaves, variegated with brilliant hues ranging from yellow to orange-pink, red and crimson. These colours are more vivid in plants raised annually.

The plants need a moist, very warm atmosphere all the time and must have good light. They should be well watered during the summer and given a weekly feed of liquid manure. They are best potted on annually in spring.

They can be propagated by cuttings at any time from the ends of shoots, inserted singly in 5cm (2in) pots of cutting compost and put into a propagator at 21°C (70°F).

Good crotons to grow are *Codiaeum variegatum pictum* and its cultivars 'Carrierei', 'Disraeli' and 'Reidii'.

Coleus blumei
Cool or warm. Coleus are grown for their colourful foliage. They should be regularly watered during the summer, and much less so in winter. A temperature of 13°C (55°F) is best in winter. Feed with liquid manure weekly from June to September. Growing

Codiaeum variegatum pictum (croton) is extremely rewarding but is not really easy to grow.

tips should be pinched out to encourage bushiness.

Seeds may be sown in February and germinated at 16°C (1°F). When large enough, pot the seedlings on into 7·5cm (3in) and then 13cm (5in) pots. Alternatively, take tip cuttings of non-flowering shoots in spring. Plant them in cutting compost in 7·5cm (3in) pots and keep them in a temperature of 16–18°C (61–64°F).

Columnea gloriosa is a beautiful trailer. Though not the easiest to grow, it is well worth persevering with it.

Columnea gloriosa

Stove. With its tubular flowers of bright scarlet and drooping habit, *Columnea gloriosa* is ideal for hanging baskets. It flowers during the winter.

It needs a warm, humid atmosphere (no lower than 13–16°C (55–61°F) during winter). Feed established plants regularly with weak liquid manure during the summer. Re-pot this plant every other year in June.

Pieces of stems root quite easily in a cutting compost placed in a propagator with a temperature of 18–21°C (64–70°F) and a humid atmosphere. The stem pieces should be taken in spring.

Cyclamen persica

Cool or warm. The modern strains of the Persian cyclamen, a popular winter-flowering plant, have blooms in shades of purple, red, pink, mauve and white and combinations of these, and variously silver-marbled leaves.

The plants should be brought into the greenhouse in September and given ample ventilation, light and a temperature of 10°C (50°F). Watering must be done carefully from the bottom without wetting the bare corms. After flowering, the plants should be rested by gradually watering less and, during the summer, laying the pots on their sides to dry off. In autumn, growth should be re-started by watering.

Cyclamen are best propagated from seeds sown in August at a temperature of 13–16°C (55–61°F). Then pot them on until they are in 13cm (5in) pots. At no stage should the corms be buried.

Dieffenbachia picta
(dumb cane)

Stove. This has dark green, pointed, oblong leaves covered with white and pale green spots. Its cultivar 'Rudolph Roehrsii' is mottled pale and dark green.

Dieffenbachia needs a humid atmosphere with a winter temperature not lower than 16°C (61°F).

It is propagated from suckers or stem sections containing an eye in a cutting compost at a temperature of 21–24°C (70–75°F) in a propagator.

Dracaena draco
(dragon plant)

The species and varieties of dracaenas are grown for their superb range of foliage. Among the more attractive species are the smaller *Dracaena godseffiana* and *D. sanderiana*. A larger cultivar is *D. deremensis* 'Warneckii', which has long grey-green leaves with two silver stripes.

The plants need a winter temperature of 10–13°C (50–55°F), rising to 16°C (61°F) at night in spring and summer to encourage

Dracaena fragrans 'Massangena' has attractive green and gold leaves and likes a warm, humid atmosphere.

growth. The atmosphere must be humid.

They are propagated from cuttings of a main stem, partially buried horizontally in cutting compost in a propagator at 21–24°C (70–75°F).

Euphorbia pulcherrima (poinsettia)

Warm or stove. This splendid plant has insignificant flowers, but large scarlet, leaf-like bracts in winter. It is also available in pink and cream forms.

It needs a winter temperature of 13–16°C (55–61°F). During the summer it needs a humid atmosphere. It should be watered freely while growing, but after flowering it should be kept just moist. Give weak liquid manure weekly from June to September, during which period it can stand outdoors.

Poinsettia is difficult to preserve from one season to another so it is better to grow new plants from cuttings taken in spring. These should be inserted singly in 7·5 cm (3 in) pots of cutting compost and placed in a propagator at 18–21°C (64–70°F). The rooted cuttings should be potted on, and feeding should begin in their final pots.

Ficus elastica 'Decora' (india-rubber plant)

Warm. This plant is grown for its rich, green, bold foliage.

In winter it needs a temperature of 16–18°C (61–64°F). Water freely in summer and keep just moist in winter. Place in a well-lit position, but out of direct sunlight. Provide a humid atmosphere in summer, with ventilation when needed, and pot on every other spring. Feed with weak liquid manure during the summer.

The plant can be propagated from cuttings of lateral shoots taken from April to June at a temperature of 21–24°C (70–75°F), or from leaf-bud cuttings.

Few plants can surpass Euphorbia pulcherrima (poinsettia) for the splendid colour it gives.

There are many beautiful varieties of indoor fuchsia, which are grown as both bushes and standards.

Fuchsia

Cool or warm. The tender varieties of fuchsia are attractive as pot plants and provide beautiful summer flower displays in greenhouses.

After resting during winter, when they should be kept in a dry, well-lit place at a temperature of 4–7°C (39–45°F), fuchsias should be started into growth by being plunged into water and kept at a temperature of 10°C (50°F). (Any cuttings required should be taken when the young growth appears.) After removing as much soil as possible from the roots, pot the plants in John Innes potting compost no. 3 in a similar or smaller pot.

During the spring and summer fuchsias should be allowed to stand in a cool, well-lit place out of direct sunlight. Real success with fuchsias results from feeding and watering well during the growing and flowering season. Spraying the foliage with water occasionally is also advantageous.

Cuttings should be taken from shoots with no flower buds and should be nodal. They should be inserted in 5 cm (2 in) pots of cutting compost and placed in a prop-

agator at 16°C (61°F) until they are rooted, when air should be allowed in and the temperature lowered to 10°C (50°F). Young plants destined to be bushes must have their growing tip pinched back to induce bushiness. This may be repeated once or twice more if necessary. For standards, the plants should not be pinched back, but the main stem should be allowed to grow, removing all laterals as they appear, until the required height is reached, when it should be stopped.

Fuchsia bushes should be pruned lightly in February. At this time, overgrown plants can be hard-pruned to reduce their size. Standards are also pruned.

Pendulous varieties, such as 'Falling Stars' and golden-foliaged 'Golden Marinka', are excellent for hanging baskets, either to beautify a greenhouse, or to hang outdoors during the summer.

Gerbera
(Transvaal daisy, Barberton daisy)

Cool. *Gerbera jamesonii* has orange-scarlet, daisy-like flowers from May to August. There are also many hybrids and varieties in a wide range of colours.

Gerbera needs well-drained soil and cool conditions, with a temperature of 5–7°C (41–45°F) during the winter. Water freely in summer and more sparingly in winter, ventilate well and provide some shade when necessary. Apply weak liquid manure at fortnightly intervals during the summer.

Gerbera can be propagated by division in March. Alternatively, sow seeds in seed compost in February at a temperature of 16–18°C (61–64°F). Prick out and pot on in the usual manner.

Grevillea robusta
(silk bark oak)

Cool. *Grevillea robusta* is a foliage shrub with pinnate leaves up to 37·5 cm (15 in) long.

It requires a winter temperature of 4–7°C (39–45°F) and can be stood out of doors from May to October. Water freely in spring and summer and keep just moist

Above: Grevillea robusta is beautiful and easy-to-grow.

Below right: Hoya carnosa is relatively unknown.

during winter. Feed fortnightly with liquid manure during summer. Re-pot in March every two years, increasing the pot size if necessary.

This plant is propagated from seed sown in March in pots of lime-free sowing compost and germinated at 13–16°C (55–61°F). Prick out into 7·5cm (3in) pots and then pot on as necessary.

Hippeastrum
(amaryllis)

Warm or stove. Hippeastrum are showy, bulbous plants with strap-like green leaves and blooms of white, pink, red or orange, sometimes striped or frilled, according to the hybrid.

Plant one bulb in a 15cm (6in) pot of growing compost with half the bulb exposed and water sparsely until growth begins. As soon as the flower bud appears, or shortly afterwards, water freely and feed weekly with liquid manure. Maintain at a minimum temperature of 13–16°C (55–61°F). When leaves turn yellow, keep dry until re-starting growth in autumn.

Propagate from offsets or seeds sown in the springtime.

Hoya carnosa
(porcelain flower)

Cool or warm. This is a climber with deep green, glossy leaves and clusters of pale pink, sweetly scented flowers during summer.

Keep *H. carnosa* at 10°C (50°F) in winter and at not less than 16°C (61°F) in spring and summer. Provide a little shade when necessary, and abundant water, except in winter. Maintain a good level of humidity in spring and summer and also spray the plant with water when hot. Give liquid manure every three weeks in summer.

The plant is propagated by cuttings 7·5cm (3in) long taken in June and July. Root at 16–18°C (61–64°F) in a propagator.

Impatiens sultanii
(busy lizzie)

Cool or warm. Busy lizzie has white, orange, magenta, crimson or scarlet flowers from April to October.

It needs a winter temperature of 13°C

(55°F). When growth re-starts in March, water fairly freely. Liquid-feed weekly from May to September and provide a little shade on hot days. Re-pot every other year in April.

Propagate from tip cuttings inserted in cutting compost at any time from April to May. Place in a propagator at 16°C (61°F).

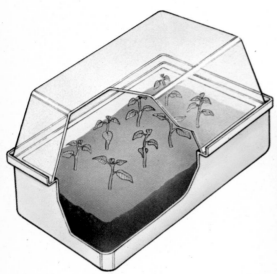

Above: Impatiens sultanii can be propagated from tip cuttings in a simple propagating unit given bottom heat.

Right: Maranta leuconeura 'Kerchoveana' is called the 'prayer plant' because it raises its leaves at sundown.

Jasminum mesneyi (syn. primulinum) and J. polyanthum

Cool. *Jasminum mesneyi* (syn. *primulinum*) has yellow flowers in spring. *J. polyanthum* has white and pale pink blooms in winter. Both are climbers.

Both do best in a greenhouse border, but they can be grown in 30 cm (12 in) pots. They should be trained up wires. In winter, a satisfactory temperature is 10–13°C (50–55°F). Keep the compost moist continuously and water freely during the growing season.

Propagate from heel cuttings and give bottom heat of 16°C (61°F).

Maranta

Stove. These are ornamental foliage plants, with leaves of various shapes marked or streaked in vivid colours. The two most strikingly coloured plants are *Maranta leuconeura* 'Kerchoveana' and *M. L erythrophylla*.

They need a winter temperature of 13°C (55°F), ample watering in summer, more moderate watering in winter, a humid atmosphere, a daily spraying and a fortnightly liquid feed during their growing season.

They are propagated by rhizome division in April or by planting basal shoot cuttings in the summer in cutting compost at 21°C (70°F).

Palms

Cool. Small palms make good table decorations, and the larger specimens are most attractive for the greenhouse and conservatory. Amongst the most excellent is *Chamaedorea* (syn. *Neanthe*) *elegans* 'Bella' (parlour palm), with elegant pinnate leaves, up to 1·25m (4ft) long, that hang down gracefully. It should be watered

Above: Groups of *Howea belmoreana* can have a striking decorative effect.

Left: Neanthe elegans is a perfect palm to grow because it requires so little attention.

freely in summer and have its leaves sprayed weekly. Feed throughout the growing season. Give partial shade: too much sun turns the foliage brown. It needs repotting only when it becomes pot-bound, and this is rare.

Howea (formerly *Kentia*) *belmoreana* (curly palm) is a palm with dark green pinnate leaves 45 cm (18 in) long and 30 cm (12 in) wide, carried on 45 cm- (18 in-)long stems.

Howea (formerly *Kentia*) *forsteriana* (Kentia palm), another excellent species, has leaves that differ from those of *H. belmoreana* only in that they droop and have fewer leaflets.

Both of these are grown in a growing compost. Ideally, they should be given a winter greenhouse temperature of 10–12°C (50–54°F); the minimum should be 7°C (45°F). *Howea* need full light in winter, with some shading in summer. Water sparingly between November and March, abundantly from April to July and moderately between July and October.

All the above-mentioned palms can be propagated from seed. Place the seed on the surface of some peat in a seed-pan, and germinate at a temperature of 27°C (81°F). Transplant the seedlings to 7·5 cm (3 in) pots of growing compost and maintain a temperature of 18°C (64°F) until they are growing.

Pelargonium
Cool or warm. Fuchsias and pelargoniums have a number of common uses, including greenhouse display, hanging baskets, indoor pot plants and summer bedding.

Among the pelargoniums there are two outstanding groups of hybrids – the regal

471

pelargoniums, among which there are some very beautiful named varieties, such as 'Black Knight', 'Lavender Grand Slam', 'Carisbrooke' and 'Nomad', and the zonal pelargoniums. These latter are commonly known as geraniums, and include several outstanding named cultivars (such as 'Cleopatra', 'Du Barry' and 'Gustav Emich'), varieties of the Irene seed strain, which is regarded as one of the best (such as 'Electra', 'King of Denmark' and 'Maximum Kovaleski') and varieties of foliage geraniums, both pendulous types and miniature ones suitable for hanging baskets.

Although pelargoniums can be maintained in a greenhouse from year to year, it is more common to take cuttings annually.

Nodal cuttings are taken in August and inserted individually in 7·5cm (3in) pots of John Innes potting compost no. 1, or in soilless sowing compost. Keep them covered with paper from seven to ten days. Normally no heat is required for rooting. Pinch out the growing tips to form good bushes when the plants are about 15cm (6in) high. Pot on into 10–15cm (4–6in) pots. Maintain a winter temperature of 7–10°C (45–50°F) and keep the soil just

Above: Pelargoniums are among the most popular and colourful plants to cultivate in a greenhouse.
Left: Zonal pelargoniums are available in many colourful varieties, all of which are most attractive.

moist. Water freely during the growing season. Keep the greenhouse well-ventilated and provide shade during the hottest weather – do not let the temperature exceed 13°C (55°F). When well-rooted feed with liquid manure until the flowers open.

Peperomia

Stove. These are mostly moderate-sized or small plants. They like shade from the sun, and grow in well-drained compost. They should have a humid atmosphere during summer and be sprayed twice daily, but they must not be overwatered and be allowed to dry out before the next watering. The best winter temperature for them is

472

13–18°C (55–65°F) and in summer 15–24°C (60–75°F).

They are propagated by cuttings inserted singly in 5 cm (2 in) pots of cutting compost in a propagator at 24°C (75°F).

Pilea

Stove. Of these attractive foliage plants, *Pilea cadierei* (aluminium plant) and *P. muscosa* (artillery plant) are the best known.

They require a winter temperature of 13°C (55°F) and a summer one of 24°C (75°F). They also need full light in winter and moderate shade in spring and summer. Water freely from April to September, very moderately in winter. Feed fortnightly during summer.

Propagate from cuttings in May. Insert in cutting compost and place in the propagator at 18–21°C (64–70°F).

Plumbago capensis

Cool or warm. This is a lovely deciduous climber with panicles of blue flowers from April to November.

While it can be grown in a pot, it is best planted in the border and trained up wires

Peperomia caperata has curious cream flowers, like shepherd's crooks, borne on light brown stalks.

Pilea cadierei is a very charming foliage plant.

or a trellis. It should be watered well until after flowering, and then kept just moist and watered increasingly as new growth appears. The best temperature up to December is 13–16°C (55–61°F); the minimum during the winter is 7°C (45°F). Feed regularly during the summer and re-pot annually in the spring.

Propagate from heel cuttings at a temperature of 16–18°C (61–64°F).

Primula

Cool. Primulas are excellent for greenhouses.

P. malacoides, although a perennial, is usually grown as an annual. Its leaves are hairy, ovate and pale green. Whorls of star-like flowers, ranging from pale lilac-purple through to red to white in colour, open between December and April.

P. sinensis is also a perennial grown as an annual. Its thick stems bear two or three whorls of pink, lilac or white flowers during winter.

P. obconica is also grown as an annual. Its light green leaves cause a rash on sensitive skins. Its winter-produced flowers are in

473

clusters of pink, red, lilac or blue-purple.

P. x kewensis, a perennial hybrid, has fragrant, yellow flowers, borne in whorls on upright stems during the winter.

All primulas require a minimum winter temperature of 7°C (45°F). Always keep the plant moist. Feed weekly with liquid manure when the flower stalks start to lengthen.

All are propagated from seeds at 16°C (61°F). Prick off the seedlings into boxes, and transplant them singly into 7·5cm (3in) pots of growing compost. Plunge them outdoors in a shaded frame for the summer. In autumn, pot them on to 15cm (6in) pots.

A very beautiful plant, *Primula obconica* must be handled with care, as its leaves affect sensitive skin.

Rhododendron (syn. *Azalea*) *indicum* is a lovely plant for Christmas decoration.

Rhododendron (syn. Azalea) indicum (Indoor or Indian azalea)

Cool or warm. This is an evergreen with many varieties which become massed in red, pink or white flowers during the winter or early spring.

In autumn the plant should be stood in a well-lighted place and sprayed with clear water. The compost should be kept moist, but not over-wet. An occasional feed with liquid manure helps to swell the buds.

After it has flowered, remove the dead flowers and put outdoors in the sun after the danger of frost has passed. During the summer keep the plant in the shade, water and feed until early October and then bring it back under the glass. If necessary, re-pot into a larger pot after flowering.

Propagate from half-ripened cuttings taken in April, inserted in cutting compost with a little bottom heat. They are not easy to root. Rooting compounds and mist propagation will be helpful, however.

Saintpaulia (African violet)

Warm. A charming small plant with pleasant fleshy green leaves and violet-like flowers, mainly pink and purple in colour.

Saintpaulia ionantha, the species normally cultivated, needs a winter temperature of 13°C (55°F). The atmosphere should be humid. Always keep the soil moist, without wetting the plant's leaves. Feed fortnightly with liquid manure during the summer.

Propagate from leaf cuttings during the summer. Place in a propagator at 18–21°C (64–70°F). It may also be grown from seed, germinated at the same temperature.

Sansevieria trifasciata 'Laurentii' (snake plant, mother-in-law's tongue)

Warm or stove. *Sansevieria trifasciata* is essentially a foliage plant, with narrow, fleshy, pointed and slightly twisted leaves edged with yellow and banded with light and dark green.

Minimum winter temperature should be 10°C (50°F). Allow the plant to dry out in the summer between waterings. Feed monthly from May to September.

Propagate from suckers potted up in growing compost.

Below: Saintpaulia is among the most spectacular of plants that can be grown in a greenhouse.

Sansevieria trifasciata 'Laurentii' is nicknamed Mother-in-Law's Tongue.

Senecio (syn. Cineraria) cruenta

Cool. There are numerous varieties which form compact masses of daisy-like flowers from December to May, according to when they were sown, in colours which include white, lavender, blue, mauve, red, pink and various bicolours.

Plant in John Innes potting compost no. 2 or soilless growing compost, and keep them at a temperature of 8°C (46°F) from October onwards, during which period the plants should be fed fortnightly with liquid manure and watered – but not over-watered – regularly.

They can be raised from seed between April and August at a temperature of 13°C (55°F). Grow the seedlings on through the summer in 7·5cm (3in) pots in an open frame, shading with muslin during hot spells; bring them into the greenhouse in September.

Sinningia speciosa (Gloxinia) is essentially a greenhouse plant, with large bell-like flowers.

There are few more colourful or easier to grow pct plants for greenhouses than *Senecio cruenta*.

Sinningia speciosa (Gloxinia)

Cool or warm. Gloxinias have large bell-like white, pink, blue and red flowers during summer and autumn.

Provide the plants with a humid atmosphere, keep them moist and feed with liquid manure weekly from the formation of buds until the last flower falls. As the leaves turn yellow, cease watering, gradually remove the dead flowers and leaves, remove the corms from the pot and store them in a dry place at 10°C (50°F). Re-start growth in early spring by plunging the plants into growing compost and placing in a propagator.

Gloxinias are either propagated from seed at a temperature of 15°C (60°F), or else they can be propagated from leaf cuttings.

Stephanotis floribunda
(Madagascar jasmine)

Stove. This evergreen, twining shrub has dark green leaves and heavily perfumed, white, waxy flowers from May to October.

It can be grown in large pots or in the greenhouse border, from either of which it is trained up wires or a cane framework. The best winter temperature is 13°C (55°F), but from April until late October it should not fall below 18°C (64°F) for long (a higher temperature does not matter). Keep the plant just moist in winter. While it is growing give ample water and maintain a humid atmosphere. Provide a little shade during the summer, otherwise let it have full light. Feed fortnightly with liquid manure from May to September.

Propagate from cuttings of lateral non-flowering shoots in a propagator at 18-21°C (64-70°F).

Right: Strelitzia is grown for its large, dramatic flowers.
Below: Stephanotis floribunda is an exquisite, sweetly scented climbing plant for greenhouses.

Strelitzia
(bird of paradise flower)

Stove. *Strelitzia reginae* is an evergreen, stove-house perennial that yields the most intriguing bird's-head-shaped flowers of green, purple, orange and blue in April and May.

In winter it needs a temperature of 10°C (50°F) and to be kept nearly dry. Water freely during spring and summer. Prevent scorching of the leaves by shading, and ventilate when necessary to lower the summer temperature to 18-21°F (64-70°F). Pot on or re-pot every second year in March. Liquid-feed fortnightly while growing.

Propagate by detaching single-rooted shoots after flowering and potting them up in growing compost. Strelitzia is also raised from seed which should be germinated at 18-21°C (64-70°F).

477

Streptocarpus
(cape primrose)

Cool or warm. These are showy hybrids with large, corrugated leaves and flowers of red, purple and white between May and October.

During winter streptocarpus requires a temperature of 10°C (50°F), and then 13°C (55°F). Water freely during the growing period and sparingly in winter. Shade the glass, and ventilate when necessary during the summer. Feed with weak liquid manure fortnightly from May to September. Propagate streptocarpus by division or leaf cuttings, or sow seeds.

Tradescantia fluminensis

Cool or warm. This species has leaves that turn pale purple underneath in bright light.

Below: Tradescantia fluminensis 'Variegata' are some of the most easily grown of greenhouse trailing plants.

Above: Streptocarpus hybrids are very popular greenhouse plants.

'Quicksilver' is a silver variegated variety. Tradescantia needs a winter temperature not lower than 7-10°C (45-50°F). The plant should be kept just moist. Water freely during the growing season. Position in good light, out of direct sunlight. Re-pot annually in April. Feed with weak liquid manure fortnightly from May to September.

This plant is easily propagated from tip cuttings at 16°C (61°F).

Zantedeschia aethiopica (Arum lily)

Cool or warm. The arum lily has beautiful large white flowers with a conspicuous yellow spadix and large, green, slightly glossy arrow-shaped leaves. It flowers from March to June, according to the temperature in which it is kept.

The handsome, large, white flowers of *Zantedeschia aethiopica* are very useful for flower arranging.

Z. elliottiana is another lovely species, with yellow blooms and green leaves with silvery spots.

After flowering, the plants are dried off and rested with the pots lying on their sides. During August and September re-pot in a potting compost to which some bonemeal has been added. Stand the pots outdoors, water them well and bring them into the greenhouse in early October. When the roots are growing well, regularly feed with liquid manure. Spray the foliage against greenfly.

Arum lilies are propagated from offsets, which may be taken at the time of re-potting the plant.

9 Garden frames and cloches

Like greenhouses, garden frames and cloches give another dimension to gardening. Although the principle embodied is quite an old one, it remains very popular and is still being developed as a current technique. Frames and cloches have common functions, but there are marked differences in the manner in which they are used. They afford protection to plants of various types against adverse weather conditions and can extend their growing season.

Garden frames

A garden frame is perhaps rather more complementary to a greenhouse than a cloche. There are, for example, many greenhouse subjects which can spend much of their time under a frame, and thus release space in the greenhouse. In fact, younger plants often flourish better in its cooler environment. Also, after flowering, plants can be transferred to a frame from

the greenhouse to dry off and rest. A frame is essential for hardening off bedding plants, and for raising and propagating many types of plant. When no greenhouse is available, a garden frame can be heated by means of warming cables.

Garden frame structure Basically, frames have base walls made of tongued and grooved timber, metal, breeze blocks, plastic or sometimes glass, on the top of which is fixed a light which is a wooden or metal frame glazed with glass or PVC.

Choosing garden frames The frame's purpose will dictate what type should be bought. For raising seedlings, rooting cuttings and growing vegetables such as lettuce or early carrots, the frame need not be very high. The more usual lean-to type, with a height of 45cm (18in) at the back and 30cm (12in) at the front, will therefore

A traditional garden frame, constructed in timber and glass, is an invaluable adjunct to a greenhouse, but it also has its own particular functions.

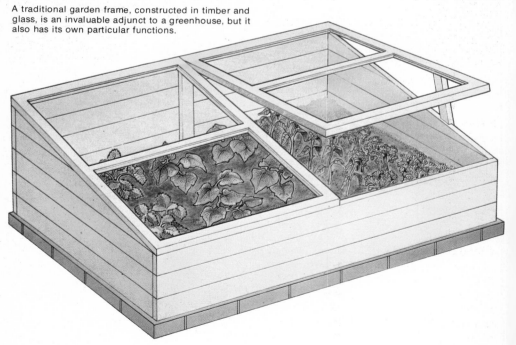

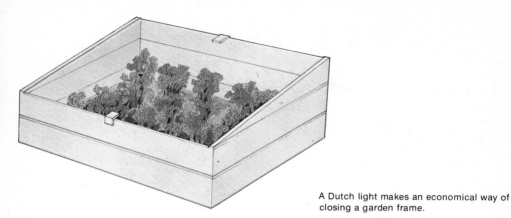

A Dutch light makes an economical way of closing a garden frame.

serve. This type is usually fitted at the top with a 2 x 1·25m (6 x 4ft) or 1·25 x 1·25m (4 x 4ft) light which slides up and down on runners. A cheaper and simpler form is the Dutch light, which is composed of a single sheet of glass 150 x 78cm (59 x 30in), held in a frame. The glass slides in rebates in the styles and is secured at the top and bottom by means of cleats.

For higher-growing plants, such as pot plants, French beans and cauliflowers, more depth is needed and a span-roof frame should be chosen. This is like a mini-greenhouse, with lights, that can be opened, sloping from the side walls to a central high ridge.

Siting garden frames The site should be well-drained, and not too near buildings or trees, which will deprive the frame of light and could be the cause of damage from falling debris. A wooden-base frame should be stood on a course of bricks. Lean-to frames are best placed against a wall facing south or south-west.

Cleanliness and ventilation It is important to keep frames free of rotting debris, and the glass clean. Good ventilation is essential when frames are in use. Both temperature and air ventilation are controlled by opening and closing the lights of the frames.

Shading Some form of shading, for example, a thin lime wash on the lights, should be provided during hot weather.

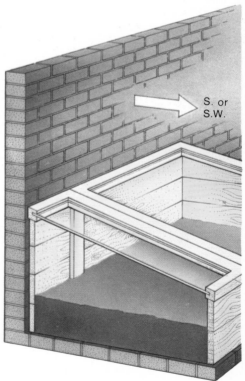

S. or S.W.

A lean-to frame should be positioned against a south- or southwest-facing wall.

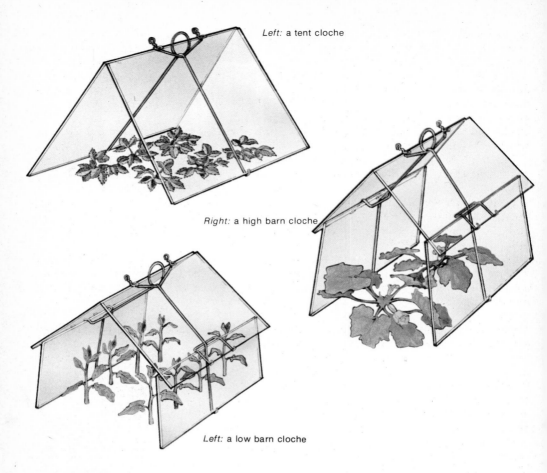

Left: a tent cloche

Right: a high barn cloche

Left: a low barn cloche

Cloches

Although many of the functions of cloches, such as propagating, protecting plants against frost and producing early and tender growth, are similar to those of garden frames, the difference between them is that under cloches cultivation is carried on in the conventional manner – planting in continuous rows – whereas frames are used more as an extension of the greenhouse. Cloches are easily moved from one crop to another, and they provide easy access to crops at specific points.

Choosing cloches There are several types of cloche available. In glass, there are three main shapes. The tent cloche is com-

prised of two sheets of glass held firmly together by means of an inverted V-shaped wire, upturned at each end, on which the glass rests. The whole is held together by a

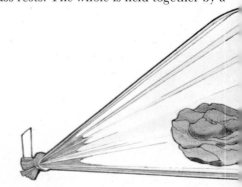

spring handle, which permits extra ventilation. The size when erected is 60cm (2ft) long x 30cm (1ft) wide x 25cm (10in) high.

The 'low barn' cloche is comprised of four sheets of glass which, by means of wire, form a cloche with two almost vertical sides at the base and a span roof. This type of cloche is 60cm (2ft) long x 57·5cm (23in) wide x 32·5cm (13in) high.

The 'high barn' cloche is similar to the last, except that it has taller sides, of 47·5cm (19in).

Plastic cloches usually take the form of a sheet of PVC inserted into hoops and secured with clips. Regular sizes are 45cm (18in) long x 30cm (1ft) wide x 25cm (10in) high; and 60cm (2ft) long x 30cm (1ft) x 22·5cm (9in) high. There are also models constructed in rigid plastic, needing no metal fittings but secured with pegs.

The three major advantages of plastic cloches are that they are lighter in weight, cheaper than glass, and unbreakable. On the other hand, they are less durable, they must be well secured or could blow away, they lose heat more rapidly at night, and condensation does not run down the sides as it does on glass, therefore light entry can be impeded.

Plastic continuous-tunnel cloche kits consist of polythene sheeting, supporting hoops and securing wires which erected, form a tunnel 9–11 m (30–35ft) long.

Using cloches Individual glass or plastic cloches should be placed end to end along each row of produce (early or more tender types of vegetables, fruit and flowers). The ends of the tunnel should be closed with glass or polythene sheets.

Siting cloches The site of the run must be away from buildings and trees so that no shadows are cast. Each cloche must be placed on previously prepared fertilised ground. The tunnel must be in place for a fortnight or so before sowing to warm up and dry out the soil so that a good tilth can be made and germination assisted.

Cloche cultivation Individual cloches can be moved aside easily at any specific point to provide access for weeding, spraying and so forth.

Cleanliness and ventilation Clean glass and plastic regularly. As the weather warms, the cloches should be opened

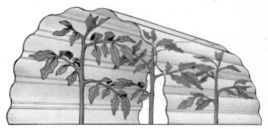

Below: The plastic tunnel, a more recent innovation, protects a row of plants as effectively as the older types of cloche and is more easily stored when not in use.

Above: A plastic cloche has the advantage over glass cloches of being unbreakable and less dangerous in gardens where young children play.

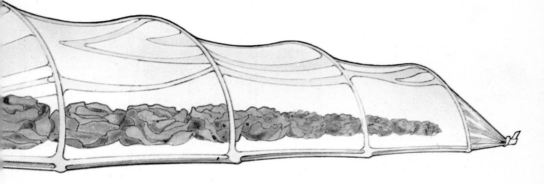

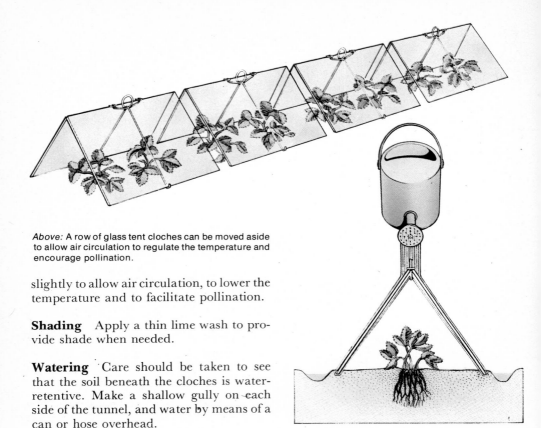

Above: A row of glass tent cloches can be moved aside to allow air circulation to regulate the temperature and encourage pollination.

slightly to allow air circulation, to lower the temperature and to facilitate pollination.

Shading Apply a thin lime wash to provide shade when needed.

Watering Care should be taken to see that the soil beneath the cloches is water-retentive. Make a shallow gully on each side of the tunnel, and water by means of a can or hose overhead.

Plants for garden frames and cloches Dates refer to the approximate harvesting or gathering time.

Plants under cloches are watered from overhead so that water flows into gullies on either side.

Vegetables

Asparagus (March)
Aubergines
Dwarf French beans (mid-June)
Cabbage (February-March)
Capsicum
Carrots (May)
Celery (self-blanching)
    (early August)
Cucumbers
Endive
Lettuce (spring and winter)
Peas (early May)
Sweet corn
Tomatoes

Fruit

Strawberries
Melon

Flowers

Anemone (winter)
Calendula (late winter)
Gladioli
Dutch iris
Lily of the valley (April)
Brompton stocks (mid-April)
Violets (October)
Zinnias (early July)

10 Common greenhouse pests and diseases

In the tables below are described some of the troubles that affect greenhouse plants.

Pests

Pest		Susceptible plants	Signs	Remedies
Aphids (greenfly)		Most	Stems, leaves and buds are swarmed with green larvae. Young growth disfigured.	Spray with formathion or dimethoate.
Caterpillars		All	Eaten or curled leaves.	Spray with trichlorphon or malathion.
Leaf hoppers		Many	Coarse mottling on upper sides of leaves.	Regular fumigation of greenhouse with BHC.
Leaf miners		Chrysanthemums, cinerarias and other pot plants	Leaves tunnelled.	Fumigate or spray with BHC.
Mealy bugs		Many	Small tufts or waxy wool appearing on leaves and stems.	Spray with dimethoate or formathion
Red spider mites		Many	Yellow mottling on upper side of leaves. Yellowing of leaves, then bronzing and ultimately leaf fall.	Regular fumigation with azobenzene. Spray with dimethoate.
Scale insects		Many	Leaves and stems become sticky; closer examination shows that stems are covered with brown, yellow or white scales.	Spray with malathion or petroleum emulsion.

485

Pest		Susceptible plants	Signs	Remedies
Tarsonemid mites		Many	Young shoots, leaves, etc., become distorted, discoloured and scarred.	No effective chemical control available, but sulphur dust or lime-sulphur sprays limit the infestation.
Thrips		Various species attack many plants	Plants become covered with black flies. Distortion occurs.	Spray with malathion.
Weevils		Begonias, cyclamen, vines pelargoniums, primulas, etc.	Plants collapse owing to roots being eaten.	Spray foliage with or add BHC, as a dust, to potting compost.
White flies		Many	Underside of leaves infested with white scales, which are im-mature white flies.	Fumigate with BHC to kill the adults and spray the undersides of the leaves to kill the young.

Diseases

Disease	Susceptible plants	Signs	Remedies
Blackroot-rot	Many	Rotting of the roots and tissues at the crown. Tissues become black.	Water plants with a solu-tion of captan.
Bud drop	Camellias, stephanotis, etc.	Buds drop off before flowering.	Often caused by dry soil condition at bud forma-tion; sometimes caused by extremes of day and night temperatures.
Carnation stem rot and die-back	Carnations	Stems rotting.	Control by spraying stock plants with captan a fortnight before and while taking cuttings.
Damping off	All seedlings and cuttings	Collapsing and dying.	Overcrowding, growing in too wet conditions, in compacted soil or in too high a temperature should be avoided. Check attacks by watering seed-boxes with captan.
Foot rot	Calceolaria, geraniums, etc.	Blackening and rotting at the base.	May be caused by con-tamination of water supply from a tank or butt. Add small pea-size lump of copper sulphate or crystals of potassium per-manganate until water just pink, to purify.

Disease	Susceptible plants	Signs	Remedies
Grey mould (botrytis)	Most greenhouse plants	Greyish, velvety fungus on leaves, etc., with ultimate decay.	Remove and burn infected parts. Give good ventilation. Fumigate or dust the greenhouse with tecnazene or spray with captan or benomyl.
Gummosis	Cucumbers, melons	Distorted fruits, sunken spots, exuding gummy liquid, which becomes covered with dark green fungus.	Ventilate and heat adequately. Burn all infected fruits. Spray with zineb or captan.
Leafspot	Primulas, anthurium, dracaenas, etc.	Pale brown, irregular spots.	Remove dead leaves. Spray with captan, maneb or zineb.
Mildew, downy	Lettuce and other ornamental plants	White tufts or downy patches, usually on undersides of leaves.	Spray with thiram.
Mildew, powdery	Carnations, cucumbers, grapes, chrysanthemums, etc.	White powdery coating on stems and leaves.	Fumigate with dinocap.
Physiological disorders	Many plants	Brown and yellow blotches on leaves, browning of leaf tips, splitting of leaves, dropping leaves, etc.	Generally improve conditions. Give adequate watering; attend to nutriments, correct temperature, humidity levels, and so on.
Rust	Cineraria, carnations, beans, apricots	Brown or black spots on foliage.	Encouraged by high humidity which should be controlled by increasing ventilation; destroy leaves and badly infected plants. Spray with thiram and zineb.
Tomato leaf mould	Tomatoes	Yellow blotches on upper sides of leaves; purple-brown mould underneath.	Good cultivation and a maximum temperature of 21°C (70°F) usually prevent trouble. Also spray with zineb, or maneb.
Virus diseases	Tomatoes, strawberries, narcissi, chrysanthemums, cucumbers, carnations, etc.	Wide range of symptoms includes colour changes in leaves and stems and flowers, distortion, wilting, stunting of growth, etc.	Destroy any suspect and seedy plants for which there is no obvious explanation for ill-health. Virus disease is spread by common greenhouse pests, so always destroy them.

487

Gardening
questions and answers

What are the best ways to screen a garden for seclusion from neighbours?

When deciding on a screen its future maintenance is an important factor to consider, and it may be wise not to cut costs. Brick, natural stone and, particularly, Californian screen-blocks are permanent and can be constructed and ornamented, perhaps with wall shrubs and climbers, to look attractive. There are many different types and designs of wooden fencing available as ready-made panels, but all need attention unless they are to suffer from rot and become unsafe during gales. Treatment with preservatives may be difficult when plants are established on or near them. Hedges must also be chosen with their ease of maintenance and ultimate height in mind.

Quick-growing, but easy to

keep neat with modern electric clippers, are golden privet (*Ligustrum ovalifolium*) and *Lonicera nitida*. Box (*Buxus sempervirens*) lends itself to elaborate trimming. Holly (*Ilex aquifolium*) is useful for keeping neighbouring children or animals out of a garden, but its spiky foliage makes trimming unpleasant, although this need not be a frequent task. Laurel (*Prunus laurocerasus*)

Berberis × *stenophylla* makes a colourful screen between a house and street.

is quick-growing and makes a dense screen. It is best trimmed with secateurs —a tedious business on a large scale — since shears or electric clippers will slice leaves with unsightly effect. *Thuja plicata* makes a fine hedge for privacy and is easily clipped, during which it emits a pleasant pine-like scent. *Cupressus macrocarpa* is often sold to form a fast-growing hedge – but is most unsuitable. It soon grows to an enormous size, forming huge trunks, and becomes quite unmanageable. Common yew (*Taxus baccata*) forms an almost wall-like hedge, but should not be planted where there are cattle because it is poisonous.

Escallonia macrantha is best suited to mild areas and is wind resistant.

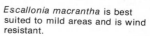

Which are the most satisfactory types of pergolas and arches available for climbing plants?

Small prefabricated and ready-made arches and pergolas are now available in wood, wrought iron and plastic-coated wire. On a larger scale they are usually made from brick or natural stone for the supporting columns, and any weather-resistant timber is used for the beams. Since the columns (or 'piers') are usually tall they need a good foundation. It is wise when building each pier to cement in strong metal rings at intervals up the sides, which will support

A pergola-covered walk makes an impressive garden feature.

any climbers (such as roses or clematis) planted at the base. Avoid homemade rustic arches and structures made from any available tree wood, for they tend eventually to come apart or rot, robbing climbers of their support.

What special features do you consider important to garden design to lend interest and professional appearance?

A major factor in designing a satisfying garden of professional appearance is to bear the style and setting of the dwelling house in mind and to see that all features blend with it. For example, a 'period' house style demands an informal garden in most cases, although certain periods – such as Tudor – do have traditional garden designs

that can be quite formal. Modern homes are happier when surrounded with formal squares, rectangles and straight lines. In all gardens, features such as ornamental pots, stone or paved steps, pools, bird baths, raised beds and so forth will add interest, and lawns are especially important in that they act like a carpet in a room, showing off the furniture. A few ornamental trees are also desirable. Where a lot of grass is impractical and paving or concrete has to be used, a pool with a fountain or waterfall always softens the harshness. If the garden is large, it is better if the whole area cannot be seen at the same time from any major point, but a good vista from the house windows is desirable.

A bank of flowers and shrubs around a focal pool creates a garden packed with interest.

How should a rose garden be planned, and can you suggest some popular easy varieties?

A rose garden often gives a pleasing effect if planned along simple formal lines, so that the roses themselves can dominate the scene. In either a large garden or a long narrow one, a rose garden can be enclosed by a surrounding wall or trellis, on which climbing and rambling roses should bloom profusely. Try to exploit the many rose forms – hybrid tea, floribunda, miniatures, bush, standards, weeping standards, climbers and ramblers. Site them to take advantage of their different heights and shapes. Blend colours carefully, avoiding clashes, and aim for striking contrast – crimson against pure white, for example. There are now so many rose varieties that it is wise to consult a current rose specialist's catalogue. However, species of shrub roses, such as *Rosa moyesii* and *R. rugosa* (which have decorative hips), and *R. centifolia muscosa* should not be overlooked.

Above: A well-head forms an attractive support for a climbing rose which may grow as high as a small tree.
Above right: A fragrant and colourful mixed rose walk welcomes visitors to the door.
Right: Floribunda roses bordering a lawn.

What can be used to make a lawn apart from grass? Is camomile practical?

For appearance and resistance to being walked on grass is unique. But where a purely ornamental effect is required, on a small scale, various very low-growing and carpet-forming rock plants can be used, such as various Thymus species. Some of these will tolerate being walked on in moderation and the aromatic ones will emit a pleasing scent as a result. Camomile (*Anthemis nobilis*) is a typical example of a fragrant 'lawn' and was popular during the Tudor period in England. It is the most practical of the unconventional 'lawns' and is particularly suitable for dry soils. Camomile lawns will not survive hard wear or drastic mowing and it is important to plant the non-flowering Cornish variety called Treneague. This should be planted on the prepared site at 0·5m (18in) intervals.

How can lawns be best integrated with garden landscaping, and when, or when not, should they be used?

Most gardens look better with a well sited lawn which acts in a similar way to a carpet in a room and shows off other features, including beds and borders, to their best advantage. 'Sweeping' lawns in garden landscaping look most impressive. Even in a small garden an uncluttered lawn will give the impression of space. However, for a very tiny garden a lawn may do little and be more trouble than it is worth, since cutting tools will still have to be acquired. The area might be better paved with natural stone and the garden devoted to plants grown in spaces between the stones and in raised beds or in pots. Generally it is best to make lawns in

Well-planned, sweeping lawns create a dramatic-looking landscape.

practical shapes and to avoid narrow or complicated shapes with sharp bends, twists, turns and corners, which may make mowing extremely difficult and time-consuming. However, straight or moderately curved grass paths are often pleasing, especially in rose gardens or other gardens devoted to flowers.

Can you suggest plants for sunny and shady sites?

Generally, most plants suited to rock gardens and dry walls like to grow in a sunny site. Other sun-lovers include plants with succulent foliage, such as *Sedum spectabile*, a popular border plant, and also most herbs and plants with scented leaves, pelargoniums for example. For bedding or border plants with a height of 30–90cm (1–3ft), choose *Achillea filipendulina* (yellow); cistus (sun rose, numerous species, many colours); cytisus (broom, numerous named forms, yellow, white, purple); eryngium (several species, usually bluish flowers and silvery bracts, can be dried); genista (several species, yellow); gazania (several forms, various colours); helianthus (sunflower, numerous excellent kinds, yellow); linum (flax, several species, blue, red, yellow). These plants also do quite well in dry poor soil. For shade, all woodland plants are suitable, but they also generally prefer a moist soil. Primulas, polyanthus, ferns and hostas are popular. Others are ajuga (blue); aquilegia (columbine, various colours); bergenia (rose-pink); astilbe (plume-like flowers); camellia (white, shades of red and pink); campanulas (bellflower, blue or white); trillium (white, pink, purple); violas (pansy, various colours). There are numerous named forms.

What bulbs do you recommend for the garden and how and when should they be planted?

Spring-flowering bulbs are planted from late summer to autumn, summer flowering bulbs in spring. For continued flowering over the years, plant in a good fertile soil. For informal plantings, scatter the bulbs and plant where they fall. Plant at about 1½ to 2 times the bulb length. Some, such as tulips and narcissi, can be planted much deeper in borders so that bedding plants can be set over the top to take over when the foliage dies down. Tulips and narcissi are indispensable for spring, together with allium, bulbous irises, chionodoxa, crocus, eranthis, erythronium, fritillaria, galanthus (snowdrop), hyacinth, muscari (grape hyacinth), ornithogalum, puschkinia, and scilla (bluebell). For summer flowering acidanthera, camassia, colchicum, crinum, crocosmia,

Boldly coloured tulips, narcissi and muscari brighten a spring garden.

galtonia (summer hyacinth), gladiolus, lilies and ranunculus (buttercup) are very popular. Note that 'bulb' can mean any storage organ – corms, tubers and rhizomes as well as true bulbs.

Can you recommend some flowers and decorative plants for winter colour?

Evergreens and conifers make any garden look less bleak in winter. There are many types of winter foliage, but few flowers. Flowers, moreover, are more prone to damage by bad weather. The following flowering plants are well worth chancing: shrubs might include *Daphne mezereum, Calluna vulgaris* varieties (heather), *Erica carnea, Hamamelis mollis, Lonicera fragrantissima, Mahonia japonica, Cornus mas* and *Magnolia stellata*; among the herbaceous perennials could be helleborus, *Vinca diformis, Viola tricolor* (winter pansies), *Primula vulgaris* (primrose), *P. denticulata* (drumstick primula), bergenias and early-flowering bulbs. In sheltered places try camellias: their blooms are beautiful and their evergreen foliage always attractive. Holly, various cotoneasters and other plants with berries add colour. So do trees or shrubs with coloured bark, such as *Prunus serrula* and varieties of dogwood (*Cornus alba*).

A Christmas rose, *Helleborus niger*, flowering before the snow has completely melted.

What flowers or plants can be used to climb and cover walls or eyesores, or to train over trellises?

For quickly covering small eyesores the following can be grown from seed sown in pots under glass and transferred in spring: *Cobaea scandens* (purple); *Eccremocarpus scaber* (orange); *Ipomaea tricolor* (purple to blue); *Tropaeolum peregrinum* (yellow). For more permanent colour the many varieties of climbing and rambling rose and clematis are popular for their generous flowering. *Abutilon megapotamicum*, with quaint lantern-like flowers, is pretty while several jasmines are good for fragrance or winter colour – note that not all are scented. *Passiflora caerulea* is a vigorous plant noted for its curious flowers and is perfectly hardy. There are numerous loniceras or honeysuckles, not all scented, but usually with delightful flowers. A notorious coverer of eyesores is the Russian vine, *Polygonum baldschuanicum*. This should be planted cautiously since it will quickly cover a whole house if permitted. It has creamy white, sometimes pinkish, flowers. For attractive foliage the variegated ivies, such as *Hedera canariensis* (Canary Island ivy), common ivy *Hedera helix* and the virginia creepers (various *Parthenocissus* species) are popular, the latter for its glorious autumn colour. Curious to look at and easy to grow from seed are the ornamental gourds which bear strange, and often large, coloured fruits.

What exotic or unusual fruits are practical for growing as crops?

Recently found to be a worthwhile crop for the home-grower is the Cape gooseberry (*Physalis peruviana*), varieties of which are known as Golden Berry. The fruit is about the size of a large cherry, golden yellow in colour when ripe, and surrounded by a papery calyx like the well-known Chinese Lantern (*Physalis alkekengii*) to which it is related. The fruit is delicious either raw or cooked, with a flavour similar to a sweet gooseberry. It is easy to grow from seed sown under glass early in the year. seed. Plant about 60cm

Grow on the seedlings in pots and transfer them outdoors to a warm sunny place when all risk of frost has passed. Worth trying in warm sheltered areas is the Chinese gooseberry (*Actinidia chinensis*), but both male and female plants must be planted for

pollination. The fruit is delicious and the flavour similar to both grape and gooseberry. It has a thin brownish skin, is about 6cm (2½in) long and 4cm (1½in) wide.

The brown, furry-skinned fruit of the Chinese gooseberry.

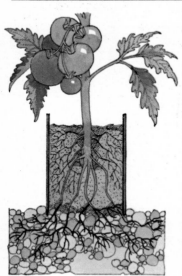

A section through a ring system, showing the ring of compost standing on a moisture-laden aggregate of ballast or peat.

What is ring culture, how is it carried out, and when is it most suitable?

Ring culture is designed to achieve more even moisture conditions and feeding for those plants that tend to suffer when subjected to wide fluctuations. It is commonly used for tomatoes, but can be applied to cucumbers and other members of the same family, as well as to chrysanthemums grown for cut bloom, and other flowers and crops. The plants are grown in a potting compost contained in bottomless pots or rings, usually made from fibre,

and disposable. These are stood on an 'aggregate', usually consisting of 'ballast' comprising both fine and coarse particles up to pebble size. The large particles give support and the fine sandy material conveys moisture to the compost within the rings by capillary action – the aggregate being constantly kept quite moist, preferably by an automatic method. Once moistened, the compost in the rings will remain that way, and only liquid fertilisers are then added, which are absorbed by the fine roots that develop. Instead of ballast, in some cases peat can be used.

What fruits do you suggest for a small garden, where there is no room for orchards or extensive planting, and general appearance is important to keep the garden attractive?

Many fruit nurseries are now selling dwarfed fruits that can be grown *in pots*, the trees or bushes staying quite small and compact. Also specially useful for the small garden is the 'family tree'. This usually has three different fruit varieties grafted on to the same tree, the varieties being chosen to solve any pollination problems. For example a pear may have the three varieties Williams, Conference, and Doyenne du Comice. Fruit trained as cordons, fans or espaliers takes up little room, and bush or half-standard trees grown on semi-dwarfing rootstock are also economical of space. Even grapes can be grown in pots as long as the number of bunches is restricted to about six and the plants are discarded after about three years and a fresh start made. Most fruit is attractive when in flower and when cropping and proves extremely ornamental for any garden. Fruit trees in pots or small tubs can be attractively used to decorate patios or terraces.

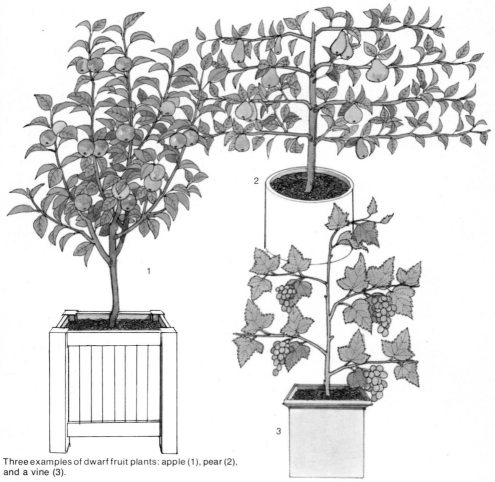

Three examples of dwarf fruit plants: apple (1), pear (2), and a vine (3).

Can you give general hints on the selection and buying of equipment for watering?

A watering-can of about 7 litres (1½ gal) capacity made from stout plastic with a rose that can be removed and replaced is generally useful. Hosing needs careful assessment. If it is to be attached to a high-pressure mains the hose must be strong, but this usually means that it will not be very flexible and may be difficult to manoeuvre. Various designs of hose reels and reel dispensers, some in the form of a trolley, are available. These should be made from stout plastic or aluminium alloy so that they do not rust. An adjustable hose nozzle to give spray or jet and to shut off completely is helpful. There are many patent fittings on the market for connecting hoses, and fitting them to taps. The best types of automatic lawn or border sprinklers are those which distribute water in squares or rectangles. This way no part of the ground gets more watering than necessary; for those which distribute in circles, there has to be some overlap. Automatic or semi-automatic watering can be done either by using drip-feed cisterns that siphon over periodically and distribute water through a trickle line, or by using an electronic system, in which a special circuit and photoelectric cell control water according to the degree of solar energy.

These methods can also be adapted for various automatic watering systems in greenhouses. Trickle irrigation is especially useful in the vegetable garden or where plants are grown in rows. To assess the degree of moisture meters are available. These indicate 'dry', 'moist' or 'wet' conditions by a meter reading on a scale. The meter works either visually, with lights, or aurally, by electronic oscillation.

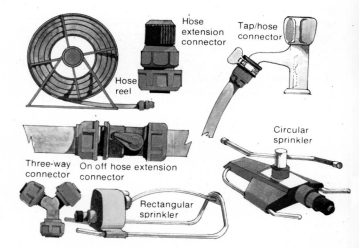

Hose reel

Hose extension connector

Tap/hose connector

Three-way connector

On off hose extension connector

Circular sprinkler

Rectangular sprinkler

Plastics are used extensively in gardening, but are they always good substitutes for other materials and for what purposes are they best suited?

There are countless different uses for plastics. Clear plastic is ideal for giving weather protection to plants easily damaged by wind, rain or cold. As it is lightweight and unbreakable, it is exceptionally handy for making cloches and frames that can be rotated around vegetable and fruit crops and also for giving protection from pests. Black plastic sheeting makes an efficient 'mulch'. Strips can be run along rows of plants to keep in soil moisture and hinder weed growth.

Plastic pots, seed trays and the like are clean, hygienic and easily sterilised. Some plastics form excellent pool liners (see page 502). Clear plastic bags can also be used to cover plants to keep them moist and fresh in the gardener's absence from home.

Have you any special hints for the care and storage of tools and equipment during the winter months?

A dry garden shed is vital for proper storage of gardening equipment. Nothing should be put away dirty, since the dirt will hold damp and encourage corrosion or rotting. Mowers and cutting tools must be thoroughly cleaned and oiled. Small tools may be wrapped in an oily rag. Various anti-corrosion and water-repellent preparations can be bought, usually in aerosols so that they can easily be sprayed on to equipment. Submersible water pumps for operating waterfalls or fountains are best removed from ponds, cleaned, smeared with grease where necessary, and stored dry over winter. This prevents damage caused by water freezing during a severe winter.

What are the best ways to sharpen tools with cutting blades safely?

Special patented sharpening tools are sold for most garden cutting instruments including lawn mowers. For a lawn mower it is best to use one of these or give the blades to an expert, especially in the case of cylinder cutters. Rotary cutters are generally simple to sharpen since they have no curvature and, being easy to get at, can be removed without difficulty from the machine. Before sharpening these blades, and those of shears or similar instruments, clamp them firmly, in a vice if possible. Badly blunted blades can first be filed to remove irregularities, then finished with a carborundum stone. Those experienced with power tools may prefer to do their sharpening with a carborundum wheel, which is best attached to a fixed motor or hand drill while the cutting blade is held firmly in the hands. Protect the eyes from flying fragments.

Shown above is a carborundum stone and a fine file. The former is used for final sharpening.

When sharpening a blade, clamp it firmly in a vice. This will give added safety.

Make sure a carborundum wheel spins away from you so fragments are carried away from the face.

What tools or equipment would you suggest might be specially useful to infirm or disabled people, or to the elderly?

All electrically operated tools are usually far easier to use, and need little effort on the part of the operator. Consider for example the difference between using an electric hedge clipper and manual shears, and between rotary mowers and cylinder types. Kneeling and bending is often a problem for elderly people, and special stools, with side arms to help the user stand up again, are available for this purpose. For digging, special spades that will take up soil and turn it over without the necessity of lifting are made. These spades work on a lever system. It is, of course, wise to design a garden especially for a disabled person, perhaps with raised beds to eliminate stooping. Gardening in pots and greenhouse gardening at staging level are also easier for both the elderly and the infirm. If a wheelchair is to be used, see that the garden has sloped access points. Paths should be of a firm composition, so avoid

A kneeling stool with handles at the sides is a useful aid to those gardeners who have difficulty kneeling and bending.

gravel and eliminate any uneven surfaces.

Can you advise on the purchase and selection of equipment for applying pesticides?

At least two sprayers are necessary, one large for severe or routine applications, and one small for the odd plant needing individual treatment. The large sprayer size will depend on your requirements, but generally 5–8 litres (1–1½ gal) capacity is convenient. The small sprayer might hold ½ litre (or a pint) or so. Fruit-growers may need a much larger sprayer, preferably of the knapsack type to leave the arms free. The larger sprayers always have a lance, usually with a finger-operated valve, and most are of the pneumatic or 'pump-up' type. Most

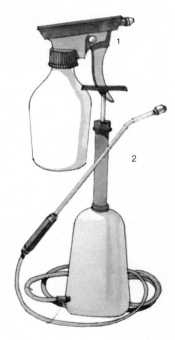

A small trigger-operated hand sprayer (1), and a pump-action sprayer (2), with a lance.

small hand sprayers also work on this principle, but there are some that are piston-pump operated and hence give an intermittent spray. However, it is wise to select a sprayer with either a lance or a long tube which can be turned upwards to support the nozzle. This is so that the undersides of leaves can be efficiently sprayed – it is there that pests and diseases usually first attack. Fumigating lamps are also available for greenhouses, but it is better to use proprietary aerosols in pressure cans or pyrotechnic fumigants. For applying total weedkillers to paths and drives, a separate watering-can *distinctively marked* should be kept, and used for nothing else to avoid mistakes.

Are water gardens and rock gardens viable features and worth the trouble of construction?

Very few really satisfying gardens are complete without rock and water, preferably used in conjunction with each other. Their construction need not be much trouble if gone about in the right way. Ponds tastefully made, stocked with plants and fish, and perhaps given a waterfall or fountain to please the eye with sparkling water and the ear with tinkling sound, will attract immediate attention. It is delightful to sit nearby and quietly watch the fish and the wildlife which the pond attracts. Water lilies are among the most beautiful of flowers, and the foliage of other marginal plants and rushes will give pleasant contrast to the garden. Rock gardens can be filled with interesting plants and in spring can become a glorious mass of colour. They are important features of many famous gardens. Moreover, most rock plants are happy with dry conditions and do not need lots of attention once established.

A colourful planting of spring flowers around a man-made pond can achieve a natural effect.

How can pond water be kept free of excess weed, and should cleaning be necessary?

A new pond invariably goes through a stage when it turns green or even brownish, but as water plants become established the water will clear. Oxygenators and floating aquatics help (page 505) Blanket weed, a fibrous weed like green cotton wool, is often troublesome. Floating aquatics tend to keep this down and when necessary it should be removed by hand. Many deliberately introduced aquatics can become very invasive, hence the care needed in choosing. Do not introduce plants collected from natural water. There is now a number of proprietary products sold for adding to garden pools to keep them clear. These are harmless to fish and cultivated aquatics, but the label instructions must be followed exactly. A well-planted and established pool should keep itself clear, although weather conditions may cause temporary clouding or greening. It should very rarely, if ever, need cleaning out. Indeed, such disturbance upsets fish and disturbs the natural habitat. However, weed will need occasional thinning and water lilies and similar plants will need division from time to time.

What is the simplest and quickest way to make a pond and what are the basic essential of its design?

With modern plastic sheeting it is possible to make a pond quickly and easily, with a result better than that achieved with concrete. However, it is important to choose the right plastic and to prepare properly. Polythene is *not* suitable for a permanent pond. Special liners made from PVC, preferably reinforced with nylon net, can be bought. More expensive but suitable for very large and elaborate ponds – even lakes – is butyl rubber. This is a synthetic rubber that is virtually everlasting. It is thick and strong and will safely take the weight of rocks. Concrete is hard work to mix, and often cracks over the years owing to expansion of ice if the

The pond foundation has a ledge for pot plants. It is lined with plastic sheeting and filled with water. The finished pond is decorated with a slab surround and marginal plants in pots are placed on the ledge.

pond freezes. It also has to
be coated, or washed for
some time, before plants or
fish can be introduced to
the pond – otherwise the
alkali it contains will kill
them. With plastic sheeting
it is necessary only to dig
the hole to the required
size, shape, and depth,
remove sharp stones if any
and spread a layer of fine
sand over which to lay the
plastic sheet. Water can
then be run in and the
edges of the excess plastic

left around the pond
covered with flat stone or
paving slabs. A pond need
be only 0·5−0·75m
(1½–2½ft) deep, and then
only in places. It should not
be too shallow or it may
freeze solid in winter and
injure fish, and it may
become too warm in
summer. A shallow shelf
around the side of the pond
will be useful for standing
baskets or pots of marginal
plants. Formal gardens
demand geometrically

Although this waterfall looks
natural it is, in fact, entirely
man-made.

laid out ponds in
rectangular, square or
circular shapes. Informal
ponds should have gently
curving sides in the same
way as borders or beds.
Don't make a pond on a site
where there are
overhanging trees or where
shade predominates.
Choose an open sunny
position for the location of
your pond.

How are fountains and waterfalls set up, and what pumps or other equipment are necessary where there is no running water?

Few gardens have the amenity of natural water at a higher level than the pond where a fall or fountain is required. Special submersible electric pumps are obtainable with outputs to suit the smallest pool fountain or the grandest waterfalls. Waterfalls are quite difficult to make look really natural. Use natural stone rather than buying a plastic version. When plastic sheeting is used for a pond, arrange that it can be taken up and under where the fall is to be constructed, to avoid water loss. A fountain should be in proportion to the size of the pool; remember that wind may blow water out of the pool area. The pump must be powerful enough to raise the water to the height of any ornament to which the jet is attached.

An electric pump raises water to the top of the waterfall.

Should fish be introduced to a pond? If so, what species and how should they be fed?

Fish will make a pond much more interesting, but they also serve a practical purpose in eating the larvae of gnats and mosquitoes which can otherwise become a great nuisance. Aquatic nurseries usually supply fish as well as plants and it is wise to consult them since they often provide collections of various species suitable for pools of various sizes. It is important not to overcrowd a pool. Goldfish are the most popular and there are a number of types, such as shubunkins, which can be obtained in many colours, some with long tails, and comet goldfish, with red flowing tails. A very beautiful fish that does well and lives for many years in a garden pool is the golden orfe. Also necessary for a pond are water snails, which help to keep it clean. A common one is *Planorbis corneus* (ramshorn snail) and another is *Limnaea aricularia*. When a pond is well established with plants there is no need to feed fish unless the pond is very small or overcrowded with fish. Overfeeding is one of the greatest causes of death or ill health in fish. If you do feed them use only proper fish foods sold for the purpose, or natural foods such as daphnia and tubifex.

Golden orfe (1) and goldfish (2) are popular for garden ponds

What plants are best for a water garden? How are they planted, and when?

All plantings are best done from May to June. To keep the water fresh and to maintain an aquatic environment suitable for fish, submerged oxygenating aquatics must be planted. Good oxygenators are *Callitriche autumnale, Elodea crispa,* Myriophyllum species and *Tillaea recurva.* Plant them by weighing them down with a piece of flat stone on

Nymphae odorata 'Alba' is a sweetly scented water lily.

Special baskets are sold for planting water lilies and other submerged plants.

the pool bottom. There are many beautiful marginal plants such as water irises and rushes. A selection should be made by reference to a specialist

aquatic nursery catalogue. Take care to choose plants suited to the size of pond, since some can be rampant and crowd out everything else in a short time. *Iris laevigata* varieties are well-behaved in this respect and have showy flowers in various colours. One of the first water plants to flower is the marsh marigold; *Caltha palustris 'Plena'* is the neat double form. Water lilies can be planted similarly but need usually at least 30cm (12in) of water, depending on variety. Marginal plants can be planted in pots or special plastic baskets sold for the purpose, using chopped

turfs with a little bonemeal incorporated. They should be planted so that their roots are just covered with water when the planting containers are submerged. Some floating aquatics, which need no planting, may also be added to pools. Water soldier (*Stratiotes aloides*) is a popular plant with spiky floating leaves. The water hyacinth (*Eichhornia crassipes*) is a beautiful summer plant, but it must be stored in frost-free conditions during the winter while the water hawthorn (*Aponogeton distachyus*) has a growth habit similar to that of water lilies.

A planting scheme (*left to right*): iris, water lily, potamogeton, bullrushes, *Pontederia cordata*.

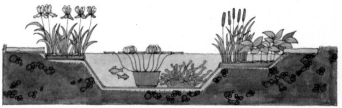

505

Can you give general hints on designing rock gardens?

A rock garden must have a sunny open site and if there is natural rising ground this can be used to great advantage. When a new garden is to be established in the grounds of a newly-built house there may be some rubbish and rubble that can form the basis for a rock garden and give it height. However, there must be a reasonable covering of good quality soil on which the rock plants can feed. 'Rock' gardens made with old broken concrete in place of natural stone rarely look

attractive. It is best to use stone all of the same type and place it with any strata lines running horizontally. Large pieces give the best effect and stones weighing less than about 25kg (½cwt) are rarely useful. Flattish stone, such as that used for crazy paving, can, however, be used on its side to give the impression of bulk; these pieces should also weigh about 25kg (½cwt) upwards. Solid squarish pieces should be laid with a slight slope backwards so that rain runs into the soil. If space permits, meandering stone paths in the rock garden are attractive.

Alpines and dwarf conifers combine in a rock garden.

The semi-trailing *Asperula suberosa* with its pinkish-white flowers and whitish foliage is ideal for rock gardens. Its dense central clump thins gracefully to trail at the edges.

Can you suggest some good, long-blooming rock plants for easy culture?

There are an enormous number of rock plants or alpines. Indeed, this is

another case where a catalogue from a specialist nursery will help. Some very popular, easily-cultivated plants are *Alyssum saxatile* (yellow), *Plumbago ceratostigma*

(blue), *Dianthus deltoides* (scarlet), *Iberis officinalis* 'Albus' (white), *Thymus serpyllum* 'Coccineus' (red), *Arabis albida* 'snowflake' (white), *Campanula muralis* (blue), *Aethionema* 'Warley Rose' (pink) and helianthemum (variously coloured named varieties). This group will also give colour from May to autumn, but it should be realised that the vast majority of rock plants are spring-flowering. Another usually long-flowering species is *Asperula suberosa* (pink), its main flowering period being summer.

506

How is a 'dry wall' made and what plants can be used to cover it?

Drystone walls can be used to retain sloping ground or banks dividing areas of different elevation. They are best made with thickish slabs of natural stone of varying size. No cement is used, the stones merely being piled on top of each other with a slight backward slope so that rain is taken into the wall. Stability is provided by using soil instead of mortar, and here and there trailing plants can be inserted into this soil. Provided large enough

stones with a good depth have been used, such a wall will be firm and stable. The wall should *not* lean forward, but on the other hand only a slight

backward slope is usually necessary. All the plants described on page 506 are suitable for insertion in the wall or along the top to trail over the edge.

A well-made dry stone wall is an attractive garden feature.

Can you suggest some ways to make a rock garden look more attractive in winter?

Choose plenty of evergreen rock plants with pleasing foliage, which may be grey, silvery or red as well as green. There are also numerous dwarf shrubs or ground-cover plants that can be dotted here and there. Most important are dwarf conifers, which can be had in various shapes, in yellow, gold and grey-green. Some good plants are *Iberis officinalis* 'Albus', lithospermums, various saxifrages, *Veronica gentianoides*, *Armeria maritima*, *Cardamine trifolia*, *Arabis albida*, *Geranium sanguineum*, *Polygonum affine*, polyanthus and primulas.

Gardens can be enhanced with a charming blend of dwarf conifers such as *Tsuga canadensis pendula* (hemlock) in the foreground.

All these have attractive foliage and flower from spring to summer. For dwarf shrubs, try *Daphne cneorum*, *Gaultheria procumbens*, *Hebe* x Carl Teschner, *Hypericum calycinum*, dwarf lavenders, pernettyas (numerous varieties with coloured berries), *Phlomis fruticosa*, *Ruscus aculeatus* or *Santolina chamaecyparissus*. Consult the catalogues of the specialist nurseries which supply dwarf conifers. These conifers are extremely attractive and embrace the genera Cryptomeria (Japanese cedar), Juniperus, Chamaecyparis (Lawson cyprus), Pinus, Abies (fir), Picea (spruce), and Thuja (western cedar).

507

Index

abutilon, 141
Acer palmatum, 46, 177
aechmea, 379, 437
African violet, 386, 393, 409
agave, 377, 378
ageratum, 103, 140, 182
aloe, 378
alyssum, 90, 94, 96, 103, 140,
    141, 169, 182, 190
amaranthus, 103, 458
Anchusa capensis, 103, 140
anemone, 380, 484
angelica, 68–9, 314, 316, 317,
    323, 328, 342, 344, 361
anise, 29, 318, 340, 345
Anthurium scherzerianum, 437, 458
antirrhinum, 95, 96, 104, 140,
    182, 190
aphids, 83, 97, 225–7
apple sawfly, 199
apples, 202–9
    frost resistance, 200
    pests and diseases, 255
    varieties, 207–9
apricot, 199, 224–5
arabis, 183
araucaria, 380, 416
artemisias, 335, 361, 367
artichoke, 263, 272, 288, 299
asparagus, 273, 275, 287
asparagus peas, 285
aspidistra, 379, 380, 429, 458–9
aster, 90, 96, 97, 105
aubrieta, 17, 93, 133, 183
azalea, 392, 393

balcony gardens, 148–51, 163
balm, 320, 321, 333, 336 –7, 345,
    361, 362, 368–9
balsam, 314
banyan tree, 379
basic slag, 59, 60–1
basil, 320, 321, 324, 325, 327,
    332, 340, 342, 345, 348, 349,
    353, 368–9
bay, 315, 320, 321, 323, 324, 325,
    348, 351, 362, 368–9
beans, 67, 262, 265, 266
    broad, 263, 270, 282
    dwarf, 283
    runner, 270, 286
bedding plants, 87
    spring, 96–7, 132–9
    summer, 100, 101–19, 140
beds of plants, 88–9, 140–3,
    156–8
beetroot, 263, 266, 269, 273, 275,
    296
begonias, 23, 96, 106, 140, 141,
    153, 183, 190, 393, 396, 424,
    459
bellis, 92, 133, 142, 183
berberis, 47
bergamot, 315, 321, 332, 345,
    356, 367, 368–9

billbergia, 379
bindweed, 82
black-root rot, 486
blackberries, 198, 199, 200,
    237–9
    pests and diseases, 255
    varieties, 239
blackcurrants, 198, 199, 200,
    245–7
    frost resistance, 200
    pests and diseases, 255
    varieties, 246–7
Bletia striata, 398
blossom weevil, 255
blossom wilt, 255
blueberries, 252
bonemeal, 59, 60–1
bonsai, 178–81, 417
borage, 326, 330, 340, 344, 345,
    346, 361, 362, 368–9
borders, 88–9, 326–9
    herb, 314
botrytis, 251
bottle garden, 423–5
bouquet garni, 363–4
Bouvardia × domestica, 460
brassicas, 262, 263, 265, 270,
    271, 276–81
broccoli, 262, 263, 272, 273, 275,
    284
bromeliads, 379, 384, 421
brown rot, 259
Brunfelsia calycina, 461
Brussels sprouts, 57, 263, 270,
    272, 273, 276
bud drop, 486
buddleia, 47
buds, types of, 74
butterfly bush, 47
bulbs, 457, 494
    indoors, 386–7, 460–1
    spring bedding, 137–9, 386–7,
    460–1
bullaces, 220
busy lizzie, 457, 468–9, 494
buxus, 47, 177

cabbages, 57, 60–1, 263, 264,
    270, 271, 272, 273, 274, 275,
    278, 281
cabbage aphis, 270
cabbage caterpillars, 270
cabbage root fly, 271
cacti, 194, 376, 377–8, 402–3,
    404
calabrese, 262, 273, 274, 279
caladium, 394, 395
calceolaria, 153, 190, 461
calcium, 56, 59
calendar, vegetable, 272–5
calendula, 98, 120–1, 152, 189,
    344
calliopsis, 121
camellias, 47, 367, 462
camomile, 325, 344, 360–1, 367,
    368–9
campanula, 183, 462
canary creeper, 131

candytuft, 98, 121
cane spot, 255
canker, 255
capsicum, 484
caraway, 317, 318, 345, 368–9
carnations, 194, 462–3
carrot, 59, 67, 263, 265, 266, 269,
    297
carrot fly, 271
castor oil plant, 116
catalogues, 40
caterpillars, 485
cattleyas, 399
cauliflower, 271, 277
celeriac, 218
celery, 263, 289
centaurea, 98, 122, 183
chaenomeles, 47
cheiranthus *see* wallflower
cherries, 184, 199, 200, 221–3,
    225–6
    pests and diseases, 255–6
    pruning, 222
    soil requirements, 200, 221
    varieties, 29
chervil, 317, 318, 324, 325, 328,
    340, 345, 346, 362, 368–9
chickweed, 78
chicory, 290
chives, 315, 316, 321, 322, 324,
    325, 326, 327, 330, 333, 344,
    346, 348, 349, 355, 362, 363,
    368–9,
chlorophytum, 383, 393, 430, 463
chlorosis, 200
Christmas cactus, 378
chrysanthemum, 98, 121, 184,
    360, 393, 463
cineraria, 106, 107, 141, 476
cinnamon, 314
cinquefoil, 78
cissus, 384, 393, 412–13
Clarkia elegans, 122
clematis, 75, 189
Cleome spinosa, 107, 463
climbers, 190, 384
    annual, list of, 131–2
    as decoration, 412–13
    evergreen, 174
Clivia miniata, 463
cloches, 67, 71, 481–4
clover, 78, 324
cloves, 314, 359
club root, 271
Cocos weddeliona, 417
codling moth, 255
coleus, 107, 141, 393, 396, 465–6
columnea, 466
compost, 32, 62–7, 454–5
cone flower, 116
conifers, 14, 16
conservatories, 439–40
containers, 20, 25, 28, 100, 160–9

    plants grown in, 170
convolvulus, 107, 332, 345
coriander, 316, 318, 332, 345,
    370–1

cornflower, 98, 122, 183
couch grass, 80
courgettes, 273, 306
cranberries, 252
crassulas, 378
creeping buttercup, 78
crocuses, 386, 387
croton, 465
cryptanthus, 379
cucumbers, 68, 270, 291
cumin, 318, 345, 370–1
currants, 245–7
   black, 199, 200, 245–7
   frost-resistance, 200
   pests and diseases, 255, 257
   red, 199, 247
   varieties, 246–7
   white, 247
cuttings, 92
   bedding plants from, 101–19
cyclamen, 377, 392, 393, 405,
   466
cynoglossum, 123

daffodils, 188, 189, 461
dahlia, 92, 96, 108
daisy, 92, 133, 143, 183
damping off, 486
damsons, 198, 220
   site, 198
   varieties, 220
dandelion, 78, 365
daphne, 171
decorative uses of plants, 410–17
dianthus, 108, 184, 360
dieffenbachia, 394–5, 417, 437,
   466
digging, 261
dill, 317, 318, 324, 325, 328, 340,
   345, 370–1
dimorphotheca, 123
diseases see pests and diseases
Dizygotheca elegantissima, 380–1,
   417
dock, 80
dracaenas, 466–7
dumb canes, 394–5, 417, 437,
   466

earwig, 97
echeverias, 378
echium, 108, 109
elder, 365
endive, 292
ericas, 177
eschscholzia, 98, 123, 185
euonymus, 176
euphorbia, 109, 392, 393, 467
exotics, 394–401

fastigiate trees, 16
fatshedera, 381, 412
fatsia, 48, 171, 178, 381, 417
fences, 21
fennel, 314, 315, 317, 323, 324,
   325, 328, 332, 345, 353, 362,
   370–1

fertilisers, 55, 56–61, 200–1
   list of, 60–1
Festuca glauca, 101
feverfew, 112, 365
ficus, 378–9, 393, 414, 417, 467
field woodrush, 79
figs, 232–3
   varieties, 233
flame nettle, 107
flax, 98, 126
flea beetle, 271
floral arrangements, 86–7
flowering plants, indoor, 386–92
   failure to flower, 388–9
   light requirements, 376, 388
   purchase of, 388
foliar feeding, 420–1
foot rot, 486
forget-me-not see myosotis
frames, 67, 71, 90, 480–1
fruit moth, 256
fruit garden, planning, 198–201
fruit trees, 199
fruits,
   listing of, 202–254
   pests and diseases, 255–7
   see also individual fruits
fuchsia, 102, 436, 468

gages, 198, 199, 215–19, 255, 257
   pests and diseases, 257
   site, 198
   varieties, 218–19
gaillardia, 184
gall mite, 255
garden centre, 41
garlic, 321, 346–7, 370–1
gazania, 109
geranium, 27, 110
gerbera, 468
gloxinias, 476
godetia, 98, 124, 185
gooseberries, 198, 199, 241–4,
   256
   pests and diseases, 256
   site, 198–9
   varieties, 244
gourd, 495
grapes, 199, 227–31, 250
   pests and diseases, 256
   site, 198, 199
   varieties, 230
grasses, ornamental, 128
greenfly, 97, 251, 255
greenhouses, 32, 33, 67
   culture 454–7
   heating, 446–8
   installing, 442–3
   pests and diseases, 485–7
   plants grown in, 458–79
   propagation, 452–3, 455–7
   types and shapes of, 437–44
   ventilation, 444
   watering in, 96, 71, 450
greens, 272, 273, 274
Grevillea robusta, 417, 468–9
grey mould, 487

ground cover, 14, 96, 358–9
ground elder, 81
groundsel, 81
gummosis, 487
gypsophila, 124
gypsum, 60–1

hanging baskets, 100, 150,
   168–9, 351
hardy annuals, 98–9, 120–32
   for growing in situ, 120–32
harvesting and storing
   fruit, 206
   herbs, 362–3
   vegetables, 269
heather, 14
hedera see ivy
hedge, 334
heeling-in, 45
helianthus, 124
heliotrope, 110
herbaceous plants, 181–7
herb gardens, 156, 323–9
   colour in, 330–9
herbs, 400–1
   in containers, 348–52
   cosmetic and pot pourri,
     356–61
   drying, 362–4
   savoury and sweet dishes,
     368–73
   from seed, 340–7
   wild, 365
   in winter, 353–5
hippeastrum, 469
hoeing, 267
honeysuckle, 356
horsetail, 181
houseleek, 187
howea, 471
hoya, 412, 469
humidity, 407–8, 422
hyacinth, 137, 386, 387, 461
hydrangea, 48
hyssop, 324, 325, 326, 328, 330

impatiens, 96, 110, 185, 469–70
indoor plants,
   care of, 393
   decorative uses, 410–17
   exotics, 394–401
   feeding, 420–1
   group therapy, 422–5
   humidity, 407–9
   hydrophonics, 426–7
   light, 402–4
   pests and diseases, 432–3
   propagation, 428–31
   warmth, 405–6
   watering, 418–19
iresine, 92
iris, 457
ivies, 27, 174, 378, 382, 384–5,
   393, 412–13

Japanese maple, 16, 43, 46, 173,
   177

jasmine, 356
jasminum, 470
juniper, 16, 367

kale, 263, 280
kalanchoes, 378

larkspur, 125
laurel *see* bay
lavatera, 124–5
lavender, 326, 330, 333, 335, 356,
  370–1
lawn, 67, 78–9
  mowing, 37
  sowing, 36–7
  turfing, 36–7
  weeds in, 78–9
leaf curl, 256
leaf hoppers, 485
leaf miners, 485
leafspot, 487
leeks, 263, 305, 342
leptosiphon, 125
lettuce, 265, 266, 293
lilac, 49
lime, 57, 60–1
linaria, 126, 185
linum, 98, 126
lobelia, 96, 111, 140, 190
loganberries, 199, 240
Lonas inodora, 126
lovage, 316, 318, 370–1
lupinus, 126
lysimachia, 185

mace, 314
magnesium, 56, 454
mallow, 124
mangetout, 28
maple, 43
marantas, 397, 470
marigold, 96, 112, 330, 370–1
marjoram, 315, 319, 320, 324,
  325, 326, 342, 348, 355, 361,
  362, 370–1
marrow, 263, 265, 269, 270, 306
matricaria, 112, 365
meadowgrass, 79
mealy bugs, 256, 432–3, 485
melon, 68, 307
  cantaloup, 307
mesembryanthemums, 111, 152,
  189
midge, 256
mignonette, 127, 361
mildew, 256, 257, 487
mint, 315, 319, 324, 325, 326,
  328, 331, 353, 354, 361, 362,
  363, 370–1
  varieties, 318, 325
moisture indicator, 69
Monarch of the Veldt, 118
monstera, 393, 410, 413
morning glory, 131
moths, 255, 257
mowing, 35
mulching, 67, 70, 268

myosotis, 93, 134, 138, 139, 142,
  143

narcissi, 137, 387, 461
nasturtium, 132, 190, 330, 372–3
neanthe, 382, 424
nectarine, 226
nemesia, 96, 113, 186
Nemophila insignis, 98, 127
neoreglia, 379, 389
nettle, 81
nicotiana, 113
nigella, 98, 127
nitrates, 60–1
nitro-chalk, 59, 60–1
nitrogen, 56, 58, 59, 454
nutmeg, 314
nutrients *see* plant foods

odontoglossum, 399
Olearia haastii 178
onions, 263, 269, 300
  salad, 294
orange tree, 400
orchids, 397–9
oxalis, 81

painter's palette, 437, 458
palm, 470–1
pansies, 93, 96, 113, 134, 153
paphiopedilums, 398
parsley, 314, 316, 317, 324, 325,
  326, 327, 328, 345, 348, 349,
  350, 353, 362, 363, 372–3
parsnips, 269, 301
paths, 18–19
patios, 9, 13, 16–17, 155–9
  plants for, 27, 174–87
  trees and shrubs for, 176–80
paving, 15, 17
  laying 37–8
pea maggot, 271
peaches, 198, 199, 225–6, 256
  pests and diseases, 256
  site, 198
  varieties, 226
peacock plant, 397, 424
pearlwort, 79
pears, 210–14
  espalier, 211
  harvesting and storing, 213
  pests and diseases, 256
  pruning, 212
  varieties, 213–14
peas, 67, 262, 265
pelargonium, 92, 101, 102, 152,
  186, 189, 378, 471–3
Pellonia pulchra, 424
pennyroyal, 318, 325
penstemon, 114
peperomia, 414, 424, 437, 472–3
pergola, 16, 491
perpetual spinach, 310
pesticides *see* insecticides
pests and diseases
  control of, 83
  of flowers, 97

potash, 58–9
potassium, 56, 454
  of fruit, 255–7
  in the greenhouse, 85–91
  of vegetables, 270–1
petty spurge, 82
petunias, 27, 96, 114–51, 186,
  188, 190
Phacelia campanularia, 29
philodendron, 393, 395, 412, 415,
  416, 417
Phlox drummondii, 114, 186
phosphorus, 56, 58–9, 454
pieris, 176
pilea, 382, 424, 473
pineapple, 379
pinks, 194, 359–60
pip plants, 400–1
Pittosporum undulatum, 424
planning a garden,
  average sized, 15–23
  large sized, 13–14
  small sized, 24–39
plant foods, 56–61
  table of, 60–1
plantain, 82
planting
  a tree, 43–5
  vegetables, 264–5
plectranthus, 414, 416
pleione, 398
Plumbago capensis, 473
plums, 198, 199, 200, 215–19
  frost-resistance, 200
  pests and diseases, 257
  site, 198, 215
  soil requirements, 200, 217
  training and pruning, 216
  varieties, 218–19
poinsettia, 392, 393, 467
pollinators, for fruit trees, 199
pollination, 199
  see also individual fruits
polyanthus, 93, 135
Polygonum baldschuanicum, 155
ponds, 116
poplar, 47, 58–9
poppy, 56, 324–5, 372–3
portulaca, 116
pot marigold *see* calendula
pot pourri, 356–61
potato, 59, 263, 269, 302
potato blight, 271
potting off, 92
powered tools, 34–5
pricking out, 91
primrose, 93, 135, 478
primula, 27, 148, 473–4
Primula denticulata, 43, 136,
  137
propagation, 90–3, 428–31
  in greenhouse, 452–3, 455–
  herbs, 340–7
pruning, 72–6
  fruit trees *see* individual fruits
pumpkins, 269, 306
pyracantha 175

510

radishes, 271, 294
raspberries, 234–6, 257
    pests and diseases, 257
    varieties, 236
raspberry beetle, 257
raspberry moth, 257
red core, 257
red spider mite, 432–3, 485
redcurrants, 199, 247, 257
Reseda odorata, 127, 186, 361
rhododendrons, 57, 474
rhoicissus, 384, 412–13
rhubarb, 253–4
    varieties, 254
ribes, 49
ribwort, 79
ricinus, 116
rock cress, 183
rock garden, 506–7
roof garden, 192–5
room pines see bromeliads
root crops, 67, 262, 263, 269,
    296–304
root flies, 271
root rot, 378, 433
roses, 75–6, 357–8, 365, 461
rotation of crops, 262–3
rubber plant, 378, 393, 417, 467
rudbeckia, 116
rust, 97, 255, 487
Ruta graveolens, 178

sage, 315, 318, 325, 326, 327,
    345, 361, 362, 372–3
salad burnet, 5, 345, 367
salpiglossis, 117
salvia, 96, 117
sanseviera, 140, 143, 383, 393,
    475
santolina, 178, 335–6
savory,
    summer, 340, 342, 345
    winter, 315, 323, 327, 348
sawfly, 257
saxifrage, 187
scab, 255
scale, 255
schefflera, 381, 417
schlumbergera, 378
scindapsus, 385, 414
screens, 21, 23, 490
seakale beet, 308
sedum, 187, 380
seed,
    sowing, 340
    for lawn, 36–7
    sowing, 264–5
    thinning, 266
sempervivums, 187, 378
shallots, 269, 321, 326, 346–7,
    372–3
shapes of plants, 380–5
shepherd's purse, 82
shrimp plant, 459–60
shrubs see trees and shrubs
silver leaf, 257
slugs, 271

snake plant, 393, 475
snakeskin plant, 397, 424
snapdragon see antirrhinum
snowdrops, 188
snow-on-the-mountain, 109
soil,
    alkalinity/acidity, 56–7
    feeding, 56–65
    replacement, 25–6
    types, 200–1, 260
sorrel, 324, 325, 367
sowing, 264–5
    vegetables, 264–5
speedwell, 79
spices, 314, 340, 359
spider plant, 107, 463
spinach, 266, 309
spinach beet, 310
spot treatment, 80
sprinklers, 70
squashes, 269, 306
stagshorn fern, 415
Star of the Veldt, 123
stardust, 125
Stephanotis floribunda, 477
stocks, 93, 96, 117
stonecrop, 199, 200
storing see harvesting and storing
strawberries, 201, 248–51
    pests and diseases, 257
    varieties, 250–1
strelitzia, 437, 477
succulents, 377, 378, 404
sugar peas, 285
sulphates, 59, 60–1
sun plant, 116
sunflower, 124
supports, 99
swedes, 269, 271, 303
sweet bay, 178
sweet cicely, 317, 345
sweet corn, 263
sweet pea, 132
sweet scabious, 130
sweet sultan, 130
sweet william, 129
Swiss cheese plant, 393, 413

tagetes, 117
tarragon, 315, 326, 342, 353,
    372–3
tarsonemid mites, 486
teas, herbal, 315, 332, 321, 326.
    344, 353
thinning,
    flowers, 99
    vegetables, 266
thistle, 82
thrips, 486
thyme, 187, 315, 316, 317, 318,
    322, 323, 324, 326, 338, 348,
    352, 362, 366, 372–3
tisanes see herbal teas
toadflax
tobacco, flowering, 113
tomato leaf mould, 487
tomatoes, 68, 263, 265, 295

tools and equipment, 34–5
tradescantia, 383, 393, 431,
    478–9
trailers, 414–15
trees and shrubs, 41–9
    bonsai, 10, 27–9
    fruit, 199
    indoors, 416–17
    planting, 43–5
    for small gardens, 46–9
trefoil, 79
tulips, 138–9, 386, 461
turnips, 266, 269, 271, 304

umbellifer, 332, 342
ursinia, 118

vegetable plot, planning, 262–3
vegetables, 276–311
    harvesting and storing, 269
    pests and diseases, 270–1
    rotation of, 262–3
    salad, 289–95
    sowing and planting, 264–5
    thinning, 266
    weed control, 266–7
venidium, 118
verbena, 96, 118
vine weevil, 256
vines, 192
viola, 113, 187
violet, 359, 484
Virginia stock, 130
viscaria, 130
vriesia, 379

wallflowers, 93, 133, 136, 138,
    361
walls, 18, 19, 26, 30, 31, 39
waterfall, 503, 504
watering, 68–71
    equipment, 498
    in greenhouse, 69, 96, 71, 450
weedkillers, 77
weeds,
    in flower and vegetable plot,
        80–2
    in lawn, 78–9
weed control, 266–7
weevils, 256, 486
white currants, 247
white flies, 97, 433, 486
window boxes, 67, 100, 150,
    151–3, 163–5, 352
    plants for, 190
winter moth, 255
wisteria, 16, 75
woodruff, 358, 365, 367

yarrow, 79
yucca, 140

zebra plant, 383, 437, 458
zebrinas, 140
zinnia, 119, 152, 189
zygocactus, 378